NOBODY SPECIAL

From a trauma perspective

Siobhan O'Regan

Nobody Special - From a trauma perspective

Copyright © 2021 by Siobhan O'Regan

Printed and bound in the United States by Ingram Sparks Self Publishing. All rights reserved. No part of this book may be reproduced or transmitted in any form or by any means, electronic or mechanical, including photocopying, recording, or by any information storage and retrieval system, without written permission from the author or publisher. Exceptions are permitted for quotations embedded in critical articles and reviews about this book.

For information about special discounts available for bulk purchases, sales promotions, fund- raising and educational needs, contact:

siobhanoregan@nobodyspecial.ca

Edited by Jeyran Main

Published by Review Tales Editing and Publishing Services

Cover Design by Maysam Boutorabi

978-1-988680-09-5

978-1-988680-08-8

This book is a **memoir**. It reflects the author's present recollections of experiences over time. Some names and characteristics have been changed, some events have been compressed, and some dialogue has been recreated.

This book is dedicated to my soul mate Yanick and all survivors impacted by trauma.

In order to empathize with someone's experience, you must be willing to believe them as they see it and not how you imagine their experience to be.

- Brené Brown

NOBODY SPECIAL

From a trauma perspective

Written by Siobhán O'Regan

trau·ma

n. pl.

trau·mas or trau·ma·ta

1. A serious injury or shock to the body, as from violence or an accident.

2. An emotional wound or shock that creates substantial, lasting damage to the psychological development of a person, often leading to neurosis.

3. An event or situation that causes great distress and disruption

im·pact

n. im-pakt; *v.* im-pakt

1. The striking of one body against another.

2. A forceful consequence; a strong effect.

3. Influencing strongly, to have an "effect."

CONTENTS

Introduction 11

Chapter One
The Pawn 13

Chapter Two
The Little Girl Who? 23

Chapter Three
Stolen Innocents 33

Chapter Four
The Secrets And Lies 47

Chapter Five
Little Girl Blue 59

Chapter Six
Access Denied 73

Chapter Seven
Freedom, Or Something Like It 89

Chapter Eight
Bittersweet 99

Chapter Nine
Nowhere To Turn 113

Chapter Ten
Lost 129

Chapter Eleven
Acceptance Has Its Price 139

Chapter Twelve
Life Or Death 155

Chapter Thirteen
Rock, Paper, Scissors 169
Chapter Fourteen
The Many Masks 185
Chapter Fifteen
False Pretenses 197
Chapter Sixteen
Then There Were Three 215
Chapter Seventeen
Three Plus One Makes Four 229
Chapter Eighteen
It Takes A Village To Raise A Child 241
Chapter Nineteen
As The Season's Change 261
Chapter Twenty
One Step At A Time 277
Chapter Twenty One
A New Beginning 297
Chapter Twenty Two
One Foot In Front Of The Other 315
Chapter Twenty-Three
Reflection 333
Chapter Twenty Four
Then And Now 347
Perspective
Healthier vs. Unhealthier Mindset 367

INTRODUCTION

I grew up accustomed to words such as rebellious, impulsive, avoidant, withdrawn, reactive, disruptive, disorderly, out of control, and self-centered my entire life. My personality type was described as oppositional, compulsive, defiant, critical, hostile, depressed, unapproachable, and damaged. This was before I evolved to being anti-social.

Ultimately, this led me to multiple diagnoses of chronic depression, anxiety, panic attacks, Bipolar Disorder, Oppositional Defiance Disorder, Sensory Processing Disorder, Inhibited Reactive Attachment Disorder, Complex PTSD, ADD/ADHD, Aarskog syndrome, Stockholm syndrome, addictive personality disorder, alcoholic and drug addict.

To all the different psychoanalysts that didn't understand my circumstances, I would like to say that I'm sure this made sense in the quest of labeling and fixing me. In reality, these were all symptomatic of a much broader issue. I was just a kid who was trying to survive. I endured 13 years of torture and abuse at the hands of a sadist whose cruelty was so severe that its aftermath will be felt for generations to come. In addition, I had a mother who couldn't connect with me because of her own mental health issues. I grew up feeling unloved and unwanted.

My mind was forced to protect its child state by disassociating itself from reality and blocking out chunks of my memory. I was left battered, broken, incomplete, and severely detached. I spent the better part of my adult life angry, bitter, alone, feeling abandoned, resentful, unattached, lost, and crippled by fear.

I was 36 when I experienced my first breakthrough and finally developed my first-ever attachment to my partner after two years of extensive therapy. Surviving my journey has been nothing short of a miracle. This book is the first step in the healing process of understanding that I was a victim. I became a survivor, but above all else, I am a fighter.

This is my story, my tale.
Siobhán O'Regan

CHAPTER ONE

The Pawn

1976 was the year Canada launched its opening of the CN Tower as the world's tallest freestanding tower. Canadian Parliament voted to abolish the death penalty. Apple computer was founded on April 1st by Steve Jobs and Steve Wozniak. The movie "The Omen" had just been released, and Rocky was getting ready to make its debut in mid-November as a number one box office hit. The summer Olympics was hosted in Montreal, Quebec. Ninety-two nations had participated, and Canada had won 11 medals but no gold. At the time, popular musicians were Queen, Diana Ross, and Abba, who had just released the hit single Dancing Queen.

It was Thursday, August 5th, 1976. Usually, it would be the 217th day of the calendar year, but this year marked the 218th day, landing on a leap year and a typical summer day in the little town in Main, Ontario. I was born at 1:20 am, and I was the third child born to Sean and Kristine. I had an older sister Beth who was three, and my brother Lorcan had just turned two.

My mother, Kristine, was the fifth of 7 children, three boys and four girls. Her history growing up was never really clear. I heard different variations of her life growing up, but what I did manage to piece together was what had been a very distant and unhappy childhood.

As known to everyone, most prominent families, back in those days, had very little to get by. According to my mother's version of the facts, she was raised by an absent father who was a porter at the local hospital. He alone supported his family of 9 on his meager earnings. My grandfather John was a Scottish orphan adopted by a German family who immigrated to Canada when he was a young lad. I remember not much about him as a child as we never gathered for Sunday dinners or holidays in the usual family tradition. My mother became estranged from the family after her mother died in the early '80s. Kristine described her father as a distant, gruff man who didn't take the time to wash before meals after a long shift. He would often eat with soiled hands.

John often preferred a nap or the company of a stiff drink over quality time with his girls, least of all my mother. John, back in his youthful days, fought in the war. He didn't win any medals for bravery, but he left a part of himself back on the battlefield bringing home pieces of shrapnel in a place where his left testicle once hung.

My Grandmother, Elizabeth (my sister Beth is named after her), was a very reserved woman who was not very affectionate and spent most of her time consumed in whatever activity she could use to distance herself from her demanding lifestyle. Like many other women in her time, she gave up on her dreams for the love of a strong, capable man with the promise of a better life, only to find out that life happens on its own terms. These terms changed more so with each prospective birth of a newborn child.

I didn't get the chance to form my own opinion of my Grandmother, Elizabeth. I only have one memory of her when I was maybe four or five. She was standing in the living room, and we began to dance to the song "Staying Alive" by the Bee Gees. To this day, that song is one of my favorites and still brings back one of the fondest memories.

Elizabeth died at the age of 57 due to complications of her diabetes combined with many years of having a stressful lifestyle. My grandmother gave birth to seven babies, but I have been told that she was pregnant several times more. Back in those days, women did what they could to get by. My grandmother eventually died due to the complications of the many things she did to her body. I mean the things that stigmatized a woman back then, detaching herself further each time from the man she loved and married.

My mother and her siblings took care of one another as they grew up. The absence of appropriate parenting and a proper upbringing paved the way for some unspeakable events, leaving each child with dark secrets. It caused them to run from the past to define and follow them into adulthood, paving the way for mental health issues, addictions, and disorders. This consumed them, and eventually, their dysfunction passed down onto their children and ultimately repeated their abuse patterns.

Kristine, my mother, would often tell me during our talks that she married my father to get out of her house. They met in high school, and the rest they say is history. Beth was born in the spring of 1973, Lorcan, a year and a half later in the summer of 1974. By the time she became pregnant with me, there was constant turmoil within the marriage, accusations of infidelity, and divorce threats. By this point, Sean sought companionship with anyone who shared his passion for the bottle, drowning his sorrows in anything that would numb how he truly felt about his life. A disease later claimed him of which he inherited from his father, Lorcan.

My biological father, Sean, was the third child and the only boy of Irish immigrants. My grandparents were born and raised in Ireland and came to Canada after their second daughter's birth. Sean, I'm told, was born here in Canada. His name came from a long-standing Irish tradition that dated back several generations. His poppy's name was Sean James (poppy is the Irish term for grandfather), and his father was Lorcan James. My father was named Sean, and my brother was named Lorcan. I believe you get the idea by now.

I'm told that my poppy, Lorcan, was a good man. He died at a young age in his late fifties, tragically like my grandmother on my mother's side. Sean's mother was a strict Catholic woman who, by all accounts, hated my mother. As such, she projected that hatred onto me. When my grandfather died, she made it a point to take me out of his eulogy and completely denied my existence.

When we were reunited, all of my behaviors reinforced all negative feelings she had toward my mother. To her, I did not exist except to tell the rest of my family what a colossal disappointment I was. As a teenager, I would waste years of time and energy to gain her approval, only to be rejected at every turn. I tried to turn to Sean for support and eventually resented him for not standing up to his mother to protect me. I called her once on behalf of my son Kian when he was little, hoping that she would change her mind and accept my boys as part of her family. I left a message begging her to give my boys a chance, but she never called me back.

To this day, I think her rejection hurt more than my adopted father's actions towards me. Eventually, I learned in therapy that to move on and forgive her, I had to first move through the grieving process, much like when someone dies. Only I had to grieve the loss of an entire family that was still alive.

I was born with a premature stomach valve and spent a great deal of my time as an infant in and out of the sick kid's hospital because I couldn't keep food down. For several months, as a result, I was malnourished, underweight, and very colicky. My valve eventually matured, and I gradually began retaining food around eight months. This was not without causing any long-term effects, and to this day, I still have stomach issues. My doctor suggested that she give me up for adoption and that I would most likely never get better. He told her that she would be better off without me.

Like her mother before her, Kristine did not conform well to the demands of being a full-time mother of two toddlers and a chronically sick baby with little to no support. Kristine spent most of her time angry and resentful towards her husband. He, by all appearances, worked hard to provide for his growing family. Behind closed doors, he spent most of his free time drinking away his burdens even when he was left in charge of us. To this day, I still bear a scar on my stomach where I was burned at the age of two. I was left unattended playing on my own and yanked the bottle warmer off the counter when he was passed out on the couch during a bender. Sean spent the better part of his young adulthood battling his addictions. Eventually, he found the support he needed in Alcoholics Anonymous (AA).

Towards the end of Kristine's marriage, she met and quickly fell in love with a man named Dean, who scurried into the role of a protector. He had no issue declaring and taking over enemy territory.

Kristine later justified the affair by holding out that Sean stepped out on the marriage long before she ever did. Several times, my mother told me about a woman named Nancy, who once knocked on her front door. This was a woman Kristine said who was a mutual friend of both her and Sean's. At the time, Nancy was six months pregnant and told my mother that the baby was the product of an affair with Sean. Kristine recalled being devastated by the news, especially since she was pregnant in her first trimester with me.

Nobody Special

To this day, Kristine claims that Nancy's baby was Sean's and that I have a half-sister out there who is only a few months older than I am. This girl who's named she cannot recall has my dark curly hair and hazel green eyes. This is the spitting image of our father, and this was an image Kristine grew to detest and often remarked growing up how much I looked like my father. A comment that took years to comprehend since I grew up oblivious to the fact that I was adopted and knowing I looked nothing like my adopted father.

I asked Sean once about Nancy, he shut me down immediately, denying any part of it to be true. Dean eventually became her biggest ally in disassembling her already failed marriage, making Sean public enemy number one. Kristine liked to talk in army terms, and I think it allowed her to bolster her ego. They were likely terms her father used to use when addressing his kids, which stuck with her as an adult.

According to both of my parents, it was Sean that left the marriage first. This is the only consistent story told between the two of them about the events that lead to their divorce and the separation of our siblings. I was hospitalized in 1977 after being bitten several times by a spider while napping in my crib. According to an entry in my baby book, Kristine writes how Sean came to the house with a woman and packed Beth and Lorcan's things and moved their belongings while Kristine was tending to me in the hospital. Sean agrees this happened for the most part but would not disclose if there was another woman and if she was, in fact, his companion.

In the late '70s, early '80s, fathers began to lobby for new legislation to acknowledge its legal rights publicly. As an unwritten rule, the courts openly sided with the matriarch. In the grand scheme of things, they felt it was best practice and paramount for the child's welfare to give full custody to the child's mother. Only in rare cases, if a mother was believed to be unfit or admittedly couldn't care for her offspring, would a father be granted full or partial custody of his children; otherwise, men had very little standings in custody proceedings. Assumingly, in our case, however, this notion, although controversial and in its experimental stages, appeared to have enough merit to the courts to set a precedent and to appease the lobbyists' stance for a change. The courts decided to split our sibling set right down the middle, thus granting my brother and sister full custody to my biological father. I assume that it was because he worked full time, and they were more independent than me. The court gave my mother full custody of me.

My biological father later told me that it was because she didn't want the two older ones and settled for me. My mother told me he didn't want me because he wasn't sure if I was actually his. Either way, the damage was done. Neither parent, for reasons of his or her own, contested this judgment. Sean told me he wanted all three of us but knew that he was lucky to get the two that he did. Kristine's grief over the loss of her two older kids eventually turned to vindictive anger and projected on me. Regardless of her reasons for keeping me, I was never the child she really wanted and made no qualms expressing this from day one. She wanted my sister Beth. My aunt Karen eventually disclosed that Kristine had contacted Sean when I was seven years old and begged him to trade me for my sister. Sean confirmed that this indeed did happen. He told her no, and added that he wouldn't pass around his children. He offered to take me from her hands, and she hung up the phone.

Kristine and I moved around a lot. I discovered later in therapy that I was moved thirty-three times and attended thirteen different schools and institutions. Our first move out of Main was when I was a toddler. This was after Kristine and Dean decided to move in together by relocating to Raymore to distance themselves from my family and to be close to Dean's work. His father landed him a job in a factory when he quit high school and moved up the corporate ladder very quickly to become a plant manager with no formal education.

There isn't much I can tell you about Dean or his upbringing, even though I grew up with him. The truth is that I actually know very little about the man. As a toddler, I can tell you that he was the second child adopted into a religious family with strong ties to the Baptist community. I do not know what his life was like before he was adopted; his childhood stories were always off-limits. As a teenager, he was in a significant car accident that required skin grafts on both his back and shoulders, and he spent some time in his late teens out west.

Dean's older sister, Laura, was by my account a decent woman who suffered most of her adult life from anorexia-bulimia. The last I heard, she was still married and only had one child, a boy named Mark and was my age. Dean's adopted parents were good people with strong ties to the community.

Nobody Special

They lived in a modest home with ethical Christian values and decided to adopt when he and his wife couldn't conceive a child of their own. Dean's father, Charles, was strict and loved his children but was devoted to his faith first. This became a huge problem and made Dean resentful because his father would donate most of his time and money to his church. It got worse when his father remarried shortly after his beloved wife passed away; Dean openly disapproved of his father's choice to move forward so quickly after his mother, Anna, passed away. He created friction between his father and his new wife after they were married. But for now, just before his mother died, Dean moved us back to Main when Kristine became pregnant. This was so he could be closer to Dean's family as often as he depended on them for financial support.

It is important for me to be precise. The fact that my mother was pregnant with my sister was not welcoming news to Dean. We found out the hard way; he detested children and never wanted any to begin with. He made it very well known to my mother when they met that he didn't want any kids, and it became more evident as time went on.

Growing up, Kristine disclosed that my abuse began well before the first beating, and that was when I was a baby. She once walked in on Dean, holding a screwdriver to my throat because I wouldn't stop crying. She claimed she pushed him out of the way covering the marks on my neck from where the tool was pressed into my skin. She also claims that at the time, she didn't know what to think and so she passed it off, hoping it was an isolated incident. She would recite to herself the same thing she would say a million times over throughout my thirteen years of torment. He didn't mean it. He loves you, and we are nothing without him.

Stephanie was born in the spring of the following year. She was the spitting image of our older sister Beth. Stephanie had pale skin, white-blond hair, and blue-grey eyes. She was, by anyone's standard, a beautiful child. Kristine told everyone, including myself, that Stephanie's identical sister died in labor while giving birth. Dean told everyone a much different story. He said that the afterbirth was so large that the doctor said it could have easily be mistaken for her twin.

Although Stephanie was not a twin, she was born with a heart murmur (a hole in her heart). She was medically fragile for quite a few months before the doctors assured my parents she would be just fine. By this time, Dean felt the pressure from his parents to do the right thing for his new family by marrying my mother. Therefore, in a small ceremony, they made their union in the privacy of his parent's living room.

Tales of Kristine's horrible cheating, child stealing x-husband was a hot topic of conversation between my mother and her new in-laws. I'm sure it was the driving force behind the next series of events that eventually sealed my fate. I'm not sure whose idea it was to have Dean adopt me, but I can make an educated guess. I suppose since Dean himself was adopted, it stood to reason that adopting me just made sense to those who stood behind the decision.

Unfortunately, the honeymoon period didn't last long. Kristine's insecure and demanding ways began to wear down the marriage. She often attributed her behavior to missing her kids. Her depressive moods weren't the only thing catching my new grandparent's attention. They also began noticing Dean's temper becoming increasingly erratic and out of control, especially towards me. I started spending a lot more time with my grandparents and most of my weekends sleeping over at their house. Dean had his parents convinced that his anger was fueled by the stress of dealing with his wife's moods as his wife was stressed out due to my biological father's actions. Everyone agreed that with my family out of the way, my mother had a chance to move on with her life.

Dean's father hired a big shot lawyer out of Reardon and went to work with the adoption proceedings. According to Sean, he received a notice to sign over his parental rights and showed up to court with my brother and sister. The judge was openly taken back by the lack of disclosure in the court's documents stating that there were siblings involved. The judge granted a remand and ordered my father to hire a lawyer. At the time, Sean could not afford one, so when all was said and done, the adoption became finalized on August 25th, 1981, just 20 days after my 5th birthday.

I remember the day well. My parents called me into the kitchen and sat me down. They told me that they were changing my name to Jennifer. This was already my middle name. At the age of five, I could not comprehend why they wanted to change it, and besides, Kristine had never called me Fallon anyway. She only ever addressed me as Gio. She told me once (when I found out that I was adopted) that she had nicknamed me Gio after finding out that Fallon was the name of Sean's girlfriend back in the days when he was a young lad in Ireland. This was during one of their family trips to the old country. She had thought of the name Gio while sorting out laundry one day, and it kind of stuck. So, they officially changed my name to Jennifer, and they gave me my mother's middle name. I received Dean's last name, and that's what I went by from that moment on.

Kristine didn't see much of my brother and sister after she and Dean moved in together. In fact, after I turned two, we hardly saw them at all. Thus, by the time the adoption was finalized, they were but a distant memory. My earliest memory to date was when I had to say goodbye to my brother and sister for what I didn't know would be the last time. I remember the mood being so somber than usual. We were all huddled in a small room. Sean was sitting on the couch in front of me playing his guitar, and I was curled up on the floor with my brother listening to him play. Kristine was holding Stephanie quietly in a corner, chatting to Beth while they watched her sleep. I remember we went for a car ride afterward to drop off Beth and Lorcan somewhere. Sean told me that I stood behind him with my arms around his neck the whole drive back (back in those days, the laws around seatbelts were not the same as they are today). I'm not sure I understood that I wouldn't see them again, but this night, for some reason, stayed ingrained in my head forever. Subconsciously, I don't think you ever forget your first real connection to another human being. For me, I think my first real attachment was to my brother Lorcan.

Our mother always paid all her attention to Beth, and she always preferred our sister over her other children. He was two years older, but I'm told he spent a lot of time entertaining himself by playing and taking care of me. Eventually, the memory I had of him faded, but in my heart, he stayed with me. For as long as I can remember, as a child, I dreamed of having a brother, a protector, a best friend, and growing up; this passion became an obsession. The feeling was always so strong, and I could never shake it off.

In many ways, I died that day when they said goodbye and thrust me into the world that would rob me of my childhood. It was the defining moment that eventually leads to a life of constant torment and fear. My father and siblings would never see that innocent little girl again.

CHAPTER TWO

The Little Girl Who?

We had minimal contact with the family growing up. My mother was really only close to one of her sisters, which was an - on and off -relationship. They were as close as two sisters could be one minute and then refuse to talk to each other for years, the next. Karen was the youngest of her seven siblings and was always thought to have some significant mental health issues, but to me, she was just Aunt Karen. Her husband Randy earned a living as a farm hand-raising chicken. They never made much money or had a place of their own. They had to travel wherever work took them. Lodging was whatever their employers provided. I can remember them living in various homes, from run-down farmhouses to a small trailer on a tiny lot just yards away from the barns.

It was long hours of back-breaking labor, and Dean would often help out in the barns on the weekends while Kristine and Karen did their own thing. Neither sisters ever learned how to drive, so sometimes Randy would drop them off in the city to shop and left us kids to occupy ourselves in the barns. Karen and Randy had two kids, Robyn, who was older than me by two months, and Randy Junior, who was one year, my senior.

Robyn was one of the only few friends that I had as a child. As we got older, she grew to have much more in common with Stephanie than she ever did with me. This closeness caused a significant source of rivalry and conflict between the three of us. Like Stephanie, Robyn was hugely revered by her mother and learned what to do to get her way at a very young age. If Robyn didn't get her way, she had meltdowns for hours until she did. This behavior eventually wore her father down as a parent. At that time, though, she was Uncle Randy's princess and always knew how to play her father for his affection. Unfortunately, for Randy, Junior and I learned a much different lesson and discovered it the hard way.

We were not in the same class as our sisters, and we eventually paid a high price for our parent's attention. Like me, Randy Junior's wants and needs always came second to his sibling's demanding ways. I can recall how high-spirited he was and how much he struggled to contain himself. Junior was still a trigger for his father's temper. Uncle Randy was not known for his communication skills and ruled with an iron fist when you didn't see it coming. Randy Senior's rage was cruel and inhumane.

I remember one Christmas when I was maybe six, and Junior was seven. We were playing in the downstairs level of our split-level home on Main. I was showing Robyn my new cabbage patch doll. I was disappointed because it wasn't a real cabbage patch doll, and Junior had knelt in front of the fireplace exploring our new toys. Moments later, it caught my attention that he was picking the teeth off of my new hairbrush. Without thinking beforehand, I cried out for him to stop! Mid-sentence, I slapped my hands over my mouth to stifle my reaction. My body seized up immediately as my eyes darted between Dean and Uncle Randy. I don't think Junior understood what he was doing because when I cried out, he looked up to see why I was yelling. When he realized it was him, he looked genuinely surprised. Junior dropped the brush immediately and tried to apologize, but it was too late. Randy Senior rushed towards him and slammed his head down on the cement fireplace, where he was kneeling, and started punching him. All I could do is shut my eyes, turn my head and listen to Junior cry out whenever he got hit. I understood precisely how he felt. This was not the first time we each other's abuse and certainly not the last. This moment was always so significant to me because, for years, I blamed myself for what happened to Junior that day, and I think he did too.

Junior would often project the anger he had for his father onto Robyn and me by constantly torturing us, and we hated to be alone with him. When we were younger, he played these games with us, where he would pin our arms down, lay on top of us, and grind up against us. I never really understood the game. As an adult looking back, I don't recall him ever touching me inappropriately, but it was still awkward.

Afterward, he would threaten to kick the crap out of me if I ever told. Not that there was much of a difference. He would always beat me up anyway. Violence could be summed up as a chain reaction in our circle, and it was something we as children had no control over. Randy Senior would beat up Junior. He would then try and take it out on his sister and often get beat up again when she told on him, so by the time it came around to my turn, he would do a number on me.

As if that wasn't bad enough, the beatings were getting worse and more frequent at home, and so I started taking it out on Stephanie. She'd then tell Robyn and also her brother. They would, in return, give it back to me again. I hated it when Robyn, Junior, and Stephanie teamed up against me. Robyn was more helpful than usual and always invited me out to the barns. We played in the bails of hay. Junior hid in the bails to jump out and beat me up. Our parents knew exactly what was going on and never did anything about it. My mother would yell at me if I came in with a busted lip, or I had blood on my shirt (like it was my fault), and as usual, nothing ever came of it. It got to a point where this was happening almost every visit, and I didn't want to go to the farm anymore. I wasn't allowed to hang out with mom and aunt Karen. I took what was coming and just went off on my own and cried by myself more often than not. No one ever came to my rescue. If truth be told, I think they allowed it to happen to explain away the bruises that were accumulating at home.

When Robyn and I were little, our mothers decided to pull an everlasting prank on us and told us that they switched us after we were born. For years neither one of us had a clue as to who our birth parents were. I can't begin to tell you what that does to a child's sense of belonging and security. Both of us were too little to know any better. As I got older, Kristine reinforced her story by telling me how much I resembled Uncle Randy. This likeness was because we both had dark wavy hair and were small-built. I looked nothing like Dean. Before things started to get really bad at home (besides getting the daily belt), I used to witness how awful Uncle Randy would wail on Junior, and I was terrified of him. Kristine abused this situation using my fear of him as a scare tactic to keep me in line, and she used to tell me that if I didn't smarten up, she would give me back to him.

Since day one, I didn't like Uncle Randy and stayed the hell away from him whenever I could. If I had to interact with him, I always tried to suck it up because if what I knew was right and sent me back, I didn't want him to hit me like he did Junior. Sometimes Dean and Uncle Randy would play rough houses with the other kids in a friendly game of tackle. Both of them would hurt me on purpose so that I couldn't play or, worse, tickle me until I cried. I never understood how tickling was fun for everyone else, and I had an adverse reaction to it. This kind of abuse affected me so badly that if anyone ever touched me, I would yell to keep them away from me. Just the mere thought was unbearable, so I sit back, cry, and feel isolated.

After dinner, our parents would sit around for hours and play cards. I loved to watch and go unnoticed. Sometimes, Aunt Karen would let me bring out the cards. I would race to the drawer, carefully take them out and pretend to count each one out as I'd seen them do thousands of times before. I often hold out hope that there was a chance that she was my biological mother, and that was the reason why Karen was pleasant to me. She was a lot nicer than Kristine ever was. It was all hopeful thinking on my part. Sometimes in the summer, our parents would switch kids for a couple of weeks; I would then pair up with Robyn and Stephanie with Junior. I would go to the farm, and Junior would go to the city. Kristine would often tell me it was because I needed to spend time with my birth father. Robyn and I usually got along pretty well when it was just the two of us, and there was minimal violence.

I once worked up the courage to ask aunt Karen if I was adopted. I made sure we were alone and stood there shaking because I was scared of the repercussions. I was taking a massive leap of faith that she wouldn't tell anyone. She looked at me with a look of shock on her face and appeared very uncomfortable by the question. She then looked around to see if anyone was coming. "No," she said in a loud voice and warned me never to bring it up again. It would upset my mother. I decided not to push it further, but for the record, I didn't believe her. I always found Karen very difficult to approach; It was almost as if she was intimidated by me and kept herself distanced on purpose. Regardless, I was drawn to her because she was the nicest to me, more than anyone else had been.

It wasn't long after when my mother and her sister stopped talking to one another for a couple of years. Robyn soon experienced some of what her brother and I were getting when Randy started disciplining both of them with the belt. Something I had become well acquainted with a long time ago was the beating. Dean began to use the belt regularly on me when I was closer to four. I do not recall how old I was when he used it on me, but it had become my usual form of punishment. I cannot comprehend what a four-year-old child may do to deserve such punishment is beyond me.

***

Nobody Special

If there were ever an event that justified everything Dean did or would ever do to me would have been just before Stephanie's 2nd birthday. Stephanie was admitted to the hospital with a virus that attacked her heart, and they told me she almost died. They always made sure that I knew it was still my fault, and I grew up thinking I had nearly killed my sister. I had a terrible habit of taking chewed-up pieces of gum off the street and popping it carelessly into my mouth. I was caught shortly before Stephanie got sick, sharing a part of second-hand gum with her. This is how she caught the virus, and it almost killed her because of her underline heart condition. For years, I wished I was the one who had gotten sick and that it had killed me rather than always having to receive their consistent anger.

Shortly after what happened with Stephanie, we were told that Kristine had to go away for a few days, and I would be staying with Dean's sister Laura. Stephanie was still recovering from her virus, so I believe she stayed with Dean's parents while he worked so he could take care of her at night. When Dean dropped me off, I remember Aunt Laura hugged me, and I yelped out in pain and pushed her away. At the time, I was not used to being embraced by anyone, and underneath my clothes, I was covered head to toe with injuries. Dean told her that the bruises were from me playing at the farm.

She gave me a small pad of paper, which I carried everywhere, and kept it close by if I caught Mark doing anything wrong so I could write it down. Of course, he never did. Aunt Laura spent a lot of time playing with her son Mark and made us homemade play-doh. I was so excited. My mother had never done anything like this with me. She was always too busy with Stephanie. Aunt Laura showed us how to make it with flour, water, and salt, and I think I ate more than I played with. Later that afternoon, Mark and I went outside to play on his slide. Mark always fascinated me. I had never seen him get into trouble. His parents never raised their voices or placed hands on him, and they always seemed to smile and wanted to be near him.

That afternoon I was sitting on the top of the slide, and he was trying to crawl it up. I was so thrilled and was thinking that I just caught him doing something wrong. All my focus went into trying to draw him climbing so I could show Aunt Laura. Out of nowhere, I lost my balance and fell backward. My arm got caught between the stairs of the slide, and I completely blacked out. I woke up in the hospital after having had surgery. My arm was suspended in a sling beside my bed. My fingers were individually attached to wires that hung from the ceiling. I had to stay in bed awkwardly for what seemed like forever. According to Kristine, I was released almost two weeks later. The nurses told me how the ladder on the slide broke my fall. They added that my arm broke in half. They told me that I was such a brave girl, and I kept begging them to repeat that story every time they came to check on me.

One day a doctor came in to chat with me. He sat down on the bed next to me; this made me feel uncomfortable. My favorite nurse was standing next to him. She was always so friendly and gave me a nod. The Doctor smiled and asked me questions about what kind of games I liked to play and told me that he thought I had the coolest bruises and wanted to know where I had gotten some of them. I repeated what Dean had told Aunt Laura and said that I got them from playing on the farm. I looked back at the nurse, who was now showing me a popsicle in her hand. The Doctor asked me some more questions, but all I could focus on was the frozen treat. After he was finished asking me questions, he left. The nurse handed me my popsicle, and I asked her to tell me my story again.

I can recall being so scared in that hospital room, alone with my mom never being there. She later told me that it was because she had a hysterectomy and was recovering at home. She said that Dean couldn't be there because he had to work and take care of Stephanie. I already hated hospitals because back in Raymore, my mom had said that a squirrel bit me. I remember having to undergo several treatments where they had to pin me down to give me a series of 21 needles.

I don't remember how long that treatment was. Still, I never managed to get over my anxiety of needles and developed such a deep-rooted fear of sleeping outside of my own bed. To this day, I have anxiety attacks when I'm forced to sleep in a strange environment, especially when there are other people in the room. Kristine eventually disclosed to us that she had become pregnant, and early during her pregnancy, they discovered that she had cancer in her uterus. She was told that she would not be able to carry the baby full term, so they took the baby and the uterus out. She then said to us that it was a boy; it made the news that much harder. I often wondered if this story was even real. If this was the brother I had. I spent many days sitting in my room and dreaming about the same boy I had pictured before. But it couldn't be. The boy I remembered was always older. I could easily describe in detail what he looked like in my head anyway.

Nobody Special

While my mother was recovering, we would stay at my grandparent's house, and there was a lady there who took care of us named Auntie Doris. She was much older than my mom and so incredibly warm. She read books and took us for long walks. Our grandmother was very sick and was bound to a wheelchair. She couldn't do that kind of stuff with us anymore. I adored everything about this woman and liked to be around her, but after grandma died, she went away too, and I missed her so much.

Kindergarten was such a tough adjustment for me. This was because I came to realize that it was not so different from home. Several significant events happened to me that year, which made it a memorable one.

Firstly, it was recognized since the first day at school that I was not very good at maintaining relationships. No matter what I did, kids didn't warm up to me. Even if they somehow managed to push past my rough exterior, I would find a way to push them away. I could be very friendly at times, but I could never stay connected with any one of my peers. If they snuck up or touched me, I react to them by shouting or jerking away. This kept other children from wanting to approach me. Otherwise, I was described as quiet and reserved and kept to myself.

One morning I was asked to take something to the office, and I took my time getting back to my classroom. Back then, it was inappropriate to interrupt the national anthem or Lord's Prayer, so if anyone was late, they had to wait quietly in the hall until it was finished. There was a young boy in my class; I believe he was Jehovah's Witness and was always excused just before the anthem. He still took his usual place in the hallway just outside our classroom.

On this particular morning, we stood in the hallway together, talking loudly and goofing around in the spirit of doing what young kids do. The principal overheard us, came running down the hall and marched the two of us off to his office. He then proceeded to lecture us on respectful behavior. At least, I assume that's what he was saying since I honestly don't recall paying any attention. I remember clearly to this day that he took out a long yardstick and had me place my hands out in front of myself. He then put his hands underneath mine and quickly removed them, striking me three times on the palm of my hands. I was then forced to watch as he did the same thing to the other boy. The principal then told us to sit on our hands while he went to conduct announcements and told us that he would do it again if we spoke even one word.

My hands stung, but it wasn't my first time getting hit, so it was normal for me. By the look on that boy's face, though, the tears streaming down both sides of his cheeks, it looked like it was the first time for him. My mom said that the boy's parents made a huge deal about having their son endure what they called 'the strap' and that he was the last child at that school ever to receive that form of corporal punishment. Ironically, this made me the second last kid to ever win the strap in that school too.

Note: Corporal punishment was not illegal until 2004 when the Supreme Court of Canada ruled that corporal punishment was an unreasonable application of force in the maintaining of classroom discipline (http://m.cea-ace.ca/education-canada/article/banning-strap-end-corporal-punishment-canadian-schools)

In kindergarten, I was only five years old. The first time I recall meeting a social worker from Child Services was when I struggled to sit down correctly in my chair. I refused to get changed for the gym. Eventually, when I was forced to, I can distinctly remember my teacher's reaction. She was gasping over the welts on my skin left behind from a belt buckle.

All the time during gym time, I wasn't allowed to play with the other kids and had to sit out. They played games like duck, duck, goose, and the fact that I could not participate in the games made me very angry. After the gym, I was told that I had to keep my gym uniform on and was escorted to the principal's office. I hadn't been back to the office since the day I was disciplined and couldn't figure out what I had done wrong to have to go back there.

In the same room where I received the strap was the principal, and next to him was a lady I'd never seen before. The strange lady started asking me a bunch of questions, and I immediately shut down. She then asked the principal to close the door and ordered me to drop my shorts. I started to shake violently and cried. Dean always told me to drop my pants just before I got the belt.

I looked at the door, but there was no place to go. The woman assured me that it was going to be all right. She came up behind me and pulled down my pants and my underwear right in front of my teacher and principal to expose the welts. I couldn't move. She stood behind me but didn't touch me, and everyone in the room took turns looking at my bare bottom. Each made their remarks. She helped me pull up my pants. My tears felt hot against my face, and my stomach hurt. She whispered to me that it was going to be all right and promised that this would never happen again. She lied! And asked me more questions. I offered her nothing and remained quiet. After they finished with me, I was allowed to join the rest of my class. I don't recall what came of this, but this was not the last time I was involved with Child Services.

During recess, I was playing outside when I saw this blond-haired girl. I vaguely remembered her, and she was with someone I didn't recognize either. They both knew who I was, and they stood on the other side of the fence, calling to me using the name Fallon.

I remembered thinking she was such a pretty girl and looked so familiar. She reached out to me through the chain-linked fence. I wanted to touch her and be close to her but didn't understand why. She told me that she and Lorcan missed me and that Dad was always sad. She then turned to walk away, looked back, and said to me that she loved me. Just like that, she was gone.

From then on, I sat by that fence every day, waiting for her to come back. I so desperately wanted to see her again. I spent most of my time on the play structure waiting for her, but she never came back. The following year I did what I always did. I took my position by the fence and watched to see if I could see her again. As I was waiting, a couple of kids were goofing about and ran into me. I wasn't paying attention, and I lost my balance and fell forwards approximately 4 feet towards the pavement below. I landed on my elbow and dislocated my bone. Both sockets at my elbow and my wrist popped out.

I was rushed to the hospital in my principal's car, where they operated on me immediately. I spent another week in the hospital with two dislocations and a fractured wrist. Only this time, it was Halloween, and I was forced to celebrate it in a hospital bed. I sat in my bed and cried, so the nurses brought me candy and sat with me to do their paperwork.-I did not want to be alone.

After this last break, the doctors told my mother that if I were ever to break my arm for the third time, it was very likely that I could never write correctly again. There was not much they could do to be able to do to fix it.

Siobhan O'Regan

The doctors suggested that I get physiotherapy to help with my recovery, but my parents never did. I had the worst writing hand until I started writing poetry and short stories on toilet paper. I would flush them down the toilet so I wouldn't get caught to pass the time. Being isolated in my room left me plenty of time to master my writing skills. Today I am forever complimented on my neatness and fantastic penmanship. I learned this all on my own.

Not long after I broke my arm, I began to notice my mom acting, how do you say, stranger than usual and watched her do some really bizarre things. I remember two instances offhand that come to my mind. Once, when she was in the middle of the living room staring off into space, I watched her played with a pushpin, pushing it into her hand and pulling it out continuously. As a child, I didn't understand what was wrong with her. Whenever I tried talking to her or called out her name, she stared right through me or pushed me out of the way.

The second instance was when we were at my Aunt Karen's, and she was eating a banana. My mother looked like a zombie and just stared off into space. Her food was oozing out of the corner of her mouth. Robyn never lets us forget that moment and likes to remind us every time she sees a banana and refuses to eat another one as long as she lives. Dean left us so many times during their relationship, and this was one of those times. He packed his belongings and walked right out the door. Kristine stood there, screaming and begging him to stay, and fell onto the ground. He didn't look back and left her wailing, repeating the words, "I'm sorry." I sat next to her in the corner of the room, holding my sister while lying in a heap on the floor.

Mom told me that we were better off without him. She lay in bed and moped around for days and snapped at us whenever we came near her. I took care of Stephanie and left my mother to do her own thing. Eventually, he returned as he always did, but this took such a massive toll on my mother. She became even more distant, especially from me. I was still so jealous of how she looked at Stephanie, and I-could never figure out why she hated me. She always looked at me like I was a burden rather than her own child, and I could never figure out why.

CHAPTER THREE

Stolen Innocents

We moved to Fields shortly after kindergarten, and I finished grade one in a new school. My parents bought a house on the other side of the town, right across from a fire station. When the doors were open, Stephanie and I would ride right through that station a few times with our bikes before we eventually got caught. The firemen were really nice about it and told me that they wouldn't have to say to our parents if I stopped riding through their station. So we promised to stay out. We did not live in that house for more than a year or so; however, I remember the neighborhood well.

A boy lived a couple of doors down from us who was several years older and always paid attention to me. I thought he was so refreshing because he had a really neat bike and told me it was something called a dirt bike. He would let me sit on it. After school, I would go over to his house, and we would sit in his room, and he would teach me to play cards. I wasn't exposed to many boys; in fact, I think Junior was really the only boy I knew, so I thought this kid was pretty amazing compared to him.

When I was over at his house one day, he told me that he would teach me how to play strip poker. I thought this game would be fun until I realized that I had to take my clothes off. I was so intimidated until he showed me that I could start with my socks first before removing my shirt and then my pants. He convinced me that it was no different than wearing a bathing suit, so we got down to our underwear, but that was as far as I was ever willing to go. We did this just about every day for a couple of weeks. I found it to be fun and exciting. He was always patient with me.

Siobhan O'Regan

Each time when I got down to my underwear, I got so nervous and found an excuse to end it and go home. One day he acted a little differently. He stripped down to his underwear before we started the game and told me that we would play it a bit differently this time by touching ourselves in front of one another. He volunteered to go first and slipped his hands down his pants, and started playing with himself. Then he instructed me to do the same; only I had no idea what I was doing; I was only 6. I still had my clothes on, so I slipped my hand down my pants and followed his lead. He told me that we were playing like we usually did. Still, since he was already down to his underwear, he was just touching himself, while I did not have to do that until it came to be my turn. This wasn't so bad, I thought, he really liked hanging out with me, and none of this actually hurt. As I got down to my underwear, he suggested that we both get naked. I told him I wanted to stop. He came closer and instructed me to touch him. I laughed nervously and pushed him away. He reached out, grabbed me, and we started to wrestle around on his bed until he pinned me down like Junior used to do.

I wasn't afraid, but I didn't feel very good, either. I asked him to get off. He didn't respond right away, so I raised my voice and demanded that he get off. He told me that he would do so, but I would have to kiss him first. As he pursed his lips, I thought that I had never kissed a boy before, except for Dean, when mom told me to kiss him goodnight. So I kissed him quickly and waited for him to let me up. He laughed at me and told me all I had to do was ask nicely and that he would never hurt me. I wanted so badly to believe him, and so far, he hadn't. I really liked him, and he made me feel good about myself. I wasn't sure I wanted the strip poker anymore but went along with it because it made him happy.

The following day he and I went up to his room. We did the same thing as we did the previous day, only this time, he said we were going to touch each other and that he would go first to show me how easy it was. He came up to me and told me it wasn't going to hurt. He then put his hand up to my belly and slipped his fingers past the elastic on my underwear. I felt so nervous. Sometimes he would let his thing peek out a bit when he played with himself, but now I could see how big it was through his underwear, and it was a lot bigger than usual. I was so fascinated by the way it grew right in front of me. None of my body parts did that, and he explained that it increased the more he touched it. He added that I did that to him.

Nobody Special

I pulled back, and that made his hand slip out of my underwear, and I started shaking. He laughed and took it as an invitation to start wrestling with me again. I was relieved that he wasn't mad, but then he pinned me back only this time; it wasn't fun. He was getting really rough, and I was scared. It didn't feel right. He told me that we were going to play a game of touch. He had to keep a hold of my arms, and the further he went without me saying stop, I would win. He started from my neck and worked his way down, stopping every few inches, saying, "touch" until he got to my underwear. I understood all I had to do was to say stop, but I froze. I felt utterly and totally powerless and had no voice. He still had me pinned and leaned on to one side while he dropped his leg over the top of mine. I was pinned underneath his body weight. Once again, he slipped his fingers into my underwear. He stopped and kissed me on the cheek and whispered "touch," and started caressing my vagina.

I had an overwhelming urge to throw up and told him I felt sick. He tried and pushed his finger up inside me. I didn't even know there was an inside to me. I started to shake and squirm around. He came out of my pants and started playing with himself while still lying on top of me. He then flipped me over, pulled down my underwear, and held the back of my neck at the same time. He then climbed on top of me and shoved something up my bum. All I could do was scream into his bed while he held my head down. When he was done, he gave me a huge hug and told me that I was the best friend he ever had, and held me as I cried.

I stayed inside for a couple of days after that until he finally tracked me down on my way home from school and told me that he missed me. He asked if I had told my parents. Of course, I had not. I played it really cool because deep down inside, this was the only friend I had in the whole world, and I didn't want to lose him over some stupid game. However, I didn't want to be alone with him anymore either.

I was sore from where he touched me (I could not tell for certain what he stuck up inside of me. I realized afterward, when I was in my twenties, what the term sodomize meant). I no longer liked the game and didn't understand it anyway. He told me that we didn't do anything wrong, and he wanted to waste time. He insisted that we didn't have to do that anymore. I told him I just wanted to play outside instead. For a couple of days, that's what we did. But if I am honest, there wasn't much a teenager can have in common with a 6-year-old. He was losing interest in bike riding pretty quickly.

Siobhan O'Regan

Even as a kid, it didn't take a genius to figure out what he really wanted to do. He started to get mad every time I refused his advances to hang out with him.

I once tried to tell my mom what had happened after he stopped playing with me. I'm not sure what my motives were for reaching out to her, but I hated it when people were mad at me. I think I might have been looking for some guidance. Regardless, the conversation didn't get very far. She cut me off and accused me of lying. I never brought it up ever again. I asked her about it once as an adult. She told me that it was in the past and that I needed to learn to let things go.

I guess you could say that I was a massive target for bullying from day one. I was shy and so badly wanted to fit in that I would do just about anything to be liked. It was my sister's 4th birthday, and my cousins were over. I was playing in the front yard when a group of boys I knew from around the neighborhood decided to pull a prank on me by stealing my bike and refusing to give it back unless I did as I was told. They lured me in a bushy area not far away from my house but far enough away that it was private. This was a place we used to hide when we played a game called kick the can. One of the boys told me to yank my pants down and show everyone what I showed my friend. I looked at him, hurt and confused. I had never shown anyone my private parts. I held my ground and tried to hold back the tears.

He gave me a mean look and told me again angrily that I had better do as I was told if I wanted my bike back then. He looked deep in thoughts for a second and started to laugh, then ordered me to yank down one of the other boy's pants and play with his wiener. I was confused and started feeling sick to my stomach. I was trapped and was completely surrounded. I looked at my friend for help, but he seemed just as invested in this prank as the rest of them and shoved me forward, closing in any gaps. He encouraged me to go ahead and that he wouldn't let them hurt me.

I'm not sure how the other boys picked who was meant to be my partner because I was too wrapped up in feelings of shame, but I do recall him covering his face when I pulled down his pants. His friends instructed him to lie down and told me to lie down beside him and to "play with it." I didn't know exactly what they meant by "play with it," but I had seen my friend play with "it" enough to think of what they were expecting. I grabbed on and started tugging it. Someone yelled out, "she fucking likes it, go ahead and suck on it." What!? I thought, why would anyone do such a thing and tried to stand up. This same kid pushed my face into his bare crotch; I started to cry.

My sister and my cousin came around the corner out of nowhere to witness my face being pushed into some kid's bare crotch. The kid who held my head released his grip and scattered with the rest of them, including my so-called friend. The boy who held my bike ransom rode off on it, and I had to walk home empty-handed, begging Stephanie and Robyn not to tell anyone.

I'm not sure to this day if Stephanie understood what had happened to me or what would happen if she told on me, but I was not privy to her version of the story when she did tell Dean and tried to hide. All I know is this marked the day I remember receiving my first beating and a moment I would never forget. Dean came at me with fists flying in a rage. Everyone was outside and had a general idea of what was going on. Still, no one came to my rescue, including my mother. I did my best to fight him off when he came towards me, but it only made it worse. When it was over, I could barely walk, and so I crawled most of the way to my room. I was told to go straight to bed. I cried myself to sleep and was in so much pain. I was confused, scared, and alone. This was about to become my new norm. That boy, my so-called friend, never spoke to me again, and I could not play outside by myself either.

During this time, my mom was getting friendly with some older kids in the neighborhood. One boy lived next door, and the others lived somewhere close by. They were all in their late teens, and to this day, I'm not entirely sure what my mother's relationship was with these kids. However, later, I found out that she was taking these long walks with them to the graveyard to smoke pot and whatever else they did to pass the time. Dean stayed back to watch TV, and it was unknown if he knew or supported her new recreational pastime. He didn't seem to care that kids were hanging out in front of our home all the time.

I started spending a lot more time in my room and didn't come out much to socialize. I did eventually meet one girl in school who lived down the street from us. She had a younger sister and three older brothers, one born with significant mental health issues. He was entirely dependent on her family for everything. Behind closed doors, her family was just as dysfunctional as mine. Still, with one subtle difference, they all openly cared about one another.

Siobhan O'Regan

I had never invited any friends over to my house before and was so happy when my mom agreed to a sleepover. Stephanie ended up liking her too, and she and I began fighting for her attention. This girl and I hung out a lot together, but most of it was spent fighting over trivial things. She struggled to get close to me, and I always kept my distance and had to be in charge to make sure I was still in control.

She was the first person ever to get a real glimpse into what my childhood was like, and every time she got close, either Dean or I pushed her away. Dean didn't like her or her family and didn't want her around, but it was one of the few times mom temporarily overruled him and allowed us to be friends. Our friendship was short-lived, but she remained in contact with us and was allowed to visit once or twice over the years. My 10th birthday was her last visit. Stephanie and I were fighting, as usual, when Dean went off on me. Initially, he forgot she was there, grabbed me by my arm, and pushed me to the ground in front of her. He then regained his composure and restrained himself, opting to yell instead, and physically escorted me to my room. This was new. He usually would have kicked me down the hallway. He told me that she was not allowed to come over again, and he meant it. She never did come back after that day. She went missing as a teenager for a few weeks, and the police began to question me, but I didn't know anything and hadn't spoken to her since her last visit.

We eventually bought a house on the other side of Fields, a place Stephanie and I called the "House of Horrors." She and I spent the next eight years in total hell. For her, it was longer. Some of the worst childhood memories I have are in that house, yet there are so many things that my mind has blocked due to the abuse I endured at my parents' hands. It established a belief in me, at an early age, that no adult could be trusted, and I was to be let down countless times by a system that was meant to protect me. I discovered firsthand the multitude of flaws in our educational system and how it ignored all of the early warning signs by openly participating in the problem rather than the solution.

Within the first week, we moved into our new neighborhood. Stephanie and I found ourselves in trouble. We had run off to the yard, which would be our first mistake, and went to explore the community. We met up with a bunch of Asian boys just down our street in a field so that they could show us a plant named head knockers.

Nobody Special

This plant was a hard circular ball at the top of a long flexible shaft and often housed a worm if you tore it open. It was native to the field it grew in. If you grabbed the shaft just right and flicked, it would sting whoever it came in contact with. They demonstrated on me and then on Stephanie. Still, one demonstration was not enough, and they started hitting us with them all at once. I ran away, assuming Stephanie was behind me, and turned to see they were still beating her with them. I ran back, screaming and yelling at them to stop. I began throwing rocks at them until they backed off. She got up and limped all the way home.

I tried explaining what happened to my parents. Her body was entirely covered with bruises where they had hit her multiple times. I so badly wished that I had stuck it out when they first started beating. I was blamed for taking her off the property and paid dearly for it.

I call most of Dean's beatings blitz attacks. There typically were no warnings, and they came out of nowhere. Many of these were provoked by simple gestures, a perceived look, or, in my case, just for merely breathing. There wasn't much that didn't set him off. These blitz attacks would be one strike if I were lucky, or it would turn into a full-blown, full-contact, anything goes blood sports kind of thing. They often lasted until he tired himself out. I was small, but I gave him a workout—an example of a blitz attack. One day, my parents were sitting at the table, playing cards with Karen and Randy. Dean leaned over and gave Stephanie and Robyn a sucker. I wanted one too, but Dean was in a mood to play one of his sick little games; he looked at me and asked what I wanted, so I pointed to the sucker.

"Oh, one of these?" he asked, holding one up. I nodded and smiled at him. "Then ask," he demanded. "May I have a sucker, please?" I said timidly. "Come here," he said. "I can't hear you." and held it out in front of me. I stepped closer and repeated in the same manner. "What did you call it? He demanded! Confused by the question but focused on the treat, I repeated the word "sucker." Out of nowhere, he backhanded me, and I flew across the floor. I knew that he had busted my lip because I could smell the iron in my blood. Kristine, Karen, and Randy looked but said nothing, and he threw my sucker to Junior, who did not hesitate to pick it up and pop it in his mouth. "That will teach you to swear," he said and turned back to his game. I picked myself up, never taking my eyes off the floor, and went into my room. I huddled up in a corner and stuck my thumb in my mouth, and rocked myself back and forth while I cried.

Dean used to accuse me of giving him a dirty look behind my bangs. He threatened to cut it all off so that I wouldn't have bangs at all. There are only a few pictures left from me growing up. They all depict a hairstyle that is short and very boyish. As a young girl, I could have been pretty, dressed appropriately, and cut my hair like a girl. I had my biological father's features, including his dark curly hair and hazel green eyes; the longer my hair was, the curlier it was, so they kept my hair short and defeminized me to make me look more like a boy.

In every picture, I had short bangs. I think he would have been happier to strip me bald. Only this time, he held true to his word and came at me with a pair of scissors. Usually, my mother wouldn't get involved, but there were a handful of times she would jump in, which was one of them. I ran into my room and tried to duck under my bed. He grabbed my leg, pulled me out, and grabbed my hair. He and I both knew if he wanted to subdue me, grabbing my hair was the way to do it. He threw me on the bed and straddled himself on top of me. My mother was behind, trying to disarm him. He positioned his knee to hold down my chest up against my throat. Kristine was screaming at him to get off me and could see that I was choking for air. He shook loose of her grip, grabbed a clump of my hair, pushed the scissors up to my skull, and started cutting. He had his knee pushed up to my throat so hard that I couldn't breathe. I was suffocating. She pushed him so hard he lost his balance, causing one of the steel blades to break over my forehead. I had minor cuts all over my scalp and a huge scar where the broken blade. My hair came out in clumps that day, and I had to miss school for an entire week until I was healed enough to get a haircut and cried the whole time. I kept getting bullied so badly at school, and to make things worse, I was forced to tell everyone that I did it.

One thing worse than the physical abuse I was enduring was mental abuse. As if growing up without the security of knowing who my birth mother was not enough, it was thinking or feeling that I was never good enough as well. In all the years with Dean, he called me kiddo maybe three or four times. Otherwise, I was the fuck up, the mistake, the good for nothing, the piece of shit, and the list went on. He rarely addressed me by my first name unless he was calling me into the house from playing outside. His words were cruel and were meant to hurt. I grew up thinking I was beyond ugly and worth absolutely nothing.

Growing up, I don't remember when our parents didn't correspond without yelling or screaming. This was mainly at us kids. Stephanie and I never learned how to communicate with one another appropriately and rarely got along. We had a love-hate relationship that eventually strained our connection, especially as adults. As kids, we depended on each other for our survival. Stephanie was a bit of a dreamer, and I always envied that about her. She would play with her dolls and just escape into her own little world by tuning everything out around her.

This was something I could never do.

I always needed to be stimulated and active. I didn't understand the concept of play. Stephanie never got beaten half as bad as I did, which grew into a massive resentment for me. I would unleash my anger out on her. I beat her up until she cried. It was a release for me, but all it did was make me feel lousy and eventually guilty for hurting her. Ironically, even though she didn't get "it" as bad as I did, I tend to forget that she was abused, too, in every sense of the word. Being his biological child did not save her from his wrath. Eventually, she experienced the same fate as I did to some varying degree.

I remember once during dinner; Dean noticed that Stephanie and I had yellow powder stains on our clothes from picking dandelions. We had already been warned not to pick them. So he decided to teach us both a lesson by replacing our hotdogs with half a dozen stems from the dandelions. He made us sit there until we had finished every last bite. Like me, she also received the belt. I'm not sure when it started for her, but we can both recall being forced to lay face down on our beds with our pants and underwear down to our ankles. He had our hands underneath us, and If we covered our bum with our hands, he would add extra strikes.

Both of us had convinced ourselves that when the initial sting was over, we grew to like the warm fuzzy feeling that would take over for a bit after the initial pain began to fade. He used to play these sick games and torture us by cracking the belt then make us turn away so we couldn't see it coming as if the fear of the belt alone wasn't enough. I preferred it when he belted us together. We would lie side by side, and he would strike us across the buttocks. If it was just me, I got hit anywhere on my body, which was far worse than across the bum. The only exception to that statement was the buckle. Its sting would penetrate my skin with such force that the effects of it lasted next to forever.

I often received the worst of Dean's anger, most of which I suppressed. Still, I'll never forget the day he backhanded Stephanie so hard she flew across the room and into our kitchen cupboards. This was the first time I saw him do that to her. This was some of what he did to me behind closed doors. It was one thing for it to happen to me, but to see it happen to her was devastating. I swore I would never allow that to happen again, but of course, it did. I jumped in and pissed him off on purpose if I thought he was about to go off on her to make sure she was safe. Stephanie had her own way of showing her gratitude. After a considerable beating, Dean would almost always take a nap, and we could still tell that he was sleeping because he snored so loud. Stephanie would sneak into my room, help me up off the ground, and hold me until I stopped crying. We made a game of counting my bruises to pass the time by. Mom did catch her a few times and kicked her out, but she never told on us.

One day Stephanie and I were outside playing and started fighting. When Dean hollered out his bedroom window for me to get into the house, it was way too early for him to be done with his nap, and so I knew our shouting woke him up. I prepared myself for the worse. I slowly inched my way up to the house, knowing what was waiting for me inside. I took a deep breath and slowly opened the door, and peeked in. Our side door had two sets of stairs, one flight leading up to the kitchen; the other flight led down to the basement. The only thing I remember is that Dean jumped out from behind the door, grabbed my hair as I peered in, then…nothing.

I woke up at the bottom of the stairs in such a daze. My head was pounding so badly that I couldn't open my eyes. My ears were ringing, and my body was frozen. I moved to get up and felt this excruciating pain in my chest and couldn't take a deep breath. I eventually pulled myself together and crawled up the two flights of stairs to my room, clutching onto my chest and curled up on the floor. I could hear Dean snoring in the next room. I lay on the floor, shivering, and fell back asleep. When I woke up sometime afterward, I had the biggest headache of my life. My chest was killing me, and I still couldn't open my eyes fully. The light was more blinding than usual. My mother eventually checked on me, and I learned from her that he had smashed my head between the door and the doorframe. This had knocked me out cold. I had fallen down the stairs, and he had just left me where I had landed. She said he threatened to do the same to her if she had touched me, so she left me there to wake up.

Apparently, I passed my mother the day before on my way up the stairs while she was in the living room playing her records. I'd be damned if I ever recall him actually hitting her unless she was in the line of fire protecting me. Otherwise, I'd never seen him lay a hand on her. They were just content to yell in an argument. Most of the time, she was entirely out of it. She was off in her own little world and let him do whatever the hell he wanted. It took several weeks of moving really slowly before I could even breathe properly again. This was not to be the only time I would have this type of injury. During my first therapy course, I learned that he likely cracked my ribs. The constant beatings kept aggravating the injury.

Ever since I was a child, I have always had food aversions, especially textures like fat and bone. My mother used to serve us the same thing every single day. We grew to hate soup and sandwiches. We actually preferred when Dean made us lunch and gave us canned pasta.

One day Dean was in one of his moods and decided to go off on me while I was eating chicken noodle soup. I had a habit of storing the chicken into my cheeks and then spit it out after in the toilet. I gagged on a piece only this time and threw up half my soup and the chicken back into the bowl. He was so angry that he told me to sit there and eat my bowl's content until it was all gone. I must have eaten and regurgitated that bowl of soup several times before I just couldn't do it anymore. I just sat there and cried.

He then took his fingers, picked up some of the chicken, forced it into my mouth, and clamped my jaw shut. He threatened me that if I spit it out, I was going to regret it. I naturally threw up again. Only this time, the liquid couldn't escape out my mouth and began pouring out of my nose and onto his hands. I started choking. Kristine started shouting at him, asking him to stop. I wasn't breathing, so she pushed past him to help me. As soon as I could pass the air again, mom sent me to my room. On the way, I threw up a couple more times on her carpet, allowing Dean to follow me and finish me off. Stephanie sat there with her eyes shut, crying as she had been forced to watch the whole thing.

Siobhan O'Regan

I swore I would take a beating before I would ever eat anything I didn't like again and would sit at the table with a blank look on my face for hours staring at the plate of food. It took a few strikes to the head when I refused to eat it and even a few throws across the table, but he couldn't break me.

I often went to bed hungry for days at a time because I refused to eat. I loved hot dogs and sometimes sneaked a package out of the freezer and hid it under my mattress in a small slit I had made significant enough to fit the entire package. I snacked on them one at a time. They would eventually turn hard, but I didn't know any better at the time, and they were a lot better than the alternative. I knew Kristine kept track of every single food item she bought, so I had to be careful and really make them last. I eventually got caught when I was taken to the hospital for severe stomach cramps. The doctor told her that it was likely food poisoning. Kristine was baffled; she told the doctor that I didn't eat anything out of the ordinary. When the doctor left the room, I confessed to my mother about the hotdogs thinking for sure I would die. She threatened to tell Dean if I said anything, so I kept my mouth shut, and so did she. From that day on, she started locking the freezer door. As a kid, I often mistook her to keep secrets from Dean as an act of kindness and held out hope that a small part of her loved me.

Kristine was so compulsive about anything and everything. We were forced to wear slippers in the house, and we were never allowed to go to bed without washing our feet with soap and water. We had to use a cloth to open the refrigerator door and turn on the stove to get fingerprints on the appliances. We were not allowed to look in the fridge without permission. We could never help ourselves with our own drinks and snacks. The food was regulated and portioned out for us. Dinner was what was put in front of us, or in my case; I went without. I understand that meals were like this for many other kids growing up, but it was to the extreme for me. I wasn't missing just a meal or two. My parents would often serve meals I didn't like as a form of punishment.

We would do housework twice and sometimes three times a week. Kristine would go over every inch with an actual white glove she had on hand for when she painted. If there was ever any dirt, we had to do it repeatedly until it was done right. Everything had its place, and if something were out of place, she would wake us up in the middle of the night and make sure we corrected it. It got so bad that I often had a reoccurring nightmare that I was washing the bathroom floor, and it would get bigger and bigger. I couldn't keep up with it. I would wake up in the middle of the night, dripping in sweat, and the only way I could fall back to sleep was if I got up and rewashed it. This was even if she had approved it the night before. We were hardly ever allowed to sit on the furniture for fear of getting it dirty, so we were forced to sit on the floor. This was even during the rare times when we were allowed to watch TV as a family. If our dresser drawers were ever messy, she would take everything out and throw it on the floor and make us fold them over until the drawers were up to her standards.

Our mother didn't hold back either. Although, I always preferred getting smacked around from her instead of Dean. Her abuse didn't last as long, but it still hurt. She often used scare tactics that were best described as sadistic. For example, there was a time when I stole $20 from her Avon to buy off some bullies with candy. She found out and took a hammer to my right hand to teach me a lesson. I am talking about the same arm that I broke twice before. I couldn't write correctly for months after that and was forced to repeat grade six due to not writing in combination with other factors. I confronted her as an adult about this particular incident, and she claims that I was dramatic. She didn't hit me that hard. Stephanie was forced to witness this as a clear lesson to anyone who would be caught stealing in our house and has a much different perspective on what happened. This was one of the memories I blocked until Stephanie recalled it in a conversation several years later.

Around this same time, Randy Senior was struggling to make a decent living. He was in between jobs, so Dean hired him to work for him at the plant, and they rented a small apartment on the other side of town. This was a rough adjustment for Junior, and it got him into a lot of trouble. He got wrapped up with the wrong crowd. He was always getting into fistfights and would get caught setting fires. This was not the first time he got caught starting fires. I witnessed him starting them when we were little all the time but knew better than to tell on him. Junior was continually getting into trouble for mostly fighting at school and was suspended multiple times. Factory life did not suit Randy Senior very well, and he took a job on a turkey farm in Reardon a short time later and lived up there for close to two years.

CHAPTER FOUR

The Secrets And Lies

Stephanie and I were little but knew that our mother was not well. I'm pretty sure that I experienced my first nervous breakdown when Dean told us that she would be going away for a long while. Just the prospect of being alone with Dean was so frightening that the thought of it was unbearable.

No one told us specifically why she had to leave. All they told us was that she needed to get some help. We came home one day, and just like that, she was gone. We were on our absolute best behavior, and I remember holding my sister while she sobbed for her mother. To our surprise, Dean left us alone to do our own thing, and for a while, he was almost like a human. He appeared calmer than usual, didn't yell at us as much, and even allowed us to have screen time. Watching television in our house was a rare treat and only ever happened on Saturday mornings when they wanted to sleep in; otherwise, it was at night, and it was always whatever they wanted to watch.

Sometimes Kristine challenged me to watch a horror movie. She liked them, but Dean didn't, and Kristine did not like to watch them alone. I had to act tough and pretend that they didn't scare me even though they did. I considered it quality time with my mother. Stephanie and I liked the show titled "Different Strokes and the Cosby Show." I hated cartoons, but you take what you can get when you are given very little entertainment. To this day, I don't watch television during the day and get this uncomfortable eerie feeling whenever it is turned on. I often plug in a set of headphones and listen to music instead.

One afternoon during one of Dean's naps, Stephanie and I were playing downstairs in the basement. We got into our mother's button collection. She hated us touching her things, but she wasn't there to catch us, so I was snooping through some old photo albums while we were playing. I came across this picture of a young girl and a boy. My heart just about leaped out of my chest, as it was a picture of the same little girl who visited me at the school before I broke my arm. The boy was the same one that I pictured in my dreams, only younger. Panic set in, and I automatically felt sick to my stomach. There was this indescribable sense of excitement followed by fear, despair, and complete emptiness. Behind another page was a document that I had never seen before, I didn't understand all of the words, but my parents' names were on it.

I read the name Fallon and a line that read "ADOPTION." I knew my former name because before I was adopted, Dean's father had gifted me bonds as Christmas and birthday presents. When Dean cashed some of them, I had to sign my old name to hand them over. He eventually stole all of me and my sister's bonds, totaling thousands of dollars apiece. There are no words to describe the magnitude of different emotions and thoughts that went through my head. I gave Stephanie a look with confusion. People always said that Stephanie and I looked nothing alike. She looked so much like the girl in the picture with the same color blond hair. Then it dawned on me, and I realized why I was being treated so differently. I remember how horrified I felt at that moment, thinking to myself, it was true that I was Randy Senior's daughter. I was heartbroken; I carefully put everything back the way I found it and swore to keep my mouth shut. I couldn't go live with Uncle Randy and Randy Junior. I just couldn't. Stephanie was so wrapped up in the buttons she had no clue what I had just discovered.

I honestly don't recall how long Kristine was gone, but she appeared different in many ways when she came back. She was no longer passing out where she sat, and she seemed alive and even nurturing. This was for a while anyway. Sometime later, she left again, and that was when I started getting really sick.

I had a lot of trouble eating and couldn't catch my breath. My fingers would go cold and tingly, and I would have really bad dizzy spells, so my doctor prescribed this medication, which my mother called breathing pills. These episodes would come on suddenly and last forever. It was exhausting, and when I had them, it would physically knock me out for a couple of hours at a time. I understand now that these were likely onset panic attacks, but my mother at the time called them something else.

Nevertheless, before Kristine left us for those several weeks, she would typically just give me a pill and tell me to sit in my room until it went away. I was never permitted to lay in bed unless it was bedtime; this was the one time that she would allow me to curl up with her to take a nap. I'm not sure if this was for my benefit or hers, but my chest felt tighter. I was gasping for air and felt so confined and conflicted. I hated anyone touching me, including her, yet I longed to be held by her as she did, Stephanie. I wondered if I would feel this way if she really were my mother.

Whenever I was sick, I did my best to keep it to myself afterward. Even now, a part of me wants to be consoled and held, but it feels too unnatural, so I don't go there. I was thankful that this nurturing side of my mothers didn't last long. Still, there was always this other side of me that so desperately wanted to have some connection with her.

One evening as Kristine was sitting in her bathtub. I came in to keep her company. I drew enough courage to whisper, "Mom…am I adopted?" Kristine didn't appear surprised by my question, but I could tell that I had caught her off guard. She demanded to know why I would ask her that. I told her it was because she and Karen always said that Robyn and I were switched. She then laughed, sounding somewhat relieved, and told me no, I was not adopted, and it was just a joke.

I didn't dare press further, but I couldn't help wondering what else she had lied about and that made me angry, as I knew that she was dishonest with me. I visited that picture so many times over the years. It was my way of escaping, and for the first time, I had something to fantasize about. It was like my little secret. As children, no one ever did tell us where Kristine went when she was gone. Still, I eventually found out later that after her hysterectomy, she had become addicted to several prescription pills and was battling with her addiction. All the time she had spent away from us was due to her going to rehab and trying to get clean.

Almost every year, in the summertime, my family used to rent a cottage up in Boreal Lake for a week. Stephanie and I always looked forward to the cottage, but what I loved the most about it was that it wasn't home, and it was so nice to get out of the city and out of the confines of my room.

My parents used to rent a small boat, and we would spend hours fishing on the lake. The year I turned seven, Stephanie was four, we were out fishing in the boat. Both of my parents smoked and used to lite one cigarette after the other. Once, out of boredom, I asked my mom if I could try one; I was surprised when she said yes, and even more surprised when Dean agreed. Stephanie got excited and told them she wanted to try one too. Before they handed each one of us their cigarettes, Kristine gave us instructions on what to do. I was annoyed because I'd seen them do it enough times that I knew what I was doing. Stephanie and I took a big haul at the same time and sucked it in. We both started coughing so hard, we were choking, and I can recall how much it burned when I breathed and gasped for air. Both Kristine and Dean were laughing hysterically until Stephanie started gagging and threw up. Kristine grabbed her and hung over the side of the boat. She was so frightened that she clawed at my mother to bring her back in and screamed between sobs. I had tears in my eyes, but what hurt the most was the burning in my throat every time I coughed. Kristine held on to my sister as she wailed between gags and finally got her to settle down after a few minutes.

I asked for some water, but Dean said no, claiming he didn't want me throwing up in the boat also. I knew better than to argue, so I sat there in agony. My throat felt so raw and burned for several days after that. Stephanie curled up with Kristine and had a good cry. We both learned a valuable lesson that day. This was not so much about smoking in general, but to be careful what you ask for because you might just get it.

Boating was not something Stephanie, and I ever looked forward to after that vacation. It created a massive fear of fishing as well. The following day when we went further out on the lake, Dean was casting out for the umpteenth time when suddenly I felt this jab of pain from the corner of my right eye along with a huge tug, and so I screamed. I startled everyone in the boat, causing them all to jump. Kristine started yelling at me because the hot ash from her cigarette burned her leg when she jumped.

Dean looked over and hollered, saying, "Fuck," and told me not to move. My sister looked at me and started screaming too. Dean's lure had lodged its self in the corner of my eye with the worm. All of the bobber's weight was hanging off the cast and had ripped the skin surrounding my eye. Dean cut the line inches away from the hook. My mother began holding me down at the bottom of the boat while he drove back to shore because I was so terrified of the worm attached to the hook that I darn near jumped out of the boat. Stephanie cried all the way back, so Kristine spent most of the trip trying to console her more than she did me. I was kept and strapped down to the bottom of the boat. We got to shore and headed up to the nearest hospital that was a couple of towns over.

While we were in the car, Stephanie and I were in the back seat when she asked me if it hurt. She then touched the wire that was still attached to the hook. I know she didn't mean to hurt me, but when she grabbed the hook, I jerked my head away, pulling the wire, and started to bleed again. I panicked and started screaming. Dean slammed on the breaks, turned around to face Stephanie, hollered at her, and slapped her across the mouth. Usually, he would only yell and hit me like that, but he was furious and directed it at her this time.

I held my breath and was shaking violently, waiting for my turn. Kristine yelled at him to keep going glancing back periodically to give me a dirty look. Stephanie was now crying inconsolably and sucked her fingers to soothe herself. At the hospital, Dean's demeanor changed, and they became incredibly attentive. He called me kiddo and held me while the doctor cut the hook to pull it out. They had to restrain me from stitching the hole, and afterward, the doctor told my parents that I was the luckiest kid alive. Most of the damage was done to the skin around my eye. The area where the hook scratched the inside of my eyes was minor, and they were confident that it wouldn't cause any permanent damage.

I had to use eye drops every day for a few weeks and cover them with a patch for almost a month, so I was glad that I didn't have school. The following year, he hooked Stephanie in the cheek the same way he hooked me and had to have it removed at the hospital. He then nicknamed me his largemouth bass and Stephanie his smallmouth bass.

One time, our cousins came down to the cottage with us. Randy Junior and I were in trouble for something as usual, and we were told to wash the lunch dishes and clean up the kitchen while they went for a walk on the beach. Junior had his dog with him, and everyone knew how much she meant to Junior. The dog was Junior's baby. I watched, amazed and silent, as he grabbed a plate, offered it to his dog, and let her lick every inch of the food. He then casually placed it back into the cupboard without cleaning it or having it touch the water. He did this with every dish while I kept watching.

Siobhan O'Regan

I was absolutely speechless. I cleared the cups and utensils, put them into the sink of hot water, and wiped the table. When they were done with the plates, he reached into the sink, grabbed a handful of utensils at a time, dumped them into the dish rack, and ordered me to dry them. He then grabbed the cups one at a time and tossed them in the dish rack as well. The pots and pans were also left for me. I had no formal training on washing dishes since my mother would have had a fit if anyone touched her beloved kitchen. I was pretty confident she would have lost it if she had seen this. It most likely would have killed her. Junior took a quick look around, smiled at me, and walked his dog in tow. I will be damned if he gave it a second thought. I, on the other hand, thought about nothing else all afternoon.

Dinner time came, and I took my place at the table; my stomach was killing me in anticipation and shaking out of fear of the unknown. Robyn set out the utensils as Kristine pulled out a stack of dog-licked plates and placed them on the counter. She took the top one, scolded Junior and me for missing a spot, scratched it off, and handed it to her sister. He then grabbed the second plate, glanced at it, and loaded it up with food. I felt like I was going to throw up, not because I was grossed out but because I was so scared we would get caught. I looked at Junior, but he was in his own little world and couldn't be happier. I couldn't believe no one noticed, and we lived to talk about it. Junior and I never brought it up, but I re-visited that moment many times as one of my happiest memories at the cottage.

In the last year, we were at the cottage. I met a boy while I was on the beach. It was just Stephanie, Kristine, and me, as Dean often went off to do his own thing. This boy was adorable and was flirting with me. At first, I was extremely cautious and didn't want anything to do with him, but I thought he was kind of cute and relentless. I desperately wanted to make a friend, and so I smiled back. I was cautious about what I did and said to him because I really wanted him to like me.

We hang out a lot over the next couple of days, and he told me that his family owned a cottage connected to the beach. Every day I looked forward to going out to see him. We spent most of our time hanging out and playing in the water. The last day before we went home, we walked along the shore, and he asked me for my phone number. I lied and told him that we didn't have a phone. He leaned in and kissed me on the lips. It was so quick that I didn't have a chance to react. He smiled and promised to look out for me the next year. I became so obsessed with him that I considered him to be my first real kiss. We never did go back to the cottage, but that wasn't the last time I saw this boy.

As we got older, my parents would send us off to summer camp every couple of years for a week. The first year, I was out taking my swimming test. Afterward, they asked me to follow the counselor to the main building. This was my first camping experience, so I didn't think anything of it. I was escorted into a small office and introduced to the people inside. I don't recall who they all were. Still, I remember the lady who had told me she was a worker from Child Services. She started asking me many questions concerning my bruises and a mark that looked like a cigarette burn on my forearm.

I was sitting in my bathing suit and my towel, looking down. I noticed that I was covered in bruises. I adjusted my towel to cover some of them, but there were too many to hide. I told her that I just got them from the swimming test when I struggled near the end and must have hit myself while swimming.

I honestly didn't know any better and didn't have enough time to develop a better story. Dean had warned me about people snooping into our business. He had taught me that the world was a lot scarier outside of our house. There were people out there who did terrible things to little girls, who didn't do as they were told. I was assured that he couldn't protect me if I ever were taken away. That was enough information for me as I didn't know exactly what he meant, but if out there was going to be worse than what was happening at home, I wanted no part of it.

I kept my eyes on the floor and told them nothing. At one point, I asked about my sister. I had nothing more to say to them and asked to be excused. She asked me a few more questions, but I kept quiet, thinking to myself, he would be so proud of me. I was finally excused and went off to search for Stephanie. I'm not sure if they questioned her or not. All I know is that I told them nothing.

Kids were a lot friendlier at camp than they were in school, but by then, I was so scared of people in general that I didn't want to connect with any of them. Therefore, I hung out with Stephanie as often as I could. By the second day in, I was so homesick; I think I was just overstimulated from being outside my environment. With so much going on, it became too overwhelming. I forced them to call my mother. I started crying and begged her to bring me back home. She refused and said that she would see me in a week and then hung up the phone.

When they came to pick us up, we were excited to see them. I had many stories to tell, but I was very relieved to be back home underneath it all. I never did tell them about the lady who questioned me. I didn't want to upset Dean. He was an impossible man to read when he wasn't angry. I spent most of my life walking on eggshells or dodging bullets. It was quite a ride home.

We were sent to camp twice again over the following few summers, and each time, it was a hit or miss for me. I had moments where I was excited and moments where I dreaded going. I liked the fact that it was not a big deal if I didn't like the food and that it was ok to ask for more if I was still hungry. I did get into trouble for taking and hiding food under my blankets in our cabin. They told me that it attracted animals, so I promised them that I wouldn't do it anymore, but instead, I just found better hiding places. The funny thing was that I liked to hoard the food. However, I rarely ate it. Just to have it was far too valuable for me. It gave me a false sense of comfort.

At the beginning of grade four, if the home wasn't bad enough, the school was really starting to take a toll on me. I know I wasn't liked at all. I had very few friends. No one talked to me, let alone played with me. I spent most of my time wandering the playground by myself or hanging out with Stephanie. This one set of Asian siblings moved in right across from the school partway through the school year. Their English was broken, but they communicated well enough to get by. Unfortunately, trying to make and maintain friends was awkward for me. I had an undiagnosed attachment disorder, and there was the fact that I couldn't even go over to anyone's house, let alone anyone come to mine.

This disconnection was a massive issue for me. Technically I could only socialize at school, and with my introverted and chronically fearful personality type, no child could relate to me, let alone connect with me on the most basic level. Once these kids understood that I was not liked and was being teased by the rest of their peers just for being my friend, they stopped talking to me altogether.

Before they left me, we all received our school photos, so I gave them each one of mine. They came late in the year, and so they didn't have one for me. I didn't care. I was so happy to have a friend to give a photo to. A few days later, I walked through the schoolyard on my way home when something on the ground caught my eye. I picked it up and was devastated to see that it was my photo. I cried all the way home. Unfortunately, I didn't get the hint very well. A couple of days later, I found enough courage to ask them to play with me. In return, they told me to go away in front of a group of kids. I was heartbroken, embarrassed, and wanted to die.

For years my punishments were strict, cruel, and demoralizing. We were never allowed to sleep in, and even though they sometimes slept in on Saturdays, we couldn't. Dean had us up every morning at 7 am. Before they stripped my room of everything, I started reading Sweet Valley High books. I began reading faster so that I could get my hands on more. I often read two books at a time as two was the maximum we could take out of the school library. I grew up thinking that being grounded lasted for weeks and months at a time with minimal to no socialization or family contact. For me, I was only allowed to attend school, eat meals, and do my business but wasn't allowed to socialize with anyone.

I was ok for the first little while and sat for hours just singing to my radio and doodling. Eventually, Dean stripped my room, taking everything and leaving me with nothing but the clothes on my back and an alarm clock that I used to hide in my drawer. This was because the constant ticking would drive me insane. He used to force me to keep it out on the corner of my dresser, and when the ticking became unbearable, I used to dream of hitting him over the head with it in his sleep.

I first heard that kids were typically grounded for a couple of days or maybe a week max in my early teens. It took me years to comprehend the concept that what happened to me was inhumane and even longer as an adult to admit I was imprisoned, tortured, and dehumanized.

In a particular beating episode, I was curled up on the floor in the fetal position weeping to describe another session of my abuse. Stabs of pain were surging through my tiny, underweight framed body where the belt and his fists had penetrated. I felt so bad that I felt like vomiting, but I didn't dare. He began to scream and demand that I get up. My head was spinning, and all I could hear was him panting heavily. I knew that he was standing near the entrance to my room and that he was well within striking distance. From experience, I knew that if I got up, he would use the door to finish me. Consequently, I chose to lie very still and prayed that he had tired himself out.

Siobhan O'Regan

I was hoping that he would go away. My heart was beating so hard and so fast, and I was forcing myself to focus on his breathing to anticipate his next move. Panic rose when I heard him take a deep breath. My body seized up as I listened to the floor creak underneath him. He was moving in my direction. I realized that he was coming back. I felt a massive blow to my lower back, and I yelped out in pain through gritted teeth. I sprawled out onto the floor with my hands underneath me, clutching the new surge of strain on my back.

I sucked in as much air as I could and held it. Nothing is worse than feeling like you're suffocating when you can't take a breath between blows, so I knew to take one whenever I could and hold on to it for dear life. I then waited. Nothing happened. The nausea was now overwhelming me, and he began yelling and cursing at me again. I slowly let some air out. I could tell that he was wearing down, and I was praying for it to be over. My eyes were shut. I always kept my eyes closed because I had convinced myself that it was easier if I didn't see it coming.

I had one arm behind me now, and one is clutching my stomach. I knew that if he hit me in the stomach, I would vomit, and it would only make things worse. I heard him walking away. I was listening very carefully. My ears were ringing, and my head was pounding, but I could still sense him moving towards the door. There was a moment where I heard him shuffling in the doorway; then, out of nowhere, there was a loud hollowed clank of what sounded like metal hitting something hard with great force. Immediately, I felt this excruciating pain, unlike anything I have ever felt before. I couldn't even scream. I couldn't breathe. My entire body was thrashing around, I reached out for my crotch, but I did not dare to touch it. I felt nothing but an intense surge of continuous pain.

I finally caught my breath and began to scream, but no sound came out of my mouth. I did not hear him leave. My body was convulsing now, and there was vomit on my shirt. I looked down at my private area and saw that I was bleeding through my pants. My hands were shaking so badly, and I wanted to touch myself, but it hurt too much. I was so scared. Still unaware of what had happened to me, my mind could only concentrate on the pain and the blood, which was becoming an even bigger pooled stain on my pants. I missed realizing the object lying on the carpet just inches away from me. The large metal wind-up alarm clock usually sat in the corner of my dresser and the only object that was left in my room. The pain was so intense that the clock went completely unnoticed.

Nobody Special

My mother later told me that I was experiencing my first period and that it was normal for me to bleed heavily. Eventually, I was taken to go to our doctor, and they told him that Stephanie and I got into a fight, and she threw the alarm clock at me. He clinically confirmed that the incident had likely broken my hymen and that this was not uncommon in active females. However, he couldn't rule out my period either since girls started their cycles much earlier these days. There was no exam conducted at the time. An exam at fifteen showed that there was severe scarring where the clock hit my vaginal area. A portion of the blood appeared from where the clock tore me open, and I probably should have had stitches, but the doctor never bothered to look.

My doctor was so old school and ended up with cancer and died a year after his diagnosis. I often thought that if he only took the time to put two and two together, he might have saved me from my parents much sooner. But as luck would have it, a much older male doctor didn't invest much time into a young adolescent girl whose mother, as it turned out, was a massive hypochondriac.

I'm not sure how often Kristine visited the doctor when I was little, but I'm sure that it was quite often. She needed to feed her addiction to painkillers, and so she was a massive hypochondriac. Kristine spent a lot of her time explaining the multiple wrong things with her and was always on several prescription drugs.

I swore as a kid I would never follow in her footsteps and, for the most part, stuck by my own convictions based on a child's perception. I was prescribed inhalers for asthma, antidepressants, psychotropic medications for ADD/ADHD, and bipolar disorder. These were some I would take for a bit, but others I wouldn't at all. My mother's prescriptions were her drug of choice and her way of coping through self-medicating. Ironically, I eventually battled my own demons in the form of addictions, but that will be discussed later.

CHAPTER FIVE

Little Girl Blue

Near the end of grade five, there was a new girl that came to our school. Her name was Chloe, and I used to be so amused by how the girls would always flock around her in hopes of befriending her.

I was jealous as I would have loved to have a best friend. Heck, there were times I would have settled for any friend. Kids in our school came and went, but I always preferred the comfort and solitude of being by myself to having their rejection any day. Therefore I sat back and watched them from a distance. We had to pair up during a class project, and we had the only teacher in school that liked to pick our partners for us. Secretly I was grateful because it saved me the embarrassment of being picked last.

I think she strategically paired Chloe and me up, figuring the new kid wouldn't know how unpopular I was yet. She was warm, friendly, and for some strange reason, we were somehow able to connect. A few girls were upset that I got picked to be her partner, and I didn't hold back to voice their disapproval on the playground. None of it seemed to phase Chloe. Truthfully, I believe the others were fascinated by wanting to know what was so special about me, making Chloe wish to befriend me.

Chloe and I would sit together at lunch and chat with one another before and after school. Later I would run home and tell my mother all about my new friend. Chloe was all I would talk about. I honestly don't remember how it came about that my mother and her father met, but they did, and I think it was the only thing that salvaged our friendship.

Siobhan O'Regan

I didn't bring her home out of fear of my father, so I was allowed to hang out a couple of times at her place. I learned that she lived alone with her father, and she was referred to as a latchkey

kid, a term I had never heard before. This meant that her dad worked long hours, so she took care of herself until he would come home from work.

There were many things about this girl that fascinated me, and this was one of them. Stephanie and I always had someone at home watching our every move. I became obsessed with her world; she was allowed to use the fridge and stove and even learned how to make Kraft Dinner (KD). I seriously didn't even know how to boil water. I was so grateful to her for taking the time to teach me (when I eventually moved out of my house, making KD became the only skill I possessed thanks to her). She told me that coming home to an empty house made her feel lonely and that she looked forward to her dad coming back.

I had a hard time believing that someone loved their parents so much that they would look forward to them coming home every night. I was the happiest when mine left me alone. We eventually disclosed some of our deepest darkest secrets to one another. I learned that her mother's husband used to do unspeakable things to her when they were alone for many years. They were the kind of stuff the boy did to me when I was six. The only difference was, the way she described it was far worse over a more extended period. For reasons I'll never understand, her mother could choose to support her partner and turn her back on her child. I listened to her stories and thought compared to her; I didn't have it so bad.

I guess my new taste of freedom clouded my judgment. I was so immersed in gratitude to be out of my house that I forgot how terrible my situation was. It was just a different bad. We would spend a lot of time exchanging war stories with one another, and I was so glad to have someone I could tell my secrets to. She indeed was my best friend.

I needed to learn a thing or two about treating people, so I made some decisions, which I regretted later for a very long time. It was always a power struggle whenever Stephanie and I interacted. If we played a board game, I would teach her how to play, and if I didn't get the way, I would threaten and intimidate her. This was the same in all my interactions, and now I was starting to treat Chloe the exact same way. There are many things to be said about the special bond between two people who share a significant trauma history. Still, our friendship did not survive because of my apparent lack of people skills and the language I developed in the absence of adequate guidance and proper role modeling. During those torment and segregation years, I developed a significant deficit in communication skills, empathy, sympathy, and deductive reasoning. You stop growing or become delayed developmentally due to some trauma, add chronic fear and mistrust to the formula, and have many personality disorders.

By the beginning of grade six, Chloe had somehow developed immunity to my unfavorable legacy. Other kids liked her, but, like me, connecting with people on an intimate level was a massive challenge. So she appeared to prefer the familiarity of my company regardless of how badly I treated her. She always was the smarter one and got decent grades, and I was barely getting by.

In middle school, we always sat next to each other in class, so I could cheat and look at her papers when it came to exams. We eventually got caught, and the punishment in our school for cheating usually meant a suspension. We were dragged into the office, and our parents were called in to have a chat with our principal. Of course, Kristine didn't drive, so that meant Dean came in. The moment they told me that my parents were called in, I started to shake violently. I knew what was happening, and he had the whole drive to and from school to decide how to execute my punishment. My stomach was in knots as lately, my tummy always hurt. It didn't take much to aggravate it, and I felt like I had been kicked several times when I was stressed out. He came into school and didn't even look at me. They arrived before Chloe's dad did and was asked to go straight into the office. I was told to follow them in. I didn't dare budge until Dean gave me the okay to move.

I sat in the office as quietly as humanly possible and continued to shake. Kristine kept giving me a dirty look to stop what I was doing as if I had any control over it. The principal agreed to an in-school suspension and told us that I was lucky, and if this were to happen again, they would send me home.

Dean said nothing to me on the way home, and I went straight into my room. I sat in the fetal position in the corner of my room, stuck my thumb in my mouth, and rocked back and forth until it was time to eat. Dinner was uneventful, but for a kid living in fear of the unknown, it was excruciating.

I preferred a blitz attack to this, any day. I didn't touch my food but really tried to eat. However, my stomach hurt too much, so mom excused me and told me to have my shower and get ready for bed.

My room was next to Dean's room, which was down the hall from the kitchen. I had to pass where Dean sat at the kitchen table to get to my room. I carefully placed my dishes in the sink and slowly inched my way past Dean. When I was on the other side of him, I scurried to my room to gather my things. During my shower, all I could focus on was my fear of what was going to happen to me when I got out. The thought was creating an even more intense pain inside my stomach. When I was done, I tidied up, as I always did. My mother had notes up around the house, giving detailed instructions on how to clean up. If there were any deviation from the list, I would have had to deal with her wrath, and the fact that I was on his radar too really scared me.

I listened for any movement in the hallway, took a deep breath, and tiptoed the five or so feet into my room. I closed my eyes and fell onto the belt strategically placed at the end of my bed. I lost it then and began crying and whispering under my breath, "I'm sorry," repeatedly until he came in.

He stood in the door and told me to assume the position, which meant panties down and lay across the bed's edge. He then instructed me to turn my head and snapped the belt a couple of times, which also meant that he was either gearing up or losing patients. It was tough for me to pull my pants down in front of anyone and stretch across the bed. I was completely exposed and vulnerable. Yet, I was forced to do this every time. I complied, pulling my Pj pants and underwear down to my ankles. I have to add that drawing them down to my knees made me feel less exposed. Still, it was also harder to move around if he was planning to hit other areas of my body, and I was to go into defensive mode.

He may not have been sexually abusing me, but beating me while I am half-naked was just as demoralizing. I heard him close the door behind afterward and went to town. I lost count of how many times he struck me. I always did when he went off on me like this, and there wasn't much of my body that the belt didn't get to know intimately. Regardless of the beating I just received, nothing hurt more than the words that came out of his mouth when he was done. As he walked out the door, he told me that I was not to hang out with Chloe anymore, and he would see to it that she understood this as well.

Nobody Special

I was curled up on my bed in nothing but my nightshirt and screamed into my blankets. I was about to lose the only thing in the world that I valued, and it was my fault. The next day Kristine told me that she had talked to Chloe's father and agreed not to be friends anymore. She also said that Dean would be calling the school to check up on me to make sure that we weren't speaking to one another. I walked up to Chloe the next day as my face was completely red and swollen from crying all night, and before I could say anything, she confirmed what my mom had said.

I was heartbroken. I served my in-school suspension sitting in a room with piles of schoolwork, alone and grieving the loss of my one and only friend. She stood by her word and didn't speak to me much after that but was friendly when she passed by me in the hall. I stayed away out of fear of what my father would do if I got caught near her. It absolutely killed me when I would see her hanging out with other kids at school, and I didn't have anyone. She did come up to me to tell me that she was moving with her dad to another town and that we would stay in contact, but we never did. I missed my friend so badly, and I don't think she ever knew how much her friendship meant to a girl like me. I did one day in the future get a chance to tell her, but I was far too damaged to pick up where we left off. And just like that, she was gone.

Chloe leaving school hit me hard, and behaviorally, I started spiraling out of control. I started stealing from my parents to buy candy in a desperate attempt to win over friends. Unfortunately, that only lasted until the candy was gone. I was even stealing from the lost and found at school, gifting the items I took, again, trying and make friends. Kids were no longer content with just ignoring me and making remarks; they would pass me by in the hallway, pushing me around and calling me names. One kid made up a name for me that eventually stuck, and from then on, I was forever known as "fish lips."

I was this skinny little kid who dressed in boyish clothes. At the time, having big pouty lips was not in fashion like it is today. Realistically, it didn't matter, as they would have picked on just about anything. Bullying back then was so prevalent. The threshold for disciplining a student for this type of behavior was much higher than it is today. So, just about everybody did it.

Siobhan O'Regan

There was only one kid who was liked less than I, and ironically, she was a child who was adopted as well. She used to tell stories about how her biological parents were royalty and how she was a genuine princess. She became the only person I could lash out on when things got unbearable.

Getting picked on became a sport for many kids at the school, and it was something I could not get away from. I remember that when the bullying turned into physical abuse, and I started getting beaten up daily, I seriously started thinking about suicide. I had thought about it so often while sitting in my room by myself, but I was such a sheltered kid, and there wasn't much I knew about the subject then. I only knew that I didn't want to live anymore. If getting it from the kids wasn't bad enough, the teachers sat back and allowed it to happen.

I had this one teacher who I really admired named Mr. Dickson. He had this way of connecting to the children and was generally well-liked by all his students. We had this assignment in class to write a poem, and I wrote mine in less than half an hour. I really liked poetry and used to write a lot of it before Dean took everything out of my room. So the writing came very easily to me. He was very impressed, and for the first time, I got an A on a project. It was so good; he asked me to submit it to be published in a book that prints kid's poems and short stories. He proudly selected mine.

A week or so later, after it came out in print, he read it out to the class. Instead of congratulating me for my accomplishment, the children began to harass me and spread around a nasty rumor that I had stolen it and copied the whole thing word for word. A couple of days later, my teacher asked me to speak in private. He sat me down in a chair and looked me straight in the eye. He asked me point blank if I copied the poem. His line of questioning shocked me. He was so proud of me when he read my poem out to the class couple of days ago. Why did he change his mind? He went on to tell me what plagiarism was and that it was illegal. He then continued saying that I would be in a lot of trouble if I did copy it and that I needed to speak up and tell the truth. I broke out in tears. I felt so betrayed and defeated. The one person who I thought was in my corner didn't believe me. I told him, "No," and I meant it. I wrote that in class when the assignment was handed out, and every word was my own.

I typically ate alone most days unless all other seats were taken, then the other children would sit at mine. In one instance, a boy sat next to me. I didn't know him well, but we were in the same class together. He took a bite of his sandwich and started yelling at the top of his lungs, "Fish lips touched my sandwich, and now it tastes like crap!" I just sat there in silence and kept my head down. That wasn't good enough, so he threw a pickle at me, landing in my hair, and shouted, "If you wanted some, all you had to do was ask." A lot of kids were laughing and chiming in now. They never used to pick on me like this when Chloe was around. A few days earlier, I was caught picking my nose in class, and now the whole school knew about it. Kids would walk by my locker every day and stick their boogers on the outside of it. They pretended to pick their noses and wipe them on me. One boy stuck his finger up his nose and yelled, "fish lips is missing something from her lunch," while pulling his finger out of his nose and wiping it on my sandwich. Kids at our table started screaming, ew! and backed away from me.

Most of the time, I could hold my own, ignore them and retreat inside my head. Other times like this one, I cried and ran out of the lunchroom. The bathroom was the only place I could hide and often retreat to. The last time I ate lunch in the cafeteria that year and instead, I just began to sit there and draw cartoons instead. I hated sandwiches anyway and only ate them if I hadn't eaten in a couple of days. I stored the sandwiches in my locker, and when the smell of rotten sandwiches began to create complaints, the principal would force me to get rid of them. The kids started to complain of the scent regularly. I decided to hang outside whenever possible and be as far off the property as I could. This taunting lasted forever and never seemed to get old; I absolutely dreaded going to school.

Before there were school buses, I had to walk nearly four kilometers to and from school. I was just within the perimeter of what the board considered walking distance. When Chloe was around, I would meet up and walk with her, but now I had to walk independently. I was walking home from school one afternoon when a car hit me less than five minutes away from school. It clipped me from behind, and I rolled down its side a few times before I hit the pavement.

The driver jumped out of her vehicle and was screaming hysterically. I felt dizzy and recall seeing spots in front of my eyes, almost like I did just before Dean would knock me out cold. This time I didn't lose consciousness. I could feel that the side of my leg was scraped from where I hit the cement, but otherwise, it felt okay, and so I got up and started limping back up the hill. The lady demanded that I sat down and told me not to move, but my head was spinning, and I wanted her to leave me alone. She was insisting that I get into her car, but I had been warned never to get into a car with strangers, so I kept walking and told her I was okay. She reluctantly got into her car and drove off.

A kid who had seen the accident walked me back up to the school and told the office staff what happened. They took one look at the blood through my torn pants and told me that they had to call my parents. I panicked and told them that they would be mad and begged them not to call, but they disagreed, and they called them anyway. I honestly have no clue what happened next. I don't know who that kid was; who helped me? Or how I got home? All I know is that my parents did not take me to the hospital, and I spent time recovering in my room. My mom took pictures of the massive bruise I had on my hip where the car hit me, and that was it.

I made several appearances at the office, all of them requiring me to go to the hospital. One time I was in the shop class, and we were making plastic key chains. I forgot to tighten the base plate on the sander, and the base tilted, pushing my hand right into the belt while it was running, sanding the skin off two of my knuckles. They called Dean immediately, and he rushed me up to the hospital, but there was nothing they could do for me. There was no skin left to stitch, and they said it would scab over and heal on its own. They suggested that if it didn't heal properly, see my doctor and then refer me to a plastic surgeon. It eventually recovered on its own, leaving behind scars, but the kids at school never let me live it down. One kid even grabbed my bandaged hand for fun and squeezed it. I never understood why they were so mean to me.

On one of my routes home, a house on the corner was rumored to have live rabbits caged held in their back yard. I passed by it on the way home and snuck a peek through the fence, and sure enough, there were about 30 of them all lined up in cages. I used to look in on them every day and would sometimes talk to them through the fence. When I was passing by the yard, I overheard a bunch of kids talking about how the people who owned the house were breeding them for food and were planning on setting them free. I felt sick, wondering how anyone could do that to such a harmless creature, so I walked up to them and told them I wanted to help. I was thrilled when they said that I could and included me in their plan.

They told me that we were going to run in, open as many cages as possible, and make a run for it. Only two of the five kids went into the yard with me, and we released as many as we could before we got spooked and hightailed it out of there. I don't know how I got caught. I can only assume someone recognized me as one of the kids running away because the police showed up at my door to inform my parents what I had done. They let them know that the owners were expecting retribution for their losses.

To say that my parents were angry was an understatement. The police questioned me, but I didn't tell them anything except that I had done it independently. I refused to give up the other two even after they said that there was sufficient evidence proving more were involved. At that age, it baffled me how they could have known that. They recovered most of the rabbits, but I was forced to apologize in a letter and work to pay off the rabbits they lost through my allowance.

I didn't even know that I had an allowance. I was punished severely and was grounded for almost six months for that stunt. I became my mother's slave to pay back the money they forked out on my behalf. The police came to the school to question a couple of kids. My two accomplices were eventually caught and were ordered to apologize the same way I did. Still, I ultimately paid the price several times over. The news got around the school that I was the one who told on them, and that made me a snitch on top of my other many beautiful attributes. The kids just hated me.

Just before the snow came, we were finally granted a bus and only had to walk the quarter kilometer to catch it. I didn't mind walking to school. I liked it, but it was getting much colder out, and the cold weather didn't agree with me. Unfortunately, the bus was a breeding ground for cruelty as now kids could do what they wanted without having to worry about the repercussions of getting caught, like that ever mattered. There wasn't a single day that I didn't get pushed, threatened, spat on, harassed, and belittled. What's worse was that my parents knew what was happening and did absolutely nothing to stop it.

Dean would often tell me that I likely did something to deserve it. I remember one of the kids pushed me once to the ground for looking at her the wrong way. She grabbed me by my coat and mushed snow into my face. It burned so bad. Then she spat in my hair (the one thing that never seemed to grow old). I only ever attempted to get up when I would see the bus coming, or else I knew that they would just thrust me back down again. One time I walked up and pushed past the rest of the kids and actually contemplated jumping out in front of the bus. I tried to do this several times over the next couple of months and chickened out every time. I don't think any of them actually understood what I was feeling, and I kind of hoped they would just push me like they often threatened to do. Sometimes I would hide behind the fence and wait until I'd see the bus, then run out like I was late.

In the spring of 1987, things had settled down quite a bit when the weather started to get warmer. Kids were still cruel when they interacted with me, but they got bored picking on me when I stopped reacting to them. During lunch, I would leave the school property and go down to the park close by. I enjoyed hanging out near the water and watched the kids play.

I met this boy named Joe, who sat next to me, chatting about nothing special. I wasn't really interested in what he had to say but remained friendly with him since I didn't have that many options. Joe claimed that we were in the same school in grade five but placed in different classes. He was a loner like me, and it turned out to be a lot for two people to have in common. We began to hang out just about every lunch hour. Joe wasn't someone I would consider attractive, but he wasn't ugly either. I didn't feel like I was anything appealing either, but the appearance didn't seem to bother him. He must have thought I was cute to do what we did.

Joe became my first experimental boyfriend. We would go behind the building on the other side of the school and make out. I was nowhere close to being developed like some of the other girls in school. He didn't look like he had that much exposure to the opposite sex either. We just let nature take its course and did what came naturally. I let him touch me, and I would touch him, and we would take in all the pleasant sensations it did to our bodies. This was much different than when I was six. We were both eleven, and this boy was not pressuring me to do anything that I didn't want to do. We both couldn't think of anything more exciting to do with our time.

We both got naked once and tried to have what we thought was sex since neither one of us had a clue what the heck we were doing. However, he wasn't able to perform. Embarrassment took over, and we decided to end the relationship shortly after our last encounter. I got what I wanted out of him in the form of sexual experience, and I wasn't the least bit concerned about what he wanted. I went back to doing my own thing, and we went our separate ways. I had become so numb I had no consideration for his feelings whatsoever. By the end of the year, my teachers notified my parents that

Nobody Special

I was failing all my classes. I needed to repeat the sixth grade. There are no words to describe the horrible sensation I faced knowing I had to face grade six all over again.

Grade six was no better the second time around. The school was constantly putting out fires as far as I was concerned, and I was being hauled into the office daily for one thing or another. My peers were continually harassing me for being the only kid in my grade to be held back a year. On the second day of school, I met this new boy I nicknamed Armstrong because he only had one arm. I became attracted to his personality right away. I loved how he walked around like he owned the place and didn't give a damn about what people thought of him, and best of all, he liked me.

One day this kid was making fun of me, and so he jumped him and started slapping him in the face playfully with his stump. He always seemed to know just how far to take things, and no one really messed with him. He had two friends he hung out with regularly named Alex and Oliver, and one of them had a girlfriend named Emily. Oliver and Emily fascinated me since I had never seen two people my age tongue joust the way they did. I often found myself staring at them as they were going at it. We went down to the river together every lunch hour, and they tried and convinced me to swim in the water with them. They splashed me when I didn't, so I always went back to school in wet clothes. They were all so carefree, and I loved how I felt around them. Armstrong was a year older than me. He was in the eighth grade and was a lot more experienced in all areas of life.

I remember the first time he stuck his tongue in my mouth to kiss me. I slapped him and pushed him away. I had never been kissed like that before, and he tasted like an ashtray. He looked at me, laughed, and remarked how I liked it rough. He did it again by wrestling me to the ground. I felt emotions I had never felt before. It was a combination of fear, excitement, danger, and curiosity all rolled into one. It made me feel very unsure of myself. My body had developed a mind of its own when he would touch me. I quivered anytime he pressed his body up to mine, but there were certain things he would do that would drive me crazy. For instance, I would get angry when he would tickle me. He would often make up for it by kissing my neck. That boy would make me dizzy; all I knew was that I liked him a lot, and he liked me, or at least I thought he did.

One afternoon we were down at the river, and I hit my head climbing on one of the rocks. I instantly felt this warm sensation streaming down my face. I recognized the smell immediately and knew right away that I was bleeding. Armstrong didn't hesitate for one second. He tore off his jean jacket and held it on top of my head until we got to the school. I walked into the office, and they called Dean right away. When they asked what happened, I panicked, but Armstrong didn't flinch and told them that I tripped and banged my head on the corner of the building playing tag. I was sure grateful that he remembered we were not allowed to be off school property. Everyone knew kids left the school to go to the park, but he also understood how much I feared my father. He didn't exactly know why but understood what it meant to come from a dysfunctional family and didn't want me to get into trouble. At the hospital, I refused to get stitches, so they agreed to try taping it instead. I thought the idea of taping was great; it meant that Dean was less likely to smack me around, given my wound could open up again and bleed all over my mother's precious carpet.

I told my mom that I met this new girl named Emily and that I was hanging out at her place. However, I was actually sneaking over to Armstrong's house. My mother never met her but bought the story anyway. I think she was glad that I had met a new friend, so I stop going on about how much I missed Chloe. We would hang out watching movies, listen to music, and make out. I loved his room. It was in the basement of his mother's townhouse, and he slept in a hammock. He almost always had company over, so we were seldom alone. On the weekends, he and his friends would hang out in the field by my house and ride their dirt bikes. I could watch them for hours. He sure knew how to maneuver his bike for a guy with one arm and gave me a crash course on how to ride one.

Things were pretty good for a while except for the fact that he was sometimes rude, disrespectful and reminded me of Dean. I would get mad when he told me things that would upset me and then brush it off. He would joke it off and make it as if it wasn't important and turn it into something funny. Only that it wasn't funny, so he would act stupid to try and make me laugh. Sometimes it worked. Other times, we would fight and argue. He was only nasty to me and said really mean things when we fought.

The thing that upset me the most was when he would grab me and slap me in the face with his stump. This made me laugh when he did it to other people, but it totally irritated me. Not only was he rude, but he was getting rough with me too. It seemed like there were more bad times than good, and he was starting to pressure me to have sex. Heavy petting wasn't cutting it anymore. It was getting harder to fend him off when we were together, and I preferred when his friends were around.

Kristine had already had a discussion with me about how sacred a woman's virginity was and that it was the best gift you could give to a person you cared about. She made me promise never to do it unless I had talked to her first. This conversation was ironic since she didn't know I had a boyfriend. She also knew that Dean had broken my hymen during a beating, which is what I understood to be my virginity at the time.

I wanted to make sure that I saved myself for that special guy, and by the looks of where things were heading in this relationship, it wasn't going to be him. It was two weeks before Halloween. In his basement, we were making out in his hammock when he started getting a little too forceful this time and wasn't taking no for an answer. He and I were alone, and his friend Alex had gone out to score some smokes. We started kissing and understood fondling was as far as I was willing to go, period. When he started pulling down my pants, I told him to slow down. He had attempted this before, so I wasn't alarmed but was getting annoyed. My panic button hit fast when he started pulling his pants down and began to shove his tongue down my throat.

I tried to push him away, but he had this way of dropping his weight on me, so the sides of the hammock came up snug around us. I told him that I had enough, and it was time to leave. It was clear that he disagreed and kept ongoing. I lied to him and said that I had been sexually active to make me look experienced because I knew that he wasn't a virgin even at thirteen. This was not how I pictured my first time and needed it to end, so I shouted at him to stop.

I knew this would get his attention because we both knew his mom was upstairs and wouldn't want her to come down. He put his hand over my mouth and told me to shut the hell up. When he released his grip, I told him to get off me, or I would scream louder. Realizing I was dead serious, he swore at me, appeared to take a moment to contemplate his options, and climbed off. He was furious and called me a cock tease. I had never heard of the term before, but I understood what it meant.

He stood there and lit a smoke with his pants undone, hanging halfway down his buttocks, telling me that I really didn't have to be such a bitch about it. I did up my pants and walked home. I swore I would never allow what happened to Chloe to happen to me. I meant it (my mind was still in denial about what happened to me when I was six); I couldn't stop the abuse at home, but I could prevent this from going too far. I refused to talk to him at school despite his many attempts to apologize to me but then reached a point of no return when he called me a cock tease, among other things, in front of our peers. I once again walked the lonely beat of the schoolyard on my own. I was so lonesome I deliberated on taking him back, but as fate would have it, the events that took place later made that decision for me.

I came home from running an errand with my parents to find a package on my back step addressed to me. I figured it was from Robyn, so I scooped it up and took it to my room. I was excited, so I didn't hesitate to open it up and immediately wished that I hadn't because inside was the biggest snake I had ever laid eyes on. It slithered right out of the box and fell onto my carpet.

I began screaming and ran out of my bedroom, slamming the door behind me. Dean came running, and I told him about the snake. He was livid. He went to the basement, grabbed some gloves, a box, and an ax, and went in after it. He caught it and took it outside, and chopped it up into several pieces. Dean's reaction to the snake was nothing new to any of us as we had witnessed him abuse our beloved pets first hand. We always knew that our pets would eventually disappear shortly after we got them. I thought for sure he was going to turn the ax on me next. My mother was in hysterics and still screaming at the top of her lungs.

At first, I had no idea who it was from until I read the inscription inside the box's lid that read, "Thinking of you, love Armstrong." I threw it out before Dean was able to see it. I honestly can't tell you if that was meant as a friendly gesture, but it nearly got me killed. I got the beating of my life that night so much that I still couldn't walk properly without a limp. Although it didn't matter much, I ended up sick and couldn't go out anyway. If there was ever a way to end a relationship, that was it. He hounded me at school, but it did not last long.

It turned out that the school and my parents had other plans for me, and I had no say in the matter.

CHAPTER SIX

Access Denied

The school's final draw was during a science project, which we were given earlier in the year. We were instructed to research our topic and to add pictures. I still couldn't draw at the time because of what my mother had done to my hand when she caught me stealing. So, right there at the table, I borrowed a pair of scissors from the librarian and started cutting pictures right out of the encyclopedia, pasting them to my project.

I was called into the office a couple of days later and was in significant trouble damaging the book. For a brief moment, I had no idea what I did was wrong. We used to cut things out of magazines all the time for projects, so I did not understand the difference. Then the principal told me that he was going to call my parents. I had a meltdown, and I begged and pleaded with him not to call and promised to pay for the book out of my allowance. I stated that if they were to find out, I would be killed. I'm sure he thought at first that I was overreacting until he saw that I had wet myself being in a state of panic. He agreed to let me pay them five dollars a week until it was paid off. Of course, I never received an allowance, so I had to steal it from home. After a couple of months, they eventually caught me in the act. It became impossible for me to steal anymore, and I knew that I would pay dearly for stealing the second time.

I didn't know that my parents and the school were making plans of their own behind the scenes without requiring any input from me. The year was 1987; I was eleven, and it was a few days before Halloween. I was told that I was going to stay somewhere else for a while. I was so scared and confused. The next thing I knew, my parents drove out of town and escorted me into a facility out in the country. It didn't take a genius to figure out that this was not your average establishment, and everywhere you looked; there were big heavy doors that locked behind you. It appeared that I was in a lockdown facility, and I was being institutionalized. At the time, I didn't even know what the word meant.

I was such an isolated kid, and this was a new concept for me. I had no clue as to why my parents would bring me here. They took me into a room where a couple of staff members were waiting, and they told me that I would be staying there for a while. I was not allowed to go home. I panicked, and my chest immediately began to feel so tight and heavy. I begged my parents to take me back and told them that I was sorry. I promised to be good, even though I had no idea what I could have possibly done to deserve this! Dean and Kristine gave me a hug and a kiss goodbye. They told me that they loved me and would see me again in a couple of weeks. I was so confused by what was happening that I didn't notice their "love parenting performance," which everyone in the room witnessed. And Just like that, they were gone.

Before I stepped foot into this institution, I hardly swore, never smoked, and only stole to survive. I stayed there for nearly a year, and that became my home. When I left, I was doing a heck of a lot more.

The following year was absolutely brutal, except that Dean hardly laid a hand on me during the entire time I was locked up. Unfortunately for me, my new housemates picked the abuse up where he left off. The abuse I endured from them was a walk in the park compared to his. There were so many kids there with behaviors way worse than mine. Kids ran away, attacking other kids for no apparent reason, and everyone adopted this kill or be killed mentality.

A girl at the Institute was sent there because she had psychically abused two children with a belt. She was babysitting them at the time. Her body was large, and compared to me, she was a giant.

I kept to myself as much as I could, but the kids tended to drag you in whether you were open to it or not. I was hanging outside on my second or third day when this girl came up to me and asked if I wanted to know a secret. "Sure," I said, thinking, great, someone to talk to. She leaned in eagerly only to spit in my ear. I was used to being spit on, but this was over the top, and I was recently struggling with a new obsession, germs.

Nobody Special

I couldn't go up and tell the staff because I'd get thumped so, I used my sweater to clean up what I could and avoided her as much as possible. My first fistfight happened with this girl who used to come up and push me around and make fun of me. She wouldn't give in. I was getting so fed up with it that one day I pushed her back.

Fights were like fireworks on the Fourth of July weekend in this place. Everywhere you looked, there were always conflicts going off. Some were pretty cool, most were dull, and if you'd seen one, you pretty much have seen them all yet; everyone still had to be front row center.

I was the smallest kid there, so if I didn't start sticking up for myself, everyone would start taking turns on me. She cocked her arm back and threw the first punch, and hit me on the neck's side. Unfortunately for her, I knew how to take a punch, and compared to Dean; she would have to do way better than that. I was used to getting pushed around, but I never fought back. This time something took over, and I punched her square in the chest. I don't think she thought I could hit back because she lost her balance and fell even though she was bigger. She regained her footing and started cussing me up and down, yelling bloody murder.

I stood there; my heart was beating out of my chest. I was breathing hard as it was cold outside, but I could feel the sweat under my clothes, and my stomach was hurting so bad from shaking so hard. I felt like I was going to blackout like I do when Dean goes off on me. When he would beat me up, I'd have these attacks where I would start to feel really dizzy, and my fingers would go numb. I felt like I was going to pass out. It was becoming a regular thing. The problem was that they would last forever and strip me of my control. I didn't feel much pain when I was in this state, but I wasn't very steady on my feet either. Luckily for me, this initiation didn't last long. A few more fights forced me to participate, but staff usually jumped in before getting too dangerous.

A lot of times, it was a new kid who came in looking for someone weaker to push around. They learned pretty quickly not to judge a person by their size. If there were one thing Dean's beatings taught me, it was that they made me a lot tougher than most kids.

Siobhan O'Regan

This was a coed facility. We had boys down one corridor and girls down the next. It was well supervised, so there wasn't much interaction between the sexes. Sometimes, kids would sneak into each other's rooms but would always get caught.

Our time was very structured. We had therapy, group therapy, chores, meals, and even school. Everything we did was in this building, and we didn't leave it very often. This place was under constant lockdown at all times. We had to ask and be escorted to the bathroom while the staff stood guarding the door. Every exit was locked and required staff to unlock it. Every aspect of your life was monitored, and it felt like a hospital prison. Each room had a sterile feel to it, and each one had a bed with a hard-flat waterproof mattress, a desk, and a bathroom just down the corridor that everyone shared.

It is impossible to describe how difficult it was to go from an environment where I was completely alone most of the time to one where I was hardly ever alone. I never thought I would long for the moments when I could be by myself in my room. Kids would often pull pranks on one another to amuse themselves. I was eventually caught writing an obscene word on another child's face using a permanent marker because I was dared.

I had just earned the privilege to go home on the weekends, and I missed going back for two weekends because of this prank. There was a doctor who often came to see us and prescribed all these medications. He checked me entirely over and took forever, documenting all the marks and bruises all over my body. He told the staff that I was extremely malnourished and underweight and told them to put me on a milkshake diet. This sounded exciting at first, but I began to have even more issues with my stomach and had a lot of trouble keeping things down, especially ice cream. Eating then became a massive issue while I was there, and it also created an enormous cause of conflict. They thought that I was making myself sick on purpose, but my body rejected the food, not me.

An older woman in our ward named Hooksy did the night shifts and often peeked her head in my room when she heard me crying during her rounds. I didn't want to like her or anyone in this place and spent nights awake trying to figure out how to end it all. I was sad that no one would miss me, not even a little bit. She would come in and sit on the edge of the bed and talk about her day and tell me for the first time how special I was. She kept telling me that things would get better. I laid there curled up on the bed in the fetal position and would cling onto a blanket that my aunt Karen had knitted a few years back. It was black and pink, and I hated the color pink, but she made it, so I tolerated it.

Hooksy noticed a couple of holes in the blanket and told me that she loved to knit. She asked if I would mind her fixing it for me sometimes. I told her that I didn't care. She was always so lovely to me, no matter how much I pretended not to care about her. One afternoon I came in and found my blanket folded up on my bed. She had repaired the holes. It wasn't the same color, but I didn't mind, and inside the folds, I found a homemade shortbread cookie. I didn't like shortbread, but I kept it with the rest of the food I snuck into my room. I had to wait until she checked in with me to thank her, and I allowed her to give me a big hug. I thought at that moment that one day I wanted to be just like her. I thought how neat it would be to make kids feel good about themselves like she did for me. I think she retired while I was there because I don't recall her being around in the months leading up to my release.

Therapy was useless. My therapist did a lot of the talking and told me many things about what he thought my issues could be. He told me that I had ADD/ADHD symptoms, Oppositional Defiance Disorder, borderline, and suffered from depression. I kept quiet most of the sessions and exercised my vow of silence. I know that if I didn't, then Dean would kill me. I laughed nervously when he asked me how I felt getting spanked. "Spanked?" I thought. "Is that what they're calling it?" I guess Dean left out a few minor details when he was qualifying for the father of the year award. He was excellent in describing his role, creating his mentally fragile daughter, whose behaviors were destroying the family dynamic. I wondered how Kristine portrayed herself in the storyline? Individual therapy was utterly pointless. The only thing I learned in group therapy was never to let my guard down and let others in. I thought to myself, why even bother? Just so I can get spit on, beat up, and laughed at? No thanks.

One afternoon I showed up in therapy, and my parents were sitting in the room with my therapist, waiting for me to join them. I was confused. Usually, I was the only one who attended these sessions. I sat down and noticed this suffocating tension in the air. My therapist turned to me and told me that my parents had something to say. I was to stay quiet and wait before asking any questions. I was intrigued. My mother fidgeted for quite a while; I assumed that she was searching for the right words. She looked at Dean, then at my therapist but didn't once look at me. She then blurted out, Gio (which was my nickname), your adopted. The words felt like tiny shards of glass stabbing at my heart. It's one thing to think it's true but something entirely different to finally have someone confirm what I already knew. My therapist looked at me with these sympathetic eyes to offer support but then opened his mouth. He told me how difficult this was for my mother to tell me this.

What!? Whose side was he on? All-time stood still at that moment while everyone sat back to gauge my reaction. There was so much anger building up in my body that I seriously wanted to hurt someone. Kristine spoke up again, announcing to the room how much she and my so-called father loved me and that they were sorry that they kept this from me. She added that they wanted to tell me sooner but didn't know-how. She went on to explain that she was my biological mother, and Dean was my adopted father. I couldn't look either of them in the eye. I glanced down at my hands and asked about the kids in the picture? There was a long pause; then, in a low voice, she confirmed that they were, in fact, my brother and sister from her first marriage and that we all share the same father.

My heart didn't break; it shattered in my chest. My whole life was a lie. I felt sick to my stomach, and now things were beginning to unfold right there, in the confines of that room. I had so many questions, but I couldn't find the words to ask and was focusing all my energy on suppressing my anger. Dean didn't have much to say, but when he finally weighed in, he tried to tell me that he was sorry about the way he had treated me when I got up and left them mid-sentence. I had enough. It felt good to finally have the courage to just up and go like that. My newfound confidence was great, knowing that he could not follow after me. My therapist came in pursuit, but I was done. He found the staff to take me to my room until he was done with my, dare I say, wonderful parents.

As they say, this was the straw that broke the camel's back, and I was about to become the demon child from hell. If they thought I was terrible before, they were in for a rude awaking. When I was finally released, I wasn't the least bit sorry to leave, and I was by far a different child than I was going in. I had gained a little bit of weight, and I had finally learned to stand up for myself.

It didn't take long after I returned home for things to go back as they were before and for Dean to start back into his old abuse patterns again. I was dreading the start of grade eight. My school was the same as usual, and all my old feelings came rushing back the moment someone yelled, "Hey, look, fish lips is back." Kids were not as physical as they were the year before, and if anyone tried anything, I was ready for them. However, they were just as cruel.

There was this new girl who lived right down the street from us who took my bus as well. Her mother was living with the guy who owned the local junkyard just down the road. I passed it every day to catch my bus. She was really tall and skinny and used to chat with me on our way home from the bus stop. It was evident that I wasn't very well-liked, but this didn't seem to bother her. She used to tell me all kinds of stories about her family and talked way too much, but I didn't care. I never had much to say anyway.

One day out of the blue, she stopped by my house to call on me. Dean answered the door and told her to wait outside. He closed the door and yelled at me to see what the heck she wanted, and ordered me to get rid of her. She asked if I wanted to come to a sleepover at her house with a couple of other girls. I had never been invited to sleep over except Chloe and didn't know what to expect. I left her outside and went in to ask my mom if I could, and I was overjoyed when she said yes. I didn't hesitate one minute as I packed my bags and left before Dean found out I was going and could overrule her decision.

The sleepover was in her stepfather's trailer in the driveway, and there were four girls, including me, for the night. We snacked on pizza and hung out in the trailer. At one point, one of the girls suggested we play truth or dare. I had never played before and had no clue what it was. That is when the girls began to talk about their fantasies and staged some sex scenes that I had never heard, let alone seen before. I watched in amazement as they acted them out. In the institution, I was told to suck dick more times than I can count. This was from the guys in the dorms, but tonight was the first time that I ever heard the term blowjob and watched as one of the girls demonstrated what it looked like on a banana. I had seen a nurse slip a condom on a banana once in health class, and that just about summed up my experience in sex education, outside of experimenting with touching and fondling. Then one of the girls dared our host to slip the banana into her vagina. I had no clue what to think. I watched in awe as she exposed herself, parting the lips of her vaginal opening and inserting the tip of the banana inside of herself.

I had never seen a mature vagina before. It was different from mine and was completely covered in coarse hair. Most of the girls my age were already having their periods and were well on their way through puberty. My body was not ready yet and didn't appear to be in any hurry to do so either.

Just two days earlier, I was teased in the changing room for not wearing a bra. All the other girls had one on, so I went home and asked my mother if I could have one. Dean mocked me by asking, "what for?" I understood his comment to mean that he wasn't wasting money on something I apparently didn't need. That was the end of that conversation.

When it came to my turn, I didn't want to be a prude, but I wasn't putting anything inside my body. According to their stories, I obviously wasn't anywhere near as experienced as these girls. I lied about my experience to save face. I was dared to shove my finger up inside me. There was no way that I could back down now, so I drew a huge breath and reluctantly did as I was instructed and was surprised that it didn't hurt. As embarrassing as it was, it felt kind of neat. I had never tried it before.

Armstrong had fondled with me down there multiple times, but I never allowed him to stick his fingers up inside me. All fun and games ended when the light bulb overheated and shattered at the front end of the trailer, and her mom came out to help us clean it up. It took a while to pick up all the glass, and much to my relief, everyone agreed to have a snack and watch a movie instead. I could never ask my mother anything about sex, so any questions I had, I was forced to find out on my own. I started experimenting with masturbation after that night and felt shameful and dirty doing it. I didn't dare leave my room to wash my hands from the fear of getting caught so, I stole latex gloves from my mother's painting supplies to do it and then hid them under my mattress. I only used them to masturbate and then disposed of them when I had a chance.

My friend's father was Jamaican, so when the hurricane hit Jamaica on September 12, 1988, she asked if I would do a fundraiser with her for the Jamaican relief fund. I was twelve years old, and I thought that it would be fun. When Stephanie and I were younger, mom let us go door to door in our neighborhood, singing Christmas carols to raise money for the angel tree fund. This was to buy a present for a child that didn't have anything. I always liked how good it felt to help people. My friend and I raised over one thousand dollars, and we were featured in an article in the local newspaper. Of course, like all my friendships, this one ended miserably. As far as compatibility went, we didn't get along very well. As it turned out, she had a very dominating personality. I didn't conform well to playing the submissive, and I always preferred to control my relationships.

I'm not sure what I supposedly said or what she thought I said, but she cornered me one day in the bathroom at school and pushed me into a space between the wall and the sink. I didn't have a chance to fight back as she was twice my size and was furious. She asked me if I spread some rumors about her. I snickered at the irony, thinking for that to happen, someone would actually have to talk to me. She failed to see the humor, grabbed my head, and smacked it up against the wall. She then began kicking me. When I fell to the ground, she leaned up against the wall and kicked me some more. I was crying now, not because of the pain but because I didn't see it coming and felt betrayed and tried to protect my head from the blows. She stopped, spit on me, and walked out.

I sat there for a long while before I was able to compose myself. I wanted to get up sooner, but I was way too confused and embarrassed over what just happened, so I just sat in silence, sobbing. Eventually, I picked myself up off the floor, cleaned up my blood from my nose, and left the school walking home. I told my mom what happened. I'm not sure what I expected her to say or do, but she turned it on me and then mocked me for not keeping a friend.

My mother's comment hurt so much that I went and hid in my room. I felt utterly alone and sick to my stomach, knowing that I had to take the same bus as her the next day, and swore I would never make another friend as long as I lived. Luckily for me, she didn't talk to me much after that. There was an exception where she laughed at me with some of the other kids. However, she wasn't liked very much either, so they took turns picking on her too.

There was a shift happening at home and began after I was released from the institution. I started to talk back and pick fights with my mother, so she began to use more physical forms of punishment to gain control. Usually, she was content to let Dean handle the physical discipline for the most part. Still, now she was coming into my room and using her fists to get her point across.

Unfortunately for me, Dean was getting fed up with listening to her bitch and complain about me, so; I started wearing on his nerves more than usual. It got to a point where beating me with the belt was no longer satisfying his sadistic need to hurt me anymore. He started using objects, and more often than not, my bedroom door was his first choice.

A short time later, my parents told me I was moving again. This time I would go into foster care under a temporary care agreement, which meant they would sign temporary custody of me to the region. My mother said she called Child Services for support when they could no longer control my behavior. She later said, if they had not sought an intervention, Dean would have likely killed me.

My first placement was with a woman named Dianne, who was married to a long-haul truck driver and was gone for days at a time. I hated that I had to go and live somewhere else again and didn't understand why my parents kept sending me away. If I was such a horrible kid, why didn't they just kill me like they threatened to do a thousand times? She seemed nice at first, but the moment my worker left, the mood changed dramatically. She walked me around the house, and within five minutes, I had learned about thirty rules. Don't do this, don't go there, don't eat this, and the list went on. I felt like I was living back in the institution, combined with the rules of the home. I thought it was a bit extreme because she locked her pantry and forbade me to go into the fridge without permission. Here we go again, I thought, this woman must be related to my mother.

One rule that was different from my house was that I was allowed to play outside, and I had free range of the neighborhood. At home, I needed to be within calling distance, and they had to know where I was at all times down to the very second. Here I could come and go as I pleased. I never had that kind of freedom before. Down the street was another foster home that took in boys. Their foster mom was so sweet, and I used to love hanging out there. She would sit and talk to the boys and joke around with them. I was so jealous watching how each one would go up to hug her, and she would hug them right back. I wanted to know what it was like, so I walked up one day and hugged her. It felt weird, but she didn't push me away as my mother would. The boys playfully teased that she was their mother.

Dinnertime was a zoo at the boys' house. It was similar to the institution but warmer and inviting. It was nothing like my house or even at Dianne's. I didn't like Dianne's cooking, and she always acted like I was an ungrateful brat when I didn't eat her meals. It almost seemed like nothing I ever did made her happy. She reminded me so much of my mother. Dianne's husband was nice enough, but I had no real experience working with men other than my so-called father. That never turned out well, so I kept to myself and avoided him most of the time when he was home.

I once overheard Dianne tell her husband that she felt like a prisoner in her own home. I remember thinking I'd just don't fit in anywhere. I loved the boys' foster parents most because she would get up every morning and make her kids grilled cheese for breakfast. I got to try grilled cheese for the first time at the institution and loved them. Dianne only fed me cereal, and I always felt like I was starving an hour later. I sat outside her house a couple of times, waiting for the boys to come out, and wished she would invite me in to eat one.

I finally got the courage to ask her one morning if she would make me one, and to my delight, she did. I was so happy that I didn't have to ask, beg or plead with her to do it. She sat down with me and asked how things were going at Dianne's, and I told her that I made her feel like a prisoner in her own home. I asked her if I could come and live with her. She said she couldn't take me in unless I were a boy but told me that I was welcome to come over anytime I wanted, and she would gladly make me a sandwich. She reminded me so much of Hooksy from the institution, who fixed my blanket and made me wish that I wanted to be just like her if I ever became a mom. I once walked up to Dianne and asked her if she would make me a grilled cheese sandwich. She brushed me off, telling me that she was not a short-order cook and plenty of cereal in the cupboards.

I was over at her place one night watching a movie with the boys and wanted to stay to the end, so I called Dianne to ask if I could stay past curfew. She sounded annoyed and told me that it was too late and wanted me home right away. I begged her for an extra half hour, but she did not cave. She told me that she was heading to bed, and if I didn't get home in the next ten minutes, I would be locked out.

I hung up the phone and started to cry. The boys' foster mom told me that I could watch the ending tomorrow and had one of her boys walk me halfway home because it was dark. I know I took my time because I was mad at her, but I was only ten or so minutes late. I knocked on the door, no one came, I banged, and I heard nothing. So, I finally gave up and went back to the other foster home and told her that I couldn't get in. The police were called and spoke with Dianne directly. I don't know what her story was, but I was finally let in and told by the police officer to go now to bed. A couple of days later, I sat at a table across from my social worker, listening to Dianne's lies. I recall my worker shaking her head and scold me for my trumped-up behaviors. After my mother heard about the treatment I had received at this home, she accused Child Services of treating me worse than she ever did. Either way, I was a sitting duck.

I don't pretend for a second that I wasn't a challenging child. After everything I had been through, up until that point, I would like to think that I was more misunderstood. Regardless of what I thought, I did hear that I would be Dianne's last placement.

That summer, they started leaving Stephanie and me on our own while they went out to run errands. The first time they left me in charge, Stephanie ended up in the hospital. She and I used to pass the time by playing this sock game where we would wrestle around to pull each other's socks off. I had the bigger bed out of the two of us. Our grandfather had given it to me so; we would play on my bed, and right next to my bed was my dresser. Not five minutes into our game, Stephanie flipped over my shoulder and hit her head on my dresser's corner.

Blood gushed from her forehead and poured down her face. I panicked instantly, and so did Stephanie. Especially when she saw the blood drip onto the carpet. I grabbed some clothes from my dresser and pressed them up against her forehead while trying to figure out my next move. I brought her into the kitchen and tried to think, but she was screaming uncontrollably, causing me to lose focus. I didn't know anyone, so I sat down on the floor with her and just held her. Ten minutes later, my parents came home. Kristine had forgotten something.

The moment they walked in, I tried to explain myself, but everyone flew into hysterics. Up to that point, Stephanie had finally stopped screaming, but she started crying again when they arrived. They took one look at her forehead, and Dean rushed her to the hospital. I got to stay home with my mother in an attempt to anticipate Dean's next move. Kristine's only form of communication that night was hollering at me at the top of her lungs for the blood trail that was all over her precious carpet. I was pushed and smacked every time I came near her. Stephanie had split her head opened pretty well and ended up needing three stitches. I have no recollection of what happened after this incident. Still, I know from the stories that Stephanie has told me that Dean and Kristine blamed me and took turns over the next few weeks taking their wrath out on me.

Nobody Special

In the spring of 1989, Dean gave in and finally agreed to let me have a paper route; he probably thought that it was better if I earned money rather than steal it. I was given a route with about thirty or so customers five blocks from my house. Part of my job required me to collect payment from my clients every week, and it was customary for me to give them a card with my name and phone number on it. I then had to stamp the card when they paid, and that way, they could contact me if there were any issues with their paper.

A couple of weeks into my route, I was at home alone with Stephanie while our parents were out running errands when the phone rang. Typically, we weren't allowed to answer it, but mom had just started talking to Aunt Karen again, so I didn't want to miss Robyn's calls. -She and I had just become friends again. On the other end, the caller was an older male and asked to speak to me directly, so I identified myself and asked him what I could do for him. There was an awkward silence, then he spoke up and ask me point blank if I liked my pussy licked. He didn't wait for my reply and told me how he would take me and described in detail how he was going to rape me. I immediately understood what rape meant and quickly hung up the phone. I was terrified, and when my parents came home, I told them what the caller had said.

Dean freaked out and, of course, screamed at me for answering the phone. Then my mother called the police for some advice. The police thought it might be someone from my paper route since they asked for me by name and suggested that I don't do my course alone for a while. They forced Stephanie to go along with me. I was upset that from then on, I had to share my earnings with her.

I had to cross a bustling street in order to get to my route. So, I would ride down one side and cross at the lights at the bottom of a big hill and start my delivery there. This roadside was usually safe, with little traffic coming and going from the clinic and a nearby gas station. There was a police station right across the street. I used to ride my bike and have the strap of the newspaper bag across the top of my head so I could ride with both hands.

Stephanie and I had just finished our deliveries. We were making our way back home for dinner when an old lady whammed into me as she quickly left the clinic. This threw me and my bike into the heavy traffic.

Siobhan O'Regan

Stephanie was ahead of me. She heard the crash and turned to witness the cars trying to maneuver around me and missing me by inches. She began screaming at the top of her lungs. Drivers, who had stopped, suddenly were now swarming around me, and all I could hear was several people yelling for someone to call an ambulance. Stephanie sped off on her bike to get our parents. I have only two positive memories of my adopted father, and this was one of them. Just as the ambulance arrived, the police had pushed back some foot traffic, and I could see him speeding up on my sister's banana seat bike toward us. He helped them carefully remove parts of the bike embedded in my leg to transport me to the hospital.

I was hit on my right-hand side, and I had landed on my left. My leg was wedged between the cement and my bike. My first ride in an ambulance was exciting. There was so much going on. I was strapped down to board on a stretcher. I kept asking them to take the neck brace off, but they couldn't until they checked my head for any trauma due to the impact. I didn't even recall hitting my head (back then, kids didn't wear helmets), and they told me that my leg might be broken, but they couldn't know until they cleaned up the blood.

It was at the hospital where they discovered, for the first time, that I had low blood pressure. When the initial shock wore off, the doctors kept checking it and asked my parents if they were aware that I had blood pressure issues. Of course, they didn't know. They did a multitude of different tests, and during one of them, a nurse commented on my bruises. Dean shrugged it off and told her it was a skateboarding accident. This was the story they were sticking to every time, yet, I didn't even own a skateboard. I was fortunate. I had minor cuts and bruises from the impact and a torn ligament in my knee. There were four cuts on my leg from where they had removed pieces of the bike. They decided to glue and tape the cuts because I screamed for dear life as soon as I heard them suggesting stitches. I was on crutches for the better part of a month. With Dean's help, Stephanie took over my paper route for several weeks until I could get around it independently.

It was on this route that I discovered my love for Archie comic books. Stephanie and I would stop at the corner store every week during collection day, and I would purchase one comic book with my earnings. She would buy a slushy with hers, and I would devour every page as I walked home. This became another reason for me to escape reality. Dean often took everything I had out of my room, so I started buying two of them whenever I could with my tips and hid them under my dresser drawers. This way, if mom tore our drawers apart to make us refold our clothes, she was less lucky to find them. Junior had some old MAD magazines, which he let me have in exchange for doing his chores. From then on, I started collecting the comics out of the newspapers that one of my customers saved for me when she was done with them. Dean eventually threw my entire collection away with the rest of my belongings. I was able to replace most of my Archie comics but could not replace my MAD magazines.

There were two people on my paper route that had a significant impact on my life. One of them was an elderly lady with Alzheimer's, and the other was a woman named Melissa, who lived next door to her. The lady with Alzheimer's would always forget that she paid me and often tried to pay me again in one week. I took an extra payment once but couldn't shake the guilty feeling that I had cheated the money from such a lovely couple. I returned the money the next day, claiming I made a mistake. Her husband was so grateful, told me. He said how amazing I was. He made me feel good by doing the right thing. I never forgot that feeling.

Melissa was a likable person who always chatted me up and saved me the comics from her paper after learning that I liked to collect them. Melissa and I had quite a few conversations. She eventually became the first person I turned to for help. Back then, I was a really messed up kid and would do and say many things that made people's heads spin. I failed to recognize that Melissa would eventually become anyone significant. One day I was talking to her, and she asked about my family. I pretended that I was with my twin sister Beth. I told her that she was around the corner and started calling out to her. When my fictitious twin didn't show, I told her that she would have to meet her some other time.

I lived in a fantasy world. I wasn't hurting anyone, and I was raised to lie about my circumstances, so I created a world where I had something to be proud of, even if it wasn't real. Who knew that she would one day meet my actual family and use this incident as a tool to assess my credibility? As I Got to know Melissa over the months, she started picking up on subtle hints that my home life was not stable or as healthy as I was leading on. I ended up on her doorstep on a few occasions, visibly upset and shaken. Eventually, I disclosed that my father was abusive. I'm not sure why she was the one person that I finally told after all these years, but for some reason, I was desperate enough to trust her.

CHAPTER SEVEN

Freedom, Or Something Like It

Dean's father passed away in the fall of 1989, and Dean stood to inherit a small fortune. I can only assume he was forced to share his father's estate with his widow and, of course, his sister. Regardless, it was enough for him to take the money and abandon his family.

Dean took Kristine grocery shopping late one afternoon. He dropped her off at the front door and told her that he would join her shortly, and left her to park the car. This was their routine. Kristine shopped, paid for the groceries, and went out to find Dean assuming that he had stayed in the car, which he had done many times before to catch a nap.

She told us that she searched and waited over an hour before she finally called herself a cab. She was absolutely furious. When she got home, a note detailed his decision to take his inheritance and skip town to go out West.

My mother was stricken with grief and went completely off the deep end. Rather than sink to the ground, cry and fall into a deep depression like she usually did, she'd lashed out on us in a rage and directed most of it at me. Eventually, we learned that he left her just enough in the account to get by for a couple of months. He had paid most of the household bills up to date and left $200 each in our accounts.

As previously mentioned, our grandfather gave us bonds for our birthday and Christmas over the years totaling thousands of dollars. Dean had us hand over the bonds to start a business that went under in a few short months. Although the $200 seemed like a kind gesture, it was a fraction of the thousands he had forcibly taken from us.

Mom was under so much stress. She had no job, no skills, a mortgage, and two kids to support. Kristine went off on me so badly one night. She started kicking and punching me, telling me that it was my fault that he left. So, I did the only thing I felt I could do and snuck out of the house to find help. I ended up at Melissa's. I showed up at her home with my face tear-stained and swollen. My shirt was torn from where my mother had grabbed me in the struggle.

I told her that my dad had left us and that my mother was having a breakdown. I didn't know who else to turn to for help. We got back to the house, and I left Melissa to deal with my mother. I went to make sure Stephanie was okay and found her hiding in her room. My mother had no friends, no family except Karen, and no one to turn to for support. I did my best to be there for her, but for some reason, just looking at me would set her off. She always seemed to be looking to pick a fight.

Melissa appeared to be an excellent support for my mother, and I thought she was making headway with her. Still, Kristine was mean, vindictive, and spiteful when she wasn't around. She would direct all of her anger at me. Kristine had this way of portraying the victim, and she didn't care who she had to cross to make herself look good. At the expense of others, for months, Melissa was only purveyed to what Kristine would tell her; without anyone disputing the facts, she did well to make herself look good in every circumstance.

I was made out to be the horrible daughter. Unfortunately, my behavior at the time coincided with my mother's ability to push my buttons, validating Melissa's tainted impression of me. One day we were sitting in the living room, and I snapped at Melissa. She leaned over and slapped me on the forehead, and told me never to disrespect her again. I was so hurt and frustrated. How was I supposed to know how to act or treat someone? I came from such a hostile environment.

At that moment, Melissa became just like the rest of them for me. I could never trust her, and I hated my mother for stealing her from me. Melissa never fully understood what happened to us behind closed doors. Up until now, the only other person who lived through every moment of the horror was my sister, and she wasn't talking either. Melissa and my mother remained friends for a couple of years. Still, just like everyone else, she eventually found out that once her purpose was served, she would be kicked out too.

Nobody Special

During the several months, which Dean was gone, things at home were terrible. Mom no longer communicated using words. She would shout and use violence to get her point across. All punches exchanged were one-sided, and I never could lash out and punch her back. The only contact I had with her was in self-defense. Stephanie, on the other hand, was getting all my anger directed towards her. She, too, had a hard time making and maintaining friends and found refuge at a local church down the street when things got unbearable.

We started venturing out on our own and would walk down the main street to the local market and further down to Red Rose Nursery. Kristine was glad to get rid of us, and that is how we got our first taste of real freedom. On Saturday, we were bored and decided to head down to the local market. Neither of us had any money. We were both starving, so we asked the local merchants if they had any odd jobs for us to do. We wanted to earn our lunch. One Merchant was a sweet senior man; he and his wife rented a restaurant's space and sold a Mediterranean delight called donairs. He told us that if we cleaned his grills for him, he would pay us ten dollars apiece and have a free lunch.

It was a dirty, greasy job, but we didn't care. We were grateful for the work and the food. It turns out that I loved donairs, and so did Stephanie. That is how we began to have steady work and free food when we didn't have any money. It was as if he completely took us under his wing; he and his wife Mary were indeed saints and, for years, became our guardian angels.

They eventually met Kristine and became friends with her and Melissa. Still, Cocherian, whose nickname was Coco, understood that there was a lot more to my family than we let on. Sometimes Stephanie and I would let out too much information when we talked to him. He managed to piece together a general idea that our home life was not as enjoyable as Kristine and Melissa made it out to be.

Mary was the type of person who treated everyone like family and got along well with everyone, especially Melissa. However, she always treated Stephanie and me with extra special attention and love. They eventually opened up a restaurant where I frequently went as an adult until the day they retired. I even introduced them to my now-partner, who loved their food and fell in love with them as much as I did. They were around to see my kids grow up and were always as kind to them as they were to us. We still see them from time to time after they retired, and they will forever have a place in my heart.

In the meantime, Kristine entertained the affections of a gentleman friend who just happened to be married and strung him along with sexual favors. In return, he helped her out financially, but the bills kept mounting up, and that forced her to apply for income housing and announced that she had to give up the house.

One day out of the blue, she told Stephanie and me that Dean had contacted her and wanted her to fly out to British Colombia to meet with him and talk about coming home. I freaked out, screaming, yelling, and punching the walls. My mother attacked me, restrained me on my bed face down, and pounded my back until she subdued me. There was no way I wanted him to come back home. On the other hand, Stephanie was young, naive, and welcomed another chance to have a father. That made it a lot easier to turn my anger on her.

Kristine called Child Services and convinced them that I needed to care until she got back on a two-week temporary care agreement. I felt like my whole world had collapsed beneath me, and I wanted to die. I was placed in a foster home dwith three other girls, and we all shared a room with two bunk beds. They had a pool, but I was too miserable to enjoy it and spent most of my time sulking to myself or picking fights with the other girls, so they knew where I stood; Stephanie stayed with Aunt Karen.

My foster mother was not very friendly and didn't do well to hide the fact that my presents threw a wrench in their happy little dynamic. I was there for the short term and had no intention of staying longer. She was nothing like the foster mother who had the boys, and I missed her so much. I wondered why they couldn't all be like her. I was given access to my Child Services file as an adult and read how the agency accused Kristine of using them as a glorified babysitter. At the same time, she went off to retrieve her long-lost husband.

Two weeks was long enough for me, and I was happy to be home when Kristine got back. Dean was a couple of days behind while he settled his affairs. She then told us that he was a changed man, wanted to start over fresh, and things would be much different this time. We had heard this so many times before, and I wanted to believe it so badly, but I wasn't buying it. The day Dean came home, we waited for him to arrive and greeted him in the driveway. Stephanie ran up to him and gave him a big hug. When it was my turn, I held out my arms but was very reserved and guarded. He glanced over in my direction, stood up, and walked right past me; my heart sunk into my chest. Stephanie came up and tried to hug me. I pushed her out of my way. As it turns out, Dean hadn't changed at all and came back with one hell of a chip on his shoulder. I also learned that he was ultimately broken. I'm not sure what he spent his inheritance on, but he had spent his last bit of change on his return flight home. It didn't take long for Dean to jump into Kristine's big defender role when dealing with my behaviors. I would once again learn to suppress my anger or suffer the consequences.

I was in the final stretch of my last year in middle school and couldn't wait to get the heck out of there. I begged my parents so often to switch schools and even threatened to kill myself if they didn't. I had found out that threatening to end my life to someone who didn't value it, to begin with, wasn't very well thought out. It was not the best strategy to get my way. Regardless, I was stuck. I threw myself into my studies. One class project required me to write a speech, so I wrote mine in less than an hour. The writing was about embarrassing moments. It was so good that they asked me to read it out during an assembly for the school. This was quite the honor since they had only handpicked one student per grade out of the entire school. I was scared to death, and my teacher thought it was good enough, but I didn't want to face the fear of stepping up in front of the entire school. I was once forced to debate history for a class project. When I stepped into character and questioned my opponent on his platform, he yelled at me and told me that he didn't want my vote and to sit my ass down.

I was so embarrassed that I took my seat and refused to continue. The class cheered and laughed and started chanting, "fish lips, fish lips." Our teacher scolded the class, but that's all they ever did. Now, I was told that I had to do it in front of the whole school. Standing in front of a firing squad would have been much more humane.

The day came, and my mother forced me to wear a dress. I hated wearing dresses cause Dean always told me how ugly I was in them. I wore my hair back (I started growing it after Dean left) and sat up on stage until I was called up for my turn. There were three speeches, and mine was last. Sitting on that stage, I felt sick to my stomach, and the pain was overwhelming. I had the same feeling when I knew I was in trouble or about to get the shit kicked out of me, which was most of the time.

My hands were shaking so badly that I could barely read my own handwriting, and I was so scared that I didn't hear a word of the other kids' speeches. I only clapped on cue when the audience did. Finally, it was my turn. The moment they called my name, I felt that I was hearing the sea of different conversations erupting in the audience. I heard someone yelling, "get off the stage and back into your aquarium, fish lips." I could listen to the explosion of laughter that followed. My teacher nodded her head to encourage me to continue. I started reading my speech, but my anxiety overwhelmed me, and I could barely get a word out.

The audience chatter was getting louder, and I couldn't focus. I began reading it so mechanically that no one was getting any of my jokes, and if there was an outburst of laughter, it wasn't because of my speech. Teachers were scurrying to calm the students down, and I could hear them threatening the kids over my own microphone. I didn't bother finishing, and I walked off stage. No one was listening regardless. I ran into the bathroom and hid in a stall, and cried. I could hear the thunder of clapping when I walked off stage, and it wasn't because of a job well done. I honestly didn't know what I could have possibly done to deserve this much hate. No matter what I did, who I talked to, everyone loved to pick on the girl whose parents sent her to the loony bin. I was destroyed.

I don't know how it came about. Still, my counselor at school told me about a girl who worked part-time in an insurance company and had to take a couple of months off while her family traveled back home to India. She thought that I might be interested in the job. All I had to do was to clean and file invoices. Dean felt that I was lying at first. I think I impressed him when it turned out to be real, so I started doing it after school.

I was good at my new job, and I liked the work. It was simple enough, and I loved the fact that I worked alone. I started bringing Stephanie with me, and she helped clean while I printed off and filed invoices. I thought I was the coolest kid in school. Not too many kids my age had a job working in an insurance company. I was so proud of myself that I made sure to keep my first paystub. Unfortunately, it was only temporary, and I was not able to keep it. They used to have a jar of loose change that they held near the fridge to purchase drinks, and we had to dip into it to pay for supper from the sub place around the corner. I'm not sure if they ever caught us, but if they did, no one ever said anything. Later I applied at an animal hospital just down the road from where I lived and got a job cleaning cages, taking care of the animals, and monitoring their health after surgery. This was a placement that I actually loved and really excelled at.

I was excited about going to high school because it meant a fresh new start. I was a little scared because I had no idea what to expect. The first day, I met this girl named Carrie, who was such a free spirit. She attended a different middle school than I and didn't think of what people thought of her. It was a large school, and even though there were plenty of kids, who didn't know me, some still recognized me. I was so embarrassed when they passed me making rude comments in the hallways.

She didn't seem to care and hung out with me anyway. I was so jealous of her because she could afford to buy her lunch every day and always bought french-fries. I loved french-fries, and she was still nice enough to share them with me. When Dean went out West, we grew accustomed to more freedom, so I spent a lot of time hanging out at her place. She had the kind of independence I could only dream of, and her family was really wealthy compared to mine. Unfortunately, Carrie's reality was that her mom and dad co-existed in a failed marriage and were only holding to their relationship for Carrie's five-year-old sister.

She had an incredible mom who drank a lot; in fact, I don't think I ever remember when she didn't have a bottle on the go. We would sneak in and out of the house almost every night to meet up with a couple of her friends searching for boys, seeking a good time. One night we snuck out and came back to find a note taped to the window that read, "I hope you girls had a good time; I can't wait to discuss your adventures in the morning."

I went into full-on crisis mode, but Carrie laughed it off. That was her style, and she ended up sleeping the rest of that night like a baby. On the other hand, I stayed awake, wondering if I would ever be allowed over again. In the morning, her mother was so cool about the whole thing. She told us how much she was worried by having thoughts about what bad things could have happened to us out there alone.

Siobhan O'Regan

Carrie dismissed her mother's concern and brushed her off with a hug and a kiss. She told her that we would never do it again. I then pulled her mom off to the side and said to her that my parents would ground me for months if they found out. I told her that I would do anything if she agreed not to tell. She laughed, likely assuming I was exaggerating. She found out soon enough that I wasn't and began to take pity on me later on.

I also envied that Carrie's mom kept a stocked pantry and that she could eat whatever she wanted, whenever she wanted. I became visibly overwhelmed whenever we went to eat and couldn't even decide what I wanted. There were way too many choices, and so she would load up her arms, and we would head up to her room. Out of habit, I was sneaking some of it and would hide it in my pillowcase. If she ever knew, she never once said anything about it. Now and then, Dean would get mad and kick me out, forcing me to sleep outside, and that was when I would show up at Carrie's house cold and hungry. They always took me in without asking me any questions.

One morning Carrie's mom did ask what was going on, and I put my head down on the table and said nothing. There was a long pause, and then she told me not to worry and that I was always welcome here. Her mother never asked too many questions but seemed to know a lot more than she ever let on. I was so grateful for her kindness and for having me when I overstayed my welcome. Carrie and I did a lot of foolish things together. On top of sneaking off, we would go driving off with some older boys whenever we got a chance. She was the first person to introduce me to alcohol.

Once, we were down in her basement, and she brought some bottles of vodka coolers. I can still remember the warm rush I got after the first sip. It felt like I was basking in the sun from the inside out. My cheeks felt numb to the touch. It was euphoric. I spend the rest of the evening chasing after that sensation, taking tiny sips at a time and relishing every blissful moment. This became my favorite pastime.

My parents rarely drank. They claimed that they used to when I was little and told me how I polished off a glass of wine they had left unattended when I was three years old. I had ended up in the hospital detoxing overnight. I can also recall when we were sick with the flu; my mother would give us a shot of whatever she had on hand. We often threw it up, and she would tell us that it meant it was working and forced us to drink another one.

Nobody Special

One afternoon I had just came home with Carrie after spending the night at her place. Melissa's common-law partner Jerry had invited Dean over for a couple of drinks while mom and Melissa were out and insisted that we all come over. This was the first time that I had ever seen Dean drink. This was the second and last decent memory I ever had of the man and the only time I ever felt any connection to my adopted father.

Carrie and I hung around and watched them pound back the drinks they were experimenting with. They made a shot called "The B52". Both of them were knee-deep and half-crocked when Jerry winked and signaled Carrie and me to drink. I didn't take my eye off Dean for one second and didn't dare touch it without his approval. I waited for the go-ahead and shot it back as fast as I could before he could change his mind. I remember Carrie telling me that she didn't think Dean was half as bad as I made him out. I bit my lip and chose to say nothing. After two or three shots, I wasn't feeling a thing and had to sit down to keep the room from spinning. Dean sat next to me and put his arm around my shoulder. This made me jump, and so he laughed at my reaction. He told me that he would take me to the Bahamas when I graduate grade eight, and we will go parasailing together.

I had no clue what that was, and I didn't dare to correct him for thinking that I was still in grade eight. I sat there so stiff when he initially touched me but eased up as time went by. I was hugging him back towards the evening. My mother and Melissa walked in. Kristine had a look of utter shock on her face to see her husband affectionately touching his daughter for the first time.

Looking back at this moment in time, I guess our actions that day only reinforced everyone's opinion that I was a liar, storyteller, and not believed. These events laid the foundation for seventeen long years of alcohol abuse, chasing that indescribable thirst to gain his approval and relive that moment I shared with Dean. This was one very brief moment in time and one that would stay archived in the back of my mind.

When Robyn came back into our lives, she and I spent many times dreaming about moving out as soon as we turned sixteen. We would both get jobs and split the rent. I don't think there wasn't much we didn't figure out right down to what we would store in our medicine cabinet. She had just moved back from Reardon, and her family was settling on a farm almost forty-five minutes away from where we lived. Junior spent a couple of months working at a gas station when Dean was in BC and talked about living with us permanently. They told us that Stephanie had to move into the room with me, and Junior would take her room. It felt cramped, but Kristine seemed to get her way about many things lately, and clearly, Dean was not happy about it. I was sure she was holding something over his head, but I never found out what.

CHAPTER EIGHT
Bittersweet

High school was a little better than middle school. I decided to participate in a school activity for the very first time by attending a roaring twenties casino night. The goal was to raise money for a charity, and I managed to find an old Halloween costume at the Salvation Army to complete my look.

My job at the animal shelter was going well. I loved working with animals, and my boss liked my work. There was, although one little problem, Dean. He was spiraling out of control again. I would take the bus two and from school, and my stomach would be in knots on the way home, not knowing what kind of abuse was waiting for me.

I was still extraordinarily underweight and still underdeveloped for my age, so tossing me around was always easy for a guy who stood 5 foot 11 with significant anger issues. It was a Saturday, and Robyn was spending the night when the three of us girls got into an argument. That is when Dean ordered us to go to bed. Junior was working the night shift, so Kristine told Robyn and me to sleep in my room and to put Stephanie in her old room.

Robyn and I were still angry and bickered back and forth when the door sprang open with such force that it made us both jump. Dean rushed and grabbed me by the scruff of my neck and threw me up against the wall. He pinned me up with his hand to my throat. I knew struggling made it more difficult for me, but I was choking, so I tried to loosen his grip to get some relief. That is when he dropped me, turned towards Robyn, and told her to get the fuck out, but she froze.

He hollered out to Kristine so that she would grab his belt. He picked me up again and tossed me behind the door, using it to pin me so he could grab my hair and slam my head in between the door and the wall. He loved this method of torture. Dean then pulled me out of the way and dragged me from the door. Robyn was screaming and crying for him to stop.

Kristine came in without the belt to get her. She stood between Dean and the door to give her a way out. After they left, he grabbed me up off the ground and started slapping me across the face. When I fell again, he started punching me. I lay there in a heap, trying to catch my breath in between blows. I knew there was no point in crying as it never helped, and the air was far more valuable to me in these circumstances. I don't know what set him off that night, but it was the last time he would ever lay a hand on me. When he was done, he told me to pack and get the hell out of his house. Dean wanted me gone before he got back.

I could hear that my mother was trying to calm Robyn down, who kept repeating that she wanted to go home and wouldn't be consoled. I picked myself up off the ground when Kristine came in to tell me that I had better listen to him. She reminded me not to get blood on her carpet and told me where to grab some plastic bags. Dean had told me to get out a few times before, which usually meant to camp outside in our backyard until Kristine let me in. Alternatively, I would sometimes wander over to Carrie's house, but this time was different. Dean never told me to pack before. I couldn't believe it; they were kicking me out. I had just turned 14; I could barely walk and had no place to go. I limped the nearly 2-hour walk up to Carrie's house, but no one was home. I waited outside for what seemed like hours before I gave up and started wandering the streets. I honestly don't know where I went or how I got there, but I ended up at a girl's house that I hardly knew from school, and they offered me refuge. I remembered that she had the most delightful brother. Her mother reminded me of the foster lady who used to make my grilled cheese sandwiches.

I had a meltdown when she said that she would call Child Services and threatened to leave if she did. We finally agreed that I would allow her to take pictures of the bruises and marks to document them and hold off on calling them to see if Dean would calm down enough to take me back.

I kept in contact with my mother and told her where I was staying. Two weeks later, I received a call from her telling me that her father had died and that I would need to attend the funeral. When I asked why, she responded that my brother, sister, and biological father would be there too. I dropped the phone and began to cry uncontrollably. My friend's mother tried to console me, but I couldn't accept her support and needed to be by myself. Other than Stephanie, no one had ever held me while I cried.

Two days later, I met my parents at their house. I was tired and exhausted. I was up all night, and fear was written all over my face. My mother made me wear the dress I wore the day I gave the speech in front of the entire school. They wanted me to look pretty for the funeral. I hated dresses, especially that one, but I didn't want to ruin any chances I had with them. The ride up was dead quiet, and I spent my time counting the faded bruises I couldn't hide under my dress.

I walked into the funeral home and kept my eyes on the floor. There were many people there whom I had never seen before, and all I could concentrate on was pursing my lips so they wouldn't look so big. I didn't want them to look at my lips and think that I was ugly. We sat down, and my mother tried to hold my hand, but I pulled away from her. I didn't care about anything other than seeing and physically touching my brother. When the ceremony was over, my mother got up and told me to turn around. She pointed to a prettier blond girl than I ever imagined and a boy I recognized immediately. He was every bit as handsome as I thought he would. He was everything I imagined he would look like.

Then she pointed to the man standing beside them whose features were so familiar that it was like standing in front of a mirror. She introduced him as Sean, my biological father. I don't remember who hugged me first, but I recall how uncomfortable and unnatural it felt when Sean held me. He was bigger than life, and I felt like I was being smothered. Sean held on to me for what seemed like forever and told me how much this moment meant to him. He had missed and told me how much he loved me. I was crying so hard and didn't want to ruin the moment for him, but I needed him to let me go.

For the next half an hour, there was a barrage of hugs and friendly sentiments. My anxiety was going through the roof. For a brief moment, I forgot that there was a funeral going on. I had only been to one funeral before when my grandma died. All I remembered was grandpa crying and wondering why Dean didn't. Had he not loved his mother? Kristine told me it was my turn to say goodbye to my grandfather and marched me up to the room's front. I glanced at the casket and looked away. I didn't understand why everyone had to stand there and talk to the guy when he was dead. I was so relieved when that part was over. Out in the parking lot, the adults were discussed where to go next when Sean took me off to the side and pressed a circular object into the palm of my hand, forcing my fingers to wrap around it. Before I could see what it was, his hands cupped mine, and he went on to tell me how important and valuable this object was to him. It represented ten years of sobriety. I didn't understand what that meant at the time, but I would soon find out. When he was done, I opened my hand to see a medallion inside representing ten years of sobriety.

We went back to Sean's house. He lived in a beautiful three-story Victorian-style home with a long driveway that stretched to the house's back. My first impression was that he was rich like Carrie. It wasn't quite as big as her house but close enough. I walked into the kitchen; it was so beautiful and adorned with wood features everywhere; it took my breath away. We all decided to sit outside to take in some fresh air; Dean sat by himself and looked uncomfortable and out of his element. Kristine was talking to Sean and Beth, so Lorcan and I decided to go for a walk.

Lorcan and I walked around for hours. The sun was out and warm against our faces. We talked well into the afternoon. I wanted to know everything I could about him. He sometimes stopped and hugged me and then continued telling me stories of when he and Beth were little, and they would sit in dad's shop, talking about what I was doing. They wondered what I looked like and talked about the day I would finally come home.

All the talk about their life without me made me sad, and I didn't hide my feelings well. He hugged me again and kept walking. I told him about how I forgot I had a brother the last time I had seen Beth and the day I discovered them in the photo album. I didn't tell him much about my growing up. I was content just talking about him. I learned that he was in the army cadets. He went to a Catholic school and hated his stepmother. I knew hating our stepparents was something we both had in common, even though Dean was actually my adopted father. He told me about his Poppy and how he died a few years ago and talked a lot about his uncle, Pete. Lorcan told me stories of all the pranks they pulled on one another.

I could tell they were close. Another person he talked fondly about was his Nan and how much he loved her. I would meet her soon enough; unfortunately, I would not share my brother's admiration for his grandmother. We walked past some landmarks I vaguely remembered as a young girl and just took the time to enjoy each other's company; I would get upset when we started walking back to the house; I didn't want this afternoon to end. We could see that Beth and Kristine were hitting it off, so much so that Kristine asked her to come back to our house for the night. We stopped by her apartment to grab a few things. Beth didn't live at home with her dad. She didn't get along with her stepmother much either and moved in with her boyfriend some time ago.

When we got back to Fields, we hung out at the house. Kristine was all about Beth and completely ignored us. It was the first time I had noticed my sister all day, and she looked miserable and left out. I went up and tousled her hair and said, "Hey, kiddo," but didn't think much of her after that. It was near the end of the evening, and I had gone to hang out in my room when Dean walked in to remind me that I no longer lived there. He wanted to know when I would be leaving. I was shocked. Appearances weren't a priority anymore. I told him that I thought I would stay while my sister was visiting, and he said no could do. Dean said to me that I had to say goodbye and be on my way before it got too dark. I called Melissa and asked her what I should do, and she suggested that I call Sean. I didn't want to call him, but I was desperate. I didn't want to burden his family, but what other choice did I have. She said she would help me explain the situation, although she didn't know anything about it.

I talked with Sean, and by the end of the conversation, he agreed to let me come live with him, but there was one issue, his wife, Julie. I'm not exactly sure what I told my father about Dean on the ride to his place, but I know I didn't get into too many details. Julie had a son who was my age named Joe. He was best described as very laid back. His bedroom was on the top floor, and he didn't socialize much. He preferred to sit in his room and smoke something called the pot.

I had no experience with drugs, and up until I met Joe, I had never been around them. At first, Julie seemed friendly enough but didn't appear to warm up very well to the new arrangement. She didn't want anything to do with me. I thought it was very unusual that they both lived in separate bedrooms. Beth once explained to me that it was because she was crazy. I'm not sure what her interpretation of the word meant. Still, I was well acquainted with crazy being raised with Kristine, so I stayed out of Julie's way whenever possible.

Moving in with my biological father gave me something I had never really experienced before, autonomy and everything that went with it. I could come and go as I pleased, and as long as I was polite to Julie and I was home by curfew, everything was okay. I was given my own room and could decorate it with whatever I wanted; this would take some getting used to as I was accustomed to having a bed, dresser, and nothing more. I didn't come with much outside of the clothes on my back. The first thing I would throw out was anything that looked or resembled a wind-up alarm clock; the rest I decided I would figure out later. This house was bigger than I expected and had three floors and a basement that my father used for a shop where he does his woodwork. The main floor had two living rooms, a large kitchen with plenty of room for a dining table. The upper level had four bedrooms, two bathrooms, and the top tier was a loft.

It was decided that I would attend the same school as Beth. I'm not sure why she participated at a public school, and Lorcan went to a Catholic one. Still, from what I understood, Beth was the family's black sheep (for now) and tended to do things her own way.

I don't know if there is any other way to prepare a kid like me for a school as dynamic as this one. I experienced a full-on culture shock. I was never liked at my other schools, not even a little bit, but at this one, everyone wanted to get to know the new girl and couldn't wait to be my friend. My brother and sister were popular and well-liked, so my status was established before I stepped into the school. I had a new identity, as well. Since the funeral, my father refused to call me by my adopted name Jennifer and called me by my original given name. When he transferred all my school records, he had the school change the name to Fallon. Fish lips no longer existed. I was a brand-new person. As such, I was getting used to kids coming up at random to say hello without any ulterior motive proving to be quite tricky at first. I started swaying back to my old patterns of isolating myself and stayed close to my big sister whenever I could.

I meant by culture shock that I was always on guard and always waited for the ball to drop. However, I most feared someone to discover my true identity and expose me to everyone as a fraud. For years I lived in a constant state of fear, thinking every time someone whispered or glanced in my direction, it was because they talked about me or made fun of me. These feeling still has lasted well into my thirties but was incredibly difficult over the next few months.

I had no idea who I was as a person or who I wanted to be. I found that the only way I could connect with people was through sarcastic humor, and that intimacy was virtually impossible. The problem with sardonic humor was that people found it very difficult to get close to me unless they shared my specific comedy brand. Those who were sensitive would often take offense. Most of my sarcasm came from watching Lorcan with his group of friends. If I wasn't at school, then I was always with him and his closest buddies. He had two best friends, Joey and Trever. The three of them grew up as close as brothers, and they seldom spoke to one another unless they were joking, insulting, or teaming up on one another. I was hanging out with the three of them molded most of my personality. Lorcan was my hero in every way. He held up to every expectation I had of what a brother should be. For the first time in my entire life, I felt like I had a genuine connection to another human being. I wanted to be exactly like him. I started smoking because of him and joined cadets to be like him. I loved my new last name and thought cadet O' Brian had such a nice ring to it.

In cadets, we would take weekend trips away, sleep in barracks and learn basic training to enroll in the Canadian Army. That is what Lorcan, Joey, and Trever eventually did. Of course, I quickly realized that I wasn't cut out for cadets or the Canadian Army. I had an underline issue with authority and gave attitude when I was given an order.

My drill sergeant was a year older than me and acted as God's gift to the uniform. While other people usually did as they were told and complained about him behind his back, I told him what I felt about his orders. Needless to say, it didn't take long before I quit. I believe that this really disappointed Sean.

The more comfortable I was around the house, the more I began to realize why Beth had moved out with her boyfriend and why Lorcan disliked his stepmother so much. This woman would fly off the handle over anything.

When Julie flew off the handle, she screamed at the top of her lungs, have a fit by throwing objects, and stomp her feet on the floor. She would then lock herself in her room and become a source of entertainment to Lorcan and his friends, who were often accused of setting her off on purpose. I didn't see it that way. I think they laughed to shrug off an otherwise awkward situation; nevertheless, to me, she was unpredictable, and her behavior reminded me of Dean. So, I stayed the hell away from her.

Siobhan O'Regan

Lorcan's new position in the Army started to take up a lot of his free time, especially on the weekends. Beth was getting sick of me hanging out at her place mooching cigarettes. Sean didn't support my new habit either, so I decided to get a job.

Finding a job when you worked for an insurance company and an animal hospital wasn't that hard at all. I landed a position as a nurse's aide in a local nursing home. I was told that my first shift would be learning how to give clients a sponge bath. I was given gloves, a bucket with warm soapy water, a cloth, and detailed instructions on how to go about executing my task. I was introduced to my first client, who I was told had an irreversible stroke, and he just laid there on his back and stared at the ceiling. I was okay with everything she showed me until she told me that I had to wash his gentiles. I watched in disbelief as the nurse pulled the diaper off this poor man and went straight to work. I was shocked that they actually gave this type of job to a fourteen-year-old. The nurse who trained me was adorable, but some of the other nurses appeared to need some time off, desperately. I grew up pretty quickly in that job and discovered a newfound respect for the elderly. Still, I felt terrible for some of them who were stuck with rotten nurses who had a miserable bedside manner.

In particular, one nurse would rush them down the hall to dinner like she would miss her break, and I often heard her yell at them. So, I started my shift fifteen minutes earlier each day to help take them down. This way, she didn't have to be so angry all the time. I didn't like bathing them at all, but I loved to chat with them, and it made me feel good to see them when I would walk in. They were excited to see me and acted like it was the best part of their day.

I ended up quitting that job on principle after coming in several times and finding out that two nurses, in particular, had been abusing the clients. I had always suspected it but never really had any substantial proof. The day I came on my shift, one of my favorite clients' body, including her face, was completely black and blue. I gasped when I saw her. The nurses told me that she had fallen on her walker. My client disclosed that she wasn't walking fast enough, and the nurse pulled her walker out from underneath her. This caused her to fall on top of it. She went on to say that the nurse's first reaction was to yell at her and scold her for walking too slow, causing her to trip. She relayed the same story to the other nurse, who helped pick this client up off the floor. I had every reason to believe this recollection of events was true. I had seen them rush patients before, and I had personally witnessed them yell at the clients multiple times.

I went to the nurse who trained me but was told point-blank that abuse was difficult to prove. It would be the client's word against the nurses and that accidents happen all the time. The last straw for me was with this elderly lady who used to carry around this teddy bear everywhere she went and would have a meltdown whenever someone took it. This lady was usually quiet and compliant when asked to do anything but didn't like anyone touching her teddy bear. One particular nurse, whom this lady clearly didn't like, purposely took the bear from her just to set her off since taking the bear only resulted in a tantrum. The client began to have one of her huge meltdowns, and that was when the nurse hit her arm for trying to reach for her bear. I called her on it and was told to mind my position. She had been working there for years and didn't need a child teaching her how to do her job. I tried to stick it out, but I couldn't sit there and watch them continuously getting treated in that manner. I guess I was a coward in some ways, but I was only fourteen and didn't know any better. When I left, I handed the head nurse a detailed letter with everything I witnessed and hoped someone noticed.

Robyn had recently run away from home and contacted me through my mother. I was so excited to see her and eager to tell her everything I had been through and vice versa. Apparently, she got fed up with the abuse, took her brothers to the lead, and decided to leave home. She stayed with friends, for the time being, so we asked my dad if she could live with us when the opportunity came up. He flat out said no. I begged and pleaded with him to change his mind, but he wouldn't budge. I think that was the first time I felt furious and thought his decision was brash and unjust. If only he knew what we had gone through together. I tried to explain that she was abused like me, but he brushed me off, and I felt ultimately dismissed. I realized that he had no idea about the extent of the abuse she and I endured as a child. I tried talking to him about it several times, but there was always this underline sadness, so I didn't get into very much detail with him. As a kid, I understood his demeanor to mean he didn't care. At the time, he was also trying to hold together whatever was left from another failed marriage, number three. I think my father had a preconceived notion of how he wanted his family to be, now that his daughter was back in the picture. He wanted to live in the moment and start fresh so severely. Still, there were just too many variables and too much undisclosed history that affected the outcome. All the issues between him and Julie predated me. Still, to a girl who was used to bearing the brunt of everyone's anger, Julie had seen an opportunity for an out and used it.

She once screamed at me in front of Lorcan and told me that the reason why she and my dad were breaking up was my fault. I was dumbfounded and didn't know what to say. Lorcan yelled back that she was a crazy old bat and needed to quit blaming everyone else for her problems. She started to cry and ran off to her room. It was the first time someone stuck up for me. Joe came down and began to yell at Lorcan in an attempt to defend his mother. All I just wanted to do was hide. Why did I always seem to cause so much conflict? Usually, Lorcan and Joe got along, but neither of the boys hesitated to take their parents' sides if it was felt that one parent was being mistreated. Beth was starting to show resentment of having to share her brother and father. She slowly began showing patterns of being a very insecure person that ironically reminded me so much of our mother, a trait she emphatically denies to this day.

Beth lived in a house that was split into two apartments. She and her boyfriend, Anthony (who everyone called Tony), shared the upper apartment. Her best friend, Lori, lived in the lower apartment with her boyfriend, Jason. They had a one-year-old son who was the spitting image of his father. Jason was ten years my senior, and from day one, I never tried to hide the fact that he was infatuated with me.

Jason found me very attractive, and Lori knew about this. She actually thought that it was cute of us to flirt shamelessly with one another, and I can only assume she trusted her boyfriend to a certain degree. I used to love the attention I received from him, and it was the first time since Armstrong, which someone made me feel this wanted. These feelings became stronger, especially when he brushed up against me.

At first, it started as harmless flirting. I adored their son, so I spent a lot of time playing with him when I visited my sister. Then it started becoming much more. I didn't find him overly attractive, but he had this allure, a dangerous sex appeal. He came up and kissed me full on the mouth one day when Lori was in the next room and slipped his tongue into my mouth. He tasted like cigarettes and stale beer, but my hormones had a mind of their own at that age. I'm not sure how my father found out, but he was furious and told me to stay away from him. This wasn't the first time I would defy him.

I was so excited when I met Lauren. She and I hit it off from day one and never left each other's side. She lived with her brother. I don't recall offhand what happened to her parents, but they were not in the picture. She, Robyn, and I found places where we could hang out and score free booze. Lauren knew a lot of people through her brother, so getting alcohol was always easy. One night, Lauren had to babysit and asked me to tag along and told me that she would get paid a bottle of vodka rather than cash. I remember thinking she knew the coolest people ever. This was the second time I ever remember being drunk. We were given half a bottle of vodka and didn't wait until the kids were in bed before we dove in. Lauren taught me that the only way to drink this stuff was straight up. She poured each of us a shot glass full. I had experienced shots before, so I was really smug about my ability to pound a few backs. I didn't hesitate at the count of three and tossed it into my mouth, swallowing before it registered that this stuff burned like hell.

I thought that I would die, and I think I stopped breathing for at least a minute before I gasped for some air. The burning in my mouth and throat intensified with the first couple of breaths, and I was instantly hooked to the warm rush that immediately followed. This was unlike any rush I had ever felt before on such an intense level. I sat there and just tuned everything around me out. I was pretty sure that I hated the taste of the foul liquid but was willing to do it as many times as it produced the numbing effect that came with it and lasted much longer than the initial burn of the shot.

We put the kids to bed and chased the first shot with a few more before realizing that I was plastered, so I called my dad to ask to spend the night. I don't know if my voice tipped him off, but when he said no and came home right away, I knew that I was in trouble. Lauren and I did one more shot for the road, and I think it was the shot that did me in. There was snow on the ground, and the sun was still out; I was blinded because of my oversensitivity to light that I walked right into a parked car and fell flat on my backside. I must have sat in the snow for quite a while cause when I got home because my pants were soaked. I don't know how long it took me to get home, but it must have been a while because my dad was pacing the kitchen and started yelling at me the moment I walked in the door. That man had such an Irish roar that made me cringe whenever he raised his voice.

He threw up his hands, and I ducked. He then started laughing at me and remarked that I was so much like my sister. I don't know what he meant by that, but one can only assume he smelled the alcohol on me and that I was visibly scared. He told me to get my but up to my room, and we were going to talk about this in the morning. I was a fool to think I could deceive a recovered alcoholic into thinking I wasn't drinking and tripped when I attempted to run up the stairs. I could hear him below laughing.

The cool weather and long walk did very little to sober me up, and by the time my head hit the pillow, I was out cold. I woke up the following day and found a shovel lying next to me in bed. There was a note telling me to shovel the driveway. He and I were going to discuss my extracurricular activities when he got home from the shop. I moaned and tried to roll over and fall back to sleep, but I suddenly had a queasy sense of nausea hit me, and I raced to the bathroom and threw up for what seemed like an hour. I eventually scraped myself off the floor after praying to God to spare my life. I promised myself that I would never drink again and slowly made it downstairs to make some toast. After throwing that up and drinking half a dozen glasses of water, I bundled up and went outside to shovel the most prolonged driveway I think I have ever seen. It must have taken me several hours in between breaks and throwing up in the snow every three or so feet. I managed to get most of it done before I came back in and went back to bed.

My father grounded me for two weeks. Unlike at home, I had freedom of the house, but whenever Robyn or Lauren came to call on me, he would turn them away. I was grateful for not being hit and sent to my room for a couple of months. Still, I became increasingly angry with my father for not allowing me to see my friends. Lorcan and his friends weren't so cute anymore and were just mean to me. I passed the time by making coffee for Lorcan for twenty-five cents a cup, and they would pull mean pranks on me if I didn't do as I was told. Lorcan would do many mean things to me, but I tolerated most of it because I thought I loved him, and they weren't that bad compared to Dean's cruel ways.

I had no skills moving into my dad's, didn't even know how to do laundry, and was too afraid to ask for help because I didn't want to look stupid in front of my brother. He had already poked fun at me for not being able to cook. Since Julie and Sean never cooked, I depended on Lorcan to make my meals and mostly ate raw wieners and toast when he wasn't around. I would wear my dirty clothes several days in a row, including underwear, and shove some of them into my brother's hamper when I needed them washed. I know he and his misfit friends used to go through my things in my room, so I began to hide my dirty underpants under my mattress. This was until he found them and displayed them all over my room to show me that he had discovered them. That's when I started washing them by hand in the sink. I hated the feel of them when they dried, so I stopped wearing them altogether. Luckily Lauren showed me how to do laundry and even helped me pull a prank or two back on my brother to get even.

We once unscrewed his light bulb in his room and strategically hung a thread from his ceiling to mimic the cobweb's feeling. We also rigged his entire floor with marbles. He was so mad at us that he smacked us around a couple of times, but he never hurt me, not as Dean did. Lauren and I were together every waking moment until my father started blaming her for my wicked ways and demanded that I stopped hanging out with her. When I refused, we got into a huge fight when I ran away from home.

I stayed with a mutual friend for a few weeks. I had no income, so she basically called all the shots, but she let me stay because she had a massive crush on my brother. She used it as an opportunity to get close to him. Lorcan came and eventually found me. He would hang out after school and tried and convince me to go back home, even though he thought of leaving home on a few occasions himself.

When Lauren and I were on the hunt for something to do, we made our way over to my sister's place. We knew that if we ever wanted to score free alcohol and cigarettes, all we ever had to do was go downstairs to visit Jason. I loved visiting him. I loved the attention he gave me. He introduced me to beer, and it was love at first sip. I couldn't get enough of it and thought beer was much better than the hard stuff.

CHAPTER NINE

Nowhere To Turn

Between my drinking, involvement with Jason, and the constant fights my dad was having with Julie, he just had enough. He decided to call my mother, sending me back to live with her for the summer.

I begged and pleaded for him not to send me and told him that Dean would kill me. I hadn't seen or wanted to see my mother since I moved, and quite frankly, I didn't care if I ever did. Dean and Kristine had sold the house and moved into low-income housing although, they were required to pay what they called market rent.

It was a nice enough place, but I didn't belong, and I wanted to go back home to Main. Dean was the same as usual, but he had other things occupying his mind and didn't bother me. Stephanie and I had a strained relationship that never recovered, and she spent years feeling abandoned. I didn't blame her, and for some reason, Beth and Lorcan never really connected with her either. She was their sister, but Stephanie never felt like she fit in with them. Beth came up to see me once, but I only saw her mother and Melissa. Lorcan came up twice and filled me in on the latest gossip. His visits made me so homesick, and he kept asking me to move back. Lorcan told me that he would work on dad.

I decided that come September, I would move back whether I lived with my father or not, and I would not be staying at Kristine's house come hell or high water. I spent my 15th birthday with Dean and Kristine, but it was the last birthday I would spend with them. It turned out that my mother was having an affair with another man named Bruce, who lived in the same housing complex. The man had a wife and two daughters.

Siobhan O'Regan

They started out as friends and walking partners, but soon one thing leads to another. Unfortunately for Dean, Bruce quickly took his place, and Kristine finally kicked him out. Their affair was shameful and so apparent that neither one really bothered to hide it. They both acted like they wanted to get caught humiliating our families in the process, and neither one gave a damn who they were going to hurt.

Poor Stephanie was caught in the crossfire having to choose between a child beater's affections and a woman who was no less poisonous than a black widow spider. Either way, she lived in total misery. She soon faced the horrible reality of a new stepfather who had severe boundary issues. She found out firsthand just how selfish, cruel, and unattached her mother indeed was.

I moved out before Bruce left his family. He moved in with my mother and convinced my biological father to take me back. He agreed so long as I promised to stay in school, obey his rules, and stay away from Lauren and Jason. I agreed to all of his terms and fully expected to follow through except for one thing. I was a full-blown alcoholic. Although it took me years to identify and even admit that I had a problem, my promise didn't change my alcohol dependency. My reasons for getting it also never changed.

My father's micromanaging method started to mimic Dean's controlling ways, and I couldn't conform to that way of living again. I felt like he was smothering me, and so all we ever did was fight. I moved out of my dad's again after getting frustrated, and he tried to pull me upstairs physically. I was being defiant, which I understand now to be a scare tactic, but at the time, that's not how I saw it. I took it as a clear threat, so I stayed with people I knew in the circles I hung out with, my tribe.

I sometimes spent my nights wandering around the streets as I had nowhere to go, but I usually would find a friend to take me in for a night or two at a time. Lauren and I met this guy named Justin at a party and started hanging out with him for a few weeks. We often hung out at his house. Justin was an unusual-looking guy. He had unique features; his eyes were spread further apart than usual, his ears hung much lower, and he had a high forehead. He was always all over the place and reminded me so much of Junior, but he was a nice enough guy.

Nobody Special

One day we were hanging out, and I noticed a photo album on his table. I helped myself by flipping through the pages for something to do. I came across a woman's photo and commented aloud, stating how much she looked like my mom's sister Judith, who I met when Robyn and I were hanging out. He glanced over, shrugged, and said, no, that's my mom Dorothy. That's funny, I thought; my mom mentioned she had a sister named Dorothy too. I looked at the picture again and back at him and asked him if he had an Aunt Kristine or Karen. He looked up over to slowly nodded. Finally, after putting two and two together, we realized that we were first cousins and that our mothers were sisters! Due to our parents not talking to one another growing up, we had never officially met until now. I thought this was incredibly neat and was thanking God that there was no physical attraction between us. Our conversations would have accelerated well beyond awkward. Regardless I was grateful to have finally met one of my cousins other than Robyn and Junior. I could now find a little bit more than just my mother and Karen's version of this family's dynamics.

I received a call from my mother telling me that Aunt Karen had gotten into a massive accident and was ran over by a tractor. Her leg was crushed, and they were living in Blair at the time, so I hitched a ride with some friends to go up and see her. Robyn had been home for some time now and had left Fields shortly after Sean sent me back home. She had a friend staying with her who, for some reason, I couldn't stand and became very territorial when she around. She would irritate me so severely that I took a swing at her during an argument and knocked her flat on her butt. This was the first time I ever remember hitting someone besides Stephanie, where I was the initiator. It bolstered my ego so much that I actually felt good about myself, and I didn't care how much it hurt her. She and I were at each other's throats the entire time I was there, and Junior had to pry me off of beating her senseless several times. Junior had moved back home after Kristine and Dean moved into the housing complex due to the lack of room. I stayed and took care of Karen for a couple of weeks and realized that I had nowhere to go, so I asked her if I could stay with them for a while. She told me that she would talk to uncle Randy, and they would let me know.

Randy Senior was such a coward. He didn't even have the guts to tell me himself. He told Karen to tell me no and said that it was because it would cause conflict between her and my mother. I headed back to Main that day, and I and didn't speak to my Aunt and Uncle again for almost seven years.

Siobhan O'Regan

One fateful night Lauren and I were bored, so we left our friend's place searching for something to do. We were already three sheets to the wind and wanted to find a place where we could drink some more, so we headed over to see Jason's. We told a couple of friends to find us if my brother came looking for me like he always did. Lorcan was doing quite a bit of experimenting with drinking himself and had a few with the guys after training, so drinking sort of became our thing. I always told Lori why we stopped by was to see their son, which wasn't a lie since I really did adore the little guy. I loved to watch Lori play with him. She was so good to him, and it made me jealous thinking; I wished that's how my mother interacted with me.

Jason offered us a drink as he always did, and Lori, who used to be a bit of a wild child herself, never paid us any mind and took her son out to play in the yard. Lauren and I partied well into the night with Jason and his friends. I think Lori went out with my sister, leaving Jason, Lauren, and me to do our own thing. I can recall Jason cornering me a few times around the house to steal a kiss, and since this was the first time we had the place to ourselves, we went right to town. I still had not developed yet and became highly self-conscious of my body after being constantly compared to my sister. The latter had filled out nicely at eighteen. So, I wouldn't let him touch me, and kissing was as far as I was ever willing to go. Besides, he was a 25-year-old man, and I was only fifteen, he made it very clear that he had other desires, and I spent most of the night fending him off. The events that then followed haunted me for the rest of my life.

Lauren often had to check in with her brother and had to leave. Sometimes she would come back; other times, her brother would ground her and force her to stay inside if she came home drunk. This was one of those occasions. She gave me a great big hug. I usually hated hugging, especially since Sean expected one all the time, but I tolerated it with her. She was my best friend. I told her to rush back and went in search of my bottle of beer. I was feeling numb at this point and stumbled into the bathroom to pee for the hundredth time. I was cursed with such a small bladder.

I relieved myself and found a brush that belonged to Lori, and started to brush my hair. Lauren had beautiful long hair, and I started growing it out to look like hers. I loved to brush my hair. It was so curly that I had to brush it often to keep it straight. I looked at myself in the mirror, admiring how long it had grown in the past year. I wasn't feeling very steady on my feet and tried to balance myself on the sink. I missed it, fell backward, and hit my head on the side of the toilet. I was on the ground, moaning and holding the side of my head, when Jason ran in.

This wasn't my first head injury, but it still hurt like hell. I tried very hard not to move and keep my eyes closed to stop the room from spinning. Jason mumbled something and pushed me onto my back, and swept the hair from my face. I felt like the world had virtually stood still, and everything started playing out in slow motion. There was nothing that would prepare me for what was about to happen to me next. He started kissing my forehead and face as if to make it all better and started kissing me hard and shoved his tongue down my throat. I tried to push him away, but he was way too heavy. He struggled a bit, then I heard him unzip his pants, pull his penis out, and press it up against me. I felt sick to my stomach, and the floor was freezing underneath me. Then as swiftly as he undid his pants, he unzipped mine and pulled them down as far as he could with his knees. I was frozen. I couldn't move. My first and only instinct was to take a deep breath and squeeze my eyes shut. There was some hesitation, and then he covered my mouth with his hands. I felt this burning and stretching sensation in my vaginal area from the outside in. It hurt so bad, like someone pressing hard on an existing bruise, and I was trying to squirm away from him, but he had me completely pinned. Underneath his mid-size frame, I squeezed the brush for dear life. It felt like I was being stretched from the inside, burning from the outside.

My lungs were also burning, and I had lost most of my air from the struggle, so I tried to move his hand to take another breath, but he had one arm pinned with his free arm, and the other was pinned between us. He was swift and quick and let out a huge gush of air when he was done that blew a wisp of my hair on my forehead. He had become so heavy, only my mouth was covered, but I still couldn't breathe, and I was panicking. He got up and pulled my pants up with his free hand first, and then he kissed my forehead, slowly taking his hand off my mouth.

My eyes were still shut. He stood over me forever; I didn't move a muscle and listened to him leave. I pulled my knees up to my chest and felt a warm pulsating sensation down below, similar to how it felt after being hit with the belt. However, the burning and cramping lingered. Tears started streaming down my face. I pulled myself up to the toilet and starting vomiting. He then came back in and stroked my hair as if to try and make me feel better. I didn't have the energy to fight him off and just laid my head on the side of the toilet in denial about what just happened to me. The smell of vomit was the last thing I recall before I completely blacked out.

The next thing I remember was waking up while I was carried on someone's shoulder. I tried to struggle, so they placed me down on the ground. I held my stomach and recognized my brother. There were others there, but I can't recall who they were. He tried to reassure me that I was going to be ok. Everything around me was spinning, and my body felt numb.

I woke up in the apartment where I was staying. There was so much commotion. They had placed me in a bathtub half full of water and left me there to soak. All I can remember was the cramping. I felt way up in my cervical area, and my friend told my brother to take me to the hospital. They took me out and let me fall asleep on the sofa. The next time I woke up, I was in the hospital. The details are foggy, but what I can piece together were the doctors explaining to me that I had alcohol poisoning and that my screen tests had come back positive for drugs. They asked me if I recalled taking anything. I told them that I didn't and had never taken drugs. The nurse explained that my brother, sister, and father were in the waiting room and needed my consent to do the rape kit. This was because Sean had told them that he was not my legal guardian, which meant that I had to sign for it myself. I was so scared and confused.

My mother had always told me that I would be nothing more than a trashy whore if I ever had sex with anyone and would be forced to marry them. I couldn't marry Jason; I wouldn't. I asked to talk to my father and showed him the consent. I had never told anyone about the clock, and the only ones that knew were my mother, Dean, Stephanie, and, of course, our dearly departed doctor.

I didn't know what to do; I told Sean that I was a virgin, but how do I explain that I lost my virginity to Dean during a beating. I reluctantly signed the consent form, and they administered the test. I was so humiliated. The test came back negative for blood or semen but positive for signs of sexual activity and confirmed that I was not a virgin and that my hymen was no longer intact.

The doctor gasped, then asked me about the huge scar in my vaginal area. I had already been humiliated enough and wanted to go home, so I refused to answer any more of their questions. My understanding of what happened next was that Sean was told the same thing. That night stole what was left of my childhood innocents. It damaged my relationships with my family. It would destroy my brother and any chance I had at a relatively healthy life. It unleashed a demon that even I was not able to contain.

Lorcan and I never were the same again after that night. We talked about it once when we were drinking alone, and although he didn't say it, I knew that he blamed himself for what happened. He told me that he showed up, and I was naked from the bottom down in Jason's bed. He got angry and demanded to know why. Lori was back and explained to Lorcan that I had peed in the closet. Without knowing what had happened to me earlier that night, one could assume that I was too drunk to make it to the bathroom.

Although subconsciously, I don't think that I wanted to return to the place where I was raped a couple of hours earlier. Lorcan and his friends carried me all the way to where I was staying and helped bathe me. Afterward, I disclosed that Jason hurt me and kept repeatedly saying that I was sorry. He put two and two together and called our dad to take me to the hospital. I tried to tell him my version of what happened, but he cut me off. He gave me a big hug burying my face in his chest, and that I never had to relive that moment ever again. He told me that Tony was going to take care of him. I'm not sure what that meant, and I didn't ask. I understood that the topic was over, and we never talked about it again. It was the first time that I felt so safe in his arms. It was one of the few times I ever felt that way with him and only wanted to be close to him. It broke my heart whenever he had to leave after a day or two.

It turns out I wasn't the only one who had turned to alcohol. It appeared that Lorcan was using it to cope and numb feelings of inadequacy, anger, and resentment towards the woman who abandoned him. He had little to no attachment to his youngest sister, felt powerless to help the middle sister, and never lived up to his oldest sister's constant needs. Now, his father was preparing for another separation and divorce. This had all began to take a significant toll on him. Lorcan was a really attentive and nurturing brother until he had a few drinks in him. Then he would become a babbling and arrogant fool who was impossible to get close to and got progressively worse until he closed himself off altogether. For me, I took what I could get, and I literally did everything to maintain any form of relationship with him. If that meant to sell my soul to the devil, I would. Beth had moved out of the house into a new apartment, so Lorcan and I hang out a lot with Tony, and all we did was drink. Unfortunately, avoiding Jason became a huge issue since Beth and his girlfriend were best friends. It was decided not to tell Lori that her boyfriend had raped her little sister. At this point, I'm really not sure Beth knew what to believe. Regardless of what everyone thought, I loved and idolized my sister. Still, I could never get close to her for obvious reasons. She was more like our mother. I projected the anger I had for our mother out on her. It turned out that Beth had her own ideas of how I should be behaving. I fell way short of all her expectations. Instead, I took on the supportive role, which became part of the problem. Eventually, she was a public enemy number one.

The fact is, she resented me for having to share her brother and father with me. She already had her own issues and was not healthy enough to support anyone, let alone her troubled sister. This eventually became a sick twisted competition of always having to outdo me. For one instant, she even tried to put Lorcan in the middle forcing him to choose between us. Her actions created resentment that I held against her, which sabotaged any attempts to salvage a relationship. We tried several times over the years, but it always failed. Later in therapy, I found out that her rejection and lack of support destroyed my opinion of her, especially after being raped. The fact is she never had it to give, and that was what ultimately become my downfall, not hers.

My drinking with Lorcan got out of hand. Over the following six months, we were arrested and detained several times for drinking underage and disturbing the peace. It wasn't all I was doing that could have got me in trouble with the law, but it was the only thing I was arrested and formally charged with. We were drinking one night and looking for something to do, so we went out and played soccer in the department store's parking lot on the main stretch. One of us accidentally kicked the ball into one of the cars, and it set its alarm off. We thought of running but were having way too much fun to stop, so we decided to keep on playing and decided to just explain to the police when they arrived. It was an accident, but no one showed up.

That alarm when off forever, and not one person stopped to investigate, so we moved to the other side of the lot and kept on playing. What turned out to be an innocent accident evolved into an idea of breaking into cars. We figured if people didn't give a damn about their property enough to lock it up, then why should we. So, on nights where we were short on cash or bored for something to do, we would break into cars and steal anything of value they had.

I mostly took loose change, some of us had our limits of what we would take, and others would take anything. One of our friends stole a garage door opener and loved to toy with the owners by opening their garage door in the middle of the night until they got wise and unhooked it. Stunts like this got him caught, but it made for some hilarious stories, and he never once told on us. I never got caught for stealing, but I didn't really have it in me to be a petty criminal. I eventually gave a pass to the idea when it came up and found something else to do.

We went over to my sister's house to hang out with Tony one day, and of course, drinking. My sister was out, so it wasn't long before there was a party in full swing. Lorcan and Lauren had been involved for a few weeks now, but Lorcan kept denying they were in a relationship. Lauren told me she was going to make him jealous and flirt with Tony. To be honest, I really didn't give a damn what they did so long as their relationship didn't affect my relationship with either of them. She and Lorcan ended up getting into a fight. He got angry and stormed out of the apartment but was in no condition to walk anywhere by himself, so I tore after him. Once outside, he wasn't walking straight. He was belligerent and clearly upset. He attempted to cross the street without looking and cut off a cab causing him to slam on his breaks to avoid hitting him. The cab driver then leaned on his horn to express his disapproval. This pissed Lorcan off. He banged on the hood of the car and started cussing out the cab driver.

I stopped screaming long enough to tell the driver that he had too much to drink and begged him not to call the police. I gave him my dad's number; within minutes, ' police were on the scene. Usually, my brother wasn't violent, but I think the driver leaning on the horn like that scared him. Hence, the cabby opted to call the police instead. I had quite a bit to drink but not nearly as much as Lorcan. Lorcan wasn't making any sense when the police came and couldn't even stand properly, wavering back and forth where he stood.

One of the officers ordered Lorcan to drop the beer bottle, not realizing he had a bottle in his hand. He held it out in front of him then noticed some beer left, so he tried to gulp it down when three officers jumped him. Now, I'm no expert, but when I saw all three jumps on him like that, I took it as a threat to them hurting him. We had been arrested before, but it was nothing like this. I was terrified and screamed at them so they would take it easy on him. I wasn't being heard. I grabbed one of the flashlights that had been dropped off the ground and then tried to hit the officer over the head with it. This was while she was restraining my brother.

It was so heavy that I lost my balance on my first attempt. One of the male police officers grabbed me before I could connect. The next thing I knew, I was being thrown to the cement with such force that it ripped my jeans and scraped layers of skin off my knees. I was restrained face down. We were arrested. Again.

In all the times I was detained, I had never seen the inside of a jail cell. I always spent my entire time in a room with a desk and chairs on either side of it. They took off my cuffs and sat me down in the chair, and I laid my head down and fell asleep. I was so exhausted. A few hours later, I woke up to the sound of my father bellowing our names at the top of his lungs. I begged the officer who came in to retrieve me, to lock me up, and I refused to go home with him.

They ended up releasing me to his custody anyway, but when we exited the building, I took a separate way; I didn't need or want his help. I felt so betrayed that I would have instead been locked up than to listen to one more of his empty lectures. It always amazed me how much he claimed to know what was right for me, yet he knew absolutely nothing about me. I walked around for a couple of hours and crashed at Lauren's for a while. I was told to report back to jail for fingerprinting the next day. I sat in the waiting area for the better part of an hour. Lauren was with me but preferred to wait outside. When they finally did call me, they told me that I didn't need to be fingerprinted after all but served me papers to appear in court.

Lorcan and I appeared in court together with our father. One of the lawyers told us that the police were accused of using excessive force in our arrest by several witnesses, so the charges of assaulting a police officer were dropped. This all went down since I didn't hit her, and they thought it best to hide the department's embarrassment for allowing me to steal the flashlight in the first place. This was our third charge of drinking underage, so we were facing reprimand.

Nobody Special

We were both given three months' probation and were told to report to the same probation officer together. On one of our visits for Lorcan's birthday, the officer was nice to both of us and gave us gingerbread. He explained that I had to go live in a group home until I turned 16 because I was only 15, had no fixed address, and refused to live at home with my dad. I begged Sean to take me back and promised to stop running away, but it was no longer an option, so I was sent to a home for troubled teens in Dwyer, Ontario. I stayed in this facility for a couple of months until my 16th birthday. This place was much different than the institution I was placed in a few years ago. I could not connect with any of the girls and did whatever I could to pass the time. The only memorable moment I have of that place was going to the theatre for the first time. I remember being angry because everyone decided to see Back Draft when I wanted to see something else. Having said that, it became one of my favorite movies of all time.

At 16, I was old enough to apply for student welfare. I only needed to find a fixed address to claim my first check. I couldn't use my sister's address because it would affect Tony's unemployment, so Tony suggested that I ask Lori. Of course, that meant having to see Jason again, but I was pretty desperate at this point, and I was sure he owed me one. A few days later, I found myself sitting in his living room in his new apartment with Lori, Lorcan, and Jason. I chose to play dumb about what happened between us, but I couldn't even be in his apartment without feeling queasy. I remember feeling so angry with Lorcan when he chatted him up like he was a long-lost buddy.

Even more so after he agreed with Lori, I stayed with them until my check came in. I followed him outside when it was time for him to leave. I pushed him from behind and started hitting him as I cried. He turned around, grabbed both my arms, pushed me back, and told me that it was just for a couple of days. If he touched me, he would kill him. He then let me go and walked away. I fell to the ground sobbing uncontrollably. I didn't want to go back into that house, but there was nowhere else I could go. Jason didn't hesitate to test me. He swept up against me on my way through to the kitchen, and I raised my voice, telling him to back off. He cornered me and threatened me in a husky voice, telling me to chill the fuck out and to stop overreacting, or I would have to find somewhere else to stay.

Siobhan O'Regan

It turns out Lori was pregnant with their second child, and so I didn't see the point of letting Lori know that he had raped me. I thought that it would put a damper on any long-term goals they had. He kept his distance. I made sure I was never alone with him and was only around if Lori or his son were there.

Lori once asked me to watch her son while she and Jason went into the bedroom for a few minutes. I understood what that meant. Their bedroom was connected to the living room, so we went outside to play until they were done. Lori came out and acted as nothing happened to giggle like a schoolgirl. Still, he came out winking and smirking at me with a smug look, and it took everything I had not to slap the stupid off of his face.

Although he didn't come near me, he still made many sexual references and innuendoes toward me. He played them out on Lori while I was there as if it was all just fun and a joke to him. I thought of telling her many times about what happened but didn't think she would believe me. One afternoon he asked me if I wanted to smoke a joint. I had never done drugs before, but I had seen other people do it, including Joe and Lorcan. However, neither one allowed me to try it, so I figured that since I was mad at Lorcan anyway, now was as good of a time as any. I remember thinking it wasn't quite as good as getting drunk. Yet, the feeling of being high was much faster and easier than drinking alone.

I had found my niche, and as much as I loathed drugs, I figured as long as I only smoked pot, then I could justify it. The funny thing was, the more courteous Jason was to me, the more my opinion of him and what he did to me started to change. I began to question if a big part of me wanted what happened to me and still found myself drawn to him. I had no real experience with men. I didn't have a true understanding of what rape was, and now I was confused about how it made me feel.

I got my check a week later, and Jason helped me find an apartment in the downtown area above one of the stores. It was a terrifying place being there on my own, especially at night, but the rent was cheap, and it was mine. A friend of Jason's was also giving away some half-mutt half-wolf puppies, so I was given one to train him to be a guard dog. There were several other apartments in the building. Still, I was afraid to be alone at night because there were always drug exchanges and fights in the hallway.

Nobody Special

One guy got beaten up so severely that there were blood and feces by the main entrance one morning. The blood and feces remained there for months while I lived there. I would see many people come and go when I came home in the wee hours of the morning, and some of them were scary-looking. Most were missing teeth, strung out, dirty, and made lude sex remarks when I walked by. One night we were partying, and I ran into my stepbrother, Joe. He had recently moved out and was having a keg party in his apartment. This was the place he shared with a couple of his buddies. I had never met them, and they lived just a couple of blocks away from me.

One of his friends showed a bunch of us a handgun he was carrying with him. I had shot rifles in the cadets before, so I knew how dangerous they could be, but I was more fascinated than I was afraid of it. He told me many people carried guns to protect themselves from threats out there, and some carried them so they could use them to rape me. I carried that image in the back of my mind and thought of it whenever I saw someone in the hall near my door at night.

My stomach would turn summersaults whenever I passed by their apartments. I would dart into mine as quickly as possible and lock the door as fast as I could. When I went out at night, I would ask one of my friends to stay with me. Unfortunately, none of them really liked staying there either, so I came home alone most of the time.

One night, Lorcan's friend offered to take me back to my place after a party, and I bought a six-pack with him. I invited him in to share his beers. He was twenty-something and charming, I was flattered by his advances, so I didn't exactly push him away when he kissed me. I had no furniture, so we sat on the floor. Against some empty beer cases, we started making out, but then things began progressing way too quickly, and I ended up lying down on the floor. He was on top, and he started undoing my pants. I immediately ordered him to stop and tried to push him away. Usually, if I made out with a guy, it was at a party where there were many people, and I could easily walk away. Making out to me usually meant kissing and heavy petting, but I never wanted to go any further than that. Quite frankly, I was afraid of the next level and men in general. I had never been with one willingly.

The circles I hung around were more male-oriented, and the ones I would meet was much older and far more experienced. I repeated for him to stop, but he just kissed me harder and moved his lips down the front of my chest. I was trembling now. It felt so good, yet alarms were ringing in my head, and I was so intimidated by his large stature. He could easily do anything he wanted with me, and I wouldn't stand a chance. He got down to my belly button, squeezed the inside of my thighs, and stuck his tongue down the front of my jeans where he had unzipped my pants. He pulled them down just a bit further, and before I could react, his face was buried in my crotch. My body took on a mind of its own and exploded into a euphoric convulsion. I experience my first orgasm at the hands of a strange man.

It felt strangely exciting, but when the gratification faded, the all too familiar presence of danger alarmed my sense of adventure, and I needed things to slow down. I yelled at him to stop and pushed him away as hard as I could; he was easily three times my size and clearly didn't want it to end. I think he realized that I was scared and appeared to back off. He assured me not to worry and lifted me off the floor, giving me a huge hug. I was so relieved when he let me pull my pants up, then lifted me and placed me on the kitchen counter.

They were still undone, and I tried to do them up, but he moved quickly. His shoulder wasn't quite square with mine, even with me on the counter, and he stood much taller than me. He unzipped his jeans and pulled his throbbing mass out of his pants, and started stroking it. He then placed my hand on top of his to show me how to do it. It was so enormous for my little grasp, so he grabbed both my hands and directed them on what to do. He went back to kissing me. His hands moved all over my body. I turned my head away from him and squeezed my eyes shut as his lips moved up and down my neck. His stubble burned as he maintained his momentum. I silently begged for this to be over.

He kept telling me to squeeze tighter and told me how much he wanted to fuck me, and started telling me in detail other things he wanted to do to me. I stopped stroking him, afraid he might actually follow through on his threats, and he told me not to stop. He was almost there. Almost where? He told me to grab his balls and wrap my legs around him as tight as possible. Tears started to weld up in my eyes, but he was too caught up in himself to notice. He finally started to grunt really loudly and grabbed the back of my hair, thrusting my upper body into his chest and my lower body into his groin. My hand was drenched in something wet, and I wanted to let go, but I didn't like the chance of making him angry, so I just waited until he was finished.

Nobody Special

When he was done, he told me that I did pretty good for an amateur. He lifted his underwear over his penis, laughed about how it would take a while to go down, and opened another beer. I seriously just wanted him to leave, but he had three beers left, and it didn't look like he was in any hurry. With all my years of dealing with men, you would think that I would learn that they were not to be trusted, and in fact, they were downright dangerous.

When he finally left, I laid in my bed, listening to all the voices coming from the apartments down the hall, and snuggled into my dog. He wasn't much of a guard dog, but he was all I had in the world, and I cried myself to sleep. Sometimes some idiot would knock on my door, waking me up in the middle of the night and laugh, thinking it was funny, but it just made me even more afraid to leave my room. If I had to relieve myself in the middle of the night, I would pee in a can. My dog was just a puppy, so he continued to have accidents on the floor because I couldn't take him out.

On this particular night, I remember thinking afterward that I would rather have this guy go ahead and rape me than live in the constant terror of staying in this apartment alone. The fear of having him do to me what Jason did was better than the unknown.

Beth and Lorcan showed up at my apartment during a time that I just happened to be home, but it was not to be a friendly visit. She came over to accuse me of spreading an outlandish rumor. I looked at Lorcan in disbelief. He just shrugged and looked around the apartment. I wasn't much of a cook, so I ate out of tin cans, and they were piling up on the counter. I was embarrassed by the condition of my apartment.

I told her that it wasn't true, and even in my darkest moments, I would never say or do anything against her or Lorcan. But I think her line of questioning was really a rouse to get what she really wanted, and that was to lash out at me and to find Lauren just to kick her ass.

The night Lorcan and I were arrested, Lauren rifled through my sister's belonging and stole her things. She had slept with Tony, so Beth was out for blood. I was again hurt that Lorcan was not sticking up for me, but he and I both knew that my sister was pissed, and just like our mother when she was angry, no one was safe.

I hadn't seen Lauren as much since I went into the group home. I started hanging out with different crowds, experimenting with more dangerous drugs. I had become a lot more adventurous than I was, with both sex and drugs, so we grew apart.

Beth forced me to call her and lure her out so she could confront her in person. Lauren came, as I knew she would, and I had never seen Beth so angry in my life. Even I was afraid of her. She threatened to cut Lauren's hair off if she ever came near her, Lorcan, or Tony again. Beth rouged her up a bit. Lauren got angry with me for quite a while, and to get back at me, she and a few of her friends came and robbed my apartment. They destroy everything I owned and kicked holes in the wall. My landlord reported me to student welfare afterward, and I stiffed him on two months of rent. I was forced out of my apartment, so Child Services got involved.

They gave me a one-time offer to be placed in a foster home just outside of Main so long as I agreed to stay in school. I was heavily reserved, given my history with foster care, but was so tired and felt defeated that I reluctantly agreed. Lauren and her posse did an excellent job destroying everything that was mine, so the only thing I had left was my dog and a few scraps of clothing. Sadly, the worker told me that I had to get rid of him. I took that dog everywhere, and I fed him before I ever fed myself. He was my one and only companion, and I was forced to give him up. He was such a fantastic dog, and I was so attached to him. It broke my heart to give him up, but student welfare was no longer an option on my own, and I had nowhere else to turn. I was relieved to get out of that hellhole, but I was angry and resentful for having to give up the only thing I truly cared for.

CHAPTER TEN

Lost

I was placed with a Mennonite couple who had two teenaged boys of their own and lived in a farm community just outside of Main; they also had a dog. I took a bus back and forth from school. At first, I made an honest go of it, but it was not my kind of lifestyle, and I was so restless all the time. I spent most of my time isolating myself. These people were gentle and kind but very rigid about everything. Their dog was even forced to obey a strict regiment and took its rightful place by its bowl at dinner. He wasn't allowed to move until everyone was done. I didn't know how to communicate with this family, whose values were based on education and God. They were two things I didn't care much about. I spent most nights in my room thinking I had been through it all and didn't see much point in moving forward. I had nothing but death to look forward to. I spent my time thinking about the different ways to accomplish this.

My foster father came to me one day when I was sitting outside. He asked if I wanted to see some horses; I agreed as I had absolutely nothing better to do. My new family was semi-modernized; they had a computer. Still, they didn't have a TV, and I knew nothing about computers. The truth was, I loved to watch the horses walk by, and I wished I were allowed to ride them. We walked about a kilometer up the road to an old barn on a neighboring property. He then introduced me to its owner and asked me if I had ever ridden horses. I nodded yes because I had.

Robyn used to live across the road from a couple that owned horses and gave us a few lessons about 9 or 10. I got so good that they taught us how to ride bareback. The horse I rode was named Macker Dacker. I fell once, and he stepped on my big toe, taking the nail clean off. I never told anyone in fear of not being able to ride him anymore. I limped around for a few weeks. I was used to limping around, so no one really noticed. I loved him so much that I would sneak into the stalls and perch myself onto the fence, just talk to him for hours. He always looked like he understood what I was saying, and I told him everything. I told him that if I ever get a horse, I would name him Koviac Kovae. It was a name I made up on the spot. I wanted something as equally creative as Macker Dacker.

His owner once told me that he was as good as mine cause whenever I came out to see him, he would light up and always come towards me. One night while I was visiting the horses, we decided to surprise the owners by feeding them. We filled their buckets to the top with a feed from the bins. We had seen them feed grain before in smaller quantities and thought it would save time if we just packed the bucket to the top so they wouldn't have to fill it so much. We didn't know that some horses will eat more than they should and that their bodies weren't built to handle large quantities of grain.

We talked to our horses for a bit and then proudly showed the owners what we did when they stopped by to check on us. We didn't get halfway through our explanation when their demeanor switched to alarm and rushed over to Macker Dacker's stall, which I admitted to feeding first. It was too late; my horse had already eaten more than half his fair share of his grain. I got scared and ran away and was halfway down the road before Junior came tearing after me in a tractor. He got out, grabbed me by the arm, and hoisted me over his shoulder, and threw me into the cab heading back to the farm. The next weekend Karen told us they weren't that angry even though they were forced to walk the horse more than half the night due to something called colic, making sure he was okay. Robyn and I were mortified and would have never done it if we knew any better. Even though they understood and forgave us, Dean wouldn't let me go near my horse again, so I sat in the corner of the property and watched him roam from across the road in tears.

I was given chores to do in exchange for the freedom to ride this one horse, and it became my sole responsibility to take care of him. I was taught all the names of the different equipment and how to use it properly. I was allowed to ride him anywhere I wanted. There were many dirt roads and open fields everywhere, so I had many options on where to go. As long as I agreed to walk him on the cement, I could come and go whenever I pleased.

Even I was surprised at how good of a rider I had become. In such a short time, I had improved vastly. From dawn to dusk, I spent every waking moment in the barns or out in the field. I was never too far from my horse. I didn't like his name, so I called him Rudy. On more excellent days, I would go out into the field and let Rudy roam while I took in a couple of chapters from my latest novel. I sometimes just read while riding him. He was such a fantastic horse, and to this day, there is nothing more euphoric than galloping across an open field. As a child, I hoped to own my own horse one day. I learned a few valuable lessons about horses through this experience. For instance, you had to walk them three times more often than running them, or else they would froth on their underside. I hardly saw him, but Rudy's owner would always praise me for how much leaner Rudy had become when I did. He always told me that I did such a good job keeping the horse's stables clean. For some reason, even though receiving compliments was very unnatural to me, I spent a lot of time avoiding eye contact whenever possible. For the first time in my life, I was proud too.

Unfortunately, my underline addictions had a more significant hold on me than my love for horses ever did. I started skipping school to drink and do drugs again. I met a girl at school named Sadie and a group of her friends. I started spiraling helplessly out of control and went back into my old pattern of behaviors. Sadie was unlike anyone I had ever met before and had two older brothers named Adam and Bryce. She was everything I wanted in a friend and more. I just loved being around her. She introduced me to her gang, and for the first time in my life, I had a sense of belonging.

She and I hung around her dad's place a lot. He was a unique man with unique interests and was more of a friend to his kids than he ever was a father but, he was a man who loved each one of them, and they all knew it. It was so much fun hanging out with Sadie and the gang that I started doing a lot more than smoking pot. We spent most of our time drinking or experimenting with drugs. We mostly hung out at her father's place with her older brother Adam. We did pretty much whatever we wanted killing time, by pulling pranks on one other. I started dating Adam, who, at first, I thought was pretty cute but was very hands-on. He kept continually touching me in a way that frustrated me. I spent more time avoiding him than I ever did, wanting to be near him, and had no idea what my hang-up was. I ended it with him a short time later.

As part of my new circle, there was a guy named Jeff. He had a friend called Tommy, and his brother was Ryan. He had a huge crush on me at the time, and he grew on me quite a bit. He was such a sweet guy and was so loveable. The problem was that he was everything I wasn't. We talked all the time about being each other's firsts and came close a few times, but I just couldn't get past the whole intimacy thing. It was one thing to make out with someone I didn't care about, but this was much different.

This was the first guy that I genuinely cared about. One of Sadie's friends who lived alone with her son let us stay on her pull-out couch when we weren't hanging out at her dad's place. We almost consummated our relationship there, but I kept backing out. This time was the last, and I broke up with him a few days later. I really cared about him, but I couldn't give him what he wanted and didn't want to keep hurting him. The fact was that I wasn't a virgin, so that it would have been a lie anyway. It was something I never dared to explain to him. What had happened to me had created this fear of getting close to people. This plagued me in all my intimate relationships.

I officially moved out of the foster home on my own after I stopped going back altogether and returned to gather my things for the last time. They were sad to see me go and told me that I always had a home if I ever needed one. I thanked them for their kindness, but I was way too caught up with myself to really appreciate everything they did for me. They indeed were terrific people. I was more upset about not being able to say goodbye to Rudy. I didn't think I could face him after I had abandoned him like that. I spent many nights losing sleep over the guilt until I learned to shut it out completely.

My new friends and I did a lot of stupid things. We were fortunate not to have killed ourselves in the process. We were introduced to oil, hash, and even acid. Whatever you name it, we were exposed to it and tried it. We accomplished everything except crack and cocaine. For some reason, my mindset would never allow me to experiment with any drug that required me to snort or inject.

Believing in this way was probably what kept me alive, given that my aptitude for trying anything just to numb the constant pain. Sadie and I went through a lot over a span of several months. She and I were there for each other in more ways than I can count. She held my hand when I cried without ever really knowing why. I was there when she met her biological father for the first time after discovering that she had a different father than her two brothers. Something I was all too familiar with. But as close as she and I were, I always had a huge resentment. It was one thing that made me feel inadequate when I was with her best friend. She would always refer to her as her best friend, and

Nobody Special

I always felt like second-best. I wanted to be important to her too. Her best friend wouldn't come up too often and didn't interfere with our initial friendship since she didn't do drugs as we did, but I understood that I was second in line when she was around. None of my friendships ever lasted. I never felt that I was good enough.

My life changed the day Sadie came up to me and told me that she was moving out of Main and going to live with her mom in Siskin. A look of horror and grief-struck me harder than a punch in the gut, and I broke down into tears. What struck harder than that was when she then asked me to move in with her. I had a hard enough time trying to find a place to sleep in a town where I knew many people and still spent a lot of time roaming the streets at night, never knowing where my next meal or fix was coming from. I couldn't survive anywhere else. Then she told me that she meant I could live with her. I couldn't wrap my head around it. My own family didn't want me, yet she was suggesting that I come live with hers.

She assured me that I would be alright with her mom and brought me to meet her. Sure enough, after we told her a bit about my history, she didn't hesitate to say yes. Sadie and I were so excited and started telling people that we were sisters. Still, I think I invested more into the facade than she ever did. I will never forget the day I met her brother Bryce. I fell so hard for him, and he appeared to be so sincere that I believed everything he would tell me. The connection was so much, so; I thought for sure that I was in love. He and I became serious almost immediately, and initially, it was weird that I had dated his brother, Adam, first. Still, we never really did anything other than a kiss, so I felt it dissolved me of any responsibility on my part to stay away from his brother.

Bryce had one relationship before me, which was secure. He was always ready for the next step, but I was way too reserved and kept him at arm's length, which, to my surprise, he completely respected. I had tried a few times to take the next step, but I was having a massive intimacy issue. After a few too many drinks, I finally decided for the day after my seventeenth birthday to be the day.

I asked Bryce to drive me home from his aunt's house, and I let him seduce me that afternoon. It was the first time I ever gave myself to someone willingly and referred to it as my first time. It was nothing like I imagined. He was gentle and sweet and very attentive. It was a moment I never regretted. Unfortunately, it was difficult for me to disclose my aversions to certain touched without knowing my history. I couldn't explain my likes and dislikes. For me, it wasn't something I looked forward to and learned that I only ever did it for him. I would later discover that instinctually, most couples bond and connect through touch. He liked to sit and cuddle, but I always felt like I was suffocating and honestly tried. Still, I couldn't sit for long periods pressed up against someone without feeling anxious, restless, and restrained.

He and I spent a lot of time together over the next couple of months. I cared a great deal for him, but my default personality type eventually kicked in, as it turns out. I spent the entire relationship weighing it down with my insecurities and negative thoughts. I always thought I would never be good enough for him. In the end, we were never able to connect, and that became the second of many failed relationships. My inability to get close to anyone was making its mark everywhere.

He talked about moving to British Colombia with his cousin. We talked about me going with him, but he clued in long before I did that he could never offer the type of security I needed and broke up with me a few weeks before he left. I was heartbroken and devastated. I spent years comparing every relationship to this one, and every guy fell short of every one of my expectations.

After Bryce, I called my mother, and I consummated our relationship for the first time, expecting her to be receptive to me, keeping a promise I made to connect with her when I experienced my first time. She sat silently on the other line and listened as I told her about Bryce and me. When I was done, she said to me that I was supposed to call before I did it, not after, and I was nothing but a slutty little tramp. She then hung up on me. I was devastated. That was the last conversation I had with my mother until just after my 18th birthday.

When Bryce moved away, I focused a lot on my grief and the loss of attachment. Just like I had when I lost my brother, I felt like a total failure. I submerged myself in despair. Living with Sadie and her mother meant that I had to be accountable for my actions and go to school. I had to limit my drinking if I wanted to remain in a family environment. It was far more complicated than I ever thought, and I spent several months living with suicidal ideations. It got so bad that Sadie was forced to sit with me while I called the kid's helpline, begging them for help. Unfortunately, I never found it very helpful, and I hung up feeling worse and more desperate than I ever.

Nobody Special

During this time, I had grown accustomed to calling Sadie's mother, mom, and I really felt like they wanted me to be part of their family, so I started playing the part. At first, I was really comfortable in the role until we were visiting some of their relatives out on a farm one day, and Sadie's aunt calls me out. I called her aunt too; she told me, in front of everyone, that she was not my aunt and that Sadie's mom was not my mother either. I expected someone to correct her, but no one spoke up.

The only lesson I learned that day was that I was naive to believe I belonged anywhere, and her words stung harder than any physical strike. We moved from Siskin to Raymore. I attended my fourth high school, and I liked it very much. It had its own swimming pool, and I always saw each move as a potential for a fresh new start. The institution that I had attended a few years ago had a pool, and I spent as much time as I could hone in on my skills as a swimmer. I thought that I would try out and swim for a team. I was surprised when I made the team! I had never been on a team before except in cadets, and we all knew how that turned out. I competed in several competitions but never won any ribbons or medals. I had the makings of a great swimmer, but I lacked the discipline to train myself properly and didn't think that I had what it took to go all the way, so I quit the team. I met my next boyfriend, Mike, at this school, and we had a relationship that stretched, off and on, over for two years.

I was outside one afternoon like I was most days, having a cigarette between classes with Sadie, when a friend came up and told me that this guy wanted to meet me. I got a glance at him when she pointed him out and thought that he was so cute. I was sure that she was making a mistake. I missed the person she was really pointing to since smoking between classes was always chaotic. It was a mad dash to suck back as much nicotine as possible and to make it to the next subject on time.

He came up to me later that afternoon and introduced himself as Mike. I even thought that he was even cuter than I initially thought when I'd glanced at him earlier.

Two things initially attracted me to him. First, the fact that he was charming, and the second, for some ungodly reason, he absolutely adored me. I was still this scrawny teenager who looked like a little kid. My hair had finally grown out, but it drove me nuts when it was down, so I always tied it back. I hardly ever wore makeup and never wore clothes that complimented my figure. My clothes were way too baggy on my tiny frame. I finally had started getting my periods three weeks after my seventeenth birthday, and almost overnight, I began to develop breasts. My body began changing at an astronomical rate. However, rather than embracing the changes, I felt more awkward and self-conscious about myself. I didn't like to draw too much attention to the way I looked.

He was a year older, well-liked but didn't have too many close friendships. He was very immature for his age, and that part of him drove Sadie and me crazy. Where he lacked maturity, he made up for in other areas, and he was a very loving and attentive partner. We spent a lot of time behind closed doors. I only had one issue that took me years to piece together. I couldn't be intimate with him unless I were either drunk, high, and numb to the whole process. Mike and I never went without it. I received student welfare again, and it paid my share of the rent and board with some money to spare. Mike always seemed to have money as well. We would buy beers off Denver, Sadie's soon-to-be stepfather.

Mike was able to purchase the drugs through his connections at school, so things were great for a couple of months until the subtle little things he did to annoy Sadie and me became harder to overlook. He always told me how much he loved me. This fact alone was a deal-breaker, as I could never say it back to him. I felt that being together wasn't healthy for either one of us, so I broke up with him in the most cowardly way possible and had Sadie do it for me on a phone call.

She was quick to oblige. I understand how poorly I treated him and the reckless regard I had for his feelings. Still, I couldn't face him because of my inexcusably shallow demeanor. He tried to approach me in school, but Sadie fended him off and told him to leave me alone. He eventually stopped trying to pursue me, but not before his sister came up to me after class one day to tell me what kind of heartless bitch I was. She said that she would beat me up if I ever approached her brother again. I had met her a couple of times before, and she was just as brazen and unfriendly then as she was standing in front of me, threatening me. The first time I met her was when she was working at Taco Bell. Mike and I had stopped in so he could hit her up for some money. She gave me a once-over glance and shot me a dirty look. Mike told me she didn't warm up well to new people and once spat in the taco of an angry customer who yelled at her for screwing up his order. After meeting her, I didn't doubt it.

Nobody Special

My sister Beth came down and spent some time with Melissa, who had moved into an apartment of her own during a short breakup from Jerry. She made a point to check in now and then. During one of her visits, she introduced me to a really nice guy who she met on the bus, and the two of them had a brief affair. He admitted to falling quickly in love with my sister, but for reasons of her own, she ended it telling him that it wouldn't work out between the two of them. She extinguished the relationship as quickly as it sparked. He approached me a couple of times, asking me to talk to her affirming how much he genuinely cared for her, but she already had made up her mind and had already moved on. A month later, Beth discovered that she was pregnant.

Robyn and I ran into each other through some mutual friends while we were at a party. It turned out that she lived in an apartment with some guys she knew just two blocks away from where we lived. She also had her friend, who I had previously beaten up in tow. Unfortunately for her, she didn't have Junior to save her when she decided to get nasty. She soon learned that I could be a lot meaner than she was and had the aptitude to back it up. Our drug of choice at the time was acid. We were popping the stuff like candy, trying every variation we could try. Robyn's friend Matt and his roommate Dave had the connections to get it whenever we wanted.

Their place was where to do it since they had their apartment, so we spent a lot of time hanging out with them. One of the rivalries between Robyn and me was the same thing that plagued many friendships. Many of our peers thought that I was the prettier one, especially now that I looked more feminine and less like a tomboy, becoming a problem. She had a crush on Matt and was in the driver's seat in becoming his girlfriend before I came into the picture. At no fault of my own, he turned all of his attention to me, which made Robyn furious.

Eventually, petty jealousy took over, and Robyn started picking fights with us over trivial things. I stopped coming around, and many of us found other places to hang out until she eventually moved out. Over the next few months, we spent every waking moment strung out on acid and watched "Pink Floyd" "The Wall" at least a hundred times to pass the time by. We even watched it several times upside down, just because we could.

Everything was okay until Matt told me that they were moving to the other side of town and asked if I wanted to move in with them. I understood this meant as roommates, and so I made him confirm this fact when he told me that it was a two-bedroom house. He and I were each going to have a separate room, and Dave was going to be in the basement.

This was a great arrangement and one constant party for over a month until I realized that my money didn't carry me very far. Matt was footing most of the bills, including the cost of our extracurricular activities. He was beginning to hint that my debt was accumulating. He was only interested in one payment, a relationship.

By already knowing that this arrangement wasn't going to work, I begged Sadie's mom and Denver to take me back, and they reluctantly agreed. By this point, it didn't take me long to recognize that I had overstayed my welcome, and they approached me shortly after, telling me they were moving. Once again, I needed to find a place of my own.

A week later, I received a phone call. It was Dean. I stood there in disbelief as he spoke. He told me there was a new woman in his life named Rachel, and he wanted to make amends for everything he had done to me. I sat there in stunned silence. I had waited for this moment all my life but never thought it would happen. I wanted to believe what he was saying so severely, but I couldn't help think that he was doing it for her benefit, not mine. I wasn't buying it.

I spent my whole life trying to win over his approval, and everything I said and done was to try and please him. Now he was on the phone trying to make up for years of torture and abuse with a single apology. I was too overwhelmed and over-eager to appreciate what it meant to accept his apology. So I told him that I did. I wasn't in the right place or frame of mind at the time to let him off that easily, but it was too late. I told him that I forgave him and didn't even get a chance to ask him a single question or express how I honestly felt.

CHAPTER ELEVEN

Acceptance Has Its Price

I moved back to Main and stayed with friends of mine for a bit. I ran into Lauren at a party; we were both too drunk to fight, so we decided to forgive one another and move on with our lives.

I looked up at my brother, as I hadn't seen him since the day I turned seventeen. He had taken me to buy my first beer in an actual bar during one of our visits. It was the town's only strip club, but it was a bar, nonetheless. I sat across the table from him, barely touching my drink. I was so happy to be sharing this occasion with him, but there was an unmistakable sadness on his face. The brother I knew and loved was almost gone, and the man in front of me was a stranger. The harder I tried to connect with him, the further he pushed me away. Dad told me that he was at a local pub, so I walked down and found him sitting in a booth nursing a beer with some people I didn't recognize. I didn't say anything to him. I just snuck onto the seat beside him and curled up to him like I use to do when we were first reunited. His eyes were glazed over from drinking, but he looked genuinely happy to see me and yelled out, 'Look, everyone, it's my baby sister!" and threw his arm around me. It was a brief moment in time, but one that I'll treasure for the rest of my life.

Some of the old gang found steady work packing campfire wood. They put in a good word for me with the owner, and I got the job. The pay was great because it was piecework. We could take as long as we liked to get the job done and worked at our own pace. I absolutely loved this job, and the best part about it was that we worked alongside one another, which made a good company. We could take breaks whenever and as often as we wanted. It turned out that our boss also enjoyed the same activities that we did and would smoke pot with us. My absolute favorite part of the job was competing with everyone to see who could get their bags done the fastest. I really liked the physical work, but it was tiring. I just needed a place to stay, and with a steady job, I asked my sister and Tony if I could stay with them. With a new baby on the way, Tony managed to persuade my sister, as they needed the extra money.

I worked long hours in the field and came home tired and exhausted, so I sometimes went straight to bed. I hardly ever got much sleep anymore because it seemed that all my new roommates did was a fight. Tony was always much nicer to me than my sister was, so if I ever was put into a position to take sides, it was usually his. One day they got into a big fight, and she stormed out of the apartment, telling him that she was leaving for good this time.

She had been riding me all week about taking showers, being a slob, and stealing food, so I was glad to see her leave. Beth had threatened to leave as many times as I can count, so I didn't take her seriously until she brought Sean back to help her retrieve her belongings. I felt so stupid. All I could do was sit there in my room, wondering what would happen to me while she hashed it out with Tony. I felt terrible for him. She ripped into him and left him where he stood. I told Tony that Beth had an affair in a moment of weakness and a good chance the baby wasn't his. At the time, I felt it was the right thing to do, and to my amazement, he didn't act at all surprised. Beth left, and the news about the baby gave Tony a reason to party, so that's exactly what we did. By the time Lorcan showed up, we had run out of beers, so I had gone with him to get more. I told him what happened with Beth.

When Lorcan was around, he always had this way of looking at the world that made me admire him. He still would tell me not to worry about everything and that everything would be okay. I so desperately wanted to believe him and invested everything I had in those words. I felt that I could handle anything so long as he was around to protect me. When we got back, I walked into the living room and saw my ghost from the past, Jason.

I hadn't seen him for over a year, and I already had a few too many drinks. Seeing him sitting there opened some very old wounds that had not been identified, let alone healed. Tony had been drinking most of the night, just like me. He jumped up and grabbed me when I started freaking out, demanding to know why he was there, and dragged me to my room, throwing me down on my bed. My head was spinning as he held me down with his hand on the chest like Dean used to do, covering my mouth with his other hand, and ordered me, in a threatening tone, to calm the fuck down. He assured me that no one was there to hurt me.

I had no choice but to comply. Tony was over six feet tall and well over 250+pounds. I barely weighed 80 pounds soaking wet and understood the drill all too well. He told me to stay in my room until I pulled myself together before joining the rest of the party. I understood precisely why Jason was there. Knowing he had all the connections in town when it came to drugs and could get just about anything he wanted, why would Tony not want him there. I also knew Tony did cocaine and such recreationally because I had walked in on him doing it before. Now that Beth was gone, he was free to do as he pleased. It was evident that I was worthless in the grand scheme of things, and the price of doing drugs outweighed any personal tragedy.

I was so angry. Tears began searing down my face. I knew better than to argue with him. I had seen him quarrel with Beth countless times, and I knew I would be wasting my time. Tony wanted to drink and have a good time, which outperformed whatever Jason did in the past. My task was to put up and shut up.

I managed to pull myself together long enough to grab a beer from the fridge and called Lauren to come over. As I just got off the phone, I overheard everyone leaving. I went out of my room in time to see Lorcan heading down the hallway. I asked what was going on; he told me they were heading out to the bar. I tried to ask him to hold up and that I had to wait for Lauren, but he was already out the door.

I took one look around and thought to myself that she would kill us if Beth were to walk in here. The place was trashed. I started picking up empties in the hallway that lead to the living room where Jason, Tony, and a couple of other guys were finishing up a joint before they headed out. Jason told me that he'd give me a hand cleaning up the bottles. I shot him the dirtiest look, which made Tony laugh. He told me to play nice and then looked at Jason, threatening him that if he ever touched me again, he would kill him. Jason just shrugged it off, obviously embarrassed by the threat in front of the other two guys. Tony headed to his room to get changed, and everyone else left to go to the bar. Jason asked me if I wanted another beer. I didn't answer him. I knew there likely wasn't any left anyway if everyone was heading out to drink. The apartment was hot, and the only breeze coming in was from the wide-open balcony door. Still, you had to be careful because there was no actual balcony, and it was one story up off the ground. I could hear Tony running his shower. Jason walked up and placed his hand on my shoulder. He asked me to listen to him in a familiar husky voice and told me that he wanted to apologize. He wanted to see if we could fix the tension between us. I wasn't afraid of him at that moment, but I was shaking. I don't know where I found the courage to shout out loud, "You raped me, you son of a bitch," and slapped his hand away.

"Ya," he whispered, forcefully grabbing both my shoulders now, "but I did it because I love you, and no one will ever love you as much as I do, ever."

My legs went numb, and I collapsed to the ground. He leaned forward and wrapped his arms around me. Tears streamed down my face. I tried to fend him off, but he was much stronger than I was, and so my helpless defeat took over. He leaned up next to me, and I buried my face into his chest, weeping in his arms while he comforted me, stroking my hair.

I regained my composure long enough to wipe the tears from my face and told him that I was okay. I stood up. He released his grip, and as my mind was a battlefield of conflict, he staged the whole scene. He tried to hug me, and I turned away. My eye caught the door, and in a split-second decision, I decided to jump off the balcony. To this day, I don't know what fueled that decision, but the overwhelming pain I felt at that moment was so unbearable that I wanted to end my life right then and there. He must have sensed my move because he stood up and grabbed me by the back of the shirt when I attempted to make a run for the door and tackled me to the ground. He held on to me and covered my mouth to muffle any screams in the struggle. He held on to me for a few minutes and told me he would let me go, and if I headed for the door again, he would call Tony. I was crying so hard that all I could do was nod yes. He then hugged me and kissed the top of my head.

There are no words to describe what it feels like to be comforted by the man who forced himself on me and hurt me in the first place, but under all that fear, I felt strangely protected. It triggered something in me that I had never felt before. I shook loose of his grip and headed towards my room. I darted out the front door, and I could hear him in pursuit. The bar was around the corner from the apartment, and so I knew where I was going. I slipped right through the front door and found Lorcan playing pool. It was dark, so I don't think he'd seen that I had been crying. He pushed me away when I tried to hug him.

I stood there absolutely bewildered. I felt so rejected, exposed, and abandoned at that moment and wanted him to hold me. I would have liked someone to tell me that it was going to be all right. I wanted it to be someone other than my rapist.

I woke up the following day in my own bed with Tony sleeping next to me. He was completely naked, but I was fully clothed. I jumped out of bed frantically, trying to piece some recollection of the night's events. Still, I didn't remember anything after we started ordering pitchers of beer.

Tony appeared confused but dismissive of the awkwardness between us. I tried to focus on my body for any sexual activity signs without leading what I was doing and felt nothing. Tony piped up as if he read my body language and told me that nothing happened and didn't offer up any explanation. He got up and walked out, fully exposed, and collapsed into his own bed face down. I sat down on my bed and buried my head in my hands, thinking about these people who were supposed to care for me. I was so confused and didn't honestly know what to think. I was perplexed.

Tony told me that I could stay out of the month but had to find somewhere else to live. With Beth gone, he was giving up the apartment. A few days later, Beth showed up with Lori stark raving mad and ready to rip my head off.

Tony had to get in-between the two of us to fend her off. I wouldn't have been able to defend myself or hit back anyway because of the baby, so I was grateful that he would intervene. Luckily the attention went from me on to the two of them, and I was spared at the moment. I felt horrible for years, thinking I was why they ultimately broke up, but she was better off and found the right partner who truly loved her in the long run. He became an amazing father to their son. I later told Beth about what happened or didn't happen to lack a better term between Tony and me. Despite what I told her, she took my confession as an omission of guilt. She convinced herself that we had an affair and used it to fuel her anger and resentment towards me for years to come.

Siobhan O'Regan

I looked high and low for a place to stay, but there weren't many options due to my lifestyle. I hung out with Lorcan whenever I could, but the only thing he ever cared about was drinking. We took every opportunity to drink over at Jason's. This ended up becoming a regular hangout.

At first, I only went there if I was with Lorcan, but that was until I met his neighbor downstairs, June. She offered me a place to stay. She lived on disability, was incredibly lovely to me, and appeared to care a lot about my well-being.

She warned me numerous times not to hang out with Jason knowing he dealt with drugs. I already knew what kind of guy he was and didn't dare disclose our history. I was way too ashamed, so I pretended to heed her warning. Lately, I had begun to see a different side of him when his son would come around, and knowing how I felt about his boy often invited me to spend time hanging out there.

I knew that Lori's second pregnancy was a daughter, and he broke up shortly before she was born. Jason would always go on about his little girl and how proud he was. Sad but true, I was so naive that I started buying into his smokescreen act and developing feelings for him. So much so that one night we were smoking pot and drinking alone when he moved in, and I allowed him to kiss me. Everything about that night felt wrong, but I dismissed my intuition by throwing caution to the wind and gave myself to him. I did so almost every night afterward as well. Not long after our relationship began, he asked me to move in with him. I agreed, but only if he told me in detail what he had done to me the night he raped me. Call it morbid curiosity; I had to know if my recollection was right, and for the most part, it was spot on.

Lorcan came over a few times and didn't seem the least bit bothered by the relationship. He told me if it was what I wanted, then I shouldn't care what anyone thought. The few people who knew our history thought I was nuts and those who didn't would talk because of the vast age difference. It wasn't so bad. First, he was charming and did things I had never experienced before, like taking me to amusement parks and teaching me how to drive. But almost immediately, I noticed a huge difference in his demeanor. I once refused to have sex with him because we didn't have protection, and he threw a great oversized fit. He calmed down almost immediately when he recognized that I was scared of him. He apologized and said that he wanted to be with me so badly; it was frustrating. I drove him crazy.

Nobody Special

He was huge into cuddling, touching, and foreplay, which I wasn't. I was starting to reject his advances and began making excuses for my behavior. Very quickly, he became aggressive and insensitive. He started making demands and told me that I looked prettier if I left my hair down. He started criticizing everything I did, right down to my clothes. He would leave little notes around the house that read "Maybe tonight?" meaning sex. When things got really tense between us, he was tired and made me jealous by telling me that he needed to spend more time with Lori and the kids for some family time.

He then would get pissed off when I didn't react to him. He got furious one night and slammed his beer down on the table very hard. I had threatened to leave him during an argument, and that made him stormed towards me. I thought he would hit me, so I instantly jumped out of my seat and backed up away from him.

I think my fear of him got him all excited because he put his hands up in the air as if to surrender himself. He approached me cautiously, then grabbed my arms and pushed me back against the wall, kissing me hard, moving his hands down my body. This got me excited, and for the first time, I can recall actually being turned on.

Sex, as it turned out, would have to be adventurous and exciting to maintain my interest. He appeared all too eager to accommodate at first, and I was shy, extraordinarily insecure, and unsure of myself. I lacked confidence and the ability to express myself. He had no issue making it about him. There was one thing I could not bring myself to do, and I know this frustrated the hell out of him. I could not and refused to perform oral sex on him, which made him angry. Unfortunately for Jason, I had lost interest in him relatively quickly, and outside of providing a roof over my head, he had absolutely nothing going for him. I think he started realizing that too. Regrettably, I didn't think I deserved better, so; I did my best to make an honest go at it.

June would try and come for a visit once in a while but couldn't handle the stairs, so most of our visits took place in her apartment. Jason preferred to stay upstairs, watched TV, and smoked his weed. He didn't really like to share anyway, so it suited us both just fine. She often remarked about how badly he treated me and that I should move back down with her, but her boyfriend was always around, and I felt three was a crowd. Jason was usually pretty friendly with her until he caught wind of her comments. He then showed his true colors by confronting her and telling her that she needed to mind her own business.

He became incredibly insecure and jealous of the guys I was hanging out with at work and forced me to quit my job, claiming it was best for our family. He liked to use that word to describe us when he pictured us as a family with his son. He knew how I felt about his son and used him as a way to keep me in line, knowing if I left him, I would be leaving him behind as well. I went back on assistance to cover my end of the bills, and he often used threats to intimidate me by hiding my cheque and controlling our money.

One night I was downstairs visiting June after Lorcan had left. They had been drinking most of the afternoon, and I took a hiatus from Jason, who was being a complete jerk lately. I knew he was upstairs entertaining a few of his friends, so I stayed out of the line of fire.

I had just gotten over the flu a couple of days earlier and was still wearing the sweater my brother gave me to keep me warm, so I was only on my first drink up to that point. When I came up to grab another drink, only one friend remained, and he was sitting on the couch. Jason was happier than usual, so I just assumed he snorted a line of coke or something. He offered to make me a drink. I had to go to the bathroom anyway, so I agreed and smiled at the guy on the couch as I walked by. When I was done, I grabbed my drink off the counter and headed back downstairs. Almost immediately, I started feeling better than usual. I remember telling June that I should get sick more often since it lowered my alcohol tolerance; she laughed. I came back up half an hour later and felt completely lightheaded. I was feeling no pain, and there was a soft ringing in my ears. My body felt numb and tingly. I didn't drink hard alcohol often because it gave me bad heartburn, so I figured it was the drink that was doing me in.

Jason offered to make me another drink, but I didn't want to push my luck and told him I'd take a beer instead. I remember lying down on the floor, feeling like I was having an acid flashback, and felt totally relaxed. Jason came in for a kiss and pinned me down in a playful manner. I kissed him back. We wrestled around for a bit. I remember getting really annoyed because he started getting rough and wasn't listening when I told him to stop. I pushed him and tried to get up. He pushed me back down and held me there. He began touching me inappropriately in front of our guest, and I remember telling him to stop. I then remember nothing after that.

I woke up the following day in a complete panic and jumped out of bed. My whole body was sore. I demanded to know what happened; he smirked and asked me, "Why, what do you remember"? I don't think I even looked at him. I was completely naked, so I threw on some clothes and staggered out of the bedroom. Clue number one was that I was naked, and I always wore underwear, a sports bra, and socks to bed even after sex. This used to drive my former boyfriend crazy. My mind was utterly blank, and I felt an overwhelming sense of alarm. I remember only ever feeling this way once before. The ringing in my ears was still there, and it was adding to my stress. I demanded again to know what happened the night before. Jason got really defensive and nastier than usual, telling me that I needed to calm my ass down. He declared that I was fucking losing it. I tried to retrace my steps, but everything went blank after I laid down on the carpet. Nothing was adding up.

I went into the bathroom as I felt a burning sensation in the vaginal area and rectum. There were traces of blood when I wiped on both ends. When I came out of the bathroom, Jason was fully dressed and came over to offer me a hug. I recall pushing him away. He mumbled a derogatory remark under his breath and took his turn in the bathroom. He left the apartment. My abdomen was so campy, and I couldn't stop shivering. I lay down on the couch wrapped up in some blankets and my brother's grey sweatshirt and fell back to sleep.

I slept for a few more hours, got up, and had a hot bath. I then went downstairs to see if June was up yet. She interrogated me right away, reminding me that I was supposed to come back down. I asked her if she heard anything odd from upstairs last night, and she told me when I didn't return a half-hour later, she came up and knocked on the door. She heard two male voices laughing and carrying on as music was blaring out in the background. She said that she didn't hear me inside. She sat and listened for a few minutes and thought that she heard Jason describing how much I liked it on my stomach. When no one answered the door, she slowly climbed back down the stairs and waited for me to come down to call on her. She explained that an hour and a half later, she heard someone leaving and could hear someone walking around the apartment after leaving.

Siobhan O'Regan

I knew full well what happened, and I couldn't believe that the son of a bitch had done it again. Only this time, it wasn't enough to do it on his own. He invited a partner to join in too. Jason was right about one thing; I was about to lose it. He had everything. It wasn't enough that I gave myself to him. He had to take it and humiliate me in the process. I broke down in front of June and told her that it was over once and for all. I meant it this time. Today was the day I would end it all. I'm sure she assumed I was talking about the relationship, but I talked about ending my life. I sat down at her kitchen table, buried my head in my hands, and wanted to cry, but I couldn't. The feeling of hopeless defeat had consumed me. I had no plans, no future, but I wasn't running away this time. He was going to know that I knew what he had done, and he would be responsible for its outcome.

I drank all day to numb the shame I felt for what happened to me, thinking how I could have been so stupid to trust him. I asked myself the question that had plagued me since I formed my first thought, and that was what was so bad about me. Up until this point, this was all I knew. My entire life, random acts of compassion were like short breaths of fresh air in an otherwise toxic environment. Every time there was a trace of fresh air, the toxicity in the room would thicken and slowly smother me, intensifying my fears and mistrusting me of the world.

My world had become so polluted that I actually believed I didn't deserve any better than what was in front of me. It drove me to find shelter, comfort, and familiarity within the arms of my childhood rapist.

When he came home, I started in on him, almost immediately asking him straight out if he had raped me again and if he and his friend had taken turns. I was by myself, I had no one with me, and he had no reason to lie.

He looked at me and told me that I was fucking nuts and that I needed to be medicated. I wasn't backing down and repeated my question again. He walked over to the case of beer he brought home and pulled one out. My keepsake box was on the counter, and that caught his attention. It was the only thing I had left in the world. It had a ring that June had given me, a picture of my brother, my sisters, a lock of hair from Rudy's mane, and a GI Joe figurine that Lorcan gave me just before he sold his entire collection. I usually kept the box in the bedroom, and he knew how much it meant to me. He asked me where the fuck did I think I was going with that, pointing to my keepsake box.

Nobody Special

I sat down on the couch and repeated the question for the third time. He sat directly across from me and said, "Yes, we had sex. We always have sex." I asked him, "What about the other guy?" He told me, "You're fucked up." Realizing I was getting nowhere, I asked him if he drugged my drink. He smiled and asked, "Why would I do that for?" I told him then that I was leaving, and I was never coming back. I called him a child-molesting bastard. I knew he had a bad temper, but he caught me off guard when he threw the entire content of his beer on me and whipped the bottle just past my head. That was it; I got up, grabbed my keepsake box, and ran for the door. He jumped up in front of me and stopped me from passing through. I pushed him with everything I had to the best of my recollection, but he was much bigger and knocked me down. I got up again and ended up in a huge struggle. He managed to gain control when he grabbed me by the back of my hair and told me to sit the fuck down. He told me that I wasn't going anywhere. I spit in his face, which lead to a second struggle, only this time, he got on top and used both his hands, trying to choke me.

I couldn't breathe and clawed at him to let me go; my body went numb and just stopped fighting him just before releasing his grip. I thought for sure he was trying to kill me. It took me a few minutes to catch my breath. It hurt, and I couldn't stop coughing. He got up and started screaming at me, telling me that it was my entire fault. My belongings sprawled all over the floor. I managed to get myself up off the floor, and I grabbed a knife off the kitchen counter. I told him that I would stab him if he came near me and then threatened to turn it on myself next.

I grabbed what I could from the contents of my box and headed downstairs. I was still dizzy and fell partway down the stairs. I ran as fast as I could to a wooded area and collapsed on my knees to catch my breath. My lungs were burning. I stared at the knife, determined to end my life then and there. I was so scared, panting hard, and was unaware of my surroundings. I positioned myself and pulled the blade over my wrist a couple of times. I wasn't scared of ending my life but was so afraid of how long it would take for me to bleed out and how much pain it would cause. Whenever I thought about ending my life, I always pictured myself overdosing on pills. Surprisingly, the first couple of practice cuts didn't hurt, but I was bleeding pretty badly. I couldn't see my wrist through the blood, so I took a deep breath and shut my eyes, embracing myself for the follow-through. I was counting down when I heard someone yell:

Siobhan O'Regan

"THERE SHE IS! DROP THE KNIFE!"

All I could see were dark shadows, but I instantly recognized the police surrounding me through my blurred tears. One of the officers slowly closed the gap between us and demanded I drop the knife. I was on my knees with the blade resting on my wrist. His voice softened. I contemplated it for a few seconds while he spoke, telling me that he knew I was just in a huge fight; he could see I was severely hurt and wanted to get me some help. I hesitated for a moment, then complied.

He rushed over to grab me, and another officer came over to look at my arms a few minutes later. They then loaded me into an ambulance en route to the hospital. The officer, who talked me down, rode with me. We got to the hospital, and a nurse assessed me right away. She tried to ask me some questions, but I had already shut down and kept staring off into space. I couldn't feel my arms, and my throat was really sore. I so desperately needed a smoke and gave the officers a hard time when they refused. A doctor came out to assess my injuries. He made a comment to the police officer about the marks on my throat. He bandaged my wrists and told the nurses that I was good to go. I assumed that meant I could leave since suicide wasn't a crime that I was aware of.

The officer, two orderlies, and a nurse escorted me onto an elevator, up to a separate floor, down a hallway, and into a padded room with a mat for a bed. Another nurse came into the room and instructed me to strip. She then handed me a standard-issue hospital gown. I started to cry and tried to run. Realizing I was surrounded, I begged and pleaded for them to reconsider, but I was told if I didn't do it on my own, they would use force to ensure I complied. Both the orderlies and the police officer waited outside while the nurses performed my first ever body search. I became angry, standoffish, and demanded they let me out for a cigarette, promising that I wouldn't give them a hard time if they did. It turns out they didn't care much for my compromise. I spent two full days in lockdown. Someone came in and checked on my vitals and asked me some questions, but otherwise, I was left alone with my thoughts. On the third day, I was brought into an office where I met my psychiatrist.

Nobody Special

He informed me that I could be released that afternoon. Still, he wanted me to sign in to the hospital's Vance wing voluntarily. This was for some intense one-on-one and group therapy. I was so desperate. I felt like I had nothing left to lose and wasn't convinced that I wanted to live, so I took his advice, and I opened up to him about everything.

He sat in silence during most of it and even once shook his head, stating that he thought he heard it all about my abuse. He prescribed me sleeping medication, among some other pills, and I spent the remainder of my first session answering his questions. I didn't know how to respond to most of them. He ordered blood work, full medical and spent forever documenting everything I told him. This doctor said that I likely suffered from PTSD and asked if bipolar ran in the family.

I spent hours in group therapy but spent more time listening to others in the group and disclosed very little about myself. The fact was, trying to kill myself wasn't a topic that I was eager to discuss in front of strangers. I found comfort hiding behind everyone else's issues. I was allowed to call my father and asked him to bring me some personal care products, but it was really just an excuse to see if he cared about me.

He brought me a baby food jar, half full of conditioner, and didn't have much to say to me. It was evident that he didn't know how to connect with me. Again, I understood it to mean he didn't care. He had become so detached from me, and it was clear that I was a massive disappointment to him. The truth was, we were never connected to begin with.

I cried after he left and threw the jar across the room. It shattered in the bag when it hit the wall. I felt utterly alone. Lauren came to see me with her friend Danny, and it was the last time I ever saw her. Danny, however, came to see me almost every day and renewed my sense of humanity. I had met Danny through Lauren and hung out at his place a couple of times. He knew I had no one and had nothing to gain from coming to visit, yet he brought me conditioner and cigarettes. He refused to let me be alone. Danny was a musician and left me notes to tell me that he had come by if I was in therapy. He signed his name with musical notes and became very important to me. Danny became someone I looked forward to seeing every day. Unfortunately, the one person I really wanted to see never visited me, and that was Lorcan.

Siobhan O'Regan

One night I waited for the nurse to do her rounds and come in to give me my meds. Being a creature of habit when she didn't show, I went looking for her. When I found her, I asked if she forgot about me. She told me that the doctor had discontinued my medication until further notice. At every session, I had told him how much I hated taking medication and asked to be taken off of it, so I figured he finally agreed. I was called in for a meeting with my psychiatrist the following morning. He motioned for me to come in and directed me to take a seat. I remember wondering if I was finally going to be released.

I had already been there for a couple of weeks and agreed to stay until he recommended that I could go. He sat back in his chair, gave me a look that has stayed in my memory forever, and got straight to the point. He started by telling me that the last blood test they did confirmed that I was pregnant, and the timeline suggested that it was conceived on the night I was raped.

All I could do was stare at him in disbelief. He went on to tell me that the police were pressing charges for physical assault. They added I might want to consider talking to them about pressing charges for the sexual assault. He and I both knew I had no actual memory of the rape, and I thank God to this day, my mind hasn't pieced together any fragments of the events that took place that night. He told me the memory was buried for a reason.

This was all happening way too fast, and I had to absorb the fact that I was now carrying my rapist child. I had no idea what was happening. Which two men were the potential father?

I was informed of my rights. To confirm the paternity, they had to test the baby through DNA. He said that there always was a possibility they could use the paternity test as evidence if there were trials, but that's all he knew. He didn't know enough about the legal process to comment further. He then asked if anyone could call since I was in pressing need of spiritual and financial support. Still, of course, there was no one, except for maybe my adopted father.

To this day, that was one of the most challenging conversations I ever had to make. It was the second time I had talked to him since I left home at fourteen. I told him what had happened. I gave as little detail as possible, and he agreed to help. He came to get me as soon as I was released from the hospital. All my belongings were at Julie's, so Danny could retrieve a few articles of clothing for me; the rest I was forced to leave behind.

CHAPTER TWELVE

Life Or Death

I was served papers at the hospital to appear in court. I have no recollection of my release except that I didn't get to say goodbye to my friend Danny or Lauren. Dean picked me up from the hospital and drove directly to Raymore. It was a quiet drive. Neither one of us had much to say to one another since we had never really conversed before. Dean did mention that his girlfriend, Rachel was a nurse at the local hospital and could help me decide what to do with the baby. To me, he was a stranger whom I feared and loathed for most of my life, and now I was dependent on him for somewhere to stay with until after the trial.

He was a building manager for a couple of apartment buildings in the region. He had a small apartment on the first floor. I was given a mattress to sleep on. This was in one of the rooms until we moved on to the other side of the Raymore, where he became the manager of two different buildings. Rachel seemed like a nice enough person. She appeared to have a good head on her shoulders, but I never understood what she saw in Dean. I really only knew one side of him, and that was the sadistic side. I always questioned his motives and never got over my initial fear of him. I continued to be hyper-vigilant of his every movement and spent countless hours studying his body language. My fear diminished slightly as we grew accustomed to one another, but I never fully let my guard down.

We talked about my pregnancy a couple of times, and Dean made me aware of his thoughts and where he stood with it. He told me if I decided to keep the baby, he would not support me and would not be available to help out. Rachel supported Dean and told me several times that there were good families out there who couldn't have children and would be willing to adopt mine. I was only 18 years old; I had no money, no support, no parental figure, and no mentor. I was completely and utterly alone, asking myself how I could raise a baby on my own.

After what I lived through being adopted, the thought had not been an option for me until my mother called -out of nowhere- to tell me that she and Bruce were considering adopting the baby. I knew the hospital had called Kristine when I was first was admitted, but I was unsure how much they had disclosed. They told me that she had asked her name to be taken off as the next of kin.

At first, I toyed with the option as to me; it seemed the only workable solution. It was out of desperation to see my child, but then reality set in, and I figured the baby would be much better off with someone like me. I wanted the baby so bad, but I had spent most of my teens homeless and bouncing between couches. Then there was my drinking, which I was still in denial about. So, I contacted a couple of lawyers for legal advice. I didn't find it very helpful. Each one told me the same thing. Their advice was to unofficially not disclose who the father was and raise this child independently.

I understood this to mean I couldn't go through with a rape trial without identifying who the father was, and if I lost, they could file for custody. I figured I likely didn't have hope in hell winning a rape trial, given my history. I definitely would lose all credibility when they found out that I had a relationship with the man. In my opinion, the man admittedly raped me, even though I doubted he would have confessed that in court. I decided to let it go for the sake of my spirit.

I suffered from insomnia for years and only recently found out what my condition was called. I hadn't had alcohol since the night I was institutionalized. With everything going on, I found myself sneaking Dean's alcohol to take the edge off and still wasn't sleeping at all.

The day of the trial came, and I walked into the courtroom alone. Dean went off to do his own thing until I was done. Jason was there, with his new girlfriend. I was told that I needed to speak to the crown attorney and say that I was not filing the rape charge. She looked confused and grabbed my file to comb through it. She was looking for something she had missed. I gave a brief synopsis of what happened that night, and she appeared bewildered and claimed to have only looked at the case over a couple of nights before. Since Jason had decided to represent himself, the attorney told me that the case was going to be an- open and shut case- unless he was going to discuss the matter of rape himself. She was only going to charge him for the physical assault. She told me to meet with her afterward concerning the alleged rape.

I had an idea of what to expect during the court proceeding. I had been to one a couple of months earlier when Jason was charged with possession. He had gotten into a fight at a concert. Once caught, he was taken into custody because the first responder ambulance attendant discovered pot in his pocket. I sat and watched in awe as his friend took the stand and lied, stating that it was his jacket and not Jason's. The judge dismissed the charges, so I knew Jason would be equally shifty and ready for me. He didn't disappoint, and the trial was an absolute joke. His line of questioning was way off base and focused a great deal on our sexual relationship. The crown ward brought the attention back to the violent events that took place, and at the bottom line, the judge wasn't buying his antics. She rendered a verdict of guilty.

I wasn't there for sentencing, so I'm not sure what punishment he received. Whatever it was, justice was never served in my case. I spoke in great detail with the crown attorney afterward and told her everything I could recall. I explained what the other lawyers had told me off the record as well. She prided herself on being a well-seasoned attorney, but she was visibly moved by the time I was finished and was more than willing to help. It came down to my understanding of the process because the medical forensics -based on what I told her- wouldn't be enough to prove sexual assault alone. The case would hinge on, he said, she said, since no one heard him confess to what he did to me. What could have strengthened the case was if the court required Dean to step up the plate and fess up to the abuse. Only that would establish my credibility surrounding the disclosure of my first rape and that I was not a virgin because of the incident with Dean.

She said that it didn't matter that I had been raped and had a relationship with him afterward. It was not unheard of. With my history of abuse and torment, it would be difficult for people to relate and understand why. Another thing that caught her attention was that I had a rape kit done at the hospital. However, no one questioned me or filed a police report. She wondered if it was because I didn't actually admit that I was raped at the hospital but said there should have been an investigation regardless of the moment they did a kit. She kept talking as she scribbled all the details of our conversation down on her pad of paper. Unfortunately, the way I understood it, the reality was that given my history and the fragile components of my mindset, a trial would have likely destroyed me emotionally. I would have to give up my baby's father's paternity. Therefore, as long as he wasn't officially named, he would have no legal standings for his child. She gave me her information and told me to contact her if I decided to move forward; she offered to support me any way she can.

I briefly mentioned part of this conversation to Dean. I wanted to get a feel for how far he was willing to support me. I left out the fact that he could be forced to testify. He told me that under no circumstances would he confess to anything and that it was, in his words, ancient history.

His demeanor spoke volumes at that very moment, and I never brought up our past with him again. My trial wasn't the only thing that had occupied his time in recent months. I found out that my sister Stephanie was arrested and was awaiting sentencing herself. She and a friend who was my age went into a dealership. They told the agent that she wanted to do a test drive in the vehicle her father was looking to purchase for her seventeenth birthday. She had all her credentials and a license, so when the dealer went out to plate the car, they pocketed the information and took it on a joy ride to Montreal. They were both arrested after getting into an accident, causing 10,000 dollars of damage to the car. Neither one of the girls was seriously injured but was facing significant changes. The biggest one, of course, was grand theft auto. Stephanie was sentenced to six months in a juvenile detention center for girls.

It was customary for me to feel alone. Still, never as much as now did I anxiously need a mother figure to help me sort out the right thing to do for my unborn child and me. I desperately needed someone to help guide me. Weeks were passing, and the pressure to have an abortion was mounting. I wanted this baby, but there were just way too many variables. I was contemplating how this baby was conceived, and if there were resources, I was not aware of them. The only support I had in making this decision was Dean and Rachel. I knew where they stood.

The time between my decision to abort and the day of my appointment left me very little room to change my mind, and before I knew it, Dean and I were on our way to the hospital. Rachel was on shift and met up with us for some last-minute advice although, it felt more like a last-minute push.

Nobody Special

Dean helped me sign the paperwork, and I was immediately taken back to do an ultrasound. The screen was pointed away from me, but I asked to see the image and broke down crying when I saw the heartbeat on the screen. I asked for a minute to say goodbye. The technician told me to take all the time I needed. A piece of me died that day, and I hated myself more than ever for what I was about to do. I prayed for God for guidance.

Unknown to me, Sean, Beth, and even my mother were praying for a different outcome. I only found out after the fact, and by then, it was too late. Where were they when I needed support in making the decision? I think it's ironic that Dean was the one with me on what became the worst day of my life. It was the day I became so detached from the world that I stopped caring about myself altogether. The situation was so bad that I diverted all the anger I had towards Dean, Kristine, and anyone else back to me.

As one of the terms of being able to live with Dean, I enrolled back into school and got a nightclub job as a coat check clerk. It was my second night when some guy claimed that I had lost his leather jacket. The number he gave me held a black coat. He was a shifty character and a real jerk. He sat there for the better part of an hour, harassing me and demanding the club pay for his jacket. No matter how much I apologized, he wouldn't stop going on about how sentimental It was to him and attached him to the stupid thing. By the end of the night, all jackets were claimed except the black one, so to shut him up, the club agreed to pay half the jacket's value and docked it out of my pay.

The best part of this job was the after-party. Every night the manager, who everyone called Jack Daniel, would open the bar to its employees and would let us party well into the wee hours of the morning. There was always a smorgasbord of drugs and booze available, and that's where I experimented with a drug called speed for the first time.

If I am honest, I don't think that I really appreciated the concept of illicit drugs. They were prevalent everywhere I went, and everyone I knew did them. The school was going ok. I had met two sisters I could relate to. They lived with their single father, and both of them did drugs. There was no surprise there, so we spent a lot of time skipping school, getting high, and hanging out at the local coffee shop.

Siobhan O'Regan

I had become a bit of a bully and had begun to push kids around. This matter just so happened to attract the type of kids who would back me up. I was sarcastic, funny, and people who appreciated my humor liked being around me. I had long stopped caring about what people thought. I seriously stopped giving a damn. I wasn't school smart, but it appeared that I was highly intelligent and street smart. I had experienced more in my 17 years than most had in their lifetime.

I had developed a way of intimidating people with my words and was well known as an intellectual bully. There weren't many people that tried to take me on, and if they did, they never won an argument against me. I learned first-hand that knowledge was power and spent every waking moment teaching useless facts and information to fuel my latest cause. If there were something I didn't know, I would take the time to learn it to have the upper hand. I knew who the influential players were and how to navigate their circles; however, I still had one disadvantage: I could not connect on a personal level. The only way I got along with people was through sarcastic humor. If someone tried to get up close and personal, I would cut them off. This made a lonely existence for me, but it was safe.

Not everyone appreciated my sarcasm brand, though, and I once commented to the wrong person, and she took offense. It was a reference to a blond joke, and my comment made it almost impossible for me to fit within her crowd. Still, a sincere apology bridged some of the animosity.

This particular group was essential to me because they spent all of their free time playing a game called euchre. I was really intrigued by the game and desperately wanted to learn how to play it. Fortunately, a subgroup played, so I learned the fundamentals from watching the two different groups play. Cards were something I fell in love with instantly and spent any free time I had learning and honing in on my new skill.

The oldest of the sisters was named Brittany; Brit, as I called her, had a younger sister named Lisa. Brit and I were closer in age, and so we most often hung out. She and I chatted about everything. I told her war stories from work and about living with Dean. Brit would tell me about the relationship she had with her live-in-boyfriend and how badly she wanted to move out of town to distance herself from her father.

Nobody Special

One Friday afternoon, we were heading out together. After school, Brit mentioned that she was supposed to meet her dad on the other side of the football field. She asked me if I was interested in meeting him. Sure, I thought. Lisa always talked about how much she hated her dad. It was something we had in common, so I was curious. We were making our way across the field when I recognized the guy from the nightclub who claimed that I had lost his jacket a couple of weeks earlier. I stopped in my tracks and turned my back to tell Brit that the guy standing was the idiot whose coat I supposedly lost. She looked dumbfounded and said that the idiot was her dad.

The guy's name was Norman, but everyone called him Norm. He was so sleazy, massive set, and dressed like a slob. I couldn't help but notice that he was wearing an old beat-up leather jacket resembling the jacket he claimed I had lost. I asked the girls if he owned more than one leather jacket, and Lisa piped up immediately, saying, nope! I didn't need to confront him, as Lisa was quick to do that for me. I could see that he was just as thrilled over our surprise reunion.

He claimed the missing jacket was won in a pool game a couple of weeks earlier and that he only wore it a couple of times before I lost it. Therefore, they didn't get the chance to see it. None of us were buying his story, and it was apparent to me that his daughters didn't have much respect for him. They didn't think very highly of the guy. I knew right away that he was lying and thought that he made Dean look good by comparison.

We went to their apartment, and I got a good glimpse of how much Lisa despised her father. We went across the hall to smoke a joint, and Norman walked in like he owned the place. He called her out on her behavior in front of her friends. She stood up and said, "Whatever!" and sat back down. He was embarrassed and tried to exert some authority telling her to get her ass home. Instead, she just laughed and grabbed the joint, blowing it in his direction. It was the first time I had ever seen that level of disrespect towards any parent. It was abundantly clear that he had little control over her and even less over Brit, who had a terrible temper and had scars to prove it. This guy was a lowlife in every sense of the word, and I had no issue giving him a hard time after what he did to me. He was going to pay me back but twice over in the long run.

Siobhan O'Regan

***

One night, I was showering when I discovered a couple of small lumps and a large one in my left breast. Both of my breasts had been tender over the last year, and some days were better than others. The doctor told me that it was because I was still developing, and they sometimes became tender around my period. Only this time, when I went in, they weren't so quick to brush it off and sent me for an ultrasound immediately. I was then told to wait for the results.

When the results came back, the doctor sat me down and explained that I had something called Fibrocystic Breast Disease. It was going to affect me for the rest of my life. My doctor said that the only way to relieve the pain would be to take a needle and take some of the liquid directly from the cyst to relieve pressure. Wishful thinking, as if I was going to let that happen.

Stephanie came and lived with her dad after she was released from custody. I heard all the horrible stories of what her life was after I had left, and for the first time, I fully understood why Lorcan had to distance himself from me. The guilt alone was eating me alive, knowing that I wasn't there to protect her.

It turns out that Kristine was crueler than I could have ever imagined with me out of the picture. She abused Stephanie in ways that could only be characteristically described as brutal. It was so bad that it had me questioning who held the title of the most vindictive parent.

Stephanie told me stories of our soon-to-be stepfather and our mother fornicating on every available surface of the house. She told me how they made lude remarks and weak references about it and laughed it off as if it were a funny joke. Bruce had walked in on her during intimate moments at a time when a young girl requires her privacy. For instance, he had freely used the facilities when she was taking a bath.

The treatment my sister was subjected to happened to be beyond my comprehension. How a mother could treat and protect her daughter this way was appalling. To make things worse, they stopped hiding their sexual advances in front of her, and she was the one who had to leave the room.

Nobody Special

Stephanie had to talk off many sleepless nights to have sex and be so loud that she had to plug her ears to drown out some of the noise.

When Dean left, Kristine had turned on to Stephanie in the same manner; she was on me when Sean left. Almost as if she blamed us for each part of our father's faults and her failed marriages. Sadly, the reality was that my sister and I lived in entirely different worlds for far too long. Both of us were irreparably damaged by our upbringing. We served our ability to establish a bond or relationship with one another. We were forced to seek camaraderie elsewhere. I did try several times in the best way I knew and tried assisting her by threatening the people she hung out with. I told them what I was willing to do if they wronged her in any way, but the more I tried to look out for her, the further I pushed her away.

I was saving every penny I had to get the hell out of that apartment. It was clear; Dean and I were never going to see eye to eye on anything. We had nothing in common, and I needed to escape his controlling ways. I moved into a hotel for a week after I was approved for an apartment and put enough distance between him and me, abandoning my sister yet again.

My new place turned into a party central from day one, and there wasn't a single day that I wasn't entirely wasted in the three months that I was there. I spent my entire rent on drugs, booze and purchased a pair of Manx kittens (Manx is a breed of a kitten that is generally born without a tail) for companionship. On the weekends, a group of us would often head up to a swimming area in a nearby town. That is when I run into my sister Beth who was there with her new boyfriend.

She was visibly shocked by my appearance as I had gained close to 30 pounds in body fat due to my alcohol consumption. I had gone up from 80 to 110 pounds since the last time she had seen me. She had her apartment now and lived across from Lorcan with her son, Joey. She offered me to meet him. A friend of mine drove me up for a day. He was such a beautiful baby and made me wonder what mine would have looked like. There was no doubt who the father was. He was the spitting image of his father, Tony, and I was so proud of her. Motherhood suited her. Seeing him was a bitter reminder of what I gave up, and as much as I wanted to spend time with my sister, I needed to put some space between us for me to heal.

Siobhan O'Regan

Some of my fondest memories were of those three months. I spent the better part of my later teens idolizing those moments. In the meantime, Stephanie was arrested for the second time. She was caught as a passenger in a stolen vehicle. She didn't actually steal it, but because she was on probation for auto theft, she was charged an accessory and sentenced to 10 months in an adult correctional institution for women. She spent her sixteenth birthday behind bars.

I was so angry when I found out that I went to the pool hall where Stephanie and her friends usually hung out. With a couple of my friends in tow, I beat up the two girls that I felt were responsible for her getting into the vehicle. They didn't have a chance to fight back. They were bigger than me, but I was high and wasn't feeling any pain. I came at them full force with everything I had. I punched one so hard that she hit the ground after only one strike. I turned on to the second one, who was still sitting, and grabbed her head, banging it several times against the wall until my companions pulled me off and dragged me out of the hall. It was not a proud moment for me, but I got the message across to stay away from my sister, and they did.

Neither one of them pressed charges, but they probably should have. I was told that I messed the one girl up really badly. I watched how fighting made people look tough, especially when they won and how they used to light up when their friends bragged about it. I expected to feel that way, but I didn't. I felt lousy, and none of it made me feel excellent about myself. I wasn't any better than Dean and made a promise to myself not to lash out at anyone in that manner ever again.

While living in that apartment, I got ahold of my old boyfriend Mike, and we started dating again. It was nice to be with someone familiar, and it was fun while it lasted, but he hadn't changed much and had no direction in his life. I was not in any position to judge, and like the coward, I was before, I ended it in the same manner as I did the first time we broke up.

Several years later, I ran into him, apologized for how badly I treated him. He had long since moved on and started a family of his own. We talked about remaining friends but eventually lost touch. I stayed where I became infatuated with a boy named Toby, who ultimately stole and broke my heart. Toby and another guy named Devin were very interested in me, but I only had eyes for Toby. As luck would have it, he recently had broken up with a girl he had a long-standing relationship with. She was still very much in love with him, but he no longer felt the same way about her. Eventually, she moved on with Devin after Toby, and I got together, and everyone went their separate ways.

I fell so hard for him that I didn't know what hit me. He did these really amazing things to make me feel special. For instance, one hot summer night, it was so humid that we couldn't sleep, and I didn't have air conditioning, so he stayed up half the night, giving me a sponge bath. It was the most intimate moment I had ever experienced with a partner. He introduced me to skinny-dipping at a local waterhole in a nearby town. I had never had so much fun in my life. Unfortunately, this relationship unleashed a type of insecurity I had never experienced before. I became overly clingy, fiercely dependent, and developed a very unhealthy attachment to him. Since day one, he had this habit of coming and going as he pleased and always left out details of where he was going and who he was with. I would get angry and become confrontational with him because of it. In turn, he told me how much I reminded him of his last girlfriend and claimed that he needed his own space to do his own thing without me.

The deal-breaker was when Toby came home and told me that he had just tested positive for gonorrhea. I was shocked and didn't know anything about STDs. He said that he contracted it from his last girlfriend and confirmed Devin had it too, which is where it originated. I went to get treated, but I wasn't sure if I believed his timeline when he and his ex-had ended their relationship. Based on what the doctor told me about the progression of the disease, it sounded suspicious. We had also just received word that we were accepted to the apartment we applied for together. Still, given that we both had issues with the relationship, we agreed to end it and moved in just as friends. I thought it was the perfect arrangement at first, but we still had some unresolved feelings towards one another, as it turned out. It mainly occurred when we were drunk. We often entertained ourselves by having sex. He favored the no strings attached approach, but the blurred boundaries played a toll on my emotions and left me confused as to whether we were a couple or not.

One afternoon after a night together, he got up and grabbed his favorite drinking mug. He told me not to wait up and darted out the door with a smile. I was so bored and mad that he didn't invite me to tag along, so I called Brit and Lisa and asked them to go out with me. They invited me to a keg party. They agreed to pick me up in an hour. As soon as we got there, we started mingling with our friends. I happened to see Toby out of nowhere. By the look on his face, he was just as surprised to see me as I was to see him.

According to mutual friends, he was there to meet a girl he was interested in. I tried to act like I didn't care, but I did and couldn't hide my jealousy well. He knew it all too well. We stayed in separate areas of the house, but the fact that I was there was beginning to put a significant damper on his plans to connect with his new love interest. By looking at things, she wasn't too impressed that he neglected to tell her he was living with his ex-girlfriend. Lisa was more than happy to disclose that part to her as well. To say we got drunk was a huge understatement. We left the place fully intoxicated and fought the entire way home.

I don't remember the detail of what happened next, but a physical altercation broke out, and we ended up in a huge fight. The entire place was destroyed, and I was beaten up pretty badly. Toby left the apartment after realizing what he had done, and I'm told that he was flagged down jumping into the back of a police cruiser. He had disclosed that he had just beaten up his girlfriend and informed them where to find me.

The door was still open when the female officer showed up. I was just picking myself up and was wiping the blood off my face from where he had punched and busted my lip. I tried to clean up and make the place presentable, but I was walking with a limp and was bracing my chest. The police officer grabbed a broom, told me to sit down, and swept up the pile of broken glass.

At the time, I refused medical treatment, but the severe chest pains a few days later forced me to go to the hospital. The doctor treated me for bruised ribs, a minor concussion, and alcohol poisoning. I remember telling him that he must have been mistaken about alcohol poisoning because I hadn't drunk alcohol for almost two days.

I forced myself to reach out to my mother, who had absolutely no sympathy for me at all. She preferred poor Toby a few times during our conversations; in fact, she ran into him at his work shortly after our break up and invited him to the house for dinner, and offered him money to paint her basement. Kristine was cruel, vindictive, and venomous. I always discovered a side of her that made me question why she was ever given the ability to have children.

Nobody Special

I never saw him again after that night. The police called and informed me that there was an order of protection in place that required him to stay away from me. He had to be escorted by police to get his belongings. I was asked to gather his things, and his parents were coming to pick them up. His mother took one look at me and couldn't hide her disbelief. She couldn't believe that her son was capable of such violence and told me to take care of myself. They said that he was jumped a couple of months later in the park and was beaten up so severely that they knocked some of his teeth out. Some mutual acquaintances questioned me if I had anything to do with it. Still, of course, I didn't and never felt any better knowing what had happened to him.

Brit had recently found out that she was pregnant and told me that her dad was evicted from his apartment for not paying the rent. She and her boyfriend decided to move to a town near a Lake to be closer to his side of the family. This left Lisa, and I told her that she could live with me since Toby was gone if her dad paid for her living expenses. He agreed to pay 250 dollars a month for her food and board and immediately move into the spare room.

During this time, her mother, who she had not seen for years, wanted to reconnect. She sent two train tickets for us to see her in Quebec. I agreed to go, but I had to find someone to take care of my cats while I was gone. Norm offered help. I figured he still owed me one, so I gave him a key to my apartment and provided detailed instructions on how to take care of them. It was an excellent weekend for Lisa, and It turned out to be a positive reunion. I was so glad that I could be there for her.

When I returned home, I was shocked to see that my living room had been turned into someone's bedroom. Norm had gone and made himself at home. He moved in by bringing all of his belongings and used my kitchen table to dress for his clothes. I demanded that he leave, but he told me it was just for a couple of days or no more than a week. I felt terrible for Lisa since it was her father, but I did not want this man living in my house.

I agreed for him to stay a week, maximum. A week came by, and he had not moved out. He had passed out on my couch after eating chicken wings. They were left out on the table where my cats could get into them, and one started choking on a bone; I freaked. I took the TV from the living room and placed it in my room, blaring the sound to show him how pissed off I was. He walked into my room and yanked out the cable from the back of my TV. I immediately called the police, but they were utterly useless and claimed that he could stay because he had given me money for rent, regardless of it being for Lisa. Above all, I had given him a key.

I officially became a prisoner in my apartment. I was a complete neat freak, and he was destroying my home. He left his dirty underwear in my bathroom, dishes were left in the sink, and he never cleaned up after himself. He smelled up my living room so bad that it made me gag every time I walked into my apartment. A couple of days later, he had moved the TV to my living room and was paying it forward by turning up the volume. I cut the cable from the wall to stop him. I lived in hell for almost two months. When he finally left, I had the landlord replace the locks, which I should have done initially. By sharing my home with Lisa, I had complicated things.

She eventually moved out. I simply couldn't put up with her father any longer. She appeared to have understood, but we no longer remained friends. I honestly couldn't tell which one was worse between all my living environments—being beaten and tormented, living in constant fear, feeling hopeless, being alone, living with a sadist, or living as a prisoner. I scrubbed that apartment from top to bottom and got rid of my couch. If I wasn't considered obsessive-compulsive before, I certainly was now. Only I still needed a reliable roommate to help cover my rent, so I agreed to let this guy I knew in my circle move in. He was pretty quiet for the most part. He and his friends spent most of their time playing a game called Dungeons and Dragons, and I loved the fact that he was clean.

CHAPTER THIRTEEN

Rock, Paper, Scissors

I didn't have a vehicle so Stephanie, and I kept in touch by writing back and forth from prison. I received a call from her probation officer telling me that Stephanie needed a place to stay when she was released. He insisted that my sister would be on the streets unless I were willing to take her in. I probably should have thought about it a lot harder before answering him, but I agreed to take her and worked out the terms of her parole. She was fifteen at the time but was going to be sixteen upon her release. I contacted the mothers' allowance for assistance and was turned down over the phone. I was told that I was not considered a mother and did not qualify for assistance in the eyes of the law. They said that she perhaps could be eligible for financial support and told me that I could also claim her baby bonus. I had no idea of the legal process to obtain this money or even what it was. When I asked my mother for the funds, she claimed that she knew nothing about it.

The day she was released, I had scraped up enough money to take her to Wonder World in Reardon and had a friend drive us. I think it was too much for her after being locked up for ten months. She was tired, and I spent the whole time thinking she was miserable.

Taking care of my sister for the next two years proved to be a massive challenge in multiple ways, and it could only be characterized as living in hell for both of us. For me, it was like taking care of a stranger who resented me, and no matter what I said or did, nothing ever changed the fact that she felt abandoned. That she never felt like she fit into the dynamics of my world. I could barely take care of my own needs and had not even begun to delve into my trauma history or addressed any of my own pains. Now I was in charge of taking care of a child with a significant trauma history of her own.

Siobhan O'Regan

Stephanie was a spirited teen who did not need or want a mother figure, but that is exactly what I had become in light of our situation. Being a person who hated authority and was a full-blown alcoholic and an addict, our relationship was a breeding ground for conflict. I had to get tough to keep us alive. For the first time in my life, I decided to grow up and lead by example. Unfortunately, my addiction challenged my aptitude as a parent, and I made so many mistakes in the process. I was no longer in school, for starters, and was forced out by the public sector when I turned eighteen. Due to my age and the level of education I had completed, I was told that I had to finish my studies in an adult program, so I decided to get a job to support us as welfare barely covered the rent.

I contacted a temp agency and worked in a factory for a couple of months in the summer. Stephanie was left to occupy her time, which gave her the freedom to do as she pleased. One of the placements I received was working the line in a BBQ factory. They loved my work so much that I could quickly move up the chain and become a line supervisor in weeks. A month later, I transferred to the paints department, and a week into my new position, I was given a new shift partner. I was shocked to see it was Tony. We chatted about many things, but what he was most curious about was Beth's son. I just so happened to carry a picture of my nephew with me. It was the one my sister gave me on my last visit. That is how he looked at his son for the first time. There was no doubt Joey was his; he was the spitting image of his father.

Tony had a son from a previous relationship and told me that he refused to claim Joey as his own without a paternity test even though he looked exactly like him. I wasn't about to argue with him. I felt responsible for how he thought about his son and knew Beth was getting along just fine without him, so I didn't press the issue. I left that job several weeks later to return to school, and it was the last time I ever saw him again. My nephew grew up to be an accomplished kid without his influence. However, we later discovered he inherited our disease of alcoholism and addiction.

I enrolled Stephanie and me in an adult program to keep an eye on her and scrimped enough money to buy us some second-hand clothes and a couple of bus passes. I took care of our finances, but we were barely scraping by, so we had no money and very little food by the second week. I didn't have to pay for my alcohol so long as I provided a place for people to drink. So, my booze was always provided for. It probably wasn't the best environment to raise a kid, but I did the best I could under the circumstances. My mother was no help financially, but she did arrange to have a care package of food dropped off at odd times. That was only when Stephanie would call her up and tell her that we were starving.

Eventually, I started hitting the food banks, and for the next year and a half, we lived off of whatever we rationed and was given to us. I had to be very careful about how we ate to make it last. Most food banks only allowed you to access it once a month. I was able to find two different resources and utilized each one every other week, so we had some food. For a person with as many food aversions as I had, this often meant that I went without food most of the time. During this time, the only protein source I had was milk and eggs, which I could afford. Otherwise, I ate the bare minimum so Stephanie could eat. I was used to going without food, but Stephanie wasn't, and it was hard enough to curve her moods lately without adding on the already added stress.

Most of the time, we picked the foods we liked and would eat them first. Because of that, we had to get creative. We put the substance in our stomachs and ate a lot of bread with mustard, pasta, and melted peanut butter. We ate dry mashed potatoes with ketchup. The last week before our checks came in was the hardest. We scavenged off our neighbors unless our mother had Bruce drop some food off. He came over maybe four times in the two years. I always tried to budget toiletries but fell short every month, especially since my period started getting worse. I often had to steal toilet paper from school or the arena down the road to get by.

The year was 1995. My 19th birthday was upon me. I had never really celebrated my birthday before or after I moved out of my parents' house. I couldn't stand the texture of the sweetness in a birthday cake. Although knowing how much I disliked cake, my mother tried to make me a strawberry shortcake once I was little. The bread had become soggy from the strawberry juice, and it made me gag when I was forced to eat it.

For years, I refused to eat anything that resembled a cake. It really wasn't a big deal when no one called to say happy birthday to me. I was used to it, so I was surprised when I received a phone call from my mother a few days later announcing that we had a new stepfather and chose my birthday to officiate their nuptials. I think that was the only time I had ever got off the phone with her, and I was grateful for all the times she chose not to call me.

Siobhan O'Regan

One of my favorite drinking buddies found out it was my birthday and popped by to take me out to celebrate. Knowing how I felt about making it a big deal, he told me that he was taking me to the drive-in to see "Water World" and passed me a couple of hits of acid. I had given up on doing drugs when I decided to become a responsible parent. I had done well with 350+ hits over the last few years and heard how potentially dangerous it was as a chemical. I didn't want Stephanie to do it. I knew if I was to preach the dangers of doing drugs and have her watch me do them, it made me a hypocrite. So, when I knew that she was looking up to me, it changed my perspective. I truly cared about her well-being, so I gave it up. As long as I had alcohol, I could manage my cravings for drugs.

I took one look at them and thought, what the hell, you only turned nineteen once and stuck them under my tongue. I knew that it was going to be the last time I would ever do my favorite drug, and I savored every moment of it. Water World wasn't my preferred choice of a movie but watching it on acid made it more entertaining than the critics gave it credit for.

This was my second time ever gone to a drive-in. My parents took us to see ET when we were little. The first movie I saw was Backdraft, back in 1991, when I lived at a Milbank's group home. I was fifteen back then. I loved the theatre and started regularly going on Christmas Day while everyone else was at home opening gifts and spending time with their families. I had nowhere else to go, so this became my annual routine. That year Stephanie convinced me to go over to our mothers for Christmas Day. It ended up being a massive disaster as I got drunk and told her what I thought of her and her new husband. She kicked me out. I had no choice but to call Dean and ask him to pick me up and take me back to Raymore. Otherwise, I had to face walking the streets all night in the cold. It was the first and last time I spent Christmas with my mother until I turned 43.

Stephanie and I managed the school as best we could. I picked up extra shifts through the temp agency when we needed some extra money for provisions. It didn't make for a glamorous lifestyle, but we got by and somehow survived. One luxury I did allow myself was a pack of cigarettes once in a while. I liked flirting with the guy who worked at the local variety store down the road from our apartment.

I had just received a horrible haircut and was nursing my bruised ego with my neighbor, who lived above me. She asked me to walk down to the corner store with her. When we got there, my face was red and swollen from crying, so I pretended to have hurt myself to explain my tear-stained face. It wasn't long before he had me forgetting about my hair. I purchased a pack of gums, which I often did when I couldn't afford cigarettes. I handed him the exact change turning to walk away only this time. He called me back, asking me to take my receipt. I didn't think anything of it until we were halfway home and talked about how cute he was. It then occurred to me that a variety store never gave out receipts. I pulled it out of my pocket to examine it and discovered it had his phone number scribbled on the back.

I called him a couple of days later. He introduced himself as Dylan and told me that he was a student at the local college. He was taking classes in accounting, and he owned a truck. He was working as a cashier to help offset the cost of school. He and I really hit it off; of course, he never got to know the real me, and I kept whatever parts of my past that weren't immediately apparent hidden from him. Obviously, I couldn't' hide the fact that I lived with my sister and came from a dysfunctional home. He eventually figured it out on his own, especially when he met my mother. After a few conversations, we discovered that this was not the first time we had met, and surprisingly it was not the first time we ever shared a kiss. I found out his grandparents owned a cottage right across the road from where our cabin was in Boreal Lake.

We had our first kiss yards away from their property on the beach. You can imagine my surprise when he told me that he was the boy on the beach I had met that summer and thought for sure Karma had just brought us back together. Kristine disliked Dylan immediately. She had no issues disclosing this to him and intimate details of my relationship with Toby whenever she could. I found that to be absurd since my mother only saw us together once when we were dating. Dylan managed to take my mother in stride and fend off most of her attacks. The truth was that he didn't like her much either. We both agreed to keep a distance from her.

Dylan's uncle was a wealthy man who inherited his father's business sense and, eventually, his business as well. He employed Dylan's father and Dylan after he graduated from college as an entry-level accountant. One thing that always disturbed me about this family was that Dylan had another uncle we often visited. He lived in a low-end apartment building with limited mobility for disabled people. His nephew took care of him while his brother lived in a mansion decorated with priceless hockey memorabilia. His parents were kind enough but managed to catch on quickly that I had significant issues, especially with alcohol, and didn't bother to hide their disapproval. Dylan and I spent a lot of time in his parent's condo to get away from my apartment. He was engaged once before, and I could always tell they preferred the other girl to me. He had two intimidating sisters at first but were the most beautiful people you ever met once you knew them. Each one loved to spoil their brother. They tried to make me feel at home with them, but I knew deep down it would never work between Dylan and me. We were just from two different worlds.

The first time I ever remembered standing up for myself was when I started dating Dylan. My rent included a parking spot as per my lease, but his car kept getting ticketed when he parked in the lot at night. I had asked the landlord numerous times to give me a parking sticker, and she refused, stating that I didn't own a car. I was not entitled to space and wouldn't budge even after showing her my entitlement in the lease agreement. She claimed that the lease was intended to imply that I was entitled to a parking space if I owned a car. Whether the fact was implied or not, my lease clearly stated I was allowed a parking space, so I decided to take matters into my own hands. I handed in my rent check deducting all the parking tickets I had received from the first time I requested my parking permit and one hundred dollars for every month I was denied a space. This was to ensure they took me seriously.

Surprisingly, they did not try to and fight it and agreed to give me a permit to give them their portion of the deducted rent back minus the parking tickets. I had done my own research and realized that I was being taken advantage of and did something about it. In the end, I didn't win any popularity contests. I always prided myself on paying my rent on time and didn't have to put up with being bullied by their company's refusal to meet their tenants' rights regardless of whatever their reasons were.

Dylan was not an attentive lover but was an adventurous one. He liked to experiment and took me well outside my comfort zone. I liked him and agreed with some of his unconventional ideas, but some things I simply didn't like. They were painful and only turned one of us on. Dylan kept insisting we try a few times, hoping I would warm up to them, but I turned him down flat. When I was dating Toby, I discovered that the very act of performing sex was becoming extremely painful in any position. I experienced jabs of pain and cramps that lasted hours afterward. I didn't always have the luxury of getting drunk whenever he wanted to get intimate, so I used to use painkillers to dull my inhabitants to be able to perform. Dylan was insistent in teaching me how to let go of my inhabitants and taught me to live on the edge.

I was prescribed birth control to help with the severe cramping and clots I was getting during my period. It was now taking me out of commission for two or three days of the month, and I required specialized medical intervention to help with the pain. I spent lying in bed and couldn't move for those few days. It was getting worse with time. My periods had only started for two years, but the pain and cramping appeared to be more severe with each cycle. I didn't have a doctor at the time, so an aftercare clinic was monitoring me. A month or two after we met, I was put on a more potent dosage of birth control to help with my periods and stopped using backup after we both tested negative for STDs.

I liked it better when we used condoms. There was nothing to clean up afterward if we were out, but he enjoyed mocking me on how I was the only girl who couldn't just do it. He expected me to pull up my pants and clean myself up afterward. He thought my quark spoiled the mood. He reminded me of Jason so much that he would criticize my weight the way I dressed and continuously complained about my smoking and drinking. These were all transparent to me when we started dating, so I started sneaking it behind his back.

A few months later, I started feeling really sick and couldn't shake specific flu-like symptoms off. I was sure I wasn't pregnant because I had got my period and was spotting nonstop, so I dragged myself back to the clinic. They took some blood and a couple of swabs from me. As soon as I got home, I received a call from the clinic telling me that I was indeed pregnant. They said that spotting and periods during pregnancy were not uncommon. Still, they referred me to see a specialist in Raymore for precautionary measures.

I couldn't believe it. I went out and bought a pregnancy test to see for myself, and sure enough, it was positive. Now how was I to tell the father? I think I cared about Dylan, but I knew I could never fit into his world, and there were qualities about him that I wasn't sure I could look away from. I made a pin out of a safety pin and beads like we used to do when we were kids and waited for him to come over. I told him that I had something to say, and we sat down on the front steps of my building. I handed him the pin and said to him that he was going to be a father. He was silent for a brief moment and said, "I can be there for you, but I will not marry you." I felt the same way but hearing such a comment from him being the father of my child wounded me.

I think he sensed my anger because he moved in and gave me a huge hug. He told me that it was going to be okay. I desperately wanted to believe him, but I couldn't help feeling completely alone. Everything that annoyed me about him intensified during the first week after I told him. I wanted to leave him then. I knew he meant well, but he kept demanding I quit smoking. I continued to hide my drinking from him. I was so stressed out with Stephanie, life, and school that I couldn't cope without it and tried to cut down after my doctor told me drinking wasn't healthy for the baby. Back then, I honestly didn't know about the effects of alcohol on babies. I never really had anyone explain to me, and I had no prenatal care with my first pregnancy. I kept bleeding and started to get worried, so the doctor ordered another ultrasound around on the 10th-week to ensure the baby was healthy and progressing well. He ordered me to rest but lying in bed all day was unrealistic for me.

Dylan and I went to one of his family BBQs, and I was helping in the kitchen. I grabbed a cucumber and popped it into my mouth without realizing it was soaked in vinegar, and it burned an existing canker sore. I was getting them a lot lately. I wasn't crying, but my eyes were watering when Dylan walked in and asked me what was wrong. I took a moment to compose myself and told him what happened. He shrugged, laughed at me, and walked away. Later that afternoon, I went home to nap and was woken up by Dylan an hour later. He was visibly angry and ordered me to get up. Still, before I knew what was going on, he accused me of telling his aunt some outlandish story about him hitting me and how he heard that I had reported it to a lady cop. He demanded to know if this was why I was crying earlier.

I was so confused; this was not the first time I suspected him lying or caught him over exaggerating details of a story, but this was way over the top. I was trying hard to keep up with him, but he wasn't making any sense. I wasn't feeling well and still felt half asleep. When I asked him to repeat himself, his story kept changing and was all over the place. I knew he had police business details since his best friend was a local police officer, but this time he had gone way too far, and I demanded him to leave. I spent my entire life hiding from my so-called life, not recreating a new one, and would have never told such an outlandish story. He stormed out and came back the next day as nothing had happened. He was extra attentive towards me but acting smug and self-centered.

We often spent quite a bit of time with his best friend, Tyler. We attended a couple of his parties, including a weekend retreat together. Most of the guests attending these parties were friends and fellow police officers, all of which were drinking and smoking pot. As a kid, one of the officers who arrested us informed us that if we smoked weed like a cigarette, we would have less chance of getting caught.

I had been around it for so often that I was not the least bit phased by watching police officers do it and continued to shrug it off, thinking, sure, why not. The next weekend we went camping, and I was driving in Tyler's jeep when a lady cut him off. He reached for his badge and flashed it, yelling at her to smarten her ass up. I always wanted to become a police officer and was fascinated by him and loved to hear his stories. We drove the whole way up to the campsite with the top down. The wind was chilly, and I froze the entire way up there. I remember being so angry with Dylan for not speaking up, knowing how uncomfortable I was. I ended up spending the night cold, bitter, and I couldn't stop shivering worrying about the baby.

Dylan had only one other love besides himself, and that was his truck. He had bought it from the US and drove it back from there a couple of years before we met. Dylan always babied that vehicle. The day he decided to trade it in for a car to accommodate the baby broke my heart. It was the first time he showed me he had the potential to love something bigger than himself.

At one point, I felt like I needed a break from him, so when Beth invited me down to visit her and Joey for a weekend, I took it. Beth and I were finally on speaking terms again, so I didn't want to miss an opportunity to spend time with my nephew and see our brother Lorcan, who lived right across the hallway. I got to spend Saturday night watching a hockey game with him. I hated hockey, especially since it was all Dylan ever talked about, but it was fun to watch it with him. He even took the time to explain some of the rules. Dylan never did that. Beth had a new guy in her life named William, and they were looking to head out on a date, so I offered to watch Joey for a six-pack of beer. I was eager to have Joey all to myself and to spend the night curled up on the floor watching him play with his cars.

I fell in love with him instantly, and he made me realize how badly I wanted this baby. I didn't know much about being pregnant, but I knew it wasn't healthy to bleed as much as I was enduring. My fear and anxiety were not good for the baby either. My spotting had gotten worse, but my doctor said as long as the baby had a heartbeat and there was no cramping, then there was no need to worry. I did my best to carry on as I usually did. I was so glad to have my sister around for some advice finally and couldn't wait to get her to myself to ask some questions. I wished she had been around during my first pregnancy, but I was grateful to have her now.

Unfortunately, Beth seemed to only care about her boyfriend, William. I was hurt when I overheard her complain to him about me. I thought to myself, nothing ever changes. Regardless, I had such a fantastic time with my nephew and asked Beth if I could take him regularly to give her a break. I promised never to drink when I had him and kept my word. William brought him down once, maybe twice, and Stephanie and I hung out and played with him the entire weekend. Having him made me happy. I prayed my son would turn out just like him.

Two weeks later, on my 20th birthday, I had severe bleeding and some minor cramping, so I had my neighbor take me up to the hospital. They advised me that it was not uncommon in the second trimester to have some cramping and that because I had bled all through my pregnancy, they were not alarmed. They released me and told me to return if the cramping worsened. When I got home, my apartment was full of strangers; apparently, Stephanie had decided to throw a last-minute surprise birthday party in my honor.

Up to this point, my whole life had been about Dylan. I spent most of my time either with him or alone. Dylan disapproved of the people I hung out with before starting dating since most were just drinking companions. They stopped coming around, so Stephanie, in her infinite wisdom, decided to invite all of her friends instead. She proudly showed me the cake she had just baked. It was given to us in a food hamper a couple of months earlier, and she had been saving it for just an occasion. Still, she was upset because she didn't have any icing.

I scraped some change together and walked down to the corner store to buy some. I needed to be by myself to have a good cry anyway. Dylan came over later that evening, kicked everyone out, and stayed the night. The next day was the same. The cramping wasn't any worse, so he went to work, and

Nobody Special

I spent the day curled up on the couch. That night I woke up at one in the morning. I was having severe pain. It was like cramping only a hundred times worse, and I couldn't take a deep breath. I paced back and forth and didn't realize that I had contractions until later at the hospital. I told Stephanie to call Dylan. Moments later, I went to sit down when I felt this gush like I passed a massive clot, and I knew right away before I even looked that I had just miscarried.

Stephanie helped me clean myself up and took special care to wrap the fetus in a small washcloth. He didn't look like much, but he was mine, and I was forced to say goodbye to another baby. By the time Dylan showed up, I was exhausted and still bleeding pretty heavily. I didn't want to be touched or consoled by anyone. Stephanie held the fetus in the palm of her hands and passed him over to me as we left. I cried the whole way, cradling him in my arms, and begged the question, why? They took me in right away and did an emergency DNC to stop the bleeding. The doctor came out afterward to tell us that they were pretty sure it was a boy. Dylan mourned his loss as much as I did. I received a huge bouquet from his sister, who had recently experienced infertility issues herself. I took comfort in knowing she was able to carry a child to full term. I tried to support him as we mourned the loss of our child, but I couldn't see past my grief. The more emotional he was around me, the more uncomfortable I was around him. I pushed him away, drawing us further apart. My son wasn't big enough to be buried at nearly fourteen weeks, but they told us that we could name him and have a ceremony in his honor. His name was Zachary James, and he died on August 7th, 1996, at thirteen weeks and five days.

Dylan and I knew it was over, but we stayed together out of respect for one another. He came over to hang out, but both of us knew the spark had fizzled, and we were now just keeping each other as companions.

By then, Stephanie met a new guy named Allan, a jerk that mistreated her. For some reason, she was still really into him. Things started to get way out of hand when he started throwing his weight around in my apartment and left me no choice but to kick him out for good. He had thrown an object at me and ordered me to get out of her room when I tried to get her up for school. He attempted to tell me I had no right to tell my sister what to do since Stephanie paid rent, so I had Dylan remove him from the apartment.

Stephanie followed suit shortly after and moved in with a friend to be close to him. She and I weren't getting along anyway. We had gotten into a couple of fistfights over something or another after I was pregnant. I was taking a lot of my anger out on her. She didn't know how to be there for me through my grief and pain any better than I did for her. She was about to turn eighteen, so I let her go. I do not claim to be the perfect parent or set the perfect example, but I did the best I could do with what I had. She was close to finishing high school, was healthy, alive, and free to live her life as she pleased. She was starting with a clean slate the moment she turned eighteen. I'd like to think I had a hand in that.

I had another acquaintance from school move into Stephanie's old room. His name was James. I found that I preferred males, especially after living with my sister. They were easier to get along with and brought that whole protection factor with them. I was almost done with school. I had slipped up a couple of times and had come to school under the influence, but they were pretty forgiving in an adult school. I was now applying for college. I wanted to be one of two things growing up, a dancer or a police officer.

I figured at my age, without a head start or the finances to back it up, dancing was a lost cause, so I decided to focus my energy on policing. The best part was that I was never caught for any of the petty crimes I did as a teenager except for underage drinking. So, I didn't have a criminal record to speak of. I figured since I had witnessed police officers smoke up on numerous occasions, it let me off the hook for the drugs too. A month or so later, I received a letter from our local college, accepting me into their Law and Security Program. A good part of my motivation to attend college was thanks to Dylan. He was the driving force behind my decision to go since he graduated and showed me that I wanted something better for myself.

I didn't always appreciate his methods of motivating me, and I was getting tired of hearing how much weight I was putting on. I'm sure he believed that he had good intentions. I applied for financial support through the government and received student housing to be close to the school. My life was finally on the right track, but there was still something missing.

No matter what I said, how much I drank or smoked, I was never happy or content with myself.

Nobody Special

Spring arrived, and the weather was getting warmer. James and I spent the usual Friday night drinking with a neighbor. Dylan was never much of a drinker but spent the night over, especially if he thought I had too much to drink. The next morning, he played hockey and invited me to watch him play. The idea was to wake me up so I could go with him. I woke up the following day to the sound of someone rummaging through my belongings. There was a box on the top shelf on my vanity. I kept money in it, and sometimes Dylan dipped into it if he needed change for coffee or something. Figuring it was time to get up, I pretended not to hear him so I could sleep for a few extra minutes. However, I got annoyed, rolled over, and told him to snoop quieter, only to see a tall stranger sifting through my belongings. I shot up in bed immediately and covered myself with my blankets. I had a sports bra on and my underwear, but I still felt utterly exposed. I must have startled him because he lunged towards me as if to silence me holding his finger up to warn me not to scream.

I shook my head and covered my mouth to signal I wasn't going to make a sound. I was instantly relieved when he backed off. I stared at him pacing my room back and forth, looking at me every few seconds to make sure I wasn't changing my mind about screaming. He motioned a look of warning. I kept my hand covering my mouth because my arms were sheltering my body. He was pacing very quickly and mumbling under his breath. I couldn't recall how long he kept pacing for the police, but I remember every minute it felt like hours. I was trying to be brave; I didn't want him to hurt me and kept my eyes down low enough to avoid eye contact but enough that I could tell how much distance there was between him and me.

I didn't get a good look at his face. I kept looking at his hands to see if I could anticipate his next move and studied his body language to prepare myself for the worse. I had never been held hostage by a stranger. I didn't know what to expect next. My mind was racing as I started preparing myself in case he made a move at me and prayed that if he were going to rape me, it would be quick and that he wouldn't hurt me beyond that. I think it was the only time I was glad that I had experienced rape beforehand, so I knew what to expect if it happened again. I was shaking but centered on my breathing for fear of setting him off and trying to determine if I could fight him off or let him do it and get it over with. I wished Lorcan was there to protect me.

Siobhan O'Regan

I wanted to close my eyes so desperately and hide like I did when Dean was beating me, but I didn't dare take my gaze off of him and kept sucking in large breaths of air in case he came at me.

I had hundreds of thoughts going through my mind at that given moment. I felt like I was running a marathon; I ran low on oxygen and was beginning to feel light-headed. He stopped pacing, stared at me for what seemed like an hour, and tore out of my room. I don't know what hit me at that moment, but I leaped out of bed and ran after him stopping to bang on James's door and screamed for him to call 911. I followed him out the front of the building and down the road before heading back to the apartment so that I could call the police. James had come out of his room, completely oblivious to what had just happened. I collapsed onto my floor, trying to catch my breath. My lungs were burning, and I told him there was a stranger in the apartment. I needed him to call 911.

The police arrived within minutes, and one of the officers told me to get dressed. I looked down and didn't realize that I was still in my underwear. I gladly complied. They told me that I was the second person to call the police and that someone had reported a young woman in pursuit of a man in her underwear just in front of my building. The police questioned James and me separately, asking if he physically touched me. At the same time, forensics searched my apartment and my room. James was so confused and upset. The cops were trying to calm him down by assuring him that this could have happened to anyone.

When my adrenalin finally started coming down, the confusion set in. I realized my cats were missing, and I panicked. Looking down, I could see he had extinguished two cigarette butts into my living room, burning holes in my carpet. Forensics had already confiscated the butts. James and I did a walk-through of the apartment. There was alcohol on the table and some petty cash on the fridge that went untouched. The cop who was interviewing me told me that I was fearless. Another stuck his head in to tell us that the local news was there, wanting to know if they could interview us for a story.

One of my neighbors had located my cats and brought them to my apartment. Dylan arrived shortly after, just in time for the news taping. He felt horrible over what happened and told the reports and me that he had all intentions of waking me up, but we had gone to bed so late he wanted to let me sleep in. He had let himself out and didn't think twice about locking the door, figuring it was a safe neighborhood. I hadn't trusted anyone with a key since the Norm incident and loaned him mine whenever I felt he needed it.

My story aired that night on the news. My neighbors in the building all saw the newscast and offered up their support to see if there was anything they could do to help. There was a gay couple that we often borrowed toiletries from. They sent us flowers and a basket of toilet paper with their praise for my bravery. I became a local celebrity for a couple of weeks.

The police came back three days later and asked me to identify the man in a photo lineup. One of the pictures vaguely resembled my guy, but I couldn't be sure. The police said they were old pictures and instructed me to do the best that I can. The officer said they caught him the next day after he broke into a church, and he was found later passed out in someone else's bed. He was strung out on drugs, had a knife in his possession, and asked if I remembered seeing a weapon. I didn't. They also told me he had a long history of mental health issues and drug abuse. I asked about sexual assault. He gave me a stern look and told me I didn't need that keeping me awake at night, and I was fortunate. He mentioned they also had sufficient evidence to make the charges stick, so it was unlikely that I would be called to testify. I asked about him coming back and was assured that it would be a long time before he would get out again. I didn't need to worry about him coming after me.

A month later, I was on the bus, and I ran into an old classmate named Bryan from one of the schools I attended. I invited him over for a coffee. One thing led to another, and we ended up having sex. I found out afterward that he had a girlfriend and a daughter, but it was too late. He was on the fence about his relationship, and I knew mine was over, so I didn't feel like I was breaking any rules. As long as Dylan and I were no longer intimate with one another, I felt fine.

Everything was okay until the moment came where Dylan felt me pulling away from him all of a sudden. He wanted to try again and tried to seduce me into sleeping with him again. I didn't know what to do and was so conflicted. I had been with Dylan for well over a year, and I felt like I owed it to him to try again, but deep down, I was done and no longer invested in the relationship. I wasn't sure I ever really was. Bryan came over a couple of times a week. Sometimes we would give in to temptation, and other times we would just sit and talk to one another. We were sorting out our issues one by one.

Siobhan O'Regan

This wasn't the first time I was the other woman and had a one-night stand with someone I knew had a girlfriend, but I was too drunk to care. The only way I knew how to connect with people was by having sex when I was drunk. Otherwise, I didn't. There were other men who I purposely left out of my book who served no purpose except to fulfill my subconscious need to connect with someone. Usually, through one-night stands or brief encounters, I never really thought that highly of myself to deserve any better, but this was the only time I had cheated on someone and didn't try to hide it.

I knew Dylan was a jealous partner, and seeing us together would make him question our motives. The way I figured, both of us were looking for a way out, and I found it. My partner in crime didn't seem too bothered because I was using him to get out of my current relationship. He used me to sort out some of his own stuff also. I knew Dylan suspected we were having an affair and started dropping by unannounced. One night he stopped by, and we were in my room just lying casually on the bed talking when he walked in. I didn't see the issue right away but having another man in my room didn't settle well, and he stormed out. I knew he was on his way to play hockey, so I met him at the arena and told him nothing was going on. This, at that particular moment, was true. We sat and chatted for a while, and both agreed that it was time to take a break. The truth was, he had his many flaws, but so did I, and even though I know I never loved him, I did care about him. He was the only person I let in this far, and although he didn't get to know me, he knew enough, and it was time for us to move on.

CHAPTER FOURTEEN

The Many Masks

I received a phone call from my mother. As it appeared, her new husband, Bruce, was in hysterics, neglected to disclose that he was an addict. He had been running around with prostitutes before they tied the knot, so she asked for my support. I caught the next Grey Hound to Fields to meet her.

By the end of the weekend, she instructed him to move out and asked me to move in. This was to help cover her bills. She recently applied for income in her housing complex due to her changing circumstances. She was then forced to uphold paying market rent to keep her townhouse until they could process her application. I was happy where I was, but living with her was short-term and was only until I went to school. I figured I could get a job and save some money, so I agreed to help her out. I also found out that Bruce was into hard-core drugs, the kind you shoot up. He disappeared for days at a time with his paycheck and had maxed out all of his credit cards. When he came back, he was edgy, and it took very little for him to become irritated and temperamental. That, of course, only slowed my mother down a little before she went after him. When she cornered him, he would cry inconsolably like a child who just got caught stealing and used whatever methods he could to get his ass out of trouble.

I had seen more drama in one weekend from this grown man than anyone in their entire lifetime. This guy had some serious issues. I spoke to my landlord, who was incredibly helpful to me since I was held, hostage. She shot an emotional performance for the camera and acted like we were long-lost friends. Her footage was cut when they aired it, but it changed the way she related to me. They agreed to let me give thirty days' notice if they could have access to the apartment to show new tenants.

Siobhan O'Regan

I forgot to mention that my cat hated strangers since the break-in. I think the guy who broke in had kicked him. When the landlord showed the apartment to some potential tenants, my cat attacked him latching on to his leg. This led to me locking up my cat and displaying a -beware of cat sign- when I wasn't home.

Kristine told me that I could only bring one pet, so I was forced to separate my cats and made the difficult decision to give up Maverick and keep Jessie. In the meantime, Bruce had convinced Kristine to give him until the end of the month. I was promised that he would be gone by the time I was to move in. I was shocked to see Bruce was there when I arrived to help move in my belongings. As it turns out, my mother was having a change of heart. She informed me a week after I moved in that she would give him a second chance. This was only if he got some help and entered a program.

Up until that point, I had really only been around him a handful of times. From what I'd seen, there wasn't much I liked about him. Mentality-wise, my first and lingering impression of the guy was that he was an overgrown child. It appeared the drugs did a number on his brain or enabled him for most of his adult life. From what I know of his ex-wife, she put up with a lot of his behaviors to keep the marriage afloat. In my opinion, he was not an attractive man, but he did woo a lot of ladies. Although I should mention, he had to pay for most of them. Dylan volunteered to help me move in and was entertained by Bruce's tough-guy routine when he tried to show Dylan up. Bruce was grabbing furniture that usually required two guys in an attempt to move it himself, just to show off. The mentality part I mentioned earlier was that even though he banged the walls, marked up my furniture, and broke things, he couldn't admit defeat and acted like he had something to prove. He then spent all night complaining about how much he was hurt and kept telling my mother not to make such a big deal about the dents in her freshly painted hallway.

Conversations were based on cars, hockey, work, and nothing else. He used his voice tone to overtake arguments and dominate conversations, especially if he felt you weren't listening or buying into his point. He had two girls who lived with their mother in the same housing complex, making some exciting exchanges. Bruce made his first multiple attempts to seek support in Alcoholics Anonymous to please my mother but always found an excuse to go out and use. To say their relationship was dysfunctional was an understatement. Still, unlike my baby sister, I could not put up with his excuses, as I knew it would eventually make me pay dearly.

My cat Jessie was, for the most part, confined to my room. She was a good cat, but Bruce's temper was unpredictable. I had to fight Bruce off of my cat a few times when he attacked her by kicking and throwing her exactly like Dean used to do. One altercation ended up with him choking me. He was a powerful man, and I thought for sure he would hold on until I passed out. I was getting really tired of men thinking they could solve all of their problems using violence. I wasn't that meek little girl anymore, and I was not going to tolerate abuse from any man ever again. When he finally released his grip, I coughed and gagged so hard that I threw up right there on the floor. He just sat there and watched with this stupid look of satisfaction on his face until I was able to compose myself. I then threatened if he ever laid a hand on me again, I would call the police myself and allow them to search the house for any drugs. Of course, I knew that would anger him even more, but at least he knew where we stood. I booked it for my room.

I'm not sure what he told my mother. When she confronted me, she told me to try and get along with him or find somewhere else to live. I reminded her that she was the one who asked me to move in with her. I had come because she needed help, not to get abused by another one of her damn husbands. She then slapped me clear across the face and pushed me backward. It had been a long time since I had that feeling of inferiority. It took every ounce of my being not to slap her back, but I knew it would end up in an all-out fistfight, and she was still twice my size. So I gritted my teeth and asked her if she was done. She came up, pointed her finger at my face, and told me not to forget who was boss around here. She called the shots, not me. It was good to see mom hadn't changed a bit. By day three, I was ready to pack my bags and move out. Still, I had already paid my rent and only a couple a hundred to get me by until I found a job, which became priority number one.

I applied and got a job at a local corner store and started out working the night shift. I liked the quietness of it and got used to having regulars. They would come in almost every night and started inviting me to smoke outside with them. Life at home sucked, but work was at least okay. We even had our own streaker. A man would come by in a trench coat and would flash us a couple of times while we were out for a cigarette. It didn't bother us, and we would just laugh at how random and awkward it was. I figured he was a guy looking to blow off steam, so I opted to ignore him, but it bothered the employees who worked at Tim Horton's in the same complex. They called the police and eventually caught him. The police told us that he was just a harmless middle-aged man with mental health issues who happened to like the attention. The Tim Horton manager came in every night and tried to offer me a position in her store. She always complimented my work ethic and how her customers were forever talking about the fantastic night clerk across the way. I loved the independence and appreciated not having someone standing over me telling me what to do. I think, at the time, being on my own Improved my customer service skills. In fact, I was slowly learning that I was developing impeccable people skills. I made sure to attend to everyone's needs.

I know that I always had a strong work ethic. I found that I enjoyed working in an environment where I could pace myself and always had something to keep me busy. I even loved to compete and outdo myself. It made the time pass much quicker, and I didn't have to deal with anyone's drama. I made a point to learn every customer's name who came into my store, and if I didn't know, I would address them by calling them sir, ma'am, or friend. I even tried it on those who weren't as friendly and found a way to build a rapport with them eventually. One guy used to come in, and he rarely ever spoke a word except to order his cigarettes and leave. When I finally learned his brand by heart, I would stick a happy face sticker on each of his packages before he came in. At first, he looked annoyed and made a point of unwrapping the plastic off his cigarettes. He threw it into the counter to show his disapproval, but I was stubborn too, and it became our routine.

One night, I noticed that the day shift had moved my stickers, and I couldn't find them. He came at the same time as usual, and I handed him his smokes. He gave me a sour face when he flipped it over and noticed the missing sticker. He was seemingly annoyed, and he walked out. The next night he came in; I had bought bigger happy face stickers when I couldn't find the small ones and when I handed him his package, he grinned for the first time. We went back to our routine. Stephanie dropped by a few times in the true spirit of a child who had recently moved away from home and needed cash. It made me feel like I was still there for her, so I would always give her whatever I had.

One night when things were slow, I was reading the newspaper. I found an ad needing volunteers to assist with a local crisis line. The training was starting immediately. I was so excited that

Nobody Special

I jotted down the number right away. It was exactly what I was looking for to fill up some of my spare time and to keep me out of the house. I called the next afternoon. Within days, I was attending my first week of training. I was well on my way to becoming a certified crisis counselor. The course was six weeks and well worth the time. We were introduced to several community members and had no idea there were so many resources out there for support. I sure wished I knew about these when I needed them.

My first shift was exciting, and I relished every moment of it. I felt so important. I received three calls that night and documented each one with careful precision. The shifts were long most nights. There was a TV and a bed if we wanted to nap, but I usually kept busy cleaning and organizing the office space. I received a letter from my local MPP leader for my hard work and devotion to the crisis line alongside my co-workers. To this day, it is one of my most cherished possessions. I volunteered once a week and loved the autonomy that came with the position. I handled calls from suicide to people identified as chronic callers. I answered calls from individuals where I was the only connection to the outside world and called to chat with us about everything. To pass the time by, I used to go out drinking with the people I met in training. I noticed that everyone had a history and had the experience to bring to the table. We all loved to unwind with drinks after our shift, so there was always someone to drink with. I never drank on the shift, and I am proud to own that. I had way too much respect for what I was doing and saved my drinking for after work. I never wanted to make a mistake with a suicide caller in case they needed me.

Dylan was still coming around to see me. He was taking his time to move on, and I liked having him around for company. He enjoyed the perks of having sex with no strings attached. I met up with him and had a few one-night stands. While I was living with my mother, I did sleep with various people I met along the way. Sex was becoming increasingly complex and painful no matter whom I did it with. Still, I made the best of it and learned very quickly that I was becoming detached. So much so that if the very act didn't do anything for me, I would stop perusing it altogether. I often wondered if I was ever attached to anyone at all. I hated intimacy and foreplay, which made one-night stand far more appealing. I was forever numb. I often wondered if I had any feeling left at all. I stopped getting emotional after I lost the baby and just didn't care anymore.

Siobhan O'Regan

Things at home became so unbearable that I spent all of my free time hanging out wherever I could. I would find a quiet place to drink and often played poker with people from the complex. I had made a friend who lived several doors down from us and used a wheelchair. I helped him out in exchange for refuge. He had a wine cellar in his basement, so I often hid my alcohol over at his house and had access to it whenever I needed it. I even drank wine at work and hid it in Fruitopia bottles so no one would be wiser. To my surprise, no one ever did. I was questioned once about smelling like wine and told them that I had a glass at dinner before coming in, and no one asked me again after that. By this point, I was consuming at least a bottle or two every day, and because I was storing it in my friends' cellar, if I ran out, I would just take one of his.

The last straw for me was when I walked into my bedroom after work, and it smelled like dirty sweat. I put my head on my pillow and felt a wet spot on my comforter, and I was sure it was semen. I didn't want to know, and I didn't ask. I had applied for a credit card a couple of weeks prior. I was approved, so I started looking for an apartment right away and found a cute one-bedroom available immediately. It was five houses down from the house I lived at and was tortured in for over seven years, but a sacrifice needed to be made. I agreed to pay the first month's rent and painted the entire apartment to cover last month's rent. I was given access right away. I didn't tell my mother and sneaked over before and after work to paint it. I then started moving my stuff one bit at a time, starting with my cat. When it came to the big stuff, I asked Dylan to help me out, and I managed to move most of it before she found out. When she did, she was livid.

Nearing the end of July, I called the college maybe four times trying to get some information concerning my enrollment. They said that I would receive it in the mail. I called my mother twice that many times to see if my mail had come in, and she told me she would call the moment it did. She knew how much college meant to me, so I had no reason to believe otherwise. I made one more ditch effort to call the school in mid-August and was told the information was sent out. I should have had it in the mail by now. I didn't change my mailing address since staying in this apartment was only supposed to be temporary. I had my dorm assignment and asked them to resend my paperwork. I came home from work. It was now the last week of August, and to my amazement, I saw a pile of mail sitting on my doorstep. I picked up the pile and shifted through it, taking out everything from the college, and opened it right away. Most of the letters were postmarked a month earlier, and some were from two months ago. I was shocked to read that I had orientation the very next day. I was way too frustrated to be mad and had to cancel work.

I called Dylan to see if he would take me since I had no other way to get there. While I was at orientation, I found out that there was a procedure to qualify for student housing. When I didn't respond to my letters, I lost out on my housing. They told me they would put me on the waiting list, but several people were already ahead of me. They suggested I call around and see if I could rent an apartment.

I stayed in Raymore for two days walking around calling places and stayed at the Tim Horton's overnight combing ads. I was still trying to sort out my finances, which were thankfully unaffected. I was able to claim them as soon as I showed proof of registration. I was completely and utterly defeated. It took two buses and a greyhound to get home, totaling $10 one way. I called into work sick for the third time that week and gave my notice over the phone, telling them that I wouldn't be able to finish out the rest of my shifts. I slept for twelve hours straight. I can't remember how, but I found out that Beth was attending the same college that fall and had moved to Fields a short time earlier to live with her boyfriend and son. It was on the other side of town. Her relationship with me had been strained for quite some time, but I had kept tabs on her.

I asked her, more like begged her for a ride, but our classes were scheduled at different times. I could get a ride if I met them at their place. So, I got a ride down with them a couple of times but had to get the bus on the way back. I was referred to a carpool board that I visited several times a day until I found someone who was offering to drive to and from Fields. I called immediately and was instantly relieved when he agreed to drive me. I was never so grateful for a break in my entire life. I was sleep-deprived and exhausted. I got to the college early in the morning and sometimes had to stay until after hours, depending on my driver's schedule.

I couldn't sleep outside my bed, so I often went days at a time without a decent night's sleep. This wasn't unusual for me since I suffered from insomnia. However, this was taking its toll on me. Working nights, I found I slept better during the day and thought the daytime tapered my insomnia a bit. It was like sleeping in a gentle hug of warmth when I finally fell asleep after a long shift.

Unfortunately for me, I lived out of his way, and he was able to find someone who lived closer to him to carpool. He gave me my notice a couple of weeks later.

I had long since given up on finding housing or an apartment that I could afford or felt safe in. There was one, however, and it was a house that was shared with three other guys. Even though I preferred male roommates, the smell of stale sex and weed turned my stomach. I didn't feel it would offer me the safety of my apartment, so I turned it down. When my student loan came in, I wanted to make sure I took care of my finance first.

First and foremost, I paid up my rent four months in advance and upped my credit limit to a thousand dollars. This helped during some rough patches until my next financial support payment came in. Unfortunately, it was the end of September, and I took the bus two and from school. The commute was costing me seventeen dollars a day, and my finances were quickly depleting. I was forced to look for a job. My volunteer job had taken a back seat to everything else that was going on, but I still managed to do one or two shifts a month and used that time to study for my tests. I was still failing miserably. I found a position at a local video store. It was good work, and the people were nice enough, but I think I was the only human being on earth who didn't enjoy watching movies all day. I kept busy dusting and rearranging the shelves instead. My boss loved my work ethic, but it annoyed my supervisor, who liked to sit around and socialize. I was quite happy with the arrangement until her pettiness started interfering with the way she treated me. She started getting rude and demanding. I followed through with most of her demands but gave her attitude, and I got the impression she enjoyed torturing me.

Dylan's visits became less frequent. At first, he came over to get some privacy or to satisfy his sexual needs. I went along with it to have some companionship. I tried to connect with some of my peers at school and even joined the track team. Their practice schedule interfered with my busy schedule, so I had to quit. Between school, volunteer, and the video store, I had no one. I spent any free time I had drinking alone with my cat Jessie, with whom I had developed a very strong attachment to. She, in many ways, had become my only true companion. I spent many hours teaching her tricks. I taught her how to sit on command, which she did for a treat every time, without fail.

Nobody Special

I bought her a budgie to keep her company when I wasn't around. It was a lonely existence, but nothing I wasn't used to. The pressure was mounting, and I was seriously thinking about suicide again. I desperately needed a distraction, something to look forward to each day. My future was bleak. I was failing all my courses and started cutting school. I was losing interest in volunteering and hated going to work because of my supervisor.

I began calling in sick just to drink and spend the whole night contemplating the various ways to kill myself. It was a week before Halloween, and my co-workers from my volunteer work were concerned that I was missing my shifts. They called a few times to see if I was okay and to see if I was interested in going to a Halloween party with them. I knew that I was scheduled to work, so I turned them down. I read the newspaper for something to do when I saw an ad for a local chat line. I was so lonely and thought to myself, why not try it. Women were free, so I figured I would give it a try. I set up my profile, thumbed through a couple of live chat messages, thinking how desperate it was. I was sitting on a phone half-crocked, looking to chat with some stranger who was probably a serial killer and was looking for his next victim.

I hung up the phone. I hadn't gone to school all week and had already determined that I was going to quit. There were talks of a bus line between the two cities, but it wasn't going to happen this year, and I could no longer afford transportation. I was grateful to have a job, but my supervisor was one more order short of finding a replacement.

It was Friday, Oct 29th, two days before Halloween, and I just got home from shopping for my costume. I found a jailer outfit on sale for only $5 at the local thrift store and was looking forward to dressing up. It had been years since I was able to get into the spirit of Halloween. I got home and had a few beers. I then decided to try the chat line again. I was going through the profiles when I heard a voice that sounded friendly. His message said, "Anyone looking to do something over the weekend?" He seemed less sleazy than the other guys I listened to, so I sent him a message to chat live. When I was setting up my profile, I decided to use an alias and choose Terry, my bird's name. I had gone back to using the name Jennifer since I started college. I only used my biological name in high school, but college required my full legal name, and so did my employment place. I tried to explain to those around me that I preferred Fallon, but it became too complicated, so I gave up for the time being. I hated using the name Jennifer, and as far as I was concerned, it was a name that struck so much shame and pain. I wanted to put the past as far behind me as possible.

I looked at changing my name back, but it was one hundred and fifty dollars at the time. I never had that kind of money at once. I had three identities, Fallon, Jennifer, and Gio. Two of them had to go, but for now, I was stuck with Jennifer. I chatted with him for a while and learned his name was Jack. He worked for his dad, and somewhere during the conversation, I found out that he used to be a supervisor at the same video store I was now working at. We agreed to meet the following night after my shift to go out for drinks. The next day I was nervous and spent the whole day picturing what he looked like in my head. I told my co-worker about the mystery guy coming in to meet with me and lied, telling them it was a blind date set up by some mutual friend. This had my supervisor's attention. She had been working there forever and knew everyone who had come and gone. She was just as curious as I was. She was unusually sweet to me, trying to get some details to identify my mystery man. I loved the fact that it was driving her nuts.

My shift seemed to drag on, and I kept looking at every guy in a questionable manner. He had the upper hand as he could pick me out from my description and was able to walk in unsuspectingly. I wouldn't know either way. It was just my supervisor that was working at the end of the shift with me. There were only a handful of customers that had filed in and out. The suspense was killing me. Only one of them was a guy my age, and he was cute. I smiled at him, but he appeared off in his own little world and paid little attention to me. I didn't try and hide my disappointment and was growing impatient. I knew he would be coming at the end of my shift and looking at the clock. I had ten minutes left, so he wasn't committed to coming in early. I started cleaning up when I noticed the guy who just came in wasn't being cautious with his popcorn. I was getting irritated as I watched him drop some popcorn knowing full, that I would have to clean up whatever he spilled. I also had a date to get ready for, or did I? I started wondering if my mystery man showed up and decided I was way out of his league and bailed on me.

I cleaned up the popcorn area and made sure the movies were organized before heading up to close the registers. The same guy was leaning on the counter, chatting with my supervisor, and acting like old friends. When I approached the counter, she stood up as if to regain her composure, and he looked over and said, "Hello -in a self-assured manner- my name is Jack." I felt relieved but annoyed by the whole scenario, given he had been there for a least ten minutes, and neither one of them said one word to me until now.

He was handsome, but I had decided that he was paying for my drinks tonight for my trouble. I told him I had to finish sweeping, emphasizing the word sweeping, so he knew I was cleaning up after him. After I was done, my supervisor inspected my work and called me back to sweep over again. I know I did a hurried job, but even my worse job could be compared to most people's best work. I hardly ever took shortcuts, but under a few racks were some overlooked popcorn pieces that weren't obvious unless you searched for them. By the time we scoured the place for every kernel and cobweb, I had already worked for thirty minutes past the end of my shift. I was angry but kept it together for the sake of the date. I had an excellent plan to make her pay for humiliating me like that.

CHAPTER FIFTEEN

False Pretenses

Jack and I went out for a couple of drinks that night. I didn't tell him too much about myself as I was always guarded about what to say. Given my life history, our first date would have likely been our last. I learned that my supervisor had a thing for him before she became engaged to her current boyfriend. He told me that she wanted to date him, but he was not interested. He left to work full-time for his father, who owned his own business. Jack was born and raised in Quebec and was the middle child of two brothers. His oldest brother, Killian, was four years older, and Léo was three years younger. His parents had split up when he was ten. I later pieced together that his dad was a workaholic. The marriage collapsed when his mother had an affair with his business partner. He moved out of the family home shortly after.

His father was an industrial designer who, after the divorce, was offered a position that gave him steady work and financial stability to raise his sons. He packed and moved to Ontario with his three boys. This was not an easy decision for him because he had strong connections to his family. Moving meant that he had to sacrifice that. Jack was twelve and barely spoke a word of English. Leaving their mother behind was difficult for all three brothers, but as I got to know them better, I think it hit Léo the hardest. He was seven at the time.

Jack told me a story that night, which I kept asking him to repeat every year on our anniversary. He said earlier that night he had told Léo he would meet me and wanted to get a sneak peek before showing up. They drove up, and he stood outside the building, pretending to make a call on the payphone just to get a glimpse of his mystery woman. He was not disappointed and said that I was the most beautiful thing he had ever laid eyes on. He hoped I was it, so he jumped back into the car with Léo and told him the same thing.

Later that night, he came in, and the rest was history. I told him I had two sisters and one brother. I didn't get into the rest of my family dynamics and told him my parents had divorced a few times apiece and left out most of the details there too. If he was to be a keeper, I knew he would eventually meet my mother soon enough and learn first-hand what my family was like.

I didn't see any point in telling him that I was five days into becoming a college dropout or why. If he wanted to find out more, he would have to stick around for it, and I was in no hurry to get involved in another soon to be a failed relationship. By the end of the date, I considered him to befriend material, meaning if we were to move forward. He wanted to be a constant in my life; we were friends and nothing more. He asked when he could see me again, and I told him I liked to walk home from work. If he was interested, he could park his car at my place and walk to meet me. He did just that several times throughout the next couple of weeks.

I called my co-workers from volunteer and went over to their place a couple of times for drinks. I wanted to give the illusion that I had friends. They lived in a complex on the east side of Fields. Jack called it Melrose Place because of the drama, and they were more like drinking buddies than actual friends, so we didn't hang out with them very often.

One afternoon we were drinking, and my girlfriend asked me about my relationship with Jack. I shrugged and said nothing. We were just friends, but the truth was I had never enjoyed someone's company as much as I did when I was with him. I couldn't stop thinking about the next step, but I was scared. I liked him, and I knew I would have to disclose parts of myself that I preferred to hide. The problem was that I put up so many roadblocks that there was no way he would make the first move, so I suggested we took a walk by the river and staged the scene for our first kiss.

I couldn't have been more flirtatious and inviting, signaling him to move in. Subtlety was not his strong suit as he was a perfect gentleman, first and foremost. I had to take the lead. Our first kiss was the moment I knew I was developing feelings for him. I had never felt that much magnetism with another man, and he was such a good kisser too. He sent my pulse racing. We went back to my apartment, and I put on some music, teaching him some moves. I had learned them when I took ballroom dancing in high school and danced well into the night. It was the first time I ever shared my passion for art with another human being, and he said the words 'I love' you for the first time during that night. At first, I was put off by his forwardness and took his words to mean a lack of sincerity, but I brushed it off. I had heard worse. I offered him to spend the night and seduced him, figuring it took two weeks to get to our first kiss, and didn't want to wait months before we made it past home plate. He was so gentle in every way, nothing like I was used to. It was different but in the right way.

We officially became an item that night, and from then on, we were inseparable. He did, however, take a trip on a planned trip to Quebec. He visited his mom and called several times while he was gone, and we would chat for hours. For our first official date, I took him to do the one thing I loved most in the entire world, horseback riding. It was his first time on a horse. I thought he was goofy, but I enjoyed every moment of it and liked to watch him, not to mention for a beginner. He did do half as bad, even though his horse ran off with him.

Almost immediately, we moved in with one another, and if he weren't at my place, I would be at his. Meeting his family was a culture shock. Jack had the type of freedom in his father's home that I had never been exposed to. I recall feeling entirely out of my element. My first time meeting his father was unbelievably awkward. Jack insisted I bring my laundry over to his house. At the same time, we hung out, and the thought of bringing my laundry over to anyone's home was highly inappropriate. He wouldn't take no for an answer.

His brother Léo was just three months older than me. He also lived with his father. Léo had two young girls, Léonia, three, and Amélie, who was just about to turn two. His dad was tending to the girls and changing Amélie's diaper up in his room when we walked in.

Jack always spoke highly of his dad, and I was so intimidated being in the presence of such an admired man. I wanted to crawl into a hole but sucked it up and walked up to shake his hand. Up until this point, I had never dared to look someone I had just met in the eyes. I usually kept my eyes down. He was already on the floor, so I looked into his face, turned away, and stepped back. Jack didn't always like to admit the admiration he had for his father. When he described him to me for the first time, he had built his father up to be this amazing man who had dedicated his whole life to his kids and grandkids. I had never been in the presence of someone so noble in my life, and I didn't want to disappoint him.

When he finished with the baby, he looked up and smiled at me, saying hello. He had such a thick accent that made me giggle. He was warm and friendly, but I didn't dare trust it and stayed back behind Jack. He stood up and sat on his bed, asking me some random questions about myself. It made me extremely uncomfortable, as Jack was no longer shielding me. He was down on the floor, playing with Amélie. I tried to provide honest answers, but it was always so much easier to lie. I never knew what to tell people, so when he asked me if I knew any French, I drew a huge sigh of relief and sat down next to him. I put my arm on his shoulder and said, "Voulez-vous coucher avec Moi ce Soir."

I instantly became embarrassed by my forwardness, and he burst out into the most prominent clasp of laughter I had ever heard come from one man. Amélie, who obviously loved her grandfather's laugh, chimed in, so we started laughing at how cute she was.

We went downstairs, and my laundry was sitting in a bag at the front door. I felt this wave of nausea take over me. Jack was so caught up in his conversation with his father that when his dad questioned what was in the bag, he shrugged and said laundry. My worst fear just happened. I was waiting for his look of disapproval, but it never happened. He completely dismissed the whole thing. My anxiety was through the roof, and I was trying so badly to calm myself down. When Jack offered me a beer, I drank it like I was dying of thirst. I often thought alcohol helped suppress my stress. I started calming down almost instantly and even more so when he offered me another one.

I looked around his room; it was an absolute mess. I was so meticulous about everything, and this guy was my complete opposite. In fact, he was an absolute slob. He and his former live-in girlfriend had just broken up, so he had stacks of unopened boxes lying in the corner of his room. There were fast food containers on his coffee table and papers everywhere. It was just looking at it that made my anxiety shoot up another ten degrees.

Jack's bedroom was downstairs, right next to an area they used for food storage, and on the right was an extra fridge. Inside the refrigerator was a smorgasbord of different alcoholic beverages. When Jack told me his family often had wine at breakfast, I thought I had died and gone to heaven.

He and I would hang out in his room and mess around a bit, but I preferred to do the sex thing in my apartment, where it was more private. Jack eventually pushed me out of my comfort zone, and we ultimately did have sex there too. We didn't do it if his dad was home, at least not at first.

I met Léo later that night; I remember thinking how incredibly handsome he was and looked so much like Jack. He was such a huge flirt too. It didn't take me long to realize I landed the right brother this time, and I was very confident that I would not repeat what happened with Adam and Bryce. I liked Léo at first very much and thought that he reminded me of my own brother back during the good times. My opinion changed drastically as time went on, and he began to remind me more like Dean.

I never really considered myself a full-fledged alcoholic because I was fully functional. There wasn't a day I didn't go without drinking. Still, I always found a way to incorporate it into my spending and included it as part of my expenses. It didn't occur to me that my alcohol costs twice as much as my groceries. So long as I had my necessities, I could justify my purchases. I didn't mind if I had to go without cigarettes, but I could never go without my alcohol. I knew Jack was picking up on my issue quickly. He would have the odd drink with me whenever I did, and I drank four or five to his one. He would often come over while I was working and make me dinner. He would always buy a particular wine with half the alcohol content than what I was used to. It drove me insane when he would suggest that we only have a glass or two then save the rest. I thought he was nuts. He would cap the top and put it in the fridge, and I would always find an excuse to take a swig. I think that's when I started hiding alcohol in my apartment to be more creative with my drinking. Except for my excessive drinking, which I had just taken care of by hiding alcohol around my apartment, Jack and I never argued and always got along. We used to hunt for things to disagree on and pretend to argue just so we could make up afterward, that is, until the day he met my mother.

I received an irritated phone call from my mother one afternoon while Jack was there. She was freaking out about some towels that had gone missing after I left. I was curt with her on the phone since I hadn't talked to her since I moved out and was still very angry about her withholding my mail. She demanded to come over right away to see if I had them. I didn't have them, but she wouldn't listen to reason and showed up at my doorstep less than ten minutes later.

I was dreading the day Jack would meet my mother, and here she was in the flesh. I can't remember what, if anything, I told him about her, but none of it could have possibly been good, and here he was about to find out for himself. She walked in, scanning the place around. She was looking everywhere, from my cupboards to my drawers and even in between my mattresses. I didn't argue with her, and I just sat back and waited for the storm to pass. Bruce was with her, and he began chatting up Jack, who was confused over what was transpiring.

I knew if I started arguing with her no matter who was around, she would embarrass me and make me feel stupid in the process. After all these years, my mother still had this hold on me that no one else did, and I catered to her every demand to save face. She always had this way of making me feel sorry for her and acted as if I owed her one for everything she did for me. We had the most dysfunctional relationship, and I took accountability for all of it. She was the only person who could treat me as badly as she did for as long as she had, and I would wipe the slate clean every time if she showed mercy in the form of random acts of kindness. I'd feel horrible for having ever thought negatively about her. I spent most of my life referencing how badly she had it even though I was always the one standing there hurting, and she appeared to get off on hurting me.

Jack came to my rescue when he sensed my discomfort. She hated Jack right away. She told him to butt out and mind his own business. "This was between her and me," She said. Mom then turned to me and asked me where Dylan was and gave Jack a dirty look. I didn't answer her and gave her one back. After tossing my apartment, she finally became satisfied that I either didn't have her towels or that I had gotten rid of them. Regardless, she left in a huff with Bruce in tow.

She called me up a couple of days later, and asked Jack and me for dinner, and refused to take no for an answer. I agreed but knew beforehand that it was going to be a disaster. As predicted, dinner was an absolute joke. I will spare the details except for the part where she went on and on for half the night talking about how much she missed Dylan. She continued to say how he was such a good guy and that she wasn't worried that we would make it back. Dylan and I had professional pictures done, and I had given her one, but she never put it up. Now it was on the fridge in the kitchen like a shrine. It stayed there for the better part of two years. I have to hand it to the woman; she sure could hold a grudge. I was never more embarrassed in my life. She was way over the top, and I fully expected him to run away and never look back, but he didn't. He acted like he enjoyed dishing it out as much as she did. I didn't care what she thought. I loved this man, and she had better get used to the idea really quickly because he wasn't going anywhere anytime soon.

Jack and I were head over heels in love. We both knew where we stood with each other and understood what we wanted. For some reason, I always felt like the bottom was still going to drop. I wasn't insecure or jealous of him. I never had to. He ever made me feel like I was number one and never had a wandering eye. I thought I would test a theory one day, and as we were driving by an attractive woman, I said, "Look at the boobs on that! I'd do her." Jack turned around to look but barely glanced in her direction and shrugged, so I teased him about being gay, and he shot me a dirty look. A couple of days later, we were watching a movie, and he said, "Hey, look at that guy, I'd do him." I burst out laughing and said, "Aw, honey, it's just not the same." I then asked him again if he was gay, and he shot me another dirty look. I loved how we could just poke fun at just about anything.

A couple of weeks after we met, I ended up with a huge ear infection that badly hurt me; I couldn't eat for a few days. Jack took me to see his doctor, and he gave me a prescription for antibiotics. He asked if I was on the pill, and I told him that I was on a strong dose to manage my period. He said okay and told me it shouldn't affect it, but we may need to arrange a backup just in case. While I was at the pharmacy, the pharmacist asked me the same question and told me to use a backup. Jack and I looked at one another and thought, what the heck. We'll let karma decide. What do you know, the pharmacist was right, and the doctor was wrong. I found out the day after Christmas that I was pregnant. I had a normal period, but I knew to check anyways since I had bled through my last two pregnancies. This one was different, and I was experiencing pain almost immediately. I was scared that I was going to lose another one. I lied and told Jack I was only pregnant once before and was honest about how I lost it. I always assumed I lost him because of my drinking. The moment we knew there was a possibility that I could be pregnant, I stopped drinking immediately. It was excruciatingly painful, but for the first time, I cared about something more than myself.

We told Léo first, and he was so excited for us. Then Jack told his dad. I had a million thoughts going through my head about what his dad must think about me. I was drinking and hanging around his house all the time, and now I was pregnant. I'm sure I wasn't what he pictured for his son. I was going to be a permanent fixture in his life and was pregnant with his grandchild. He took the news better than I thought he would. I guess we have Léo to thank since he broke his dad twice before I came along. Regardless of how he felt deep down inside, he was supportive in every way and accepted the fact that he was going to be a grandfather again.

Meanwhile, Jack and I decided to move in together officially before the baby came. We just got approved for a one-bedroom apartment. We were due to move in after we got back from our trip to Quebec to meet his mother for the first time. I was excited but not exactly thrilled to have to sleep in another strange environment. Léo and the girls were going too, so I was told it would be cramped. I still hadn't fully got used to sleeping at Jacks's place, so I had to prepare myself for a week of little to no sleep. Jack was eager to tell his mother the good news and was beyond excited that he would be a father.

I was looking forward to the distraction and had to get my mind off of work. They had called me at the last minute before the holidays and told me that I was fired because I didn't get along well with my co-workers. That comment was meant for my supervisor since I got along well with everyone except her. I had recently confronted her about a rumor she had spread about me. Apparently, I was hostile in my dealings with her. She couldn't handle the fact that I was direct, and it became apparent she was jealous of my relationship with Jack. Thanks to Jack, I learned the ins and outs of my role and started refusing to do extra tasks when my shift was over, especially when she knew he was waiting for me.

I stopped going above and beyond as I did when I worked with the other girls, and it didn't help my case that she was close to the owner. It stood to reason that I just had to go. Ironically shortly after I left, the business went bankrupt. I saw her again serving in a restaurant when Jack and I once went out. I enjoyed watching her squirm when she had to be extra nice while seating us. I was polite to show no hard feelings but enjoyed her discomfort, and Jack made a point to tell me he admired my restraint.

We talked about everything on the trip down to Quebec. By all appearances, we were having a fantastic time, but I was under so much stress. I was tuned in to my body more than ever, and I knew something was wrong. I was in so much pain on my left side that I couldn't ignore it and had to separate myself to deal with my anxiety and discomfort. I wanted this baby and couldn't bear the thought of losing another one. Being with Jack made me feel better, and I wanted to tell him how I felt, but I was not used to sharing my emotions with anyone. I didn't want to take his excitement away from him. That's why I bottled it up most of the time.

My first impression of his mother was that she was kind enough and appeared to be genuinely pleased to meet me, but it was all an act. Her partner Vincent knew enough English to carry on a conversation but mostly kept to himself. I spent the visit occupying my own time for the rest of the trip. I hung out with Jack or played with the girls. Later that night, we told his mother about the baby, and I didn't blame her for being shocked. We had just met two months earlier, and she gave out a shriek that annoyed me for years. This was followed by her favorite words, 'Mon diuex.' Léo went and helped himself to a beer, and my stress level went through the roof. It was not half as much as when his mother Eline offered me one. I told her, "No. Mercy, because of the baby." She (Jack translated) said that it was okay to have one if it was early enough in the pregnancy.

I remember feeling so angry, thinking she was trying to hurt my baby. I had been working so hard not to drink, and it was like a constant record going off in my head that I couldn't shut it off. I gave into temptation that night, stopping after a few sips; the guilt was overwhelming. I hated myself, thinking if I allowed myself to drink, I would be signing this baby's death certificate like I did my last child.

That night set the stage for many performances between his mother and me. Most of them were away from Jack. She had this way of showing her disapproval without actually saying anything, using our language barrier as a way to exercise her ignorance. I never felt comfortable in her home. Although my mindset at the time may have obstructed my overall view of her, she let me know loud and clear that I would never be good enough for her son.

Subconsciously, I agreed, and I still hated her for it. From day one, Jack and I disagreed about our mothers. It appeared that we both had our blinders on when it came to seeing and identifying characteristics in each of them that the other one did not. The next night was New Year's. I was having a hard time adjusting to the environment and keeping a positive attitude. I was having cramps all night and felt like I was suffocating from the smoke in the air. I couldn't sleep. Everyone smoked in the house, and there was a fog that always lingered. It was the dead of winter in Quebec, so there was no air circulating throughout the home. We grew up with our parents smoking in the house, and I always felt sick around it.

Being a smoker myself, when I moved on my own, I smoked outside except when I lived in that horrible apartment in Main. Knowing now that I am hypersensitive to certain stimuli, I understand what may have felt uncomfortable for some and felt like torture. Jack's mother lived in a little village an hour outside of Le Goulet, so there were very few if anyone who spoke English. I depended a lot on Jack to translate what he could just to keep up.

I didn't watch much TV, but there weren't very many English channels even if I wanted to. I spent most of my time playing with the girls or sat alone. I also didn't drive, so I was utterly dependent on Jack for everything. Eline was preparing her annual New Year's dinner. Usually, I would have liked to help to keep busy, but everything was done. Neither one of us spoke enough of the other's language to give or follow the most straightforward instruction. I was either drunk or institutionalized when I would have taken French in middle school, so I never learned how to communicate on even a basic level.

The party consisted of Jack and me, Léo, his two girls, two of Eline's brothers, and Vincent's sons. By this point, I was tired. My mind was preoccupied. All during dinner, I put on my best face. I tried to be pleasant and inviting, but everyone at the adult table chatted in French. Not one person spoke one word to me at all.

Jack and I got into our first argument that night over his family's lack of hospitality. During this heated conversation, I disclosed for the first time that I had been raped and lost two other children before this one. I told him that I was cramping and was so scared to lose this one. I learned that he had a secret of his own. He said that a schoolteacher who eventually befriended his entire family to be closer to his prey had also abused him. Another teacher finally rescued Jack when she became overly curious about why this teacher took such an interest in Jack. Jack was supposed to go camping with his abuser and his younger brother that weekend while his dad was on a trip to Quebec. When Jack was apprehended at school, his father drove the seven-hour trip in less than four hours just to get to him.

Nobody Special

To this day, Jack never did get closure and has never fully disclosed in detail to me, or in therapy, what happened between him and this teacher. In conversations I have had with his dad, he held a lot of guilt and remorse over what happened and blamed himself for not figuring it out sooner. It is a secret they both choose to keep from Jacks's mother.

The drive home was my favorite part of the trip. I finally had him all to myself, and we conversed all the way home. It was during one of these conversations that we decided on a name for our baby. If it were a girl, I was going to name her Beth. If it was a boy, we were going to call him Kallan. Later that night, I found myself in excruciating pain, and it was not subsiding. I was Immediately admitted after I went to the emergency room. We were introduced to Dr. Grace, who told us our pregnancy was likely ectopic. He scheduled me for surgery the following morning.

I didn't sleep and cried well after Jack left. I know he wanted to stay with me and was devastated too, but he had to go to pack the rest of our things. We were moving the next morning, so I tried to be strong for him. He kissed me on the forehead as this became our signature, and he promised to be back in time for the procedure. The following day, they came in to wheel me into ultrasound. I was tired, exhausted, and still hadn't come to terms with what was happening. I still held out a small ray of hope that they could somehow save this baby. The technician positioned his monitor away from me and told me to relax, but all I could do was hold my breath. A few moments later, he looked over at me, told me to breathe, and showed me his monitor. There, in the middle of the screen, was my baby's heartbeat, and it was precisely where it should be. I was never so relieved in my life. I was taken back to the room when Jack showed up, but it was too early to celebrate until we got our doctor's results. Dr. Grace came in almost right away and explained the pain on my side was a torn ligament from having a tilted uterus. She still wanted to keep a close eye on me because of my last pregnancy's bleeding and complications. I had disclosed It all during my examination. She scheduled a follow-up at her office. She ordered me to take it easy, not to move anything heavy, and that everything would be fine. I so badly wanted to believe her, but I had heard it all before.

Jack and I settled nicely into our new apartment. I got a job working for a local sub shop, and we got our first dog, a Siberian husky named Sadie. For the first time in my life, things were better than okay. I dare say I was happy. We talked a lot about getting married since we both figured we had a grasp on what we wanted in life. Jack was raised with good Catholic values and wanted to do right by our child, and I wanted him to grow up having a family. One day he walked into the apartment and handed me a bouquet of long stem white roses. They were one of my favorite colors, and he stood back, waiting to gauge my surprise. I had seen the ring almost right away but waited for Jack to make the first move expecting him to go down on one knee and traditionally ask me. Etiquette, it appeared, was not his strong suit as he took the ring, untied it from the flowers, and asked me point-blank to marry him. I shrugged off my expectation of the perfect proposal, hugged him, and said yes.

It was a beautiful ring, with a tiny and delicate stone that I'd seen when we were out at the mall one afternoon. I was not a big fan of jewelry, so, to me, it was perfect. Jack forced me to call my mother and to tell her the big news. Her only words were, 'Won't Dylan be disappointed?' She then hung up on me. For the first time in my life, I didn't care what she thought. The only thing I wanted in the entire world was to move forward with my life and leave my past behind me. Not being one to stand on ceremony, I decided the best way to officiate our union would be to take my name back and start over. Jack and I both agreed that before we got married, I would change my name back to Fallon and that he would take my last name, O'Brien. It meant so much to me to finally have my name back and to keep it this time. I was happy that our child was going to be raised as an O'Brien too. However, when we found out that we were having a boy, his father approached him and asked him to talk to me. He wanted Jack to keep his family name. The reason being was that our son would be the last remaining child to carry on his family name since his brothers all had girls, and he was the only one to have boys. With Léo having girls, Killian not yet married, the pressure to secure the name fell on us. I was so conflicted. I understood what it meant to Jack's dad.

To carry on the family name was important, but I had been robbed of my birthright. I desperately wanted to take it back. I reluctantly agreed to change it and felt sick since I had to wait until after getting married to change my name officially. It was no longer a priority. Unfortunately, this took a back seat to many other events and caused a great deal of resentment for me. I hated being called Jennifer. To me, that girl was dead, and I wanted to forget her, figuring that so long as she was gone, I would not have to continue to live in the past.

Nobody Special

I enjoyed working at the sub shop, and I adored my boss and his family, so much so that I even invited them to my wedding. I worked straight days and loved getting to know my regulars. My boss was always praising my work and was such a good man. My co-worker and I would compete for his approval and often tried to outdo one another on the job. We got along for the most part but had our moments. I was starting to show, so moving around began to be a little challenging. I continued to enjoy the fast pace. My boss came up to me one night and asked if I would cover the night shift. The part-time staff had called in sick. I had to tell him no after Jack argued that it was too dangerous. I was annoyed with him thinking he was being unreasonable but didn't want to stir the pot, knowing my pregnancy concerned him also.

My co-worker gladly accepted. I hated it when I let her show me up, but the truth was that I was tired, and I had been spotting more than usual. I knew better than to take it easy. The following day, I found out we had been robbed at gunpoint. They found the rifle in the ditch outside the back of the store after the robber fled. The guy was eventually caught and was the suspect in several other robberies in the area. My co-worker was roughed up but otherwise unharmed, and my boss told me it was fate that Jack stepped in when he did and that I had karma on my side. From then on, we were not allowed to work alone. Jack and my boss only agreed to let me work the day shift.

Since the engagement, I got a hold of Robyn to uphold a childhood promise we had made to stand up for one another at our weddings. I hadn't spoken to her in years and was shocked to find out she was married and had a daughter. I was so excited to introduce her to Jack and ask her to be my matron of honor. My first impression of her husband Gordon was a young guy who was head over heels in love with his wife and worshiped the ground she walked on. He would cater to her every whim. He had a dark side that reminded me so much of Bruce but got along well with Jack, and that was good enough for me.

I was thrilled when Robyn agreed to stand up for me, and we started making plans and discussing the details of my wedding. Jack and I originally wanted to elope but decided on a small affair so his parents could attend. I didn't really have anyone to invite on my side of the family, so I asked my aunt and uncle to be there for me. I invited my mother out of obligation, and Jack (without knowing my full history) convinced me to invite Dean. I later asked my sisters to come. Beth agreed, but Stephanie was still too angry to show up. I hadn't seen her since the last time she hit me up for money. I didn't have it to give her.

Jack had it much easier than I did and had plenty of families who wanted to be there for him. He asked his best friend from high school, Kale, to stand up for him. Picking the flower girls was easy, and Jack's mom offered to make their dresses, so all we needed to pick was a date. I was pregnant, so we needed to work fast. Unfortunately, planning a wedding on such short notice was not going to be comfortable. It was important for Jack and me to have a bilingual minister.

Astoundingly, the only one we found that could marry us before my due date was available on June fifth. That was my mother's birthday. It was a coincidence, I assure you. We wanted to get married outside but settled on doing it in the justice of the peace chapel. We couldn't afford any extra preparations if it rained on that day. Dean gave us something I never expected. He gifted $500 to use any way we wanted towards the wedding. This was not a welcome gift since it did not come close to the money he took from Stephanie and me as children. It also certainly didn't make up for the years of torture. It just made me feel obligated, and I asked him to walk me down the aisle. I sold my soul to the devil when I took that cheque. My heart was broken since, at first, I wanted to ask my brother to be the one giving me away. However, the money would go a long way for two kids who didn't have two cents to rub together, so we took it.

Jack's dad wanted to help us out financially and had a good heart. We only wanted to have a BBQ when we planned the meal and have a fun party afterward. My mother's gift was to sign out the hall from her complex and to decorate it for us. It would have cost nothing to set up a BBQ. He still wanted to buy everyone dinner at a nice restaurant, so I lost yet another battle. Still, all things considering, we were very fortunate.

My streak of bad luck started when Robyn told me three weeks before the wedding that she had to step down because of her anxiety. I was dumbfounded and, worse, stuck trying to find someone to fill her position. The only friend I had left in the world was a guy named Trevor, who I had been in contact with on and off for years. I asked him to fill in. Initially, he said yes, but called me a week later and told me that his girlfriend disapproved. He said that a guy standing up for a woman was embarrassing and untraditional. I didn't even say goodbye. I hung up the phone and just cried. I suppose I could have asked my sister, but the truth was I always thought she was much prettier than me, and I didn't want all the attention on her. Kale's girlfriend heard about what happened and offered to step in for me. Lila was such a nice person, and we eventually became close for a time, but she had a best friend, and I wanted someone exclusive to me. I realized that I didn't have any other options, so I gratefully accepted her offer and chose to move on.

The night before we got married, Lila and Kale came over. Kale was taking out Jack and a few of their friends. Lila and I went and did our own thing. Before leaving, I gave Kale $50 I had saved. I told him that if they were going to a strip bar, buy Jack a lap dance, and better behave. I found out later that Kale told Jack about the money. They took it to buy steaks and stayed in to have a BBQ at his father's instead.

I was seven months pregnant, so drinking was out of the question. Lila and I decided to go to the bingo hall instead. We stayed for a bit but got bored. My mother lived right around the corner from the bingo hall, so we headed out to see if she wanted any help decorating the hall. When we got there, and she was angry, irritable, and just plain nasty. I was well acquainted with this side of her, and with other people, her attitude and behavior were hit or miss. This was the first time Lila met Kristine, and she received a good dose of what my mother was really about. She was rude; she called us names and attacked every effort we made to follow her instructions. It was supposed to be my night, and I spent most of it reassuring Lila that she didn't mean anything by her name-calling and criticism. I told Lila that she was just stressed out. We didn't stay long, and I held back the tears for the most part. There are only so many times you can take being called a stupid fuck up in front of your one and only friend. I spent the rest of the night crying after Lila left.

The following day, I woke up, and I was tired. There were bags under my eyes from the lack of sleep, and my face was swollen from crying all night. We had an appointment at the salon to get my hair done, so I spent most of the time with a cold, wet cloth across my face listening to Kristine go on and on about how hard it was to put the decorations up by herself. She had no one capable to help her there.

When we got back to the house, I realized that I had forgotten my bra. I only had my sports bras. I asked my mother if she could get it, and she said that there was no time. Mom offered one of hers Instead. The one she handed me was too big and lacy. I couldn't wear lace with my SPD. It drove me nuts, so I had to settle for wearing a sports bra underneath. I bought my dress off a clearance rack in a bridal store. It wasn't fancy, but it was all I could find to cover my belly.

I didn't care, and I was proud of my stomach. My son was tucked safely inside. I wasn't even sure I would make it to seven months, so to me, nothing else mattered. The only nice shoes I had were black, but I had a long skirt to hide them easily. I did my own makeup, and when it was all put together, I didn't look bad. Jack insisted we rent a limo since he knew he could get a good deal. It was supposed to be just Kristine, Lila, myself, and my flower girls. My mother decided to invite her border, girlfriend, and other random people to come along without my permission. What was supposed to be a spacious ride became cramped and uncomfortable. Inside the limo was a bottle of champagne for afterward chilling on ice. She took it, opened it, and helped herself to most of the bottle. I had a small glass to calm my nerves. By the time we got there, she was drunk.

We made our way inside, and Dean was waiting in the main lobby. He was expecting to fulfill his fatherly duties when Kristine started verbally attacking him. She told him that she should be the one walking me down the aisle, not a child beater, and reminded him that I wasn't even his kid.

I was so embarrassed that I told them they could both do it. The ceremony was about to start. I took a quick peek inside the hall, and my heart sunk when I didn't see my brother. I knew he probably wouldn't come, but there was a small part of me that hoped he would. I prayed that he would be okay wherever he was and that he was thinking about me. Jack's brother agreed to be our videographer, and we handed out disposable cameras to our guests to take pictures.

One of the many things I still, to this day, resent towards Léo was the fact that he only videotaped his girls coming down the aisle and not me. I was anxious and so insecure that it took everything I had to be in front of everyone there. It was supposed to be my moment, and he robbed me of capturing it. The ceremony was nice and had some funny moments, but my son woke up and kicked throughout the ceremony. When all was said and done, I married my best friend and the man I vowed to spend the rest of my life with. In the end, that was the only thing that mattered. We took some nice pictures just before dinner, but my family refused to take part. The photos were mostly with Jack's family.

Nobody Special

During dinner, I started to get bloated, and my dress was getting uncomfortable. I had to undo the zipper and put on one of Jack's t-shirts. I was making frequent bathroom breaks as well. During one of these breaks, I came back, and Jack told me that my mother made a huge scene when Dean took a bottle of wine off her table. I didn't want to believe him since I knew he was already upset about the bottle of Champaign she had drunk out of the limo. Before dinner, he set the camera up at the back of the room and caught the whole ugly incident on tape. I have no good memories of my wedding day. I did put on a smile for the cameras, but deep down, I was so miserable.

CHAPTER SIXTEEN

Then There Were Three

It was a hot summer, especially for me; being eight months pregnant and having no air conditioning was really hard. Our building had an outdoor swimming pool, but the building manager told me that I couldn't use it if my water broke. With the baby coming, we needed to move into a bigger space, ideally with two bedrooms. We started out looking for a nice place to raise our son. We found a beautiful Victorian house just on the other side of Fields around the corner from where my sister lived. The upper half of the house was for rent. It had wood features, built-ins, and skylights, situated on a quiet street in a nice neighborhood. It was precisely within our price range. The only issue was that we were allowed to keep my cat but were told that we couldn't bring our dog. We had to make the difficult decision to find our dog another home. That was a tough sacrifice, especially for Jack, who loved that dog. We chose to put our family's needs first, which was the perfect home to raise our son.

I was incredibly grateful to be able to carry my son, but I hated being pregnant. I had developed gestational diabetes and gained close to thirty pounds of water in the first three months. This was amazing at the time since I could barely keep anything down due to morning sickness. It kept happening at night times, which was very tiring. Dr. Grace kept a very close eye on us to make sure he was developing normally due to the periods I was having throughout my pregnancy, especially when I was experiencing heavy bleeding.

When I was just under three months, I was having cramps and started bleeding badly, so I called the doctor on call, who told me there was nothing he or anyone could do. They told me to head to the hospital if I miscarried. Being through this once before, I was, of course, devastated and called Dr.

Grace first thing. She told us to come in immediately. Sure enough, there he was, with his heartbeat as strong as ever. We were never so relieved. I found out that I was also a carrier of GBS (Group B Streptococcus), a natural bacteria in the intestines that some women carry in their vaginal area. This can cause serious illness and even death in newborn babies.

His original due date was September 2nd, but given the GPS complications, my doctor set a date to induce me on August 25th. I started having contractions on the 23rd instead. The worst part of my pregnancy wasn't so much what was happening to me, as I'm sure I wasn't the only one to experience these types of complications. It was the fact that I had no one to turn to for answers and was entirely on my own. I had no friends, no mother figure, or mentor whatsoever. I had Dr. Grace, but she had never been pregnant or given birth and could only answer my medical questions. I had to figure out everything else on my own. Back then, I didn't know how to use a computer, so the book "What to Expect When Your Expecting" became my bible. I depended on it for everything. It was great for answering the clinical stuff but didn't prepare me for what I would be facing emotionally.

Pregnancy for some women is a beautiful experience. Still, it changes your body in ways that only a woman who has been through it can explain. I had no one to get advice or comfort from. I would have appreciated some support through the tough stuff or someone to hold my hand when I was scared and unsure of myself.

I reached out to my sister, Stephanie, for some family support close to the end of my pregnancy. She agreed to be there during the delivery. Her role was to tape Kallan's birth but was asked to assist when I pushed him out. That never happened. My labor was not progressing fast enough, so they induced me and broke my water on the morning of the 25th. By then, I had barely slept for over seventy- two hours. After twenty-seven hours of continuous labor, I passed out in between contractions. This was during the last two hours it finally took me to push him out.

Labour was excruciatingly painful. I had the most unsympathetic nurses, and they had very little patience for me, displaying any discomfort. I always thought I had a high pain tolerance due to my ability to take a beating. Still, the pain became unbearable even with the epidural. I panicked when they fitted me for my central line, and they had to put numbing cream on my hands before they could try again. They still had to restrain me from putting it in. I tried everything I could to pull myself together but kept falling into that place of fear and knew I had panic attacks. How do you tell them you're a trauma survivor and need compassion, not belittling and constant criticism? I didn't know it at the time, but I suffered from complex PTSD (post-traumatic stress disorder). My labor brought me back to my trauma state, and no one there understood what I was going through, least of all myself.

Kallan was born at 5:27 pm. I was tired and exhausted, but to me, he was absolutely beautiful. I was so caught up in the moment that it didn't dawn on me right away that he was different. He didn't even cry. He just looked around as if to take everything in even after the nurses took him from me to clean him up. One nurse gave him back a short while later to have me breastfeed but immediately realized that he had teeth. I tried to tell the nurse, but she was too consumed by her work to pay attention and said it was nonsense. It was just some extra flap on his gums (whatever that meant) and dismissed my concerns.

I also noticed how flat his face was and asked if it was from the forceps. She didn't even glance over at him and told me that he was just fine and went about her task. After we were done, Jack and Stephanie left to make phone calls. Another nurse escorted me into the shower. I was left on my own to clean myself up. When I was done, I called for someone to help me. No one answered. I waited for a few minutes and screamed some more, but no one came. My legs were still numb from the epidural but could slowly inch around if I held onto the wall.

I was moving slowly and could feel where they cut and stitch below. I looked down and saw the trail of blood behind me, but I just wanted to get back to the bed, so I ignored it and kept walking. I came around the corner and saw Kallan alone wrapped up in his bassinette. There were no nurses, no doctors, and no one around. A few minutes later, Jack came up after he made a few phone calls and saw that I was standing there half-naked, visibly shaken. I was upset and standing in a pool of my own blood. Realizing his wife was left in the shower, and his son was lying in a room unattended. He helped me to bed and went looking for a nurse to demand an explanation.

The nurses were displeased when we insisted on seeing Dr. Grace and were even more annoyed when they were reprimanded after the appalling care they gave my newborn son and me. Dr. Grace stated to them that a parent or nurse had to be with Kallan at all times and demanded to know why I was left in a shower after giving birth alone. We also found out that it was against hospital policy to leave a patient alone in both of our cases.

I wasn't the only one who hadn't slept since Jack was by my side. He had been wiping my forehead during my entire labor. He had laid next to me when the nurses brought Kallan in for another attempt to feed.

I was still having trouble convincing the nurses that he had teeth since no one bothered to look into his mouth long enough to see them physically. The nurses waited until Kallan was latched on and then would leave the room.

Kallan was such a cute little creature. I was studying his face when he started to choke one day and was no longer passing air. I tried to turn him over and pat his back, but he stopped breathing altogether. I began to panic and yelled at Jack to get up and to get a nurse. Kallan was turning color, so I jumped out of bed to wake Jack up and cry out for help. A lady who had given birth a day earlier heard my cries and was already making her way to the nurse's station. Jack woke dazed and confused when one of the nurses who attended my labor ran in, grabbed him, and threw him over her arm upside down. She started administering blows to his back. Whatever was lodged came out almost immediately and cleared his mouth with her pinky finger.

When she was satisfied that Kallan was breathing, she threw me the dirtiest look and said, "That's what happens when you…" she stopped herself mid-sentence. Her face softened, and she told us that she had to take him for observation. She was going to get my doctor right away, and then she glanced down at the blood that was pooling beneath me and walked out with my son.

I was sobbing uncontrollably, thinking that I had done something wrong and that God was punishing me. I prayed that Kallan would be all right. I told Jack to follow her and tried to sit down but realized that I had torn my stitches when I leaped out of bed to wake Jack. I had Dr. Grace take a look at them. She told me that she should re-stitch, but I refused after discovering it meant more needles and agreed to let her redress them. The girl who heard my cries came in and tried to comfort me. I was still crying, waiting for Jack to come back. I just wanted to know that Kallan was going to be okay.

Nobody Special

My family doctor came in a short time later to see us, and I showed him Kallan's teeth. He couldn't believe it and said that he had heard of it but never seen it in his 22 years of practice. He told me not to worry and that it shouldn't affect him latching on. Of course, he failed to mention his latching off. Kallan caused significant damage to my nipples, and so I was forced to switch to formula.

The nurses made me feel completely incompetent and less of a mother for switching. Still, I bet none of them ever had to deal with an infant biting down on their nipples while they nursed. Over the next two days, we had several nurses and doctors stop by to look at his teeth for themselves. They made references to how unique Kallan looked and made several comments on his facial features.

Shortly after he was born, he was seen by a specialist who told us that our son had some unusual characteristics and needed to be seen by a geneticist. He pointed out how he always kept his hands folded into fists on top of his unique features. He also drew our attention to his turned-in ankles, informing us that he needed special orthotic shoes to walk correctly. Jack and I couldn't wait to leave the hospital. The videotape Jack took the day we were released as we got Kallan ready spoke volumes as to how solemn and anxious we were to collect our child and leave.

I was only able to breastfeed Kallan long enough to make sure he got the coliseum. My nipples had sustained so much damage from him latching off that I couldn't continue to feed him anymore, and his teeth had become loose in the process. We were scheduled to see a specialist in Raymore to look at his teeth after being told that they were just sitting on his gums and were afraid he could swallow them.

Jack had a meeting in Lonsdale just before the appointment and was running late, so we sped to cover some distance when we were pulled over by the Ontario Provincial Police (OPP). The officer had a dumbfounded look on his face as we explained why we were racing. We told him that we couldn't risk missing this appointment with the specialist. The officer chuckled with skepticism when he accepted our offer to take a look for himself. We then laughed at the shocked expression on his face when he finally believed us. He then asked if he could take a picture saying quote, "My wife is not going to believe this one." and snapped a photo with his phone, with our approval.

Siobhan O'Regan

He ended up letting us off with a stern warning and wished us luck. We made it to our appointment a tad late, and it was recommended that we have his teeth removed. I cried even harder than he did during the procedure, so they took a picture as a keepsake. I absolutely could not handle any procedure where they needed to do things like this. I thought it would hurt my son, and that would put me in a state of crisis. If they required needles, it was even more challenging for me. Jack had to be there to do it. Kallan was two weeks old at the time, and he was not the doctor's youngest client.

Kallan was such a content baby. He would only scream when he was hungry. This was from the moment he woke up until we could get the formula to him. We could hear the liquid hitting the bottom of his stomach. It sounded like a hollow drum. His screaming was not indicative of a fussy or impatient baby; it was more alarming and sounded like he was in dire pain and never appeared satisfied for any length of time.

Our doctor told us that it was colic. Still, we weren't buying into it. Two weeks later, we decided to fortify his formula with a pabulum to give it some substance and couldn't believe the immediate improvement. I put him on a strict regimen and stayed on top of his nutritional needs. I was amazed at how quickly he stopped fussing and crying altogether.

We later find out from his geneticist that Kallan had a condition called SPD, sensory processing disorder. This meant that whenever Kallan's brain registered, he was hungry, he would go into overdrive. He would feel like he was starving, and the part of the brain that was supposed to tell him that he was full was not responding. As he got older, we also discovered that this disorder affected other parts of his body, making him not feel pain like normal kids. We had to watch him when he hurt himself and made sure he was dressed appropriately. It didn't register with him if he was too hot or too cold.

After we solved his feeding issue Kallan hardly ever fussed unless a noise bothered him like a toy horn, I always got a kick out of this because he could be in the greatest of moods. Still, as soon as he heard the horn, his bottom lip would stick out, and he would let out a wail of disapproval and cry until he became distracted again.

Nobody Special

Kallan had such amazing strength and could hold his own head and body weight at only three days old. He was active in a jolly jumper by two months. He was always moving around, and I found that he was beginning to struggle during feeding times. I could not keep his attention long enough to get food to him and had to let him shred paper towels to keep his hands busy long enough to drink a bottle.

He was not an affectionate baby and spent hours at a time arranging his things in order and lining his sheets and toys around his crib. As he got older, he did this with his cars and lined them up around the room or objects. He would wake up between 6:30 and seven every morning. He only napped for an hour or so in the afternoon and stayed up well past 11 pm. As a toddler, I couldn't entertain him with television to save my life and could only have him settle down at night. He always curled up in his dad's arms to watch Teletubbies until he passed out. This used to drive his dad and me nuts. I always felt like our child was in permanent overdrive.

Kallan appeared to be double-jointed. He had crooked fingers that seized upon him and kept them curled into fists whenever he wasn't using them to grasp things. This also got worse as he got older. As mentioned before, his ankles were deformed and wholly turned inward. He had to wear special orthotic shoes to attach and screw together at night to keep his legs strategically placed. This helped reshape his ankles from the time he was born until he was two years old. At the time, we didn't have insurance, so each pair cost us several hundred dollars to replace every time he outgrew them.

Kristine came to visit Kallan every once in a while. This was when Jack was at work. She even told him once to leave when he came home early, stating that she wasn't done with her visit yet. To her expression, he was intruding on her visitation with Kallan.

Kristine became so unjustifiably angry and bitter with us that she only addressed Kallan as her child. She told Jack several times that Kallan was not his and that he was Dylan's child. I couldn't imagine how hurtful those words must have been to him and was worried that he would start believing her. I told him that I wanted to do a paternity test to put any doubts to bed. He assured me that it wasn't necessary and that he knew that Kallan was his.

Siobhan O'Regan

We understood Kallan was special, but neither of us cared so long, as he was healthy. Kristine kept telling everyone he had Down syndrome, but he didn't have any physical characteristics to support that claim. Our pediatrician sent us to Lonsdale's sick kids' hospital and eventually diagnosed him with something called Sethrayshotsen syndrome. It's named after the two doctors who discovered the syndrome. With nothing more than a name and a few documented characteristics, we had little to go on. We found out afterward that they assessed our son using what they call a clinical diagnosis. When he turned seven, he was hospitalized with something called the Rotavirus. The attending pediatrician sent him for further genetic testing at Dwyer's sick children's hospital. There they discovered that he was misdiagnosed the first time, and he had something called Aarskog syndrome.

When we went back into his medical history, we discovered that Lonsdale's sick kids' hospital originally thought of Aarskog but eventually sided with Sethrayshotsen due to his SPD. With the first diagnosis behind us, we decided to move forward. This baby was everything to me, and we decided to tackle each challenge as it came.

Kallan turned out to be a brilliant speaker and could strings words together like "good to go" by ten months. He could recite and identify his ABC in French and English by the time he was two. His ability astonished anyone who caught him reciting letters out loud. He would read one letter at a time and flattered even the most distinguished gentleman folk when he used his manners. He was oblivious to the attention he got when he'd say, excuse me for passing someone.

I bought flashcards and spent hours with him flipping through them, and he learned every one of them off by heart just days after we got them. He loved the repetitiveness. As brilliant as he was at memorizing things, he proved to be very high maintenance and always seemed to get himself into mischief. Watching my one-year-old was a full-time job in itself and needed constant supervision. Not a month after he started walking, he learned how to climb out of his crib, and we had to put him into a toddler bed for his safety. We bought extra safety gates around the stairs when I caught him trying to climb the railing several times.

I tried to nap when he did, but he wasn't always cooperative, so I would curl up in his toddler bed while he played in his room. One afternoon, I woke up, and Kallan was standing next to his room window. His back leaned up against the screen, pushing outwards. I leaped out of bed, grabbed his shirt, and yanked him off of the windowsill, knocking us both to the ground just moments before the screen fell two stories to the cement below. My neighbor, who witnessed the whole thing, told me that it was nothing short of a miracle. I was lucky to wake up when I did, and he was fortunate to be alive. It was sure nice that karma was looking out for him. I was forced to put pressure-mounted safety gates up in all the windows. I had Jack install air conditioning, so we didn't always have to leave the windows open to get some air.

Another time I was bathing him in the tub and warned him several times to stay seated. He caught me off guard when he jumped up and slipped, banging the back of his head on the tub. He trusted his head forward, hitting his mouth on the track of the shower doors and hurting himself. I called my sister in hysterics while holding him directly in front of me. My shirt drenched in his blood, holding a towel to his upper lip.

At the hospital, the nurse offered to start a chart on me. She wanted to give me a sedative because I was beside myself in grief and kept blaming myself for him being in pain. Kallan had ripped the skin clean off, which was attached to his gum, and there was nothing they could do about it. They told me it would eventually grow back and released him. I was assured it was an accident. No amount of reassurance would ever make me feel better over what happened to my son that day, and the guilt haunted me as I relived that scenario a hundred times over in my head. I kept beating myself up over the outcome. I never understood that day. How anyone could purposely hurt a child, knowing that I would die before I would ever intentionally hurt mine.

Jack and I raised Kallan almost entirely on our own with very little help or support from either side of our family. Maybe a handful of times, Kallan was watched when he was a baby by Jack's father and twice by my mother. We stopped allowing Kristine to have unsupervised visits after discovering that she would go against our wishes and do the opposite of what we asked. For example, the night before his genetic testing at Stollery Children's Hospital, we were explicitly told not to feed him any sugar, especially juice, and gave my mother strict instructions to follow orders. We later found out that she had provided him with ice cream. She said it was only for the taste, but he was only four and a half months old. I didn't find out until after the fact. On top of her other behaviors, such as continually referring to Kallan as her baby and mistreating Jack, this problem made us agree to have her see Kallan under our terms.

We didn't like to impose on Papa too much since we knew Kallan could be a handful. Still, it became a huge resentment factor towards Léo, who I felt often dumped his girls' responsibility on his father. He would up and leave for a night or two at a time when things became overwhelming for him or if he needed to tie one on. Léo had a custody agreement between him and his girls' mother and had them most weekends but lived with his dad. We sometimes would help pick up the slack and take the kids home to give his father a break, which seldom ever gave us a break.

Beth lived right around the corner. We were on friendly terms, but only those in our immediate circle knew we were actually sisters. We hung out a couple of times and managed to get ourselves into a bit of mischief. I found out during our discussions that she was convinced I had slept with her boyfriend, Tony. No matter how much I denied it, she never did get over the betrayal. She insisted that I had an affair and continued to resent me for it.

We visited my mother together one night for something to do and to see her new house. We got caught in the rain on our way over there. Kristine offered Beth some warm, dry clothes in her infamous glory but took one look at me and told me that she didn't have anything in my size. It was her way of pointing out how much weight I had gained. Beth couldn't believe that a mother could say that to her own daughter, given Kristine was a heavyset woman herself. I had grown accustomed to her abuse. I guess in the long run, it didn't matter as this was to be the last time Beth ever saw her mother on friendlier terms. She had no issue telling everyone that she had made Melissa her surrogate mother in place of her own.

Kristine claimed she stopped talking to Melissa after she accused her of stealing her daughter. Beth did try to form an attachment with her mother a handful of times but always found that she had a lot more in common with Melissa and developed a stronger bond with her than she ever would with her own mother. There was also the fact that Melissa and Bruce couldn't stand one another as well. They stopped trying to get along after Bruce physically attacked Melissa and tried to choke her during an altercation. The truth was, Beth started begrudging her mother, a long time ago, for the way she always put down her father and stopped talking to her altogether after this last visit. According to my sister, all she ever did was tell her how bad Sean was and the horrible things her father allegedly did to her. Beth never accepted this as part of the relationship and shut her out completely. Between us, the topic of Kristine became off-limits as well.

    I already knew first-hand how dysfunctional my mother's relationship was with her husband. After she caught him having sex with a prostitute on their couch, I still received another reminder of it. I left the baby with Jack and raced over to support her, figuring they would likely kill each other if they were left to their own devices.

    What I learned that night, no child should ever be exposed to or know about her parents. It was disclosed that Bruce was once again into some hard-core drug-related activities and had come home many nights roughed up and sometimes covered in feces. He had run up every one of their credit cards with cash advances to buy drugs and was admittedly hanging out with a dangerous crowd.

    This was not the first time Bruce was caught with a hooker. He was also having a long-time affair with a woman who just so happened to live across the street from yours truly. There are absolutely no words to describe what it felt like to be there standing in that house with my mother in hysterics. Bruce was cowering in the corner of the kitchen in the fetal position with his head down, like a child who was being struck.

    A couple of bottles of wine sitting beneath her microwave stand caught my attention. Without hesitation, I helped myself. I downed the first bottle within minutes finishing the second one only slightly longer. The events that took place later that night were a blur. There was crying. Bruce was on his hands and knees, groveling. Both of them were screaming, yelling threats of suicide. Objects were being thrown, and then there was me. I was front row center and drunk. I had promised myself that I wouldn't touch another drink after Kallan was born but, this was way too much for any sane person to take in. I took it how I took things best. This became a saga that plagued my family for years. It turned into a vicious circle of deceit, lies, empty promises, addiction, and abuse. To make things worse, I was forced to take part, compelled by my loyalty to support my mother through each one of her many crises.

Siobhan O'Regan

I started drinking again after this incident and justified it by only doing it on the weekends. It took up going to the bingo hall during the week to curb my urges. I became hooked immediately after I won my first jackpot and couldn't get enough of the activity. I lied about Kallan stressing me out so that Jack would let me go to unwind.

Back when I first started playing, the bingo hall allowed smoking. I would sit in the upper non-smoking section and met a really quiet woman who I grew accustomed to sitting with because she didn't say much at first. After a while, she warmed up, and we started chatting with one another. I learned that her husband had recently died on what was supposed to be Kallan's actual due date. She lived on her own, with her closest family member living several hours away.

Her name was Jessie; she eventually started to grow on me and began sharing her late husband and her family's stories. I loved telling her all about Kallan's latest antics. We enjoyed the idol chit-chat, and I liked the adult conversation without getting too personal. What started as two people sharing a table eventually bloomed into a friendship. She became the first person I ever considered as an extended member of my family. I included her in all of our family functions. We were two lost souls who found companionship with one another, and she became the grandmother I never had. In exchange, I took care of her like she was my own. I liked feeling needed without the burden of getting too attached and liked the idea that I could pull out anytime I wanted if things got too intimate.

I learned very quickly how to play my husband to get my needs met. I figured out exactly which card to play and when to play it to get my way. It got to the point where I was going to the bingo place three times a week just to escape my element. I understand now that I was replacing one addiction with another in the quest to get outside of myself. If it wasn't one, it was always the other. My extracurricular activities were starting to take a significant toll on our finances. As long as I got my fix, I didn't care where Jack got the money.

I eventually figured that I would win it back. As long as Kallan's needs were met and the rent was paid, I could take the "what I don't know won't hurt me" stance until the money ran out. That is when we fought about money. Jack became the classic enabler and started selling off some of our belongings. Still, then he started writing himself extra paychecks to cover our expenses and maxed out our credit cards to buy groceries and pay the bills.

Nobody Special

Jack was pretty good at maintaining the finances, even though he hadn't paid his income taxes in a couple of years. He owed the government close to $10,000 in taxes. His problem was that he didn't know how to say no to his wife. Robyn and Gordon had recently claimed bankruptcy and referred us to their agency that offers couples in financial strain help. We were hoping for a fresh start. We had accrued the bulk of our expenses when we had Kallan since we had to purchase everything on our own. Jack's dad always helped us out whenever he could and tried to give us a head start. Still, seeing how much Léo depended on his father financially, we were determined to do what we could for ourselves.

For the most part, we bought everything we needed out of our savings and used up our credit for the rest. Until I was invited to my first baby shower, I had no idea that people held parties to help one another out with gifts for the baby. I was completely unaware of the whole process watching as the guest of honor received everything from diapers to cribs. Of course, in my case, I didn't have any family or friends to invite anyway. When we claimed bankruptcy, we did it on twenty-one thousand dollars, which for a couple who had nothing, it was a substantial amount of money. Five thousand of that figure was mine. I couldn't claim my student loan, so that sum remained with us until we paid it off ourselves. With our finances in place, we started to talk about having another baby. Léo's girls were twenty months apart and were the best of friends, so we talked about having our kids relatively close together as well.

CHAPTER SEVENTEEN

Three Plus One Makes Four

Getting pregnant was easy the second time around. We conceived two months after we started trying. I was relieved. Sex was becoming unbearable no matter what position we tried. My second pregnancy was just as complicated as my first one. I only lost a great deal of weight this time because I couldn't keep anything down the first several months. That, and having to chase Kallan all the time, was enough to lose weight. My pre-pregnancy weight was one hundred eighty-five pounds, but I delivered at one hundred sixty. I then dropped down to one hundred fifty after I gave birth. I lost a total of thirty-four pounds. Quitting drinking was more problematic the second time around, but reminding myself that I lost a child in the second trimester was a good motivator because of my drinking.

Unlike my first pregnancy, I obsessed with drinking with this one, and the pain of not being able to drink kept me up at night. As hard as it was not to, I didn't dare touch one drop of alcohol. Beth got pregnant and gave birth to a daughter right around the same time I got pregnant. We bounced names back and forth. One of the names we came up with for a boy was Kian. She liked it too but was convinced she would have a girl, so I claimed the name for myself when Carly was born. Beth wasn't happy and threatened to buy a dog and name it Kian so that I couldn't use it. Sometimes her cruelty reminded me of our mother.

We told Léo first; then, we told the news to Jack's dad. He took the news better than we thought he would since it was the second time around. He was a good man with strong family values and supported us no matter what he thought.

Siobhan O'Regan

My only fears about having another baby were that I grew up knowing I was never anyone's first, second, third, or even fourth favorite. Knowing how much I loved Kallan, I could not imagine what it would be like to love two children the same. The prospect of loving one over the other scared me so much it was debilitating, except for Jack's father. I had never seen anyone treat their kids equally and watched from the sidelines as Léo favored one of his girls over the other.

I didn't want to bring another child into the world and not love them equally. This thought haunted me throughout my pregnancy and made me doubt my parenting abilities. It made me apprehensive about my unborn child. Taking a step back, I sometimes beat myself up for the way I thought back then. I often forget that I need to have compassion for that person and understand she didn't always know better.

We had an ultrasound and found out that we were having another boy. Jack really wanted to have girls like his little brother did but adjusted very quickly to the idea that Kallan would have a baby brother. He jokes to this day that Kian should have been a girl. We talked at great lengths about having this baby in Main, given what we went through during Kallan's labor, but were told we would have to give up Dr. Grace. She was well aware of our complications, understood our issues, and I trusted her. This was a difficult feat for someone like me, so we remained in Fields.

Jack asked Léo to be in the delivery room with us so he could tape the labor since I missed the birth of my first son. Leo saw it as an opportunity for him to redeem himself over the wedding fiasco. Because of the GBS, we were told that Kian would have to be induced as well. His due date switched back and forth between the thirteenth and seventeenth. We finally settled for the sixteenth. I was so excited to meet my son. Meeting him gave us something to look forward to.

We checked into the hospital, and they prepped me for a central line using numbing cream on my hand. I was scared, but I had mentally prepared myself for hours of intense labor. Dr. Grace came in to reassure me everything was going to be all right and told me if all goes well by later that evening, I should be holding my son. The first hour and a half were uneventful, and I was progressing slowly, so Dr. Anna ordered them to increase my meds.

Nobody Special

The nurse came in to dial up the Pitocin, and within a half-hour, I was in full-blown labor. I started having contractions. They were coming continually and wouldn't stop. The nurse was such a sweet woman and was nothing like the nurse who cared for me when I gave birth to Kallan. She was visibly worried when the contractions wouldn't stop and called my doctor for an emergency consult. Dr. Anna rushed in, took a look at the monitor, and demanded to know why the Pitocin was up so high. She then turned to Jack and told him that she needed to order an emergency epidural and left.

The nurse gave me some gas to take the edge off, but that only made me vomit several times over. My first epidural took hours to administer. This time the doctor was there within moments and ordered me to turn on my side. Unlike the first one, they didn't need to wait until I had a contraction to administer it. I was so tired and exhausted from the pain and was still throwing up from the gas. The nurse told me they were treating me for a shock. Léo was practically huddled in the fetal position in the corner of the room until things had settled down.

Dr. Grace told me that it was almost time to start pushing. She was worried that they didn't administer enough antibiotics in time but that it was too late, ready or not, he was coming. From the moment they put in my central line to the time they placed him in my arms, my labor took less than two and a half hours. I would have traded all of it in for the twenty-seven hours I had with Kallan any day. I experienced nonstop contractions for close to twenty-three minutes straight without a break. Usually, that kind of labor takes hours under normal circumstances.

All my fears and apprehensions melted the moment I took one look at that beautiful face. I felt like I was looking at a self-portrait. He was the spitting image of me in every way down to my eyes. He was twenty-one inches long, six pounds twelve ounces, with light blond hair and dark grey eyes. He had ten fingers, ten toes, and I held my breath as Dr. Grace looked him over. He said my son wasn't showing any physical characteristics of his brother's syndrome.

Kian had a huge birthmark that spanned the entire left side of his neck. With the support of a nurse, I was allowed to hold my Kian for a brief moment. I watched as Léo congratulated Jack and found myself wondering how it would have felt if my brother was there to share this moment with me. I wished to know how proud he was of me.

Siobhan O'Regan

The nurses took Kian to clean him up and to weigh him. They brought him back to me to breastfeed him and made extra sure this one had no spare teeth. Afterward, they told me they had to take him for observations while I got cleaned up. I didn't question them and assumed they were taking extra precautions, especially after the last time. Even Jack waited to make his calls until I was safe in my room. An hour or so later, they brought him back to me. I was surprised to see he had been fitted with a central line and was attached to a machine feeding him antibiotics. I was concerned that neither one of us was there to hold him as they put in the line, but the nurse assured me that he was in excellent hands. The doctor was to come along shortly to explain to us what the medicine was for. Dr. Grace explained that Kian had tested positive for the virus. It was likely because his delivery went so quickly that they couldn't administer the antibiotics in time. I understood that the virus was potentially fatal and read that babies had died after contracting it. My doctor said he would be okay. All my faith was then placed in her expertise.

Two days passed, and we were due to be released. The doctor wanted to speak to me about our sons' prognosis. Jack was at home with Kallan, so I asked Stephanie, who popped in for a visit, to keep me company while I was waiting. I was fine until a lady walked in and identified herself as a bereavement counselor. She asked to check in with me and if the doctor had been to see me yet. I shook my head. Stephanie and I sat up straight and looked at each other and asked why. What was wrong with my son?

Before she walked in the door, I had no idea what a bereavement counselor was or why she was there. Still, after explaining her role, I started panicking and demanded to see my son. Usually, the babies stay in the room with their mothers. Still, Kian was under constant observation and stayed in the nursery. Stephanie set out to find the nurse. Moments later, we sat across from the doctor, asking if I wanted to wait until my husband was present. I demanded he gets right to the point.

He went on to explain that Kian was not responding to the antibiotics and that there were other medicines they could try. They needed to do a few tests first. They were going to put him on a more potent antibiotic cocktail, and that the next twelve to twenty-four hours was crucial.

I started losing it and called Jack. I tried to explain what the doctors had told me while I cried. Stephanie sat there in silence while the counselor wanted to reassure me that they were doing everything they can. They asked me if I wanted to go to the chapel to pray, but I just wanted to be alone and politely asked her to leave. Stephanie took her up on her offer, knowing full well I needed my space. The next twenty-four hours were an emotional rollercoaster. I was clinging to the edge of my seat and silently praying that he would come out okay.

I had unlimited access to him, and they gave me a room to sleep in, so I didn't have to leave the hospital. Stephanie could stay with me as well, and we slept in shifts. Jack came and stayed with me whenever he could, but I understood he needed to keep busy. I was jealous. I wanted a distraction and wanted to drink so badly, but I was too afraid to leave my baby in the hospital.

Three days later, I was sleeping on the chair after a long night of pacing. Stephanie was passed out on the bed. They brought him to me for a feed. It took me a couple of seconds to snap out of it when I realized that he was no longer attached to a machine. His weak tiny little arm was wrapped in a sling to hide the bruises where the needle had been the last five days.

I scooped up my child and held him for the second time without having him attached to tubes and wires. I wept my heart out as he lay in my arms. The nurse told me, so long as he ate, I could take him home. I called Jack right away and told him they were releasing our son. Kian was jaundice, but so was Kallan when he was born. We knew just what to do. Unfortunately, we learned the hard way our son was super sensitive to the sun. He broke out in hives the moment we put him directly into the sunlight. They said it was a side effect of the medication, and it may go away with time.

Stephanie was the same way. When Kian got older, he blistered on his shoulders and neck with second-degree burns as she did. If he were exposed to direct sunlight for any length of time, he would burn without protection. So, we had to keep him out of the sun for the first two years until he could start wearing sunscreen. Adjusting to having two kids after an experience like that was no issue. It gave me perspective on how much I wanted to be a mother. I had a better understanding of how much my boys meant to me.

Kallan loved his little brother and wouldn't leave his side for a minute. He kept calling him "my baby." Once after I was done breastfeeding Kian, Kallan asked to hold him. I set them up and left the room for thirty seconds. I wanted to grab my camera, and as I came back, I found Kallan trying to get

Kian to latch on to his chest. Kallan told me that he could feed him too. I had never laughed so hard and was such a proud mama.

Kallan was less than two years old when he stopped napping just before Kian was born. I found myself working on both shifts. Since I was breastfeeding, I was up all night with Kian and up all day with Kallan. On top of that, Kian had caught a nasty virus that he couldn't shake. He was spiking high fevers, wasn't eating, and was fussy all the time. He wasn't sleeping, and I was irritable from the lack of sleep. If that wasn't bad enough, three days after he was home, I went to get him out of his crib when I completely threw out my back. It was so bad that I couldn't pick him up and had to call Beth to help me.

Jack had to work; ironically, Jack's dad had thrown out his back the same time as I did so; Jack went to work to be close to his father and help him out. I was angry with Jack for years and clung to a lot of resentment and anger regarding this. Knowing his dad had three sons, and I only had one husband, really upset me. I mostly needed him at home, given I had two special needs kids and couldn't function independently.

I sucked it up like I always did when it came to my needs and let my sister help whenever she could. Beth was still there when I needed her, but it became clear that she was there out of obligation. She didn't want to be stuck having to take care of us, so as soon as I found a way to take care of them without help, I let her go. I lived with severe back issues on and off for years. I was out of commission with limited mobility for weeks at a time. The specialists believe the injury might have initially been caused by the epidural. Still, the chronic issues were because I didn't seek medical attention until a year later.

Kian was a fussy baby since day one, and we soon discovered that he had some unique quirks, some of which made us laugh. One of them was that he refused to nap unless he had a hat on his head. We also discovered that he had aversions to certain stimuli, especially to certain textures and bright lights. He would cry until you took them away. The problem was the process of elimination and trying to figure out which stimuli caused his discomfort. He was so hyper-vigilant about everything he touched and required things to be very specific all the time. We started spending a great deal of time in and out of the hospital. We discovered that he had contracted something called meningitis when he was released. He was treated with several antibiotic cocktails. Afterward, we found out that he contracted meningitis from the antivirals they had given him at the hospital to counteract the B-strep that he contracted during his birth. Meningitis crippled his immune system and made him chronically sick for most of his childhood.

Kian was such a happy baby when he was in between infections and loved to laugh and play. Other times, when he was sick, he just wanted to be held. This became impossible sometimes since he was sensitive to touch and couldn't properly communicate his need to be in different positions.

Kian never learned how to crawl and came up with this incredible way of sliding on his bum to get around. I loved it. One of our department stores had a policy that they would replace it for free if they outwore it before they outgrew it. Since Kian kept wearing out the bum in his PJs, I didn't have to buy him new PJs for over a year. With Kian being sick and Kallan not napping, my doctor threatened to hospitalize me for exhaustion if I didn't manage myself better. Jack came up with a solution to build a playroom next to his office. This way, he could take Kallan to work with him, and so I could rest. I even looked at daycare for Kallan, but when the lady told us that he was too young to go without naps and suggested she could lay down with him until he fell asleep, I couldn't help but get upset. I thought I already tried that. That was not her role. I decided he wasn't ready for daycare, and he was better off with me instead.

At a year and a half, Kian wasn't walking, hardly talking, and we started noticing how he would stop breathing in the middle of his sleep. We were sent to see an ear, nose, and throat specialist. He diagnosed Kian with sleep apnea and told us he could not hear and was more than ninety percent deaf. This was affecting his center of gravity, which explained why he wasn't walking. We were told he required surgery to correct his hearing and needed several tubes in his ears. They added that these procedures would help with further infections. Within months of the surgery, Kian started walking and picked up speech faster than we could relay it to him.

The specialist told us that his hearing was so bad that it was like talking to him with his head underwater. The doctor explained that his tonsils caused his sleep apnea and that when they become infected, their swell becoming enlarged. He said they usually shrink in-between infections, but they never had time to shrink and continued to swell because he had so many of them. Taking them out was our only option.

We received a call from the hospital days before his surgery. All elective surgeries were postponed until further notice due to an outbreak of SARS syndrome (severe acute respiratory syndrome). Over the next eight months, Kian's tonsils grew so big he couldn't sleep without one of us supervising him. Jack slept with him over the following year so he could turn him when he stopped breathing. I had him napping on the couch to keep a close eye on him during the day. It got so bad near the end that when a neighbor stopped by one afternoon to say hi, she left in tears because she couldn't stand to watch as Kian's chest cavity sunk, heaving inward every time he gasped for air during his afternoon nap. We documented several hours of videotaping him sleeping and showed his doctor how much he was suffering. Within weeks, nine months after he was initially scheduled for surgery, his case was prioritized, and Kian had his tonsils and adenoids taken out.

His scabs were so large that they had slushed off on the third day. After his surgery, while he was on the potty, he smiled up at me when blood started pooling from his mouth. It tapered off when we got him to the hospital. Otherwise, his results were immediate, and despite the pain from surgery, he slept for the first time in well over a year.

The last time we counted the prescription receipts, we estimated that Kian was administered over 80 different antibiotic cocktail courses. This was to fight off various infections from when he was born until he was close to twelve. He started tapering after he hit puberty. He had missed close to a month and a half of school one year due to various sicknesses.

Kian never did anything on a small scale. I remember when he and his brother contracted chickenpox, Kallan had maybe twenty poxes spanning his entire body. Kian, on the other hand, had them so bad that he ended up in the hospital. He had them in his eyes, in his mouth, on his penis, and up to his rectum. The poor kid went through hell, and there was very little we could do to make him comfortable. He suffered the long-term effects of traumas and sicknesses and developed his attachment and severe anxiety disorder as a result.

Nobody Special

As a small child, he grew to depend on the attention he got when he was sick, and because of that, we thought it was in his best interest to put him into preschool. It was for a couple of days a week to help him develop social skills. Unfortunately, keeping him at school when he was always ill was the biggest challenge. He kept catching viruses and everything, including the pink eye, three separate times.

He was coming home three times a week. By the time he started Maternelle, he was still significantly behind with his social skills. He preferred adult companionship to his peers in a core French school. He often latched on to a teacher and even the school secretary for comfort, shying away from the other kids. Up to this point, Kallan was his only connection to developing his social skills. Still, he preferred solitude to play with his younger brother. He was never openly affectionate. One pediatrician suggested that Kallan might be autistic but refused to have him tested out of fear of having him labeled at such a young age. I tried introducing Kian to playgroups and joined mommy classes, but he was always too sick to attend them, and I couldn't connect with the other moms. Kian missed a great deal of the formative years when kids develop most of their social skills.

He met a wonderful young boy named Tremore, who loved him for who he was in the face of everything. They developed a friendship that followed them through grade school. I became fiercely protective of this friendship, given my hardships and knowing what Kian had gone through. Making friends was easy for Kallan, who all his peers instantly liked. For Kian, he was shy and withdrawn. He was the type of kid who would only develop a few close and meaningful friendships. We treated Tremore like we did with our children and included him as part of our family.

Watching my son suffer both physically and socially has always been one of my biggest challenges. I have felt so inadequate as a mother because no matter how much I sacrifice for my children, there is nothing more debilitating than knowing there is absolutely nothing I can do to take away their pain. I had to learn to just be there for him and to help get him through it. For a person with control issues, keeping it together, some days took everything I had. When there was nothing more to give, I had to reach even more profound.

In 2014, we had both of our boys assessed by a psychologist. We learned that Kallan had been diagnosed with several learning disabilities. He was going to struggle in school and was likely never able to make it far academically. Not without extensive support, of course. As one of my therapists once pointed out, most kids with spectrum disorders such as Down syndrome or Asperger's have developmental delays that are generally the same across the board. They don't identify as being different from everyone else. Kallan, on the other hand, has what they call pocket delays. He is not considered on the spectrum and is identified as having autistic tendencies but does not qualify as an autistic child. He has too much empathy. Kallan is right where he should be developmentally, but his cognitive delays are becoming more apparent.

Kian was diagnosed with three subtypes of anxiety disorders from all the various illnesses as a child. The lack of family support, having a brother who couldn't emotionally attach, a distant father, and an emotionally unavailable mother contributed. It pained me to see him struggle, and I am so grateful to his Papa, who remained married to his children. He eventually had grandchildren after his move to Ontario and modeled for them. I always wished I had someone like that. I badly wanted someone, just for me. Only I was too blind to see he was still there right in front of me. He was patiently waiting in line for me to pick him.

Kian has no learning disabilities but, as you know, suffers from severe anxiety. He has been seeing a psychiatrist for the better part of a year now. He is on antidepressant/anti-anxiety medication that helps regulate his anxiety. There is no telling how long he will require medications. In 2017, we had him reassessed, and they determined him to be bipolar, like his mother. He also sees a psychiatrist to help with the social part of his anxiety. He uses cognitive behavioral therapy and Dialectical Behavior Therapy (CBT and DBT) as learning tools. He was in his third high school. This was after he was bullied in his two previous schools.

Kallan was always well-liked and never had an issue making friends, but making friends has never been easy for Kian. It didn't help that he and his brother attended the French Catholic school on the opposite side of town for obvious reasons. They were bussed to and from school. Usually, kids bond in school, on the playground, or in sports, and Kian didn't quite know how to navigate either one. We had a couple of kids in the neighborhood, but Kian didn't connect with any of them and found refuge in the game called World of WarCraft instead.

Nobody Special

When his playing got out of hand, I did what I thought any good parent would do and started restricting how much time he could play. I realize I had overlooked a familiar pattern in his behavior and that he had become addicted. When Kian began lashing out aggressively, we put him in an anger management course to taper his aggression. I taught him some useful tools in managing his anger. He still has his moments, but anyone who understands him knows he is such a fantastic kid. He has a fierce determination. His psychiatrist has recently suggested getting him a service dog. Still, when I asked about one, the waitlist was over a year and a half and cost a small fortune.

Looking at him is like gazing into a mirror. He and I are like carbon copies from our looks, right down to our stubbornness. I also see my addictive personality in him, so I do my best to stay two steps ahead of him at all times.

One of the things we learned in therapy was attunement. It translates to how well you know your child and to what degree you accept him for who he is. I discovered that I was not half as attuned with Kian as I was with Kallan. I accepted Kallan for who he was a long time ago. I accepted his syndrome's limitations. Still, I had much higher expectations for Kian. I discovered that there was this part of me that didn't like things about him. I learned that the things I didn't like about him were things I didn't like about myself because of our similarities.

I was projecting my feelings onto my son. I didn't favor one child over the other or love them any differently. I just couldn't connect with the parts of Kian that triggered me and would shut him out. To him, this came across as rejection and feelings of inadequacy, worthlessness, and I was unaware that I was causing him to feel this way.

With Kallan, he was so independent and full of life, but Kian was the complete opposite. He was needy, reliant, and relentlessly demanding. He had this way of draining your energy, yet there was just something so exceptional about him that drew you to him and could always make you laugh. The rare times he wasn't sick, he was such a happy and content child. He reminded me so much of his brother. He loved to interact, chatter and just enjoyed being the center of attention.

A great deal of my therapy was based on the heavy burden of guilt I carried, not being able to meet all of his needs, and had to learn how to cut myself some slack. I accepted that I had limitations too. As a mother, I had a high expectation of myself, which I could never achieve. That made me feel incompetent, so I shut down and numbed myself with alcohol. It took me a while to break free of that self-defeating thinking. I then began looking at it from a healthier perspective. It took me time to understand that, as his mother, he was the type of personality who would need to make his fair share of mistakes and experience things for himself. He had to learn and grow. I knew that I would love him unconditionally and attunement was the one thing I was going to give him. I promised myself this would get him through it all.

When looking back at my experiences, I would say that the lessons I learned were through my children. If I had to pick a turning point in my life, I would say it was through watching them grow and taking those moments to view the world through their eyes.

With Kian's fierce determination and perseverance, he will be very successful in just about anything. Whatever he put his mind to, he will pursue it. My job will always be to keep his energies focused on the right path. Having three subtypes of anxiety disorders is not easy. There are times when I think I would lose control of it all but, he always made it back to me, and I admire his strength more than he will ever know. After everything he has been, though, he is a tough kid. He has a personality that will inevitably change the world. I am always so proud of my boys and know I don't tell them that nearly enough.

Being a large family, we are often busy, so I try and connect with them by writing them personal notes on napkins. I place it into their lunchbox and come together every night for dinner, just before they asked to be excused. I ask them to share the best part of their day with me and something they are grateful for. These kids are masters at picking out what's wrong with their lives, so I try to show them that no matter how bad your day is, there is always something positive to reflect on.

If you look hard enough and gain gratitude, you have a state of mind that needs no lecture. It does need to be taught. I tuck them in every night, and even if it's a high five, that is their moment carved out just for them. I tell them good night, I love about you, and I will see you in the morning. I do this even if it's been a tough day of behavior.

CHAPTER EIGHTEEN
It Takes A Village To Raise A Child

On September 11th, 2001, when Kian was just four months old, I was downstairs having a cigarette when my neighbor yelled out the world was coming to an end. She told me to turn on the television. I ran upstairs and flicked on the TV to see the burning towers, the World Trade Center, showing on every channel. I called my sister, and she rushed over right away. We sat and watched in horror as the second plane struck the twin towers. Both of us were in tears. Beth was distraught until she got a hold of Leroy, who was on his way home from Reardon. They closed all the major roads to the airport. There are two days I will never forget where I was or what I was doing; one is at 9/11, and the second day is when Princess Dianna died in August 2007.

    I was losing much of my connection with Jack. I became irritable and distant, especially if he didn't give me my way. Even sex between us was non-existent unless I was drunk enough to detach and dull the pain. I preferred a smoky bingo hall to the company of my husband, who now preferred spending most of his time on the computer. Jack and I were drifting further apart, especially since Kian was born. Our lifestyle gave me too much idol time, so my anxiety became irrepressible. I loved being a wife and mother. I never wanted anything more in my entire life, but there was always a massive void in my life. No matter what I did, where I went, or what I drank, it never went away. It was an indescribable need that I could never quite put my finger on, and I always felt this lingering sadness.

    Our first trip to Quebec with Kian ended up with him in the hospital. He contracted something the French called Scarlatine, which translates to scarlet fever. He had contracted this disease once before. The doctor told us that the smoky environment, which our son was exposed to, was not a good fit for his immune disorder. This caused him to be more vulnerable to all strains of a different virus'. Jack and I both smoked and tried our best to use care when handling Kian. We made sure never to smoke in the house, so he was not always exposed to it like he was at his grandmother's. Taking care of a chronically sick baby took its toll on both of us. We didn't always agree on how to handle our stress, but we both knew if we were going to visit his mother, they would have to agree to smoke outside while we were there.

Jack was hesitant about making this request, knowing how stubborn his stepfather was, but claimed to do it for his son's sake. Unfortunately, communication didn't come easy for Jack. I was not fluent in French, so I don't know how much of my communiqué she heard. I can tell you for sure that this became the most significant source of conflict between his mother and me. She may not have understood me, but she realized when I got angry concerning this particular subject.

As I mentioned before, Vincent was much set in his ways and didn't like or appreciated anyone telling him what to do in his home. When we came to visit, no matter how much his mother assured us there would be no smoking in the house, he always did anyway. I remember getting so angry with Jack, who always tried to play Switzerland in the quest to keep the peace between his mother and me. Their take on the situation was that exposure to smoke once or twice a year wouldn't kill him. My take was that it wouldn't kill them to take it outside if they wanted us to come to visit. I was amazed that they kept showing no concern for their grandson whatsoever.

One thing was definitely apparent. Vincent had little regard for anyone other than himself, and Eline cared more about her partner than she did for her grandchildren's wellbeing. I had a hard time believing Jack when he told me that he had dealt with his mother. I decided to gloss over some essential details when I laid down the law since I always preferred the direct approach, and he did not. I had a hard time with second-hand smoke, so I couldn't imagine how tough it was for Kian, whose tiny body couldn't fight off infections.

I have always struggled with expressing myself and became overwhelmed when I felt backed into a corner. I often threaten to leave if he didn't deal with his parents. I found the only way I could deal with them on a good day was when I was drunk and spent most of my trips do just that, drinking. On a few occasions, they came down to spend time at our place. I did my best to make them feel welcomed and even gave up my room for them to sleep in and went out of my way to make sure they were comfortable. When the roles were reversed, I felt like I was mistreated and ignored. I used to dread going to Quebec and only ever went for Jack and the kids' sake until we started spending New Year's with Jack's dad's side of the family. Splitting our time between the two families made going down more bearable.

The way I saw it, Léo was a carbon copy of his mother, and they both displayed all the characteristics that reminded me of the things I detested in my own mother. It was the selfish, egotistical, self-serving, narcissistic personality types I resented. I later explored with previous therapists how the anger I felt towards my mother had manifested onto Jack's mother due to transference. I would have to confront the root of my bitterness and one day forgive her for being able to move on. My biggest argument with myself was and always has been the fact that Jack's dad and his brothers were all the family my children had and would likely ever have. All I ever wanted to be was for them to treat my boys with the same dignity and respect they would have had for their own children, and they were not budging.

Having two special needs children was starting to take a significant toll on our finances and transportation. The fact that I was dependent on Jack for just about everything didn't help either. Jack took a substantial amount of time off work between the multiple trips to Milbank Children's Hospital and regular doctor visits. Unfortunately, his time was paramount in his work line and meant if he couldn't bill his hours, he wouldn't get paid.

Jack's dad suggested I get my license to transport the kids to and from their appointments on my own and offered to pay for all the expenses, including the driving course. I was taken back by his generosity. Neither one of my parents had ever given me anything close to this magnitude, even though it was to everyone's benefit. He always tried to make me feel important and part of his family. He and I grew close over the years. Well, as close as I was able to let him but significantly closer than I ever was to any adult figure in my life. I later let him in on a level that no human, other than Jack, had ever explored before. After I disclosed some of my darkest moments, he told me that he and Jack were my family now and insisted that I only call him Papa.

I only wished his values had rubbed off on his son since Léo hated the relationship I shared with his father. He often became angry with me and reminded me that it was his father and not mine. On the other hand, Jack's brother Killian was such a pure soul and only ever lived in the moment.

He loved to flirt with the girls and made people laugh. He was in a major car accident when he was sixteen. His girlfriend and her best friend were driving back from the mall after buying some safety equipment for a bike ride at the time. Back then, you didn't use helmets, but it was recommended for this event. Killian was in the back seat, trying on his new bike helmet. His girlfriend was driving at the time and was taking her turn to advance through a four-way stop when a larger vehicle ran the stop sign and smashed into their car. The two girls in the front seat were both wearing their seat belts but, Killian was not. The collision sent him flying headfirst through the side window, coming to rest halfway through the opening. His doctors say, had he not been wearing the helmet, he would have died instantly. Killian suffered a severe injury to his brain and was in a coma for two weeks. When he finally came out of it, he had to learn to walk, talk, and eat again. To this day, there is no telling how much permanent damage was done. He made a full recovery by all accounts, but I'm told he was never the same after the accident.

Beth and I continued our love, hate relationship. She had this neighbor who practically worshiped the ground she walked on except once when she complained to me about how Beth treated her like a slave. She was complaining about when she offered to help out with her wedding. I gave her advice based on the information she presented to me and told her to take it up with Beth. If Beth didn't appreciate her hard work, then she didn't deserve her support.

I'm not sure what variation of the story Beth got, but she was furious and told me to butt out when she called me. It was a case of her word against mine, and I lost by a landslide. I figured they deserved each other. A couple of weeks later, I was outside having a smoke and saw my next-door neighbor turning from my sister's street, walking past me with something tucked under his shirt. He usually said hi, but this time he kept his eyes on the ground. He was completely preoccupied with what he was hiding. I piped up and asked him if he had an animal tucked under his shirt, and he laughed nervously, saying, "Ya." He continued walking. I didn't think anything of it and continued to go about my business.

Nobody Special

An hour later, I received a distraught call from my sister claiming she had just been robbed, and after hearing the details of what was taken, it didn't take a genius to put two and two together. I told her that I knew who did it. I showed up just after the police arrived and was surprised to see Tyler standing in the middle of her living room. I hadn't seen him since we went camping with Dylan back when I was pregnant. We took a few minutes to catch up until my sister rudely cut us off and announced that it was no time for a reunion. She pointed out again that she had been robbed.

Oddly, this played out exactly like the Roseanne episode where her annoying neighbor, Cathy, got robbed. Gil, the police officer, came to take a statement recalling old times. The only difference was, this was not a show, and this was happening in real life. Tyler took my statement while forensics went over the scene. I learned he was recently married with their first child on the way, and I told him about my boys.

I know there were always questions surrounding whether or not Kallan was Dylan's, thanks to my mother. I invited Tyler over to meet Jack and my boys. One look at Kallan and his dad, and I knew there would be no question about who fathered him. Tyler only stayed for a few minutes since he was on duty. After he left, I breathed a sigh of relief, knowing full well he would go back to Dylan and tell him, with a degree of certainty, that he was not his father. This chapter of my life was finally put to bed.

A great deal of my time at home was spent taking care of my boys, so when I was asked to take on my nieces for nine consecutive weekends, I welcomed the change. Léo and his ex-girlfriend, Bryn, had split up when Amélie was just over a year old. They had agreed on joint custody of the girls. Bryn was just fifteen when she had given birth to Léonia. By her own account, she was a product of a dysfunctional family herself. She did the best she could to support her daughters.

The relationship between Léo and herself could best be described as highly toxic, and the girls were in the center of it all. I didn't think Bryn was half as bad as Léo made her out to be and got along with her fine but, I was not involved in their history, so I stayed out of their issues for the girl's sake.

She and Léo approached me and asked if I would take care of them on the weekends, and they offered to pay fifty dollars a week for the job. I gladly agreed. I loved the girls and thought it would be fun to hang out with them. We had a blast, and for the first time in my entire life, I got to experience what it was like to be a kid. We danced, laughed, and played. I took them out for special treats and learned very quickly how much I loved kids. It brought me back to when I had Joey to take care of. Léonia gave me a clearer glimpse of what it was like to be in the middle of her parents fighting, and I just sat back and listened. I held her when she talked about their latest fights.

Amélie was her father's favorite, although there was no question he loved them both equally. He and Amélie had that special bond, so I would take Léonia out and spend extra time with her. We developed one of our bonds, just the two of us. I sat down and wrote letters to Santa with the girls and helped foster their creativity by playing dress-up and starred in their plays. Those weekends meant everything to me and even brought Jack and me closer together for a while. We often talked about adding on to our family. Still, we didn't want to risk another chronically sick child, given what we were going through with our kids. We agreed that Jack would have a vasectomy to ensure no unexpected pregnancies and look into adopting when the boys got a bit older.

I always saw myself as a driven individual who would one day go back to college to make something of myself. Instead, I put everything on hold because my kids were medically dependent on me. My father-in-law also felt strongly that the boys should be raised by one parent in the home whenever financially possible. His view was based on seeing the girls bouncing back and forth between their parents. Léo forced me to stop writing letters to Santa with the girls for reasons that are his own, claiming I had no right to continue it since I was not their parent. He accused Jack and me of spending too much time with the girls and put a stop to us watching them.

When I asked about the money he owed us for watching the girls, he told us that we shouldn't expect payment from family members. We depended on that money and even lowered it to three hundred fifty dollars to entice him to honor his end of the deal. We spent a lot of money doing activities with the girls when we might not have otherwise been able to if we knew he wouldn't pay. Although this may be seen as cliché, it landed when we needed the money to cover some of Kian's medical expenses. Jack was self-employed and just started paying into a medical plan that only paid eighty percent of his medications. It didn't cover the rest of his pain or fever reducers. Papa ended up covering the money for Léo after we approached him for a loan. He was puzzled and asked about the money we were supposed to receive from Léo for babysitting. I wasn't going to lie for Léo, especially since I asked Papa for cash. That alone was exceptionally humiliating to do from someone I respected so much.

I sometimes found myself tired, angry, and resentful towards Kian for the time, energy, and money we invested in him. Every time he got sick, I was upset, especially when I needed a break and couldn't get one. I always stood by the fact that my addictions always came second to my children and that their needs always came first, but everything else was a distant third.

To this day, the shame and guilt attributed to getting raped and stripped of my dignity. The freedom for years was nothing compared to knowing I willfully resented my child for something that wasn't his fault and was out of control. Inside I was a raging ball of fury and anger, but rather than take it out on my children like my adopted father used to do, I directed it inwards. Whatever spilled out was lashed on Jack, and sometimes Léo also took it from me as well.

I could justify all the anger I had towards Léo for all the nasty things he said and did to his brother and me. Jack and Léo always had a love-hate relationship, even as children. Jack used to torture his little brother, and Léo always looked up to Jack, wanting to be like him. I always thought it was because Jack was like his father, and Léo was like his mother. The two of them always clashed. It didn't help the situation that I, too, disagreed with Léo and projected years of anger onto him. Where most people could take him or leave him, I took his rejection of me very personally. I had always thought of him as selfish. Still, since developing a deeper appreciation for those who suffer from trauma and knowing how hard it is to reach their developmental milestones, he, like me, was just stuck. We both had a lot of growing up to do.

We were forced to move after staying in our home for almost two years. Our landlord decided to sell the home. We loved the house and told them we were interested in buying it but quickly changed our minds when the next-door neighbor to the right of us said that he would take us to court to fix the fence.

Initially, we were friendly with this neighbor. We hired his daughter to babysit our sons a couple of times until a trip we took to Wonder World overwhelmingly changed our opinion of him. We were all getting along great and were having a good time until we met up for lunch. Someone had parked too close to his hatchback, and he couldn't open his tailgate. He decided it would be fun to key his car and let the air out of his tires. I was shocked by his audacity for such extreme measures and told him exactly what I thought. He told me to chill out, and the owner deserved it. Jack said nothing and didn't back me up. I was so angry with him that it ruined most of our afternoon.

Afterward, I learned that it was because he was our only ride home, and he didn't want to get stranded in Reardon and would settle it when we got home. His idea of settling it was to ignore him subtly. Jack didn't do conflict and strayed away from it whenever possible. In return, I thought that it was incongruent of the lad portrayed by Kale, Jacks's best friend. He described him as a badass tough guy when he was a teenager. Regardless, I had become quite brazen since I started drinking again and wasn't shy, so I told him exactly how I felt. Unfortunately, this meant we would have to forgo buying our house since he was not the type to let go of a grudge that easily.

We found a house on the other side of Fields. It was a quaint little 3-bedroom bungalow, and it was clean, but I hated it. Bungalows reminded me of the house I lived in all those years where I was tortured.

At this point, Jack was either working or tied up playing on the computer. I was left to drown my sorrows in whatever alcohol I could get my hands on. Like thousands of alcoholics before my time, I managed to elude my immediate family and hide my disease by mastering the art of manipulation. I only casually drank when we were out in public or at family functions to duct suspicion.

Papa always received a wide range of alcohol from his friends and family at Christmas time, so it wasn't unusual for him to pass along a few bottles to us. This year he gave us an entire case of unopened liquor. I hated drinking hard alcohol unless it was tequila because it gave me heartburn, so it sat in the basement forever. This was until Jack started to argue about my frequent alcohol consumption openly. I usually got my own alcohol, but after I had my first drink, the car keys somehow always disappeared and, I had to depend on him to get it for me when I ran out. This ended up in threats and intimidation if he didn't do as I say. So, after a while, I started hiding wine throughout the house and dipping into the liquor if my stash was depleted.

I think this gave him a false sense of superiority. Our arguments had decreased significantly, and I was now just avoiding him altogether to avoid getting caught. For six months, there wasn't a day that I didn't fall drunk and used it as a way to cope with the constant demands of a chronically sick child and an impossible three-year-old. Fortunately for me, Léo was doing his own fair share of stealing alcohol, amongst other things, so it was easy to hide my tracks when we started taking Papa's stash. This was until he decided to lock up his liquor cabinet. He assumed Léo was the only one taking it, so he entrusted Jack's key's whereabouts.

I can recall very few memories over the next five years except bits and pieces I can pull together from Jack. He tells me what I was like, and I carry the burden of guilt like heavy sandbags through every step during those formative years of my boys' young life. I remember once I was so frustrated with Kian. We had just spent two long weeks of sleepless nights with him and had conducted a couple of trips to the hospital, trying to keep his fevers down.

He was finally just starting to nap in the afternoon, and I was anxious for him to go down so I could get a moment to myself. My hands were shaking in anticipation of my next drink. Kian wouldn't settle and was miserable when he was tired, so after the third attempt to get him settled, I slammed the door to his room. The three-tier shelves I had just installed came tumbling down to the floor.

Kian let out a piercing scream. I can still hear this day, and I rushed in to console him. I held my baby in my arms for hours until he finally passed out, exhausted from crying. I later found out his fever had spiked again from another infection.

Being sick did have its benefits. It even saved my marriage at least once. One thing about having an attachment disorder is that when the tough went going, so did my all-or-nothing mentality. I think giving up is the only viable solution and the best way out. The first time Jack and I separated was when I asked him to leave. I was so fed up, unhappy, and felt like none of our issues were ever resolved (not a wrong assessment for someone who had no idea of what her concerns were or how to solve them in the first place). We agreed he could pick the kids up for an hour after work and have open visitation on the weekend until he found a place of his own, and until then, he would stay at his dad's.

Siobhan O'Regan

A few days later, both Kallan and Kian came down with something called the Norwalk virus and threw up for 24 hours straight. Then I came down with it, and that was when I had to admit defeat and asked for Jack's help. He then caught it himself another 24 hours later. The following 72 hours were complete and utter hell as there was no clean piece of fabric in the entire house, and Kian caught the same virus a second time over. We managed to put our differences on hold and supported each other through this crisis and agreed to work things out in the end. To start, I would cut down my drinking, and he would make himself more available to help out with the kids, and we agreed that I could attend Bingo once a week to get out of the house.

We made several trips to the clinic and hospital over the next few years with both our children. Still, We stopped going to the clinic altogether after they made four grievous errors that ultimately cost my family dearly. We found out the hard way that you cannot sue doctors in Canada, and not too many lawyers will try without a considerable incentive first.

When Kian was about five months old, he was developing a chest infection. When your infant son is sick as often as mine was, you get to know the signs and when to enlist medical attention. It must have been the weekend since it would have been the only reason our family doctor wouldn't have seen him so, we took him to the clinic. Typically, my doctor's amazing secretary, Becky, could get my boys an appointment that day due to their many health issues. This time, my doctor was booked entirely just before the weekend or on the holidays.

The clinic wasn't busy, so we got in relatively quickly. I noticed right away that the doctor was in a mood, and he cut me off when I was explaining to him what was wrong with my son. He demanded to know if I was a smoker. I was taken back by his harsh tone and nodded yes in response. Without looking up at me, he told me to use my words rather than nodding my head.

He took Kian and placed him on the table. He took out his stethoscope and pressed it up against his chest, and started lecturing me on my smoking taking brief pauses as if to listen to my son's heart. In all the time I had gone to see doctors, I had never seen one listen to my son's chest through three layers of clothing, his sweater, sleeper, and undershirt. Then he turned to me and told me that my son had asthma, and I should be more considerate of my child's health. He suggested I quit smoking and wrote out a script for two inhalers.

Nobody Special

I was devastated. I didn't get in one word the entire time we were in the office. I walked out to the parking lot, took one look at Jack, who was chatting with his dad on his phone, and broke down into tears before I even reached the car. After briefing him on what happened, Jack asked his dad for some advice and told us to immediately go to the hospital for a second opinion, so that's exactly what we did.

We had the doctor examine Kian before we told him what happened and showed him the prescription the other doctor wrote. A nurse makes a photocopy of the prescription for Kian's file telling us that Kian had a chest cold and an ear infection. He said there was nothing in his findings that would support a diagnosis of asthma. We were so relieved, but I held on to that prescription and handed it over to our lawyer. I don't for one second pretend that smoking with a chronically ill child was ever a good idea. Back then, I did not have the information to know about what effects smoking has on a child, including transference, that they teach you today.

I still hold out that education serves a much higher purpose than making someone feel guilty or stupid for their choices. I firmly say shame on anyone in an authoritative role who chooses to abuse their power of authority rather than exercise compassion for those; who they dedicated themselves to support.

The second time was when Jack went to the clinic with a sore throat. They took a swab and told him they would call if there were a positive result. A week before this, he had gone to a sleep clinic. The sleep clinic results suggested that he had severe sleep apnea, and they told him that they would need to revoke his license. He was still feeling incredibly lousy, so he went to see our doctor.

A couple of days later, he received a call from Becky telling him to get a prescription for antibiotics because he tested positive for strep throat. Jack asked if that could affect a sleep apnea test, and she confirmed with the doctor, saying yes. He called the clinic to inquire about the first results and was told by the reception that his findings were positive and was told someone should have notified him of this and did not. Jack was able to keep his license after proving his results were tainted because of his strep throat and the clinic's negligence.

Siobhan O'Regan

The third time was with Kallan when he was about four years old. We were at the park and slid down a huge wooden ramp. A huge sliver ripped through his pants and lodged its self in his left butt cheek. The part of the sliver we could see was approximately a quarter-inch long, so; we knew we had better take him to seek medical treatment. We rushed him to the clinic because it was closer, and he had to travel in the car with his face down over my lap in the back seat. He couldn't sit down in his car seat for fear it would lodge further into the skin. When we arrived, the waiting room was full of people. I walked in and tried to explain to the receptionist what had happened to our son. She barely glanced in my direction and told me they couldn't take him because they were full. I was asked to head up to the hospital. I tried to explain how we were forced to transport him and was told it didn't make a difference. I told her I would not risk his life further and that if he had to go to the hospital, they needed to call an ambulance.

She then pointed to the front doors and said there was a payphone outside and to help me. I was ready to tear her a strip when a lady stood up and placed herself in the middle of us. She told the receptionist that she had some nerve sending away a needy child and that he could take her place. I was so overwhelmed at that point I just thanked her over and over again. She walked up to Kallan with his tear-stained face and told him to hang in there, and walked out shooting the receptionist a dirty look. We waited our turn for over two and a half hours. I held him and had him stand on his own until he managed to find a comfortable position leaning over a chair on the opposite butt cheek.

A few minutes later, a man stood up and started yelling at the receptionist. He and several others overheard her tell her colleague how ironic it was that he couldn't make it to the hospital. Still, he could seat himself in a chair. This gentleman overheard her comment and publically reprimanded her for it. Those left in the waiting room backed him up. Jack and I couldn't believe someone could be so nasty to a 4-year-old boy and were never so grateful that a stranger came to our rescue. Shortly after, we were taken in shortly, and his doctor, an older lady, took one look at Kallan's wound and told us there was no way he should have had to wait almost 3 hours to be seen.

They tried to freeze the area, but it was lodged in pretty far, and he screamed every time she tugged on it. She finally pulled it out on the third try while his dad and I held him down. The sliver part that was embedded under his skin was three-quarters of an inch long. Afterward, we were told that they should have probably x-rayed him first and maybe cut him open to retrieve it.

The doctor stood there, shaking her head as we told her about the treatment we had received while being in the clinic, and she was appalled. She apologized profusely, promising us that she would take care of it. I believed her. I asked if we could have the names of the two people who supported my son that day, but they couldn't for privacy reasons. We went back to the clinic a few more times, but we never saw that receptionist again.

The last and final straw was when Kian was three years old, and he had been fussy for days. He was already on antibiotics, so; we took him to the clinic to see if there was anything else we might have missed. We went in, and Kian wouldn't sit still. He was crying, and the doctor wasn't very patient. He snapped at Jack and me to hold him down so he could examine him, but Kian kept turning his head and covering his ears. The doctor was rough and thrust the scope into his ear, and out of know where Kian let out a piercing scream that I had only ever heard once before. He fell silent as he drew in a huge breath; he screamed again. The doctor backed off and told us he couldn't examine him. We were to follow up with our doctor after the weekend.

Kian was thrashing around and clawing at his ear. I took him from his father and tried to calm him by holding him tightly. We left the office, and it was in the waiting room when I noticed a puddle of liquid on my shirt that was oozing from his ear. Kian was sucking his fingers now, trying to console himself, and I told Jack we had better take him to the hospital.

They didn't hesitate and took him in immediately. He had ruptured his eardrum, and they administered pain meds right away. The doctor said that the clinic's physician likely pierced it with his instrument when he examined him. Any seasoned doctor would know exactly what had happened. If our account was accurate, then we should file a grievance. We had the document that we had just come from the clinic. The time-stamped the rupture and booked an appointment to see a lawyer. Our lawyer was very sympathetic to our case but told us that malpractice suits were far and few between. They were challenging to win in Canada. He told me how to write up a letter and follow up with one of his own. I never heard back about what happened with their disciplinary committee but was told that my letters were forwarded. He assured me it would not be taken lightly. All I could do was let it go and move on. We never stepped foot into another clinic again.

When Kallan was six years old, he was hospitalized with something called the Rotavirus. I was entirely dependent on my drinking by then so, I stayed with him during the day and went home to drink at night. His attending physician at the time was a pediatrician named Dr. Calome, who told us to point-blank that our son was odd-looking.

I laughed at his forwardness and told him that he was diagnosed with Sethrasyshotsen syndrome as an infant. He shook his head and said no, and that he would bet his years of experience that he was misdiagnosed. He told us he wanted to send Kallan to Dwyer's sick kids' hospital. This was for genetic testing, where we discovered he had a rare condition called Aarskog syndrome.

When he was diagnosed, I read somewhere that there were less than two hundred documented cases in the entire world. This particular syndrome was first described in 1970 and is an inherited mutation of the X-chromosome. It is transferred by an affected mother who has a fifty-fifty chance of passing it down to her son or one in four chances of passing it down to her daughter.

We were well past the shock stage of knowing our son had a syndrome. Still, now his characteristics were finally starting to match his diagnosis, and we finally had something to go on. Kallan's geneticist supported the original diagnosis of SPD. Dr. Calome clinically diagnosed him with ADHD/ADD, which is a well-known characteristic of the syndrome.

I did as much research as humanly possible, but I could find very little information about his syndrome. I couldn't make a connection with anyone whose child had it until Kallan turned twelve. I eventually found an online support group through Facebook called Aarskog Syndrome, which currently has three hundred and thirty-eight members from all over the world. They either have the syndrome or are a parent/ family member of a child who has it. We have shared so many stories and have found some overwhelming similarities that are not yet recognized or documented. We hope our sons will get a chance to meet one day. Kids with Aarskog are born with one or more physical abnormalities, specifically to their hands, face, feet, teeth, and genitals. The majority of our boys and their carrier mothers are smaller in stature and have been diagnosed with or have ADD/ADHD symptoms. Some were born with an ascended testicle, but most of them have varying degrees of behavioral issues, learning disabilities, and mental health issues ranging from moderate to severe. Some have even been diagnosed with autism.

Cognitively Kallan was very bright, and he excelled in math but was significantly behind in language. He looked at things very logically and seldom grasped the concept of sarcasm. Kallan tended to act on feelings and mimicked what he saw. It was quite brilliant. One time, I gave him trouble for something, and I stopped for a second to collect my thoughts. He blurted out, "I like pie." I was so caught off guard that I laughed and completely forgot what I was giving him trouble for. It took me a while to process it, but it would appear that he had somehow correlated my love for pie and used it to defuse the situation. Kallan himself hated pie but had seen me indulge in it earlier that day and used my own words to change the conversation's mood. From then on, whenever a situation got tense, he would yell out, "I like pie!" and completely zone out.

With Kallan, things came randomly, and you never knew what to expect. Sometimes he used his catchphrases when they didn't fit into a conversation. We often laughed at how arbitrary he was. He is a very finicky boy and had to have things done or lined a specific way. He liked having his bedsheets smoothed out before he could crawl into them and wanted it like that, even after being in bed (I am the same way). He could not have his food touch on his plate or refused to eat it, so we had to serve him one item at a time and clean his plate in between. It was a battle to get him to eat meals such as shepherd's pie, but he learned to adapt as he got older.

I still giggle to this day when I see him separate the food on his plate and eat it one item at a time. He does not even realize that he does it. Once, we were sitting at the dinner table having our meal, carrying on a conversation about their day, when Kallan suddenly blurted out, "I learned what a vibrator is today." He said it with absolutely no effect and went back to eating, utterly oblivious to the reactions around the table. Jack's face was priceless.

Kallan's syndrome could have made him the perfect target for bullies. He was fortunate enough not to be raised in a tight-net school setting. Kids were taught and modeled to be open, accepting, and supported by a great team of school officials. He had such a love and talent for sports, so he didn't have any trouble fitting in so long as there was a game going on. For this reason, we decided to give

Kallan the one thing his father and I never had, and that was the stability of growing up with his friends.

Due to his ADHD diagnosis over the following year and a half, Kallan put on several different stimulants, all of which took away his spark and made him lose a significant amount of weight.

Our son was slowly disappearing, and even though there was a massive improvement in his attention, he was becoming, in my opinion, detached and too depressed.

He would sit at the table and mope, often cry for no reason. Kallan often cried when he was overwhelmed or frustrated, but this was excessive, even for him. Kallan always struggled to pay attention in school and was forced to switch seats closer to the teacher. He had his desk attached to hers for one year so she could keep a direct eye on him. I didn't find this out until after the fact. I attributed some of his behavioral issues to him being segregated from the rest of his class. All of his teachers would tell us what a sweet, considerate, and helpful boy he was. However, he was reprimanded continuously for distracting the other students and always putting objects into his mouth.

We had a massive issue with this at home, too. We realized we had a problem when we discovered that he had worn down his teeth to nubs by gnawing on his wood bed frame and anything else he could fit into his mouth. One specialist told us that he had a condition called Pica, which is still unknown if it is a characteristic of Aarskog syndrome. Pica is characterized by eating substances with no nutritional value, such as string, dirt, wood, sand, plastic, and ice. The list is endless. It is neurological and is attributed to a chemical imbalance or iron deficiency in the body. Those with spectrum disorders such as autism would have it, and I used to have a bad habit of chewing on things myself. I tended to bite on straws, pens, pencils, my nails, the skin around my nails, and even my clothes.

We knew we would have to monitor him closely but didn't realize how close until one day he came home from school, and we could see right away he wasn't himself. We figured he was having an off day. During dinner, he started wobbling back and forth. Food began spilling out of his mouth, and he was slurring his words. We rushed him up to the hospital only to find out he had suffered a massive concussion. Kallan couldn't offer up any useful information, so we played detective and managed to piece together what happened after getting the medical report and talking to the school. Apparently, he fell several feet from the monkey bars at the last recess and hit his head on the wooden platform below. The impact knocked the wind out of him, but he managed to get up, catch his breath, shake himself off, and tore off again.

A teacher made note that he fell based on what some students had told her. She didn't see the accident herself but recalled thinking his injuries must have been minor given he got up. She did ask him if he was all right, and he didn't mention to her that he hit his head. Since he appeared fine, she allowed him to join the rest of his friends. We had to make sure to have a protocol in place and have the school notify us whenever he hurt himself, no matter how minor the injury was, so we could have him checked out.

Kallan never did anything on a small scale. He once tripped at school, and they called us in to take a look, and wouldn't you know, he had a rock embedded in his knee and had to go to the emergency room to cut it out. We were glad most of his incidences happened at school with our bad luck, where it was witnessed and documented.

Along with our mothers, Jack suffers from severe migraines, and he passed this down to our son. He wouldn't get them often, maybe once or twice a year, but it knocked him out of commission for a day or two when he did. He once got one so bad that we had to postpone Christmas when he was six because his head hurt so much, he couldn't open his eyes, let alone open his presents.

We found if we caught them early enough and administered pain medication right away, they didn't last as long. This occurred after he got get the Rotavirus, just before we got his Aarskog diagnosis. Simultaneously, Jack discovered one night when Kallan was coming out of the shower. He appeared only to have one testicle.

A trip to a specialist confirmed Jack's suspicion, and we found out that he had an ascended testicle. He required surgery to bring it down. During the ultrasound, the doctor discovered a mass on the viable testicle and told us that he would monitor it for growth. His surgery went well. The aim was to bring down the testicle (called Cryptorchidism). Still, we were warned that there was no way of telling how viable the testicle would be for hormone production. We had to wait until he reached puberty, and even then, he possibly needed some hormone therapy. It was all too soon to tell.

The testicle was much smaller than the other one but appeared healthy. In the meantime, Kallan's recovery did not go as smoothly as his operation did. He ended up splitting his incision, and we learned that he couldn't get stitches again. He had a massive scar where his first incision was. It was six months later, after keeping a close eye on the mass of the right testicle, when it was determined that they were looking at an active tumor. We were sent back to Lonsdale Sick Kids Hospital to have a urologist take a closer look. I will never forget the day we went to see the specialist. He and his team of doctors were looking him over, feeling around the tumor. As they huddled around in a circle discussing their findings, Kallan sat up and boldly announced to the room, "How am I supposed to know the difference between a good touch and a bad touch when clearly everyone is touching me?"

Everyone stopped, turned to him with stunned faces, and laughed in unison. "Clever kid, you got there!" one of the physicians chuckled and went back to discuss their findings. Kallan became outwardly aggressive. We had brought this up to his pediatrician several times over the past year or so had. He thought it could be the meds and switched him to a different stimulant. This accounted for several changes to his medication. Kallan's urologist took particular interest in this information and told us, after the biopsy, that Kallan had a Leydig Cell Tumor. The tumor created its testosterone, and the extra testosterone explained why Kallan was having issues with his aggression. They said it would go back to his normal in due time. He also informed us that had they not discovered the tumor when they did, Kallan could have gone into complete puberty by the age of ten. They said that even though the cells surrounding cancer at the time were benign, his chances of developing malignant cells and tumors were more than double. This was especially given due to his current history of an ascended testicle and his diagnosis of testicular cancer.

Under normal circumstances, they would have removed the tumor and the surrounding tissue. Still, they decided to extract the tumor in my son's case and place the testicle's remainder back into his scrotum. Not knowing how viable his other testicle was, they wanted to make sure they gave him every opportunity to reach puberty independently. By the time everything was said and done, Kallan weighed in a total of forty-three pounds at seven years old post-cancer. We decided to take him off all of his appetite-suppressing stimulants and seek other methods to support our child with his ADHD. We began taking parenting classes using a technique called Cognitive Behavioral Therapy (CBT) to manage his behaviors. Kallan continued to see his specialist regularly and was released from Lonsdale for close to five years in remission.

We decided not to put Kallan back on medication after realizing that we would have to start from the beginning, experimenting with different stimulants and doses. We wanted to give him a break. We found a treatment-based course that gave us an entirely different perspective on what effects this disorder has on the person who suffers from it. It trained us to identify and act based on the symptoms of the disease, not the child. We discovered creative ways to get our son to follow through on the task. We developed a better understanding of his strengths and limitations by becoming more aware and in tune with our child's behaviors and triggers.

CBT, putting it simply, accepted that Kallan had ADHD/ADD and meant that we took his limitations and figured out how to work with them rather than against them. Rather than depending on a pill to moderate our son's behavior, we were going to have to do the majority of the legwork. We had to learn how to talk to our son and learn how to communicate based on his language. We had to conform to him within his limitations rather than have him adapt to ours.

I was happy to see we were on the right track with the sports and making sure he had an outlet for his pent-up energy. I thought I knew a great deal about nutrition but learned a lot more about how different types of food impacts Kallan's body. I learned how it triggers his behaviors, what foods to use to enhance his calm (as his dad likes to put it) and what foods to avoid altogether. As Kallan got older, his diet consisted of nutrient-dense whole foods eliminating sugar and refined or processed foods altogether. This was emphasizing lean meats, whole grains, fiber, unlimited fruits, vegetables, and calcium.

In school, Kallan was placed with an Individual Education Plan (IEP), which allowed us to understand our son better. This was so we could help him reach his potential by meeting his specific needs. As a goalie, I used to tell him learning was like playing hockey. For him, sports came naturally, but for some kids, they had to work twice as hard to get where he was. I taught him, with the right tools, anything was possible. He had to work twice as hard at school with him, but he was just as capable as the next guy and only needed to be aware of his limitations with the proper tools.

Putting it all into perspective, a friend once told me if you look at our society in the context of a tribe back in the day, ADHD/ADD was just as prevalent back then as it is today (minus what is caused by improper diet by today's standards). Since they didn't have pharmaceuticals back then, they were often sent out to forge for the tribe. Yet, now we expect them to conform to the unrealistic standards of sitting in a classroom for eight hours a day. It's unnatural, cruel, and inhumane, in my opinion.

CHAPTER NINETEEN

As The Season's Change

We lived in the bungalow for almost a year when we started looking to purchase our own home. Unfortunately, due to not working and the bankruptcy, it wasn't going to be easy. We were fortunate; Jack's dad came to the rescue again and offered to cosign for us to qualify for a mortgage. They gave us a preapproval rate, and we set off to find a home. We searched several places and even looked at buying a brand-new semidetached house. Still, the place didn't have air conditioning, and we would have to install a driveway. This was going to cost us too much.

We tried searching for older homes, but they all required a lot of work, which meant additional money we didn't have. Things looked bleak for a while until we came to a freehold townhouse. An East Indian couple owned it with their three kids. It was within our price range and was only three years old. It even came with all your standard comforts, including air conditioning and a water softener. The only issue with it was that it had a six-month closing date. That explained the reason behind the price and for it being so much lower than the market rate. It also included a finished basement. To a young couple just starting, it was a dream starter home.

We were allowed three visits to the home to ensure it was well maintained and everything appeared to be in order. A month before we moved in during our last visit, they asked us to extend the exchange for a couple of days just before we took ownership. Our lawyer strongly cautioned us not to for insurance reasons, and we needed the extra time to paint, so we told them no.

The day we moved in, I sat in the middle of the living room and cried. The house was destroyed. There were stains and grease marks on the carpet where they wheeled out their big-screen TV. The upstairs and downstairs carpets had unrecognizable stains that wouldn't come out. There was garbage littered around the entire house, and we hauled two truckloads to the dump. There was paint spilled on the garage floor. The fridge was broken. We were missing all of the warranty papers for the appliances, air conditioner, and water softener. The key to the mailbox was also not there. Our realtor and lawyer told us that we could go after them, but we were better off to move on. I was getting sick of people telling us to move on. Everyone kept taking advantage of us. We spent years building up our credit to repair many of the damage they did, from replacing windows to adding new floors and everything in between. By the time all the repairs were done correctly, the house cost us considerably more than the agreed asking price. I often tell myself if only I knew then, what I know now, I would have done things much differently. I was always so grateful for Jack's dad and could always turn to him when we needed support.

I remember the first time I entered AA; my father took my brother and me after we were arrested for drinking underage. I was fifteen, and Lorcan was seventeen. I received my first twenty-four-hour recovery coin and had kept it to this day. Jack and I were no longer functioning as a couple. We were merely coexisting and co-parenting. This meant that I took care of the kids during the day, and he would take over at night. We hardly spoke to one another unless we were fighting. I admittedly threatened the one thing that held any value to him, and that was our relationship. I understood how much our marriage meant to him. I knew how much his parent's divorce hurt him.

On the other hand, I did not understand how someone could value something they spent most of their time trying to avoid. I didn't believe it when he would tell me that he loved me and that I was beautiful. This was because I had gained a considerable amount of weight and didn't feel good about myself at all. I preferred it if he told me I was ugly and worthless. I understood those words. Jack was never one for compliments, and I wasn't used to hearing them. On the odd chance he expressed any emotion, I immediately rejected them. That is why he stopped putting them out there altogether.

He wasn't poetic or romantic and didn't compliment a job well done. He was your typical guy who thought nothing, said I love you like a topping off the gas tank, and ensured there was always an unlimited supply of windshield washer fluid. I was way too caught up in myself to appreciate his brand of affection. Neither one of us was turned into the other, so any attempt we made to connect turned into an endless sea of conflict.

Jack was more immediate and a fixer. I was a chronic runner and an intellectual bully. I used to dominate conversations and became an expert at pointing out all of his faults. I blamed him for the problems of the universe, especially the ones within our marriage. Jack was a pleaser and hated conflict, so he would deescalate a situation by giving me my way. I used this to my advantage.

The only problem was that he didn't know how to gauge or when to back off during times when there was no quick fix. I, on the other hand, could never measure how far to take things. Our fights would end up with me trying to kick him out and ending the marriage, while he would beg for forgiveness and offer up a truce by taking the brunt of the blame and promise change

Things only escalated to violence when Jack felt justified enough to invade my personal space. This was to overpower me physically and to get me back down. It was an attempt to get his point across. This only led to an all-out panic attack, and I lashed out the only way I knew how. Since I couldn't fight back physically, I threatened to leave if he didn't. Based on my all-or-nothing mentality, I meant it.

The one thing about having an attachment disorder is the need always to have power and control. This often meant following through on threats based solely on principle. Only the conflict was when the dust finally settled; I never actually wanted him to leave. I cared deeply for him, and I wanted to work things out. I never knew how to express myself or relay what I needed. Writing this reminds me that saying sorry was not about admitting you were wrong. It was telling the other person they are worth more than your ego.

Jack attached such high value to the words he would say. For Instance, "I love you" was recited several times a day. He expected me to reciprocate it back. Only every time, it reinforced my inability to trust him. How can he possibly love someone like me? If he ever tried to approach me sexually, my stomach would turn. I questioned how he would ever want to have sex with someone as fat and hideous as me? I spent countless nights drunk, huddled in a fetal position on my bed, just praying for the strength to end it all. I had no other options left and truly felt as if everyone would be better off without me. I had never felt more alone, yet he was right there. He was no more than a few steps away. He was gentle and kind, and I couldn't let him in.

In the moments leading up to my darkest hour, I spent several days researching suicide. I learned how to prepare by double-checking my insurance papers. I wanted to make sure there wasn't a suicide clause to leave this world knowing Jack and the boys were financially okay. That night, I held my boys tightly and said goodbye. I had no intention of waking up the next morning. I had a plan and was going to see it through. I forced myself to stay sober that night, to write them all a letter. It was important to me that I write it with a sound mind coming from the heart.

Nothing had ever prepared me for the indescribable pain I felt writing those letters and realizing that I was about to inflict the same amount of strain on my family. It was a glimpse into my mortality, and it forced me to take a long hard look at what I was going to do to my boys. None of them deserved what I was about to do to them. It was the first time I felt something in a long time, and it was by far worse than any physical pain I had ever endured. I realized that I was hurting because I wanted to live, not because I wanted to die. Had I not been sober, I likely would have missed my moment and followed through that night, ending my life once and for all.

I wanted the pain to end but not at the expense of destroying my kids. They had been through enough, and I couldn't let them face the harsh realities of life on their own. At that moment, I recognized I truly loved something outside of myself, and my purpose was to be there for those boys. Through my experience, I adopted the reasoning that someone out there had it far worse off than I ever did. I forced myself to appreciate what I had, even if I couldn't feel it for myself. I had to do it for them. This reasoning kept me alive all of those years leading up to my sobriety.

I had watched how AA transformed my stepfather into something almost human. I still thought of him as an overgrown child, but he had some sobriety under his belt. I was desperate so, I figured I had nothing to lose.

I drank before the first meeting I attended. In fact, for close to five years, I wouldn't participate in a single meeting unless I was drunk. Jack came with me for support. A man in a cowboy hat walked up, shook my hand, nodded at Jack, scooping me up, and gave me a long lingering hug. He reeked of cologne, giving me an instant headache. When he released his grip, he smiled. He tipped his hat and told me I would blend in much better now. I guess I didn't have much appreciation for how much my body reeked of alcohol. After the meeting, I somehow felt empowered, but the feeling was short-lived. I couldn't wait to get home to have a drink.

I started using AA as a way to smooth over Jack when we would fight over my drinking. I remember Jack peeked his head into the garage one night after a meeting and was surprised to see me in my usual fashion. He asked me why I had a drink in my hand when I just left a meeting. "Simple," I responded. "I'm an alcoholic. It's what we do." I gave him a shove and closed the door. I had no issues admitting the first step. Heck, that was easy. My biggest challenge was trying to figure out how to keep Jack buying into my attempts at recovery.

For close to five years, I struggled with the whole God concept and finally used it as my excuse to make my exit. I was determined that it wasn't right for me and figured I paid for my regret. I understood I needed to quit drinking and thought I could do it independently but never got very far. I spent the majority of my time doing something known in my circle as the three-step waltz. The problem was every time I drummed up the courage and determination to get sober, the more desperate I became to chase after that last drink. It was a vicious circle of endless conflict within myself. Near the end, I found myself hoarding alcohol and purchased it from several different stores so I could elude any suspicion of anyone discovering my deep dark secret.

Since my wedding, I had been talking to Lila regularly, and we had spent hours at a time on the phone just listening to one another. I chat about everything and absolutely nothing. She was someone I could always depend on and never felt judged. Lila was such a wise soul, but I was so reserved about our connection because I was never considered her number one as close as we were. She already had a best friend, and I always needed to maintain my all-or-nothing attitude.

She and I talked at great lengths about dieting. Our relationships work and inspired me to go out and get a job. To get out of the house, I figured I could use the break. I found a job working with exotic birds at a local pet store and liked working with animals again. The job was minimum wage, plus commission so, I enjoyed competing with myself to see if I could beat my previous time and get my chores done. I could feed, play with the birds, and get upfront with the customers.

Siobhan O'Regan

My co-workers instantly liked me and enjoyed my witty sense of humor. Still, our work ethic kept clashing and drove a wedge into our working relationship. This caused several differences in opinion. We were supposed to stay within our perspective departments. Still, I was always being asked to cover for everyone when they went on break. If someone called in sick, I was to cover for that as well. So, when someone asked me for help, I wouldn't think twice and assist. Apparently, I was cutting into other employees' commissions, so I was asked to only assist in whatever department I was in at the time.

I was even reprimanded for selling sand to a customer who purchased it for their bird because it was sold in the reptile department. I went so far to help customers that I gave the commission to the people in the department. I was then reprimanded again when a customer complained that I should get the commission.

There was a lot of petty bickering between employees, so I often kept to myself and ignored the gossip. I found that even that isolated me. Everyone always wanted me to pick a side, and I found that they projected their upset at me when I refused to get involved. I always went above and beyond for my customers and treated them exactly how I wished to be treated. I enjoyed being busy. It made the time go by super quickly. I ended up purchasing a Green Cheek Conure because he was aggressive, and no one wanted to handle him. I named him Jake, took him on as a pet project, and worked on him several times every day. It took a lot of blood, sweat, and tears as he was one stubborn bird but eventually, he calmed down enough to hold him. I even trained him to step up, but he wouldn't let anyone else near him. They gave me a considerable discount to take him off of their hands. Of course, when I got him home, he found more of a mate in Jack than he did me and only behaved for him. Birds are creatures of habit and tend to mate once in a lifetime. Once they choose their human mate, there was little you can do to change their mind.

I got a call one day that the water main broke, and our store had flooded. Sure enough, everyone was wading knee-deep in water, so Jack slipped over to Canadian tire and bought a wet-dry shop vacuum out of our pocket. We spent the day sucking the water out of the store and didn't once complain when my time was not compensated.

Nobody Special

Jack thought I was a pushover, but I didn't mind. I considered it volunteer work thinking I was well compensated when we bought our bird Jake who cost a lot more than what I paid for him. Unfortunately, my new responsibilities didn't do much to curb my appetite for drinking. I showed up for work hungover and stashed alcohol in my lunch to curb the shakes until I could go home and have a couple of bottles of wine. My drinking started affecting my job, and I had several accidents at work.

I once fell off a ladder from three feet up and had to take a week off of work and put on light duty for another two weeks. I tore a ligament in my knee and sprained my arm. I found out that if I drank vodka and chewed gum, no one was the wiser. I was never called in under suspicion of drinking. I was just an overachiever. I quit that job about six months later. I couldn't handle the recent turnover and hated how badly management treated its employees. I also caught my boss and his supervisor making out in the back behind the fish tanks. They ended up making commission accessible to all departments before I left, and I was thrilled to have been the driving force behind that change. I preferred the animals' company than I did the people I worked with, so it was time to move on.

Jake was a magnificent bird and a great talker. He tolerated our kids and nipped them a few times, but big daddy was always there to console him when I gave him a what for. A year later, he flew out the door when Jessie let the dog in and planted himself about forty feet into a neighbor's tree. The owner refused to let us climb up to get him due to liability issues. Jack sat at the bottom for hours to try and coax him down. Sad and defeated, he was forced to give up after Léo came and convinced him that he would eventually fly down, and someone would catch and return him. A half-hour later, Jack heard him outside, saw him on the roof, and was able to retrieve him safely and sound. Jack was so thrilled to have his buddy back, but their reunion was short-lived. Three weeks later, we ran an errand and came home to see that he had passed away in his cage. He got caught in his bedding and had a heart attack. At least Jack was able to get closure but missed his companion.

When Kallan first started playing hockey in our local league, I was told there were ample volunteer positions available. I figured that I would see if I could be a good fit since I wasn't working. When I first approached the organization about volunteering, I was offered a hockey mom position. Still, I wanted a more challenging role that was less of a cliché. I was asked to consider the role of a convener, and the rest is history. My first year was met with a lot of challenges. As a female convener,

Siobhan O'Regan

I was not exactly welcomed or respected in a male-dominated field. I had the fortune/misfortune (depending on your perspective) of working alongside a coach who, when I approached him on behalf of another coach due to player misconduct, told me point blank that unless I had his credentials as a coach, I had no business telling him how to do things in his field. He refused to work with me, and I was mortified. I toyed with the thought of resigning several times that year. Still, I decided with my junior house league director's support, who told me not to give up. Instead, I stepped it up and did exactly what he suggested. I got my coaching certifications and took a crash course in refereeing to learn the signals. I read every manual I could get my hand on and obtained my trainer's level 2 certification.

This helped my job tremendously as I often helped in the lower levels when there was a shortage of coaches and trainers and was able to fill in. Over the span of six years, I attended a multitude of broken bones from players to referees, accompanied parents to the hospital with their kids, supported one parent with the tools to get on the road to recovery from alcoholism, supported a couple of kids, and their families through the loss of a parent, and fundraised to support a family in financial crisis to allow their boys to continue playing after they lost their father to cancer. I had one team in Atom who couldn't win a single game. Their coach was worried about their confidence, so we conjured up a plan and told them I would make their coach do a pushup for every goal they scored until they won a game. They finally won their game but not before making their beloved coach do five pushups throughout four games.

In my entire time in the field, I had never seen a group of kids as motivated as they came together as a team. I can guarantee their winning was not their only objective that season. Solution-focused thinking and teamwork helped get these youngsters focused on what really mattered without even realizing it. Back when I started, we did everything old-school and built teams by hand without using a computer. I could skate but couldn't stop saving my life, so I threatened my parents if I was short on the coaching staff that I would be the one coaching these kids. Getting volunteers was never a problem after they had seen me slam into the boards a few times, but it usually only took once.

In the six years of being a convener, I had never received a single validated complaint. I had only been forced to write up two coaches. One reason was for being intoxicated while being behind the bench. The other was for using foul and offensive language to a player on his team. Unfortunately, there were many negatives to the job, and I became a bit of an expert in dealing with conflict, especially when it came to parents.

As a rule, it is rarely a good idea to exert authority. I found out that validating them always provided a higher satisfaction rate for me. I realized that modeling reasoning and compassion fostered more positive outcomes. Most often, all they want is to be heard. Sometimes you come across a passionate parent who was impossible to please no matter what you did. That's when I would send them up to my chain of command. I had never met a single board member outside of my work during the regular season. I attribute a great deal to being efficient in dealing with issues and getting to know my parents personally.

I was a sucker for the little kids. Jack and I dressed up one year at Halloween as Darth Vader and Princess Leia to give out candy to parents and kids in the stands. I'd seen one child who read Archie books in the hallway and would bring her a new one every week out of my collection. As much as I valued my books, I was never upset when I didn't get one back. I knew someone out there loved them as much as I did and was glad to share that with her.

Sure, there was always one issue or another. However, compared to other levels, we were still very fortunate to have excellent communication skills. With my credentials, I had the skill set to be hands-on.

In my last year's convening, before I tenured my resignation, several things played out. For years we had numerous complaints about one of the facilities our organization was renting ice from. The previous year, we brought forth our concerns to the Senior House League Director, which lead to a letter to the facility on behalf of the board. I followed it up and was told that the facility was following through in making some repairs. This caused us to lose ice time for two weeks.

The repairs, we were told, were done to the satisfaction of the board. The following year I heard more complaints from several trainers and coaches whose teams used the facilities for practice in both of my divisions (I was convening in both Peewee and co-convening in Bantam). Both Jack and I addressed our concerns verbally and in emails to our director but were dismissed. The coaches were told they could continue practicing. So, at the urging of our coaches, we went with several of them to document the issues by taking photos ourselves. Not only was the facility unsafe, but it was also a death trap. In the interest of safety for our children, Jack and I went straight to the city with our documentation containing several coaches' signatures. This resulted in the facility being closed to our organization's use. The facility was sold to new owners who renovated the entire facility before reopening it to the public. My son Kallan ended getting hired by this facility when he turned seventeen. This was under new ownership, and he loved his work environment. Jack and I went to several areas over the tri-city to see if we could get some ice time for our players and told the board that there was no money in the budget.

Their finance director sat in my living room and said that the real reason they had dismissed our primary concerns and didn't follow up by investigating the facility themselves (unofficially) was that they needed the cheap rent to cover the ice times. Our budget was almost nonexistent! For the rest of the season, our kids were deprived of their ice times. The time that their parents had paid for.

Over the years, I was asked to address coaches on behalf of the directors in charge. I wrote emails on their behalf and spent countless hours putting together, writing, researching, and creating training manuals. I put it all into binders for new volunteers to reference. They knew everything specific to their roles of coach, trainer, assistance coach, and convener for every level. When I started, there was no training, so everything was by trial and error. You were only as good as your mentor. The more I did with my director, the more he backed off, which suited us both fine. I learned the ropes by building a rapport with the coaches, refs, and parents.

The final straw for me was when they asked for co-convene and train Bantam's new convener. I had been asked to do it multiple times and had taught several new conveners. At one point, there was a massive controversy between a parent and a coach that lead to the parent taking matters into his own hands and threatening harm to the coach and two ice officials. He and his son were suspended for three games as a result. I was at the arena that day and deescalated the parent before he followed through on his threat. At the end of this suspension, my Senior House League Director and co-convener asked me to attend the game upon returning this player and his parent. Given I already had a rapport with this parent, I was glad to help. When I showed up to the game, my co-convener (Ward) told me that our president might show up to support us if we needed it. I asked him if he had ever met him, and he said no. I told him that I had never met him either. Ward and I discussed our roles and went our separate ways. Just before this game, a child went down on the ice seriously injured. We didn't know at the time, he had broken his leg and was waiting for an ambulance to take him off the ice.

Several grave errors were made when treating this child, so I was left in charge of dealing with the crisis and the ice delay while keeping an eye on everything else. Twenty minutes later, the referees and I decided to call the next game off. The ambulance had only just arrived and needed to do damage and crowd control. I was well within my authority to make the call. We told the parents the game was canceled, but those who wanted to practice were welcome to stick around, so those who wished to could leave. Long story short, one of the coaches complained to the president. He then overturned our decision afterward, and I released the players. The president, who I had never met, never communicated with, completely undermined our entire process, someone who had never worked frontline. He decided to overthrow his authority based primarily on the complaint of one coach who had a well-documented history of being a chronic complainer. So, I did as my position instructed me to do and approached my concerns via my command chain.

I officially quit after the vice president failed to support me in a manner where I felt heard or validated. I was unable to offer a solution or resolution to my inquiries. He had never once spoken to me in person. I finished out the season, but because of this and other similar incidences with parents fighting in the hallways, I spent the rest of the year enforcing a very strict - no parent clause - passed down to us by the board. I was asked to apply it with no support and spent valuable time babysitting the hallways as instructed.

There were much controversy and complaints by both parents and coaches who did not support this decision. When parents got angry, and they did, I directed their criticism to upper management. Their solution to defuse the situation was to point their fingers at our approach as conveners. I have long since moved on and am grateful for the experiences working in this field had taught me. I was eager to move forward. Volunteers often don't get the credit they deserve and are saints to do what they do and a high five to them. I had a great year to cool off before I decided to get involved again.

After some massive cuts that affected my son, I tried to offer up some solution-focused ideas, but it fell on deaf ears. I decided to take a proactive approach by reaching out to my local newspaper for support and found out that I wasn't the only one who was extremely unhappy with our organization. I have now taken a step back after the last board turnover.

During my second year convening, I came across an ad for K9 security guards. I can remember how excited I got and wanted the job so bad. It was likely the closest I would ever get to being a police officer, especially with my history. I walked in with a resume and was interviewed. I was hired on the spot. The training was a lot of fun, and I loved working with the dogs. I immediately developed a rapport with my dispatch team and often killed time, making them laugh with my sarcastic humor. I felt right at home. I had many assignments, from security to watching a hole in the ground. Even if there wasn't much to do, I always had company, so the most tedious jobs weren't bad. Most of my first shifts worked nights and weekends, so it wasn't unusual for me to come home after a shift and drink my usual before I went to bed. If I didn't have any alcohol, I would make Jack sneak some out of his dad's house after he went to work.

One morning Jack was in a mood and refused to go, and I was desperate, so I headed over myself. Papa was just getting up, and I heard him heading into the shower, so I slipped past the line of vision and bee-lined it downstairs to do my thing. When I came up, he was sitting on the stairs waiting for me. He asked me in a thick but calm accent why I was grabbing a beer in the morning. I looked down at my bag. I couldn't hide that distinctive clank as they tapped against one another. I started shifting weight from one foot to another, searching for an appropriate answer. The silence was deafening. I told him that I had just got off shift, and the beer store didn't open until ten. I flashed him one of my, 'did you buy it?' smiles. His face softened, and he told me straight out, "I think you may have a drinking problem." In a moment of utter shock and relief, I let out a big sigh tilted my head off to one side, and said, "You just figuring that out now?" I then spun around on one heel and high-tailed it out the front door. I was feeling very uneasy about what just happened, and I knew he wouldn't chase me. The cat was finally out of the bag.

Despite my drinking, I still had my strong work ethic, and it didn't take long for me to secure a full-time position for a well-renowned trucking company in Reardon. I became site supervisor in less than a month, which dispatchers told me was unheard of. My job description was unlimited, and I didn't mind one bit. I worked with the most fantastic group of truck drivers. Most of them were of East Indian descent, and there wasn't a day I didn't come onto shift. My desk was lined with coffee and baked goods from their families. They were in appreciation for, in their words, my kindness.

There was one truck driver, a chubby blond fellow, who fast-tracked my first experience dealing with sexual harassment. He got off by telling me what he would do to me if we were ever alone. He had an obvious thing for a woman in uniform. I was not the least bit threatened or intimidated by this guy. I knew I was safe. I was amused but wasn't going to allow him to think I condoned his filthy behavior and felt he needed some straightening out. We usually were not allowed to turn our dogs on without threats of physical harm. Still, in this case, I made the exception. I told him if he ever tried to act out on his impulses, I would sic my dog on him so fast he wouldn't be able to identify his male parts to be ready to sew it back together. I gave my dog the instruction to protect, which he did right on cue.

This particular company used the Doberons breed, which closely resembles Doberman's. The dogs looked just as scary when they were in attack mode. He got my hint loud and clear but still loved to test my boundaries by making his lude gestures from a distance. I would just ignore him. However, I did inform dispatch of my encounters with this guy but wanted to handle him personally and was given the okay to do so but still had it documented for future reference.

One of the company's higher-ups was a former police officer with one hell of a chip on his shoulders who didn't like anyone, least of all me. He never once spoke to me but yelled at me instead. A few times, I knocked him down a few pegs when I told him that I required him to talk to me in a humanized manner. I told him that I would forward a formal complaint if this continued. One time, he had a visitor come unannounced, and I was forced to make him wait while I called him since all visitors had to be preapproved as per his orders. He was not on my approval sheet. I didn't get an answer the first time, so I called back. He got on the phone and shouted, "Can't you see I'm busy?" and hung up. I relayed exactly what I was told but in a more professional manner. I informed the visitor that the office was swamped and he would contact him later. This visitor just happened to be a significant client and left very unhappy. Of course, I did not get reprimanded for this because I did exactly what my job instructed me to do. Regardless, this guy had one hell of hate on me. I'm positive that he even tried to run me over a couple of times when he had to wait for me to open the gate manually. Everyone I talked to had a few unfortunate run-ins with this guy and had many stories to back it up. I wasn't going to put up with him or anyone else's abuse.

I'd love to tell you we kissed and made up, but sadly he never grew to appreciate my excellent work skills. I was the first person to stand my ground and not get fired for it. Of course, I was also a subcontractor. I didn't work for the actual trucking company, so he didn't have much authority over my employment. I did come highly recommended. I loved the commute. I often drank until I went to bed after a long shift and woke up still buzzing. I often wondered if I was still drunk, but the six a.m. drive was often prolonged. A shot of vodka and a stiff coffee was usually enough to keep me alert. I always knew when it was quitting time. Things got worse when the shakes got worse, and my craving for a drink became more than a thought. I bordered on obsession. On a Friday night, the commute home was always the worse, and it often took close to three hours to get home. It was a weekend, which made it less painful, and I knew I didn't have to get up the next morning.

I knew that Jack and his dad were slowly closing in on me about my drinking. My days were numbered, and I knew the only reason I got away with it was that I concealed my drinking for the most part. I pretended my life was manageable. There were so many signs and indicators, and Jack did not disclose my addiction to anyone. This included his father. Jack was a true classic enabler. He didn't tell him that I was drinking so much and attending AA on and off for years. He always cleaned up after me with one excuse or another. I had gotten so wrapped up in my work and with drinking that I was completely neglecting my family and especially my kids. I had left their care to their dad, who hated that he was becoming a single father, and his work was strongly affected negatively.

When another job opportunity opened up that offered me more flexible hours and more pay, I took it. Another trucking company had used our lot to store a couple of its tracks. Somehow the company lost one, so; I calmly explained the situation to them on the phone. When my relief arrived at the end of my shift, I searched the entire lot and eventually found their truck. They were looking for someone to run their company from home and book routine freights. They offered me the position claiming they were impressed by how I handled their concerns over the phone. They asked to meet with me in person to discuss the details.

The office was based out of their home. They had six trucks, and it was a family-owned business. There were three brothers, and most of my job entailed doing the bookkeeping, making sure I kept a handle on their coming and goings. They taught me how to make bids on the computer and to confirm loads. It was easy enough, I thought, but they wanted me to start as soon as possible. I placed a call into my dispatch and told them I was leaving active immediately.

They were shocked and disappointed and asked for their two weeks' notice. I felt awful for leaving them the way that I did, but I thought it was the right move at the time. I loved my job, but there were a few things that we disagreed on, the gas being one of them. This company provided gas if you worked a certain number of kilometers away from where the company was located. My job site fit just within the parameter, so I didn't qualify. Gas at that distance on minimum wage ate a good portion of my paycheck, so I justified my leaving on short notice by taking care of my own needs. I acted just like how the company took care of theirs. I didn't last more than two weeks on the other job. It was the same distance as the trucking company. Still, I almost got into a significant accident on my commute to work one morning and ran off the road. As luck would have it, this was by a truck, and so I got spooked. I called them and told them I would not be coming anymore.

CHAPTER TWENTY

One Step At A Time

Over the next few months, I sank into another one of my deep depressions. I started drinking so heavily that I was experiencing a blackout almost every night. One night Jack told me that I was standing in the kitchen, and with no warning, I let out a huge grunt. He said; my eyes rolled to the back of my head, and he caught me just as I was about to hit the floor. I started seizing, and it only lasted a few minutes. He thought I might have taken something and ripped our house apart in the desperate search for a clue but found nothing.

Our doctor told us that he suspected it was an alcohol-induced seizure. He also said that my liver was so enlarged that I would die in less than two years if something didn't change drastically. Over the last couple of years or so, I had gone to see my doctor. I made trips to the hospital several times for drinking-related incidences. They were all aware that I was an alcoholic.

Jack had thought about doing an intervention, but there wasn't anyone on my side of the family who would bother to show up. Reaching out to his family for help was not something he knew how to do. For years he suffered in silence. The day Jack approached me about my drinking was a pivotal moment for me towards my recovery. I knew it was coming and would be a moment I will never forget.

We fought for years about my alcoholism, and each of us made our fair share of empty threats. We both knew deep down that we depended on each other, but everyone had their breaking points, and I think he had finally reached his. He sat me down, looked me in the eye, and told me that things would be different if they were just us. He then reminded me about several previous discussions we had where we agreed to put the kids first. He told me that he will always love me no matter what, but he had to do what was best for them. This meant either I changed, or he would have to leave and take the boys with him. My heart broke, but I knew what he was saying was right, and for the first time in my life, I didn't argue with him. Tears began streaming down my face. I hung my head down and quietly whispered, "Okay." As we both wept, I began to feel fear.

We searched for rehabilitation centers together and found one in Activia, just down the street from the hospital. My doctor didn't hesitate and was more than happy to fill out the appropriate paperwork. I was called less than three weeks later and was told that they had a bed available. They were willing to take me in right away. The only drawback was that Christmas was just around the corner. I couldn't bear the thought of being away from our boys over the holidays, but I knew it was what I needed to do.

Our medical insurance paid most of the semi-private room cost, but my father-in-law spent the rest. The place had a hospital setting with a cafeteria and a strict schedule of groups and counseling. It reminded me of the time I spent in the Vance wing when I tried to commit suicide back when I was seventeen. I was terrified when I walked in and spent the first twenty-four hours in my room but had to come out to have my vitals checked every thirty or so minutes. I was also given medication to help with my withdrawal. I was allowed to use the payphone in my free time, so I called Jack several times that day and cried while he tried to assure me I would be okay.

I met my psychiatrist on the second day. He spent the first half an hour explaining why I was there and why I would not be able to quit drinking on my own. He discussed what alcohol was doing to my mind and body. I did not choose to be an alcoholic, and that my genetic makeup was predisposed. No matter what I did, I would never be able to drink again safely.

He seemed kind enough, but if only he knew what I had gone through and how deeply rooted my issues were. That night I sat in my room thinking about how cold and sterile my room felt. My roommate was snoring loudly, and that was triggering me. My body was seething with rage, and I wanted to smother her to get her to stop. Since she was twice my size, I figured she was likely going to overpower me and lay one hell of a beat down. I decided to put in headphones and popped a movie into my DVD player instead.

Nobody Special

The next day I still had the shakes and was extremely irritable. My body was so sensitive that even sitting down was unbearable. I was told that this was a normal part of the withdrawal process, and it would eventually taper off. They said the meds would help, and I was medically cleared to attend therapy and group sessions. I didn't sleep very well and tossed and turned all night. I was tired and exhausted, and everything around me seemed to be setting me off. It took every ounce of fight I had to stay calm and in the moment.

The group was raw, vulnerable, and left you feeling completely exposed. I felt picked on and that everyone's attention was on me. It brought me back to how it felt when people were continually whispering and talking about me. When confronted with a new situation, I tend to take a step back and observe my survival mode surroundings. I assess the dangers before I embark on them. Back at the institution, kids had a way of taking your secrets and then used them against you. This was when it benefited them, and now I was being told to expose my darkest moments and express my feelings. It was more than unnatural, and I couldn't wrap my head around it.

There were things I hadn't even told my husband. Yet, I was expected to jump in with both feet and trust the process. The following morning was even worse. There was one councilor there. I think his name was Dan, he kept accusing me of not opening up, so I completely withdrew and shut down. My anxiety levels went off the charts. My mind was racing a million miles a minute, and I couldn't hold one rational thought.

I understood that I had signed up for thirty days of voluntary treatment, and he was stripping me in front of everyone. He told me that my stay would be significantly longer if I didn't get involved. Rather than fight back, I shut down completely. Later that morning, during a smoke break, one of the guys in my group pulled up in a stretch limo equipped with several cases of beer and offered anyone who wanted a drink to come for a ride. If it weren't that I had a family depending on me, I would have jumped in with the half-dozen or others, but I chose to ride out the rest of my sentence instead.

I was present in my classes for the rest of the day, but I was not in the mood to participate in the activities. I was forced to leave one group when I didn't recite the serenity prayer. I was told if I could not make an effort, then I needed to leave. I called up Jack right away and begged him to pick me up. I tried to tell him what was going on between sobs, but all he understood was defeat and utter desperation. He agreed to talk to me. I was gathering my things when he arrived. My counselor asked to join him with another gentleman in a small office in the hospital's underbelly.

One look at me had Jack concerned, and he could tell I had been crying a lot. I looked like I hadn't slept at all. I tried to talk, but I was quivering between sobs. Jack relayed to the councilor some of what I told him on the phone. He responded by sitting back, grinning with arrogance through every accusation. I could feel him staring at me even though my head had remained down. Almost as if on cue, he just like that started attacking me until his supervisor stepped in and told him to take a step back. He even started in on Jack when he chimed in. The councilor got up into Jacks's face forcing him to stand just to equal with him. I started crying even harder. Jack told me to gather my things and said if this was a display of how I was being treated, he was taking me home. He called his father immediately and told him what had happened. His dad agreed that it was the right thing to do.

I was glad to be home and agreed to work on staying sober but was back at it later that night and every night after that. I tried to subdue Jack by attending AA meetings during the day whenever I could. One lady there told me about a rehab center called Serenity. She explained that's where she got sober and told me to let them know she referred me.

I went home and called them right away. Within two weeks, I was interviewed and told that I would likely get into the next cycle the following month. They instructed me to attend 5 AA meetings a week and to abstain from alcohol three days before entering their program. I was also informed that I couldn't bring any of my prescriptions with me because it wasn't a treatment program. I had to wean myself off of my anti-depressants before I entered their program.

I got a call a week later that I was approved for their program and that I would be entering cycle one hundred seventy-six on Jan 30th, 2006. Unfortunately, no matter what I did or how hard I tried, I couldn't abstain from alcohol. I called them up three days before the treatment and told them that I couldn't do it. They told me to join the closest detox, but there was no way I could voluntarily bring myself to do that. This was due to my debilitating fears of sleeping in strange places. I told them that I did everything else they asked. They told me there was no room for compromise and warned me that I would have to wait until the next cycle if I couldn't abstain. The following day the director called me back after speaking to my doctor and told me that I didn't drink the day I was registered to enter the program. They would allow me to begin the treatment.

Saying goodbye to my kids was worse the second time around, and Kian gave me his most prized possession, the stuffed Simba doll we had given him for Christmas when he was two. This toy was with him through every surgery, procedure, and hospital visit. He cried for three days straight when he lost him at a sick children's hospital in Dwyer until we found him the replica on eBay.

I had not yet accepted that I was doing any of this for myself. I was doing it all for them. As soon as they left, I instantly felt alone and miserable. The girls all seemed kind enough, but I was only invested in doing my twenty-four days and had no interest in connecting with any of them. I immediately threw up my walls. It took some severe adjustment the first few days, but it wasn't so bad once I got into a routine. It was a house out on some wooded property, so it didn't have that traditional hospital feel. The staff seemed friendly enough, but they could be overly strict on things that I felt were over the top. Things like keeping your feet flat on the ground during check-in could last up to an hour. It was extremely uncomfortable and unnatural for me.

We were on a septic system, so we could only have scheduled showers and take turns doing laundry on certain days. One thing I could not bring myself to do was to eat the food. It was nutritionally balanced, but they served many foods like pork chops and deli meats with fat and bone. They had a lot of hamburger-based meals too. There was rye and pumpernickel bread that I could not stomach the smell, let alone eat, so I only ate white or whole wheat bread when they served it.

I seldom ate bread with butter or margarine and usually put mayonnaise on it from back in my food bank days, but they wouldn't allow me to have it if it was not served with the meal. I had to eat my bread dry instead. I ate many salads and lost close to seventeen pounds during the twenty-four days I was there. The only thing I looked forward to was my phone calls and letters from home.

Jack wrote to me every single day and told me how he and the boys were doing. He let me know about their routines. I didn't receive them every day, but he would write to them and send a few at a time. I looked forward to my one phone call since we were only allowed a ten-minute call per week. The first was listening to my boy's cry about his bearded dragon, who passed away earlier that morning.

Siobhan O'Regan

The second week I was behind in my chore and was forced to miss the first five minutes. I had a meltdown when they cut me off from talking to my boys. I threatened to leave the program if they didn't let me call them back. They reluctantly did, and I was okay with the rules, but they had to be fair for me to respect them.

I pretty much kept to myself the entire time I was there. I tried to get along with the other girls, but I hadn't much in common with any of them. My roommate was very eccentric, and communication was usually hit or miss with her so, I kept everything on an acquaintance level. Some of the girls tried to take their drama out on me or drag me into it. As much as I'd like to say I was innocent, I made some mistakes and apologized for my part as well.

The therapy was done in groups, and most of the material was relatively easy to comprehend. I found groups to be especially tricky. I often wanted to walk out on them when the subjects became overwhelming, but I managed to stick them out for the most part. One activity involved us unwrapping a gift several times over and had instructions like give this gift to someone who makes you laugh.

I was upset when I didn't receive that one and was devastated when each girl unwrapped it several times, and I didn't receive it even once. Of course, I pretended that it was not a big deal, thinking I should be used to it by now. At the time, the director felt sorry for me and gave me a diary as a consolation prize.

The next few groups were centered on how I was unapproachable and how I couldn't let anyone in. No one could get close to me. My sarcasm was just one of the many masks that I hid behind. I was so fed up. All I could think of was how horrible and worthless I was. I became overwhelmed by the constant insults and putdowns. I didn't see anything constructive about being ganged up on all the time. I got up and announced to the group that I was officially leaving the program once and for all. I was in such a dark place. My only thoughts were to go and find a quiet place to be by myself. I wanted to end my mystery once and for all.

Nobody Special

One of the councilors and the director followed me into my room and tried to convince me to stay. That is when I broke down crying so hard I collapsed to the ground. I had no more fight left in me and nowhere left to turn.

I understood if I left, there was only one alternative for me, and that meant death. I backed off of them when they tried to console me, and I must have blurted out what my intentions were. They now seemed alarmed, and I didn't like or want the attention. I wished I could take it all back. I just wanted to be left alone.

After many crying and threats that involved taking me to the hospital, they broke me down. For the first time, I finally disclosed the big ugly secret that I had been carrying all these years. Afterward, all I wanted to do was to end my torment. I didn't want my kids to suffer, but I had finally had it.

In a moment of weakness, I finally found the courage to tell someone what happened to me all those years. Knowing what I did, I didn't think I could face my husband and kids again. I wasn't thinking about whom I was going to hurt in the process. The room was in dead silence, and Sue turned to me, huddled up in a corner. She told me it was no wonder I was so closed off and guarded, but I would have to face my demons, or I would never start the healing process or move on.

For the first time, they broke the rules and had Jack come up as soon as I was ready to face him. They offered to be there for support. In all the years, other than death, I never had to face anything so scary in my entire life. I was so terrified he would up and leave me. I was going to be completely and utterly exposed, vulnerable, and alone. I wasn't sure what they told him to get him up there, but when I walked into the room, I could see the concern written all over his face and wanted to disappear when he tried to hug me.

We sat down, and Sue told him just to sit back and listen. She asked him not to say anything or touch me until I was done. I couldn't look at him and didn't want to see the disgust on his face. It took me a long while to spit it out, but I told him everything. I disclosed the extent of my abuse, my rape, and the most difficult of all, the fact that I had a relationship with my rapist. I let him know that my rape didn't just happen once but twice. I explained the suicide attempt after discovering I was pregnant and the abortion, not knowing who the child's father was. I knew I had told him bits and pieces during our conversations over the years, but most of the details had been kept to myself. I was crying inconsolably and curled up as if to protect myself. I waited in agonizing silence as he tried to process everything. I heard him take a deep breath; he placed his hands on my arm and whispered, "Okay."

There was another long pause. He lifted my chin for our eyes to meet, but I couldn't look at him, so he tilted his head to mine and said, "Where do we go from here? I am here for you, and I'm not going anywhere." I buried myself in his chest. Everyone was pleased with the outcome and gave us some privacy to be alone for a few minutes. I allowed him to hold me while I sobbed uncontrollably but, all I wanted was to crawl into a dark hole and die. Afterward, I took him to my room. We joked about having conjugal visits even though he assured me everything was going to be okay. I felt very unsure and extremely unsafe.

Jack came up with the boys the following weekend and brought my father-in-law with him. It was just before Valentine's Day, and Papa gave me a gold locket. He told me how proud he was of me. It was the first gift I had ever received from anyone just because they were proud of me.

He and Jack were asked to do a group session to give them some perspective on what life would be like for me and what to expect when returning home. I sat with my boys and just held them while they talked. I missed them so much. Their leaving was again agonizing. I wanted to go with them so badly, but I understood I had to stay to have a fighting chance of staying sober.

In the next two weeks, I focused a lot more of my energy on getting better and retaining as much information as I could to better my chances of success. I managed to get a little bit closer to the girls but stuck true to my nature and kept them at arm's length. We had one outing in the community for the afternoon and went to get pedicures. I hated it and didn't like anyone touching my feet. They were so sensitive I had to get her to stop before she even started.

Overall, we had a good time; none of us drank and kept each other in check.

We attended several AA meetings on and off property, but I still couldn't get a feel for the whole God thing. I didn't have a clue what I believed in. I knew I believed in something greater than myself, but I did not believe in the bible, and we were told to pray to the God of our understanding. I felt conflicted. Then I realized I was getting caught up in the word all these years and decided to attach another meaning. I changed the name to karma since I was brought up to believe God to be biblical. It was all I understood the word would mean. I was out on one of my daily walks when I came across my favorite tree. Everywhere I go, I always pick a favorite tree. I would usually select a weeping willow. It was my way of creating a space just for me. I would go up and hug it. It wasn't soft, moldable, or hugged me back, but it was something outside of myself that I did not create. I didn't manipulate or control it, and right then, mother nature became my higher power.

As I started becoming healthier, I was evolving too. I have become more spiritual in my thinking. I would take bits and pieces from every culture that made sense to me and incorporate them into my belief system. Putting it simply, I believed energy attracts energy. Being the change I wish to see globally, I began treating every little thing with respect. I tried not to impose my thoughts and ideas out onto others and to lead by example. I am the first to admit; I was not perfect, but I tried, and I threw my heart and soul into everything I did. Ultimately, I strived to be the best person I could be and continued to be humble because no matter how much I knew, there was still so much I was unaware of.

We were allowed a twenty-four-hour reprieve on my last weekend, where we could go home and spend time with our families. They spent a good couple of days preparing ourselves for some of the challenges we would face in the real world. I went home, spent time with my kids, and had a hot bubble bath. I just curled up with my husband. This was something we hadn't done in a very long time.

Going back was hard, but I needed to appreciate how much I wanted to be home and gain perspective on leaving permanently. If I ever decided to drink again, Jack and I both agreed. I would be sacrificing my place in my family and would go willingly until I got some help. That was motivation enough for me. My drinking days were behind me, but I had many challenges and obstacles to face over the next few years. Each one tested my strength and loyalty to staying clean and sober.

Upon leaving, we were instructed to attend sixty meetings in sixty days. At first, I wasn't thrilled with the idea and thought about what kind of life I would have? My counselor challenged my thinking and asked me what kind of life would I have if I chose to drink instead?

Siobhan O'Regan

I stayed connected with some of those girls for a while but eventually lost touch. We were offered two years of aftercare, but I had no reason to keep coming back. Jack handed me an envelope the night he dropped me off back at the rehab. He instructed me not to open it until the morning I was to come home. It read, "Hi, honey. If you have followed my instructions on the envelope, then it's Friday 8:15 am, which means: See you in two hours." I will admit that I am the luckiest woman alive, but I know all too well when you shut yourself off to keep the bad stuff out; you also shut the good things out.

We went to dad's place to get the boys. They were finishing up lunch, and Léo was there. I was distraught to see there was wine on the table. Léo tried to take it out of sight right away, but his apology afterward fell on deaf ears. I remember thinking how typical for him to greet me in his selfish Léo manner. This sparked a long-standing resentment towards him that was fueled over the years by his ignorance.

Perspective was the most amazing gift I received on my road to recovery. I attended every one of those sixty meetings and more. I sat across from a lady who changed how I'd seen the world in a few short sentences. She went on to say that her husband had been sick. The house wasn't selling, and things weren't going well at work. Then she paused. She looked up as if to look at me and said, well, at least my husband will get better. I have a house to sell and a job where I work with good people. Her words hit home when I so desperately needed to make sense of some of the things in my life. Now I had something to lead me in the right direction.

The first thing they tell you to do is find a sponsor. It had to be one of the same sex, preferably, only I usually don't mesh well with women and found it impossible to relate on any level. I sucked it up and approached a couple of them in the spirit of doing what has worked. They had lots to offer the right individual, but neither one had the support I needed. The only thing we had in common was that we were alcoholics, and we were women.

I spent more time listening to their issues than I did addressing mine, so I started looking at more senior members to mentor me. There was one individual I talked to a couple of times, but she wasn't the right fit either. I needed someone more like me. I needed someone who had a fun spirit and could build me up and draw me in. I found such a person in a 70-year-old man named Ed.

Nobody Special

Typically, the group frowned upon anyone sponsoring someone from the opposite sex. They called it the 13th step, but I figured that we were pretty safe given our age difference and direction in life. He was such an incredible man. He really knew his program, understood exactly how far to push me, and didn't put up with my crap. The funny thing was I didn't really like him and thought he talked too much, but somehow, I respected him.

Once when we were sitting in a meeting, a man staggered in and sat down beside me. The smell of body odor, stale cigarettes, and cheap beer made me gag. We were already listening to a guy speak who had already gone way past his time. I could feel my anxiety accelerate. I got fed up, and so I stood up and walked out. Ed was hot in pursuit. He caught up with me as I quickly approached my van, and he demanded to know why I was in such a hurry. I wasn't in the mood to explain myself, but I knew better than to ignore him. I blurted out that I didn't come to sit next to some drunk, and I was tired of listening to the same old-timer talks the same shit over and over again. I felt other people had more important things to say. "I see," he said, and then he sat down on my back bumper. I became instantly annoyed, knowing that meant I was in for one of his long, drawn-out speeches.

"Did you ever actually listen to what that man has to say?" he asked. Ed went on to tell me how surprised I would be over how much knowledge, strength, and insight he had. All I had to do was just open myself and listen to what he had to say rather than judge him and everyone around me. Ed went on to say that's why God gave me two ears and only one mouth. I could listen twice as much as I spoke. He had a way of putting things into context, but I was angry at his last statement and thought he came across harshly. He then went on to tell me a story of a young woman whose eyes told the world how hard she had it without ever speaking a word. She was in so much pain and lived as if she was utterly alone, yet; she had a companion who loved and adored her. Everyone could see she was unreachable. Ed recited how gentle and kind she was to anyone who needed her but never learned how to ask for help. She didn't know how to let people trust them. Ed then continued the only way she could cope with all her fears was to numb the person within, and the only way she could confront herself was when she came to meetings drunk. He told me she sat next to him several times throughout the years and sobbed silently to herself. Ed wanted to hold her and let her know that she was going to be okay. Ed saw strength in her that he recognized through his own years of sobriety. It took a few moments to realize that he was talking about me, and I shut down.

Siobhan O'Regan

He didn't need to know about my history to know how much I was hurting and understood me on a level that no one else did. That type of intimacy scared me and was why I put a lot of distance between the two of us. I think he understood on an individual level and was always there when I needed him. Ed set me up for my fourth step inventory just before he died. I had asked one other person to sponsor me, but we never stayed connected. No one tolerated me as Ed did.

The first year was the toughest for me. I was twenty-nine when I sobered up right before my thirtieth birthday and spent my entire birthday locked in my bedroom. I had given up on birthdays a long time ago, and celebrated special occasions was not another one of Jacks' strong suits. I was content to get drunk just to spend the day alone. Only this was the first time in sixteen years, and I wouldn't be able to get drunk (minus the year and a half I was pregnant with Kallan and Kian). I found I was getting way too caught up in the AA big book's wording and found it coming from a male-oriented perspective. I was given a copy of the NA big book. I loved it as it was written in a language I understood and could relate to. I even attended a few of their meetings.

I found I was much more at home with NA meetings but struggled to fit into the younger group. They all seemed like a tight net community, and I was still such an outsider. I couldn't warm up to the idea of needing people for support. One of my favorite places I used to go frequently before I got sober was the wine stores in my local supermarket. This was because it was close to my home. It was convenient and was a place that knew me well.

I had gotten to know the employees quite a bit over the years, chatting each other up. After walking by and waving several times, I decided to go in. I made my first disclosure. I told my favorite wine lady about my disease and my decision to get sober. She appeared genuinely happy for me but looked confused for a minute, then burst out laughing, stating, "Good God girl, all these years we thought your husband was the one with the drinking problem."

As it turns out, I went to several places to duck suspicion, but Jack was going to the same store, day after day. He would go once, sometimes twice a night, over several years. Ed was there to help me celebrate my one-year birthday, as they call it. They gave me a medallion that had my boys' names and my two nieces engraved on it. This was to remind me of why I sobered up in the first place.

Nobody Special

Jack was there with our two boys. Papa brought Léonia, and my mother showed up with Bruce. It was by far the most precious metal I had ever received, and it meant everything I had gone through getting it. I ended up giving it to a fellow member who told me how close he had arrived, but he couldn't quite make it to one year. I gave him my medallion in the spirit of fellowship and told him to hold on to it and to give it back to me when he got one of his own. I still haven't received it again, but I am hopeful that someday I will. Until then, Jack bought me a ring that I wear over my thumb as a daily reminder of my accomplishments, and I never take it off.

Over the years, I have heard many slogans that were meant to motivate and inspire. Still, one that will forever stand out in my mind is when a fellow member stood up to speak on my birthday and said that he would always have another drunk in him but, he wasn't sure if he had another sober. Meaning, it would be easy for him to slip up and drink, but he wasn't sure he'd have the strength to make it back into recovery again. I completely understood what he meant and couldn't help but think that if I ever relapsed, I likely wouldn't be able to sober up again. I just fully understood how much work it took to get where I am now.

It is admirable to know how long it has been since your last drink; what's even more important is knowing how close you are to your next one. These two slogans and, of course, the serenity prayer is what have kept me in line. In my late thirties, just before my 40th birthday, I tattooed the serenity prayer to the left side of my torso. I love it, and it stands as a reminder of how far I've come.

Kallan and Kian were seven and five when I sobered up and, I have met with a great deal of criticism involving them as much as I have in the process. My critics believed that it would negatively influence them. Still, I feel the process has done just the opposite and brought everyone closer together. It helped them have a better understanding of who their mother is and where I have come from. Kallan loved going to the open meetings and was disappointed when he couldn't attend the closed ones. He appeared to understand why when I explained the difference between a public and a private meeting. Except for one day, Jack mentioned he was heading to a business meeting when Kallan asked excitedly, "Is it an open meeting or a closed meeting, Daddy?" My kids were forever making me laugh.

Siobhan O'Regan

In the first year of sobriety, they say to get a plant; if it lives past a year, then get a pet. I loved gardening, but I wanted to keep busy, so I bought a Golden Retriever. I named her Kové (ko-vay). It was a name I thought up to when I was a kid. This dog and I became inseparable, and I spent every waking moment with her. We became best friends. She was a bit excitable but a fantastic companion. I lost Jessie shortly after Kallan was born. She didn't adjust well to having a baby around and soiled all of his belongings. She pooped in his room, and we spent hundreds of dollars on vet bills trying several different treatments to get her to stop. In the end, I had to choose my son over my beloved companion and was forced to give her away. I wailed inconsolably when they came to take her away and felt like I had lost my one and only friend. To a person with attachment disorder, it was a pain that stung for years to come. Nothing ever replaced the love I had for my cat, but this dog had an extraordinary place in my heart.

We had been hanging out with my cousin Robyn and her husband James for quite a while before I went to rehab. In the days leading up to my treatment, we mostly sat around, played cards, and got drunk together. She introduced me to the casino. Her life began spiraling out of control, and she attacked her husband with a knife and kicked him out of the house. With nowhere to stay, he came and stayed with us for a while.

One thing that always intrigued me about their relationship was that he loved her no matter how toxic and dysfunctional they were together. The more she mistreated him, the more he seemed drawn to her. The entire time he stayed with us, he was absolutely miserable and pined away for her. He even took her back after she had an affair and got pregnant.

I had some significant concerns about the well-being of their daughter. Jack and I had witnessed her being mistreated. She was getting smacked around multiple times at the hands of both her parents. We had gotten to know a different side of James over the years. He unnecessarily once stoned a baby skunk to death in front of my boys when we were out fishing.

He had a brother who was in a long-term relationship and had two kids together. He had a weakness for the ladies and was always running around on his girlfriend. He had recently been in a fatal car accident and was the driver in a head-on collision. His passenger was a young minor with who he was sleeping with. He had just found out that she was pregnant with his child. She died from the impact and was declared dead at the hospital. He had some internal bleeding, but his injuries were minor compared, and he would make a full recovery.

Both the boys came from a broken home, and when he married my cousin, he took her last name. He wrote off his past along with the rest of his family except his brother. There are so many things that I can look back at now and question, but I was too invested in keeping the peace. Jack and I sat down and had a long talk with my aunt and uncle about our concerns. Our conversations lead to when I was a child. Both of them, to my utter shock, were very open and forthright about Kristine and Dean. They validated just about everything I had told Jack up to that point about my abuse. All these years, I lived with the burden of what my family had done to my sister and me, and now, I finally had someone to back me up. Of course, they weren't as forthcoming about their involvement in abusing their own kids.

Jack asked them the question that plagued me for years, and I wanted to know why they sat back and did nothing. I always figured it was because of Karen's mental health issues and that Randy was hitting his own kids. They told us it was because Dean was crazy, and they were too afraid of him to get involved. I wanted to scream at them, interrogate them, and question why they went along with pretending we were switched at birth. Why did they beat their children too? Why didn't they take me in when I desperately needed them the most? Why had they been so terrible and unlovable towards me? We left shortly after, and I cried all the way home.

The last time we were over at his house, James went off on his daughter and pinned her up against the wall by her throat. Her feet were dangling off the ground when she gave him an attitude. I decided that I understood would destroy any relationship I had with my cousin and called Child Services. It was one of the hardest decisions I had ever made. Still, I wasn't going to allow the cycle of abuse to continue any longer. Robyn completely cut everyone out of her life for good after being investigated, but nothing ever came of it. She gave birth to a son, and the last I heard, they were still living with both her parents on the farm just outside of the city where we live.

I ran into my cousin Randy Junior a few years later in Martin Beach. It was like looking in the dead eyes of a stranger. He had fathered multiple children, all by different women, and I could tell he lived a hard life. I smiled at the little boy in the front seat of his pick-up truck. He was the spitting image of his father and told Junior to take good care of him. I hugged him and told him I loved him, but I had no clue who that man was. I only remember him as a child. I understand at some point that he had to take responsibility for his own choices, but I was there and witnessed first-hand how they were raised. I couldn't help him at that moment and felt nothing but guilt that I was able to fight so hard to rise above everything we went through. I'd seen how my cousins and even my sister had turned out. It just didn't seem fair.

Stephanie and I never recovered our relationship. She was there through the end of my pregnancy and stuck around for a couple of months after the boys were born. Stephanie never really had anything to do with them after that. She always told me that I was overbearing, unfeeling, controlling, and all I ever did was boss her around. To me, she was unapproachable, insecure, jealous, and always resented me for having abandoned her. I don't blame her. I can't imagine how badly she must be hurting. She eventually met a guy she married. I was not invited to the wedding due to a falling out with my mother. She had agreed to finance their wedding event so long as they followed her rules.

My understanding was Kristine revoked all support if she invited me to the wedding. Her fiancé was a single father of two, a boy and a girl. Knowing how badly Stephanie wanted to have a family, he did not disclose that he had gotten fixed after his second child. He waited until almost a year after they were married. He seemed like a nice enough guy, but like my sister, he came with a lot of baggage, and even though I was her kin, she made it clear that she didn't trust anyone around him. It was to the point where even I couldn't be alone with him, ever.

When they met, she was independent and working. She had just gotten her license, bought her car, and had a place of her own. Anyone who got close to her understood immediately how deeply seeded and insecure she was. Yet, when things got tough, her husband bailed on her leaving for weeks at a time. He left no clue as to where he was or where he had been. Like my mother, this pattern of abandonment just about destroyed her. She later told me that he had a significant drug issue. She spent all of her energy trying to get him clean and sober but eventually gave in to the lifestyle. She was not a stranger to abusing drugs and experimented a lot as a teenager through the crowds she hung out with.

She called me several times when he bailed on her, and I tried to help her pick up the pieces. He always came back, and no one was allowed to judge or criticize him. Like a classic enabler, she made excuses for his behavior. I was very protective of my sister. I was also very opinionated and authoritative around her after raising her all those years. I have always been very domineering when addressing her. I had run into her a few times and offered advice when I found out how they had been struggling with the kids. Being a stepmom took a toll on her. I even offered to take the kids for a night if they needed a break, but she would not allow me to get involved. She always shut me out completely.

I recently found out that she has completely given up her license. She had left her position at the company she worked at after twelve years to spend more time with her husband. When I called to make sure she was okay, I couldn't get ahold of her and was forced to file a missing person's report until she finally got in touch with me. She and I talked about reuniting, but she called and backed out at the last minute, stating she was not ready and needed time to figure things out. When I questioned her about her license, she told me that she suffered severe bouts of anxiety and was too nervous about driving.

I told her about my diagnosis of attachment disorder, bipolar, and complex PTSD. I told her to find someone to assess her and get some help knowing full well that she was likely to suffer from these disorders. Stephanie has been on her own most of her life, and although I have tried to keep in contact with her, our psychosis would prevent us from ever connecting. I reunited with my childhood friend Chloe through Facebook in 2010 and found out that she worked in the same building as my sister. Although they never spoke to one another, I was able to keep tabs on her until she left her job. Kristine accused her of stealing money from her after she visited her a few years ago. An accusation Stephanie emphatically denied and stopped talking to her mother, cutting her out of her life completely. Something I wish I dared to do a long time ago. Everyone, including Kristine, knows Bruce likely took the money. Still, for reasons only our mother knows, she decided to use this event to abandon her youngest daughter, further reinforcing her abandonment issues.

My brother was struggling as well. He had separated from his wife and took custody of his son Sean. He was living in our sisters' basement. I found out that Beth did an intervention on him and called Child Services when the family felt our nephew was in danger. Sean was placed with my sister as a kin placement. I shuttled Lorcan and my sister-in-law back and forth from one city to the other to attend meetings and court proceedings.

The plan was for Lorcan to sign over custody of Sean to his mother, Demi, until he got the help he needed. There was some apparent bad blood between Demi and my sister Beth, but I was nothing more than the middleman. I had no involvement outside of supporting our brother. Still, my sister saw this as an act of treason and had Leroy call me to make sure I couldn't plan on trying to come with Lorcan and take custody of Sean.

I remember getting off the phone and wondering if there was ever any hope of repairing our relationship. We seriously needed to work out some of our trust issues. Lorcan was scheduled to show up for a meeting with the family worker at the agency in town, so I picked him up and went together. I could immediately smell the alcohol on the worker's breath, and so did Lorcan, who reeked of it himself. The worker tore right into Lorcan, criticizing him for smelling in her words "like a brewery." He struck back at her how ironic she was calling him out yet; she smelled like a winery herself. The two of them went at each other like wild animals. The worker told him that she wasn't the one with the drinking problem, and she was entitled to have a glass or two of wine in the evening on her own time. The worker ended the conversation by telling him that no visitations would be in his sons' best interest. Lorcan would have to undergo random drug testing. She advised him to get some help and shape up before their next meeting.

I bit my tongue and let him fight his own battle, even though I thought the worker was extremely unprofessional. She reeked of alcohol while attending a meeting with an alcoholic client. Regardless of the outcome, two things were inevitable. I could guarantee you she had more than a glass or two of wine the night before. Looking at my brother, as much as I felt for him, I couldn't disagree with her about having open access to his son, especially in his condition. Although I don't always see eye to eye with my sister, I admired her for putting our nephew first. She knew how much it would hurt Lorcan and their relationship. Placing our nephew's needs ahead of her own was the first time I really respected her.

On the way back from court, it started to snow one afternoon, and we spun out on the road. I had my father-in-law's car and was scolding Kian for playing with the windows for the umpteenth time. I was just before my exit when we hit a black ice patch and spun out into the ditch. Just before we started spinning, he pushed the power window down, and the momentum forced snow and grass into the window. When we came to a complete stop, I immediately turned to check to see if he okay and saw he was completely covered in grass and snow from head to toe. I yelled at Lorcan to make sure he was all right, trying to reach for him under my seatbelt restraint. Just then, Kian started clapping his hands and shrieked with joy the words "Again, again!" He was utterly oblivious to what had just happened. He was quite content to do it again.

This was my first accident. After I was assured Kian was safe, I lost it and called Jack right away. He showed up twenty minutes after the OPP arrived and witnessed my officer's witty sense of humor. The officer asked me if it was my car, and I told him, "No, sir, it was my father-in-law's car." He started to laugh. I wasn't as amused and demanded to know what was so funny. He blurted out, "I guess we'll see what kind of a relationship you have with your father-in-law now, won't we?" He kept chuckling to himself.

As it turned out, I wasn't going to be charged for the accident because the tires on Papa's car were bald, and it's what caused the skid. Papa wasn't mad at all and felt terrible for the accident. He took most of the responsibility and didn't let me pay for any of the repairs. Regardless, everyone was okay, but it left a wrong impression on Demi. She, to this day, refuses to let me see my nephew. She calls me, in her words, "unstable." Demi won custody of her son but lost him again as a teenager. She went to live with his aunt (her sister) before moving back in with his father when he turned seventeen. Lorcan failed half of his drug tests. One visit showed me a birthday card from the drug test lady and told me it was the only one he had received. I thought it was sad. The last I heard, Lorcan and Sean were doing very well. I am grateful for that.

CHAPTER TWENTY ONE

A New Beginning

I decided that I needed to get out of the house to learn how to cope with living in a sober world. I needed a distraction, so I took up playing euchre and got a job managing a video store. It was just over the river from where I lived. Euchre became more than just a game and is most known for its competitive side and conflict. I played with a mature crowd who didn't care much for the hotheaded girl with the apparent chip on her shoulder. I eventually warmed up to some of them. I fell head over heels in love with the game. I discovered that I was vastly competitive and highly territorial. I didn't like new people right away and often gave them the cold shoulder or criticized their playing. This was earning me the reputation as a cold-hearted bitch.

I have long since learned that I need to warm up to people. I am aware that I use intimidation tactics to show them who the alpha is. I used this technique in a way to cover up my insecurities. I liked how I intimidated people and kept them at arm's length, but I didn't like how it isolated me. My peers always told me that I was very unapproachable at first, but I'd be the complete opposite when they got to know me. It took a while for them to get used to my sense of humor.

On the flip side, when working with the public, the dynamic was much different. I loved my job, and I stayed with it for the better part of a year. It was working nights and weekends, but it was minutes away from where I lived. Jack kept bringing our boys to see me if they missed their momma. A husband and wife team owned the store. Gary was a decent boss who liked and utilized most of my ideas for the store. Trish, on the other hand, was much harder to get along with. I could always tell when things were rough within the marriage when she started projecting her anger out on me. She hated it when I called her on it.

Siobhan O'Regan

Most of our issues started after I disclosed that I was a recovering alcoholic. She appeared not to have a problem with my recovery but treated me as if she was doing me a favor by hiring me. I had no worries about losing my job. I often spent my spare time cleaning and organizing the store and got along great with the customers. I knew most of them by name and their movie preference. I loved that I worked by myself and took care of the store as if it was my own.

After a year, I started looking into taking some college courses and figured that now was a good time to go back to school. I looked into going back to Reeves College in the fall until I came across an ad for Wilhalm College. It was a private college in Ontario, and I could get in right away. We had some issues paying off my first student loan and could not bury it when we claimed bankruptcy. I still had five thousand dollars outstanding so, we remortgaged the house so I could attend. I gave my notice at the store when I found out I was accepted into both of the programs I wanted. I decided to choose my major as 'community outreach' over 'police foundations.' This was partly because I found out that I would have to be sober for five years before any police force would ever consider me.

College was one of the most rewarding experiences of my life. I had one of the most intriguing teachers. They challenged me in ways that had me questioning my perspective on so many levels. I didn't always agree with his philosophies, but they taught me how to open my mind to different outlooks. I learned how to appreciate those whose opinions differed from my own. I met and connected with some of the most diverse personalities who I came to respect and admire. One such person joined our class halfway through and had quite a bit of influence on me. She rejected me when I reached out to her. I took it very personally until I realized she had her own attachment issues. She was coming to terms with some life choices of her own.

For me, though, she was the first of a handful of friendships that I tried to cultivate and discovered that I was turning to emotionally unavailable people. Fortunately, I was able to make quite an impression on a few of my teachers and classmates. I had no issues disclosing that I was in recovery and started to take credit for some of my accomplishments.

I facilitated a recycling drive at the school and had the city donate the bins. I helped a fellow student sober up long enough to receive his diploma. He was my first official sponsee, and I took him in, offering the support he needed to get through the last couple of months of school. He was a gentle soul who lost his beloved wife to cancer some years back and led a troublesome life after losing her. He wanted to give back so much but didn't quite know how to help himself first. When he had a grand moll seizure in front of our entire class, he had a terrible accident at school and spent a few days in the hospital. He banged his head off a desk then fell on the floor. I took him in and gave him a place to stay. I gave him nutritious food and rode to and from school. In return, he agreed to stay away from drugs and alcohol. He attended all his classes.

Jack wasn't sure he liked this arrangement initially but understood my need to help him out and agreed that he could stay so long as he didn't pose a danger to our boys. He fit in well with our family dynamic. He did so well that our boys treated him like an uncle and got them interested in the guitar, teaching them a few cords. He eventually graduated and moved back out to live on his own. After we graduated, I lost contact with him, but I heard that he started working at the homeless shelter and was doing well for a while.

That year was the beginning of one of the worst years of my life. It was a true testament to my commitment to staying sober. Within just three short months, I had two procedures that ultimately lead to a full hysterectomy. My van got smashed from behind by a teenaged driver while I was parked on the road. This led to many automotive issues. I witnessed my father-in-law have a series of mini-strokes that changed his life forever.

My son was diagnosed with a tumor, and my brother Keagan passed away from a fatal heart attack in his son's arms. This was just months shy of his fortieth birthday. Keagan and I didn't grow up together. He was Lorcan and Beth's stepbrother from our father's second marriage. Still, we grew close over the years leading up to my getting sober and was the driving force behind my decision to attend rehab. He was the one I turned to for support and advice.

Getting sober didn't just mean giving up alcohol. Still, it also meant giving up temptation in the form of triggers, and that meant my brother, Lorcan. I had so much guilt surrounding my brother, and we both put up a massive wall toward each other. He visited me frequently over the years, and we sat in my basement, got drunk, and talk about how we would have done things differently. We exchanged sarcastic insults until he had to go home. Next to Jack, Lorcan was the only man I had ever loved, and the thought of giving him up nearly destroyed me. Keagan and Lorcan remained brothers after our parents divorced, and he introduced me to him when I was a teenager. I spent a lot of time hanging out at his place. After being raped the second time, he reached out to me and was there for me when I needed him.

I'm not sure how he found out exactly, but I'm sure he reached out in the absence of our brother. Over the years, we kept in touch, and he helped me understand what life was like for them growing up. He offered insight into why my sister and I could never get along and told me not to worry about Lorcan. He told me that he would take care of him while I took care of myself.

I know he had issues, especially with drugs and alcohol himself, but he was there when it counted the most. Now he was gone and left behind four boys. At the funeral, I met his mother, Mary, and his biological brother for the first time. Despite what I heard about Mary, I felt for her. No parent should ever outlive their child, and it made me appreciate Kallan's outcome that much more.

I didn't get to mourn my friend. I didn't think it was to my right because I didn't know him as well as my brother and sister did. Although I didn't grow up with him, we were close. It was a different kind of close, and I spent the entire day taking care of everyone else needs rather than my own. Even Jack undermined how much his death affected me since I didn't share with him too closely what he did for me. Keagan was the first person I ever cared about who died. Jack knew we chatted regularly, but we never really discussed the details of our conversations. He knew I was struggling with losing Lorcan and how much it upset me to talk about it. He didn't bring it up and assumed I came to terms with it on my own.

As much as I appreciated Keagan for years, I resented him and was jealous that he and his brother took my rightful place in my family. For years after his death, I was riddled with guilt for being so angry and had to forgive myself, knowing he would want me to move on. I have yet to come to terms with what his death has meant to me and feel closed off and numb. I know I cared about him, and I should feel something, but I just don't.

I required some time off of my studies during those three months, but my teacher Alex didn't cut me any slack to finish a final project. He told me that if it weren't one thing, it would always be another. I struggled with his rational thinking. I knew anyone going through even one of the things I mentioned wouldn't be able to carry on with the assignment. I was now facing several life-altering events. Although Alex said he felt for my situation, he told me I needed to decide on taking time off or finishing out my studies. I remember being so angry and thought he had it out for me. Still, I realized that I needed to pull myself together and focus on what was important in my life.

Kallan and Papa were out of the woods for now. I was so close to finishing my studies, and so I trudged forward. Looking back now, I probably should have taken time off but, I left it in the hands of karma to decide. I found the strength to pull myself together and moved forward.

I don't know if that was Alex's motive all along or if he had an entirely different agenda, but, despite everything going on, I graduated with honors and was at the top of my class. I finished with an overall average of ninety-three percent. This grade was essential to me, and I busted my ass, studying for up to seven hours for every exam. Alex tried to convince me that classes were not everything, especially when I had a meltdown after receiving a less than ninety percent grade on an exam.

Initially, I didn't trust him concerning the grades and had to be stubborn, but he ended up being right. Not once has an employer ever asked what my grade point average was. For someone like me, it meant I was capable of a lot more than anyone gave me credit for. He was trying to get across to me was not to lose sight of the overall goal and not to let it become my only focus.

Alex supported me in pursuing my internship at a youth rehab center for young offenders and troubled teens. I walked in with coffees for all the secretarial staff. I took my resume with me and was in for an interview soon after. I was offered the position on the spot. My diploma required two hundred hours of intern hours. I completed close to four hundred to show my enthusiasm and commitment to my chosen field. I fell in love with the job and the kids immediately. I was submerged in my work. To say these kids broke me in was a huge understatement. I became very efficient in handling crises really quickly.

There were a girl's side and a boy's side at the location. I immediately realized that I preferred working with the boys. I thought they were a better fit for me than working with the girls. One of the boys, Jonny, was the first to teach me a valuable lesson. He taught me what it's like to overthrow my power of authority. I learned it the hard way and understood how to approach and treat these kids with dignity and respect while still maintaining my leadership role.

When I asked one of the boys to clean up a mess, I supervised kitchen duty and was approached by Jonny. He was the resident in charge of clean-up. He had paid his dues and earned his rank as a kitchen supervisor. He told me it was his job to assign chores. I said not to worry and that I wouldn't keep him long. I suggested he go about his business and walked away from him. He protested, but I, in my infinite wisdom, assumed he was on a power trip so, I ordered him back to the kitchen.

I failed to recognize that he worked hard to establish himself in his role. Even though he was a young offender, I suspect he felt like I was treating him like everyone else who labeled him. I just stripped him of his rank in front of the other boys, which was a big mistake.

After that moment, anytime I asked him to do something or required him to follow through with a task, he and his fellow minions refused. I used my power as a failsafe to threaten him with loss of privileges and consequences, which ended up in a vast power struggle. I was never going to win. After sitting down with him one-on-one, he made me realize how I completely undermined his authority. I realized how I owed this young man an apology.

I asked him how I could have approached it differently, and his words of advice were not to come in headstrong. He told me to get to know the kids before throwing my weight around unless I have to. I agreed to apologize publically during a group session. Although it was challenging to do, I experienced a massive shift of positivity on a bigger scale. We developed a mutual understanding. I had earned his respect, and in return, I took his advice. From that moment, I made it my mission to build a rapport and get to know the kids whenever possible. I have never sat face to face with a child and not find one thing I like about them to this day.

One of the senior staff members swore a lot around the kids when he was addressing them in a group. This was when they became loud or disrespectful. I got upset thinking; I did not sign up to motivate kids this way. I drummed up enough courage to ask him why. He seemed genuinely impressed by my question and was happy to answer it. He began telling me that talking tough was all they knew for some of these kids, and sometimes you had to speak their language to get their attention.

He told me as soon as he had their attention, he would tone it down and lower his voice, so they were forced to listen.

I was so fascinated and couldn't get enough of watching him interact with the kids. I even noticed that out of all the staff there; he was the only one they approached and respected the most. I learned a lot from watching him work and latched on to him as a mentor. He sure knew his stuff and was always eager to answer my questions. He took me under his wing. There was this crown ward with one hell of a chip on his shoulders, who was court-ordered into the program. This is where I first started learning about the ins and outs of Child Services. He poured on the attitude anytime anyone would approach him and was placed on my caseload.

After about the second week, I was still trying to figure out how to reach this youth3 and got some hints from my new mentor. This kid loved to bully anyone who approached him. Every day I sent him a nod and asked how his day was going. He would shoot me a dirty look or ignore me, but I kept smiling at him anyway.

He reminded me of the guy who used to come in to buy cigarettes. I was a clerk at the local corner store, and how I used happy face stickers on his pack of smokes to connect with him. It turned out that he was a decent guy, but no one bothered to get to know him. Underneath, I had no doubt this kid was like that guy, and he was a decent child beneath the behaviors.

One afternoon, he was doing his chore and banging his mop against the walls. He was slapping it against the floor. I just spoke to his work and knew he had only been rejected for an immediate transfer. I knew he was looking for someone to project his anger on. I was walking past him and kept a flat affect. He looked up at me and spoke to me through gritted teeth, "If you ask me how my day is, I'm going to take this mop and shove it up to your ass." I replied, "I had no intention of asking you how your day was." I then asked if it ever occurred to him that he may not be the only one having a bad day. I then lowered my voice and told him, "It didn't matter where you shove the broom. I am going to make you clean it anyway." I then winked, walked away, tried to hide my smirk, and sat down in the mess hall. He came in a few moments later, leaned up against the wall, and asked me what the hell my problem was. I smiled and told him nothing. I usually get cranky when I'm hungry, so I popped a handful of grapes into my mouth. I smiled and turned to my paperwork. I watched him study me out of the corner of my eye. Finally, I thought I had established contact and was finally getting somewhere with him.

My immediate supervisor didn't think highly of me and often criticized me more than she ever mentored me. She especially picked on my clothes. I wore a lot of plain clothes. They were mostly jeans and turtlenecks since I was still very unsure about my new figure. I had lost the bulk of my weight, totaling close to eighty-six pounds. I wasn't used to the attention I was attracting, so I downplayed my looks. I thought her criticism was unwarranted, considering she always looked unkempt. However, she was fantastic at teaching me how to do paperwork in the spirit of taking what I need and leaving behind the rest. I learned how to do case conferences and even got to write my own occurrence reports. I discovered that I excelled at it. I was assigned to create manuals from their policy and procedures for new students and employees. I was credited for a job well done and for my impeccable organizational skills.

At the end of my internship, they asked me to transfer to the girl's side to gain some experience. I wasn't thrilled at first and hated change since it was a completely different dynamic than the boy's side. Still, I found something I liked about each program to help with the transition. I had noticed the girls were especially rowdy at night, so I use to sit in the hallways and read to them. They particularly liked a few chapters out of Chicken Soup for the Soul. The boys used to pretend to fight with the girls over who got to have me as a counselor, which made me feel special.

This was a French-based company, and the fact that I was married to a Frenchman didn't hurt. It had become the subject of many conversations. The director sure took a liking to me and gave me a lot of responsibility when we worked a couple of shifts together. He called me into the office one afternoon to offer me a full-time position starting immediately. Unfortunately, I had to decline immediately because I had been postponing surgery and needed to take three months off to recover from a hysterectomy. I knew I would not be able to function long-term without it. He assured me that the job would be waiting for me when I got back. He sealed it with a gentleman's agreement, in the form of a handshake, and agreed that I would return full time when I received my doctor's okay.

Shortly after discovering Kallan's tumor, I found out that I had a ruptured cyst on my left ovary. This led to the discovery of endometriosis and explained the primary reason for all the pain I experienced in the past few years. It was the reason why I suffered unbearable menstrual cycles in my last few periods. I had ended up in the hospital bleeding badly and had to have Jack bring me a change of clothes as I had bled through several pads and two pairs of pants. This included a spare I brought just in case. I was passing blood clots as big as my fist.

My last pap test came back abnormal, so I had to repeat the test and was ordered to go back within three months to do it over again. Dr. Grace performed a laparoscopic procedure to deal with the cyst and get a closer look at my uterus. She discovered that I had endometriosis covering a large portion of my uterus. When I sat in her room, the first thing she said to us was that it was a miracle the kids had made it to full term. I was fortunate to have them all together. I asked her if it might have been the cause of my miscarriage in its second trimester. She confirmed that there was absolutely no doubt. I took one look at Jack and started sobbing. The news was bittersweet. It meant that my drinking was not the primary cause of my miscarriage, even though I wouldn't have ruled it out as a factor. My fear, guilt, and shame kept me from drinking through my subsequent two pregnancies.

She also told us that I likely had multiple miscarriages over the years and wouldn't have realized it. Most women in my condition never carried a baby full term, and it was a miracle that I did it twice. She also confirmed that labor would have been excruciating under these circumstances. She advised that a full hysterectomy was the only logical way to go. It would eliminate my chances of developing cervical cancer, which they monitored with my abnormal pap test. I agreed to the procedure but would have to bear it until I was done with school. I always had a hard time coming to terms with circumstances where I lost my other two children. I never thought I would ever fully let go and allow karma until I realized this fact about my body. I believed in what the children meant to me while I was pregnant with them in the true nature of spirituality. The fact that they are with me now and waited to be born to love parents, their souls bounced from vessel to vessel until they found their way to us; it was karma's way.

Jack got a girlfriend pregnant when he was a teenager. She chose to have an abortion, so he also understood what it meant to wander and grieve the loss of a child he would never meet. I never felt like my family was complete and always sensed pieces were missing. Jack and I often talked about adopting. Since Kallan's surgery, we were already warned that it was doubtful that he would father children of his own. For this reason, we talked to our boys about the family. Kian was to give us lots of grandbabies, and Kallan was to adopt us lots of grandbabies.

I was asked to be valedictorian of my graduating class. It was the first time I set foot in front of an audience since I was heckled off stage during my grade eight speech. I was petrified and had substantial anxiety attacks, but I refused to let it control me. In front of a couple of hundred people, I took a breathe and started my speech. "Hi, I'm Fallon, and I'm an alcoholic. Oops, wrong meeting." Half the audience gasped in disbelief; the other half laughed and cheered. My biological father was leading the pact. In attendance were my father, Sean, Papa, Jack, and my sister Beth. You know, for a person who disliked me so much, she oddly did always seem to be there during my most important milestones. I had the audience hanging on to my every word. No one heckled me. Everyone laughed at my jokes, and people liked and respected me for the first time in my life. My fathers were so proud, and I looked great in my pictures. I had lost the bulk of my fat and weighed one hundred twenty pounds. I had such a bright future ahead of me, yet; I still felt so empty, as though there was always something missing inside.

The night before I underwent my surgery to have a hysterectomy, I didn't sleep a wink and was so scared. I wanted my mommy so severely. Of course, maybe not my mother but someone to tell me I was going to be okay. Jack was a worrier as well, but he was the type of guy who could fall asleep getting his hair cut and even fell asleep in the waiting room during Kallan's surgery to biopsy his tumor.

The following day, we headed down to the hospital. They put the cream in my hands, and we waited while they prepped me for surgery. I put on my big girl's face but was shaking like a leaf. They came to get me, and Jack was allowed to walk me down the hall, but I had to walk into the operating room alone. I gave him a huge hug, bit my lip so I wouldn't cry, and followed the nurse in mouthing I love you to him. Inside they laid me down on the table and told me not to worry about anything. They attempted to feed me a central line but couldn't find the right-sized vein to go into my hand, so they told me they had to put it on the side of my thumb. I panicked and refused to let them. I told them they had to go through the hand. My anxiety went from zero to a hundred in less than a second, and I went right into crisis mode. I attempted to jump off the table when they tried to insert the needle into my thumb, screaming for Jack and then for Dr. Grace.

Nobody Special

Several of the staff grabbed me and held me down on the table. I was so terrified that someone put a mask over my face during my restraint. When I woke up, I was still in panic mode, and the nurse rushed over to calm me down. She assured me that I was okay. I was buzzing and was disoriented. I was still reeling from my experience. I looked over at my arm and saw that they did put the line down my thumb. I could again feel where their hands were when they held me down. Apparently, the staff did not identify a trauma victim. It was unaware of the signs when someone is in substantial fear for their safety. At the time, I didn't know how to identify it, let alone explain what was happening to me. I still have fears that plague me every day of life, which I am slowly trying to identify and overcome one at a time.

After recovery, they put me on a self-administered morphine drip. Within the hour, a nurse walked in to do her rounds and walked out immediately, and returned moments later with my doctor in tow. I could read the look of concern on her face. She smiled and asked me how I was feeling. I told her that I felt hot and itchy. She giggled and said, I could see why. I was having an allergic reaction to the morphine. I looked like I was sunburnt and completely covered in hives. Due to my addictions, we talked ahead of time about what pain meds we used and agreed I would not use anything highly addictive. Since the morphine didn't work, I was given a painkiller with a slightly more potent derivative of Advil and was ordered to take it easy.

My doctor forced me to stay and wouldn't release me for at least three days. Jack brought the boys and our nieces to see me. Even Beth and Sean stopped by for a visit. The highlight of my surgery was the card Beth gave me that read, "Sorry you lost your girly bits." I usually don't keep my cards but, this one I held on to. The worse part of my stay, minus the surgery, of course, was the woman they brought in the second night. She was up at three a.m. yelling at her partner on the phone. I had to get up out of bed and request that they move her to another room. I thought it was absurd they decided to move me since it had been my room for two days. They should have moved her, but the trade-off was that I got to have my own room for the rest of my stay.

Dr. Grace tried to convince me to stay one more night, but I had had enough and wanted to go home. I was managing on my own, so and in my mind, it was time to leave. I had to sleep elevated in the hospital, so I was more comfortable with my lazy boy when I got home. I spent the better part of a month sleeping in my living room. Unfortunately, my bathrooms were not on the main level, so I trained my dog to help me up and down the stairs. I was independent enough for Jack to return to work a week later.

I was having some massive trouble with dizziness and knew my iron was low. I had experienced this almost every time I had my period, but this time I couldn't shake it so, I never attempted the stairs without her. She was such a lifesaver. From the moment I got home, I used extra strength Advil to take the edge off and doubled it when I needed to sleep. Other than that, I didn't use any other pain relievers and attributed my fast recovery to having to get up and down the stairs several times a day. I thought if I had depended on pain meds and had been on the same floor as my bathroom, my healing time would have been much longer. The rest of my recovery went well. Jack was very attentive, although I would have liked him to be home longer. I thought he took excellent care of me. I was finally given the okay to start driving around the two-month mark but was only allowed short trips since my stomach muscles had not fully healed yet. I was surprised at how much you depend on your stomach muscles to drive. Breaking was something to get used to over again. I learned to drive standard, and I hated that we switched to automatic, but this was the one time I was grateful for the switch.

On my last visit to see Dr. Grace, she told me that they were able to save one of my ovaries. She said that I would likely need it taken out in a few years but left it in for now, so I wouldn't need hormone therapy for as long as my body held out.

I sent several emails to the program and updated them about my recovery. But when it was time to go back to work, they informed me that they could only hire me part-time. It was all they could afford in their budget. I was crushed and was looking forward to going back. I had student loans to pay off. The commute was an hour and a half both ways, and I needed stability, so I declined their offer of part-time to pursue elsewhere. I found a job working for another program that worked with disabled adults but found the situation wasn't right for me. I found the women who worked in the program were catty. I watched how nice they were in person but talked nasty about another behind their backs.

Nobody Special

They did have one lady who worked the night shift who was incredible, and I used to stick around and chat with her when she came on shift. The other thing I couldn't accept was the treatment of the clients. One client was utterly dependent on staff for everything and, during his bath time, would sit in a pile of his urine and feces while they dumped water on his head. They told me they didn't get paid enough to do PSW (personal support work). They never really bathed him.

I remembered enough from my nurse's aide days to bathe him and was forced to do it every shift after that. At night, I would sit on the edge of his bed and sing to him. He would grab my arm as if to show his appreciation. I would sit and sing a while longer. I found out I was the subject of a few nasty rumors, so I stood up for myself and confronted them about it. I was not the least bit surprised when they pointed the finger at one another.

I spoke to the supervisor, who was well aware of the dynamics of the house and offered to move me to another program with some people I met at a picnic. She wanted me to join their team, but I had already been placing feelers out there and applied to other group homes in the area. During my interview with a program centered on working with youth in group homes, I was asked to fill out a scenario and explain what I would do in a crisis. When I was done, the interviewer shook her head and told me she had never had someone fill one out so accurately and full of detail. They hired me on the spot and were excited to place me immediately. During my first shift, the house had erupted into chaos, and there were three restraints that day. It was not the best circumstances to be walking in on your first day of training. A day later, I found out a sister company had hired two of my college classmates and me, so I decided to go with them instead and turned this program down.

My first experience with this particular organization involved meeting one of the instructors named Toby during UMAB training. He was flirtatious and insisted that my classmate and I join him in his program. We figured he was just overly friendly and brushed him off.

My first assignment was working with a youth who had severe behavioral issues. This was to be on a one-on-one basis. As challenging as my job was, it was not half as challenging as witnessing this youth's mistreatment who had Down syndrome under individual staff supervision. This staff used to yell, scream, and holler at them. She tried to convince me that the only way to communicate with them was to be hard, forceful, and direct. I agree that sometimes you need to be firm and maybe even raise your voice but, at no point is screaming and belittling an acceptable form of communication. This particular staff used to pound on the bathroom door relentlessly when this youth was relieving themselves to make a point about disturbing others.

I approached the coordinator and was shocked that she supported this treatment and agreed that we needed to be firm with this client. I wondered if she was fully aware of this youths' treatment and watched in disbelief how much my co-worker's demeanor changed around this coordinator from sickly to sweet. She pulled out a bloodied drop cloth during an outing and told this resident to sit on it if she soiled the seat. I questioned where the blood had come from. She shrugged and told me it was from a nose bleed. I refused to allow her to sit on it, pointing out that it was an obvious biohazard. She refuted by stating it was her vehicle, and she would do whatever she felt was necessary to make sure it wasn't soiled on. When I wouldn't budge and told her no, I knew I was declaring war. I didn't care. I was seriously beginning to lose faith in humanity and wondered what I was doing in a field where this type of treatment was tolerated and accepted.

I talked to one of my college classmates, Alex, who worked in a different area of the agency. He told me that they experienced a high turnover rate and inquired about the program through my current coordinator. Within a week, I got a call from my director, who told me that I came highly recommended and was transferred almost immediately from part-time to full-time. The work consisted of seven days on and seven days off. I thought I just hit the jackpot. I received a call from the supervisor, who turned out to be our UMAB instructor, and they told me it was a very relaxed program. My instructor added that I could bring it on over without any hesitation if I had any laundry to do.

I instantly loved the program and immediately clicked with my new primary shift partner Matt. He was just appointed to the new coordinator position. Matt was so much fun and pushed me out of my comfort zone in so many ways. He used to poke fun at things I was subconscious about. I made mistakes, and he made fun of them until it got old, and I realized they weren't such a big deal after all.

He was such a huge guy and stood well over six feet tall. He completely matched my sense of humor in every way. It was the first place where I discovered a lot of who I was as a person and who I aspired to be. I would have to say this is where I experienced the most growth.

Nobody Special

We used to pull pranks on one another, and I still hold the crown for rigging the toilet seat with an alarm that I bought at the dollar store. The joke became epic and was talked about in our circle for months. The other staff was a net close group that welcomed me with open arms. Matt and I were considered week one. The other shift consisted of a week two coordinator named Georgia and my former classmate Alex.

From day one, I began building a rapport with these kids and found out that it was simple. Once you took an invested interest in their lives, finding their individual and unique qualities was natural.

There was this particular youth on my caseload that changed my life forever. They taught me some of the most valuable lessons I ever learned in working in this field. This bright young individual pushed all the limits to the extreme and was written off by everyone, including themself. By the time I had gotten ahold of them, they had a very dim outlook on their lives and, in their mind, nothing to look forward to. They were not attending school. They threw their weight around to get what they wanted, and the only person they truly cared about in the world was ashamed of them and didn't want anything to do with them. This group home was all they had to build them up. However, no one could reach them. Our supervisor Toby called them an impulsive manipulator and wrote them off. Still, to me, they were children with particular needs. Rather than call them manipulative, I preferred to look at them as resourceful kids using whatever tactics they could to meet their needs. Their behaviors were simply their language. I worked with this individual for over a year. I brought them home, included them as part of my family, and was able to bond with her on a level that most thoughts were impossible.

Unfortunately, it was a short honeymoon period. We started discovering that med errors were not being documented. Staff who were knowingly burnt out were still working shifts and were not conducting themselves professionally, especially in front of the youths. Youths were not getting their clothing allowance. We paid out of pocket to celebrate holidays like Thanksgiving and Halloween. One of our youth was supposed to have one-on-one, and no staff was ever assigned to them. Most of our time was tied up in restraining them. This youth was also very dangerous when they were in their trauma state. They were considered cash cows. They were more medical than group care, but this individual came with high needs. The problem was that Children's Services built an enormous wall of support for this individual. They helped finance in every step, but they never received them. The agency owed us several months of back mileage.

Mileage sheets were manipulated. I discovered that my supervisor was conducting fraud by charging distance for youth using the bus or train and overcharging Child Services. A team consisting of five other staff and me sent ten pages of grievances to our director. Promises were made, but there was no follow-through. When one of the coordinators was transferred, I took on the responsibilities without title or pay. These youth had noted, saying that they felt like they lived on welfare. Their supervisor, who made decisions on their behalf, wasn't bothering to take an interest in them at all.

One night, I noticed two of my youths were unusually off and knew right away that one of them was strung out and high. I questioned them and demanded to know what they took. I managed to coax the answer out of them. The girl and another resident had taken a bottle of Oxycodone to attempt suicide. The other one passed out downstairs after taking half of the pills. I attribute my expertise to my field of addictions, which allowed me to identify the signs. We rushed the youths to the hospital. Olivia (Night shift) and I stayed with them for over thirty-six hours until they were released and were told our intervention saved their lives.

This organization initially refused to pay for the time we spent with the girls and said we did not get prior permission for the time and a half. I threatened to quote them to the ministry, the youth's parents, and anyone else who would listen if they didn't pay up. They reluctantly did.

The weekend shift was asleep, so we often split the nights. I seldom ever got to sleep since I had a hard time sleeping in strange places. I discovered the youth were doing everything but sleeping; I had caught them engaging in sexual acts together and sneaking out of the house. Suddenly, our dangerous occurrence reports starting going through the roof. These were all things that were happening behind closed doors, but no one had noticed until now. I had asked for a meeting with my director Ellen to discuss the fraud after confronting my supervisor. I was surprised when I was called into her office and was immediately offered a position supervising my own program, title, pay, and was told to talk it over with my family. I was to let her know before she left on holiday.

Nobody Special

I talked it over with my husband and with my team. I spoke to my father-in-law, who suggested I talk to a lawyer. I took his advice, talked to a lawyer, and handed everything I had on the company over to him. He briefly glanced over the material and told me not to take the promotion, and warned me that I could be held equally liable if I did. He told me to expect getting fired and document everything I could. He suggested I take everything I had to the Ministry of Child Services. I pretended to mull over her proposal and declined it, telling her I felt my place was with my team. She told me she understood and she would speak to me when she returned from the holidays. I did as my lawyer suggested, and I turned everything over to the Ministry of Child Services.

The day after Ellen got back, I received a call asking me to come into the office. It was my day off, and it was my thirty-third birthday. I brought Kallan with me and a couple of coffees for them. I knew the moment I walked into the room that it was terrible news. Just by the atmosphere, I took a deep breath as I walked into my dismissal. During my meeting, I was taping our conversation. My new supervisor and Ellen was present. She turned to me and said that I had so much potential in this organization and wished she had gotten a hold of me sooner. She wished I had taken the promotion. When she was done, I thanked her and told her she gave me grounds for wrongful dismissal, warned her I had Toby for fraud and gave her a brief overview. She didn't look surprised, which told me she had received my report, the same story I handed over to the Ministry of Child Services. I asked if I could say goodbye to the girls and was told no. She told me she would give me a raving review about my work with the girls when they overdosed but nothing more. I tried to contact her multiple times for this reference, but she never returned my call.

CHAPTER TWENTY TWO

One Foot In Front Of The Other

After I was let go, I fell into another deep depression and felt like I was mourning yet another loss. It felt like I had been stripped of my identity and didn't know where to go. I was so good at what I did and loved working with kids. I understood them at a very deep level. I poured so much of myself into the job that I had no idea who I was or what to do with myself when it was all gone. My shift was seven days on, seven days off. Although I never saw seven days off, I now had nothing to show for it.

I tried looking for another position somewhere else, but all I could get was entry-level nights and weekends. My lawyer told me to go on unemployment and take some time off to figure out what I wanted to do with my life. After a while, I started hitting the casino and eating to self-medicate my self-loathing. I particularly enjoyed the casino because it was repetitively stimulating, and I could completely zone out. I disagree with the belief that it was a compulsion driven by the need for gambling since I would never play more than my allotted maximum bet. It was an addiction since I would require more each time to chase my desired disassociation.

It was never about how much money I could win since I never won any. If I did win, it was more time I could spend escaping my real world. As a kid, I never had an issue with food unless I was hoarding it. Even then, I hardly ever touched it. It was far too valuable, and I was forced to give up sugar when I was diagnosed with low blood sugar in my early twenties. It was likely due to my alcoholism, and now I was having an issue with portion control. On Halloween 2009, I picked up extra boxes of chocolate on sale and polished them off. I finished my boy's candy in a matter of weeks. All self-control went out the window. Gaining a multitude of weights set me back quite a bit. I experienced what it was like to live in a world of insecurity, shame, and hate all over again. The weight emotionally destroyed me, and the cruelty that went along with it did not give me a fighting chance.

I had all but given up on going to the AA but decided to return for a few months and stopped going again after people started assuming the weight gain was because I was drinking again. I single-handedly broke up a fight between two men, disarming one with a shovel after trying to attack the other with it. I guess after being attacked countless times in the group home desensitizes ones' lack of judgment. Mind you, I liked how accomplished I had become as a speaker and loved how everyone hung onto my every word and nodded in agreement to my viewpoints. It made me feel important.

I was approached after just about every meeting and was told that I inspired them, but I never felt deserving of their praise. I tried to help out a few people, but the only ones my age were males. Even though I only had the best of intentions of supporting them, it was seen as something different from the distortion of a closed mind. I once ran into an older gentleman who was from a neighboring town. I wanted him to sponsor me so badly, but I never dared to ask him and lost touch with him. I tried to stick it out, but I was forced to take a step back between the fighting and the rumors. I realized I needed people who were going to build me up, not tear me down. I did well enough of that on my own. I simply had no use for further drama in my life and no longer had any tolerance for it.

I talked to Jack several times over the years about fostering. I made it clear from the day we met that I wanted to take kids in and talked about it from time to time, but it never went any further. I was asked to consider being a kin placement for my primary child in the group home but didn't feel that they were a good fit for my house's dynamic. I deeply cared for them and knew they didn't take the rejection well. Still, I understood my situation, and I had to consider the influence this individual would have on my boys.

The topic of fostering came up a few times while working in the group home, and we considered it with a couple of different kids. Still, again the dynamics weren't favorable for them or us. We talked it over with our boys, but they didn't quite grasp the concept of fostering and automatically assumed everyone I brought home was their new foster sibling. We had some interesting conversations, but that was their mindset at the time. I often brought the girls home to hang out with my boys. They played games and swam. They loved it here, and it gave them a sense of normalcy. The girls never wanted to leave.

Jack always appeared to be on the fence about it. However, I still held out that he had to be ready and one hundred percent on board with the prospect of opening our home to fostering children. I took his lack of interest in the subject to mean he wasn't ready. We had one child we were looking at from the group home that was an excellent fit for our family. Still, the entire process was terminated after I got fired. I have to assume karma had its directive, and it was not meant to be for a reason.

I received an unexpected call from my sister's best friend, Lori, who wanted to stop by for a visit. I hadn't seen her since Keagan's funeral while I was in Main. Lori was married now with two younger girls and was having trouble with her middle child Becki. She was sexually active and had fallen into the wrong crowds, doing drugs. Lori heard what I did for a living and needed some advice. We had a long conversation about her daughter. She was desperate and considered calling Child Services to turn her over for support.

One thing was sure. She loved her daughter very much. Given my childhood experience, I thought a change of scenery, structure, and discipline would be just what this child needed for a while. I could provide that for her. I also had to keep in mind that she was my rapist's daughter, and I had to figure out how much that would trigger me. Jack and I sat down and discussed the logistics of taking her in and what it would mean for me. Knowing the father of the child was hard. I needed to set aside my personal bias. Since she had nothing to do with that ugly truth, we agreed to take her.

Having Becki with us was just as therapeutic for me as it was for her. I often wondered what her sibling would look like since she looked so much like her father. I had come to terms with my decision to have an abortion when I determined the soul of that child was with Kallan. She was an incredible kid who loved her mother but couldn't adjust to her mom moving on with her life. This was even after she got married and had two more children. The fact that she didn't get along with her stepfather didn't help.

The most challenging part was sitting back and listening to how much she idolized her father and how his multiple personalities took effect. We both knew a completely different front of him, so

I was forced to see him through her eyes. I got some satisfaction knowing that his lifestyle did catch up with him, and he served several years of jail time for blowing up his apartment and trying to cook crystal meth.

I wasn't why he served jail time, but I liked to think that karma was looking out for me and sought justice for him being a predator. I prayed that I was his only victim. I would be lying if I didn't want to warn her about her father. It wasn't my place, and I decided earlier that I wouldn't cross that threshold. Only if I thought he was hurting her was I going to take it up with her mother. The funny thing was, during our conversations, I found out that she had an excellent grasp of what kind of man her father was. In the true nature of unconditional love, she justified all of his actions and was so starving for affection. When he did pay her any attention, the blinders went on, and in her eyes, he could do no wrong.

Becki stayed with me for several months. I got her off the drugs and had her looking forward to school again. I had suggested she transfer down here to attend school, but her mother understandably wanted her daughter back home. I did as she wished and let her go. I went down to Main with my family that Christmas to watch the Santa Claus parade. My brother-in-law's store was right off the main street, served hot apple cider, and wine to anyone who came looking to get warm. I was with my family, and for the first time, I had a sense of belonging. I was happy.

Becki eventually became pregnant and had a son. Lori sent her to a home where she could learn how to care for her baby independently, with her support. I kept in touch, and I visited her after she had the baby. It turns out she was a good mother and took great care of her little guy. Becki had gotten married and added to her growing family. Her brother still held a special place in my heart and had led a tough life. His father introduced him to drugs at an early age, but with his mother's love and support, he could get the help he needed. He has since fathered a child of his own, and I hope that he continues on the right path.

I ended up going to the Santa Claus parade two more times. I wanted to capture what I did in the first year. Unfortunately, when I went, they warned me that Jason was lurking around, so I left before Jack found out. Knowing how he felt about what happened to me, I couldn't chance them sounding off on one another in front of the kids. We left, and I didn't go back.

Nobody Special

A couple of years later, I attended my cousin's wedding and had a brief chat with Lori, who was there as well. During our conversation that sparked over a passing comment, she found out that he had raped me and only thought we had a messed-up relationship. Jack liked having Becki around. He had bonded with her and had started fostering the conversation again.

I called my agency as I already had a relationship with them. This was to see if a family in the area could use our baby items after my hysterectomy. I was no longer in need of them. I had a strict policy never to sell our belongings after I vowed to give up the remainder of my addictions. I always gifted them to someone who couldn't afford it.

When I called, the intake worker told me that she would mail me an information package, but the package was in my mailbox the next day. We live in an area where our mail is delivered to a central box to our neighborhood, so I knew it was hand-delivered. This made me feel special. I placed the application on my fridge, where it stayed there for a few months.

For years, I was either wrapped up in my addictions, working, or going to school, so we decided to invest our energy into some much-needed family time. We discussed activities we would like to do together and came up with camping. We loved it so much that we eventually bought a trailer. Some of our fondest memories are out on the lake, and we made some long-lasting friendships with some of the seasonal campers there. Our boys love the outdoors, and Léo even joined us a few times, but we always got into petty arguments. Once I played poker with the girls who insisted on playing with their allowance. I, for the record, initially disagreed, but Léo asked I let them play. I won and took their money. It was as a lesson to both of them, and Léo demanded I give it back. At first, I refused until he threw a big fit, so I gave in. We eventually stopped inviting him.

One year Kian jumped out of the van, ran fifteen feet, fell, and lodged a pebble in his knee. I instantly knew we would have to have it surgically removed. We headed up to the nearest hospital. I was never more impressed with a hospital than I was that day. He was taken in right away. They opened him up, removed the rock, stitched him up, and released him within an hour and a half. His nurse practitioner was male and was terrific with him. The staff was so lovely and accommodating.

The following year I met up with a woman my age. She and her boyfriend were at the campsite next to us and started chatting with us when my dog Kovè wandered on their campsite. We started conversing and found out that she had a son who was a couple of months older than Kian. We instantly became acquainted and learned that she and her son were struggling. After many discussions, I invited them to stay with us for a few months while she got on her feet. While she was with me, her father passed away unexpectedly, and it destroyed her. I think my purpose was to see her through her grieving process and be there for her son. We put him into hockey to curb his aggression.

Unfortunately, she had issues beyond what I could do to help her, and we went our separate ways. Not long after they left, I cleaned the top of my fridge and found the information package. I left it on the table. Jack picked it up and said; we should fill it out. Within weeks, we were communicating with the agency and registered to take a training called Pride.

The entire process took less than a year from when we made our first call to our first placement. During my interview stage, I was determined to be as honest as possible. What usually took one interview took several as I disclosed everything. When Ed helped me with my fourth step to take personal inventory, I wrote everything down in a letter format that spanned across thirty-three pages. It disclosed just about everything. I used Alanon's fourth step inventory, covering every topic from finances to intimacy and reading each word to the worker. It took well over an hour to read. Afterward, I found myself wondering if I would be accepted given my history and called my sister-in-law, who was a psychiatrist. I asked her if she could refer me to a therapist giving her a brief overview of my history. This was something I had not disclosed to her before, and she gave me the name of a doctor who might be able to help. It took several months to a year to see this particular therapist. Still, I was shocked when I was invited to come in and meet with her immediately after my initial phone call.

Jack and I met with her, and I felt an instant connection with her. She identified me as a survivor based on the information I gave her during our brief meeting. I told her about all of my previous assessments and diagnosis especially, attachment and bipolar disorder. She told me that I was not completely damaged and that if I trusted the process and did the work, I would eventually be ok.

She was a couple's therapist and only agreed to see us if we came together. She explained her three-phase program, called Inter-Generational Trauma Treatment Program. The first phase was a six-week course that taught us the fundamentals of the materials we would be covering. Phase two surrounded attachment, attunement, and containment, just to name a few. Attendance was mandatory, and I wasn't able to enter phase two unless we completed step one. Phase two was one-on-one counseling for an undetermined amount of time, and phase three involved our children after we worked through our repair. I took all of this information back to my resource worker, who supported us in attending this program as a training tool with her supervisor's approval.

The first six weeks were very intense and hit home in a lot of ways. I was astonished to learn I was on the right track about many things and held out some hope that I wasn't a lost cause. Jack and I tried counseling several times over the years. It worked temporarily, but nothing ever seemed to get resolved. At first, I thought this was all primarily for me, but I soon learned that the healing process involved us. For me to heal, I needed to develop a primary attachment to my significant other. In doing so, I could bridge some of the developmental milestones that I had missed. I could especially salvage the ones that were severed during the most influential years of my life. That is when most kids are developing. I was just trying to survive.

Our therapist was also a medical doctor, so the government covered our therapy. Even though the treatment of this magnitude was generally for one year, depending on the individual's needs, we were in phase two for two years. This was until she announced her retirement of thirty-seven years. They informed us that we would be seeing two therapists Dr. Shannon and her colleague Amy (MSW), who sat in on all of our sessions.

We delved deeper into my attachment disorder and were told, with some intense therapy, how to be more open. We worked hard for me to develop an attachment to my husband. This was something most people take for granted. Jack and I learned that we stayed linked through our humor, but we had very little emotional connection. We had no intimacy whatsoever. Due to the attachment disorder, any rare form of affection would instinctually cause me to retreat and separate myself from him. I always subconsciously started a fight to sour our connection. It took several months before I could release some of my anger out on a punching bag. I was overcome by fear and anxiety just by the thought of hitting something on purpose.

We learned that our anger was manifesting on the inside, and it was the cause of a lot of our health issues. This was hard, especially for Jack, who spent years appeasing me to keep the peace. He often told me it was worth sticking around for after seeing glimpses of the woman he fell in love with. He chose to wait out the storm to see her amid a calm.

I discovered that I'm more of an implode and that my brain is systematically set on high alert at all times. My flight and fight response was at a moment's notice. My PTSD was the root of my hypervigilance. I had OCD, and I had so many difficulties with social interaction and maintaining relationships. Both of my therapists validated my SPD (Sensory Processing Disorder). They Informed me of my extreme sensitivity to touch, sound, and light. Our sessions were done with the light off, using only the natural light that came in from the windows. It is unknown how much of my disorder was due to nature since both my boys suffered from it in varying degrees as well.

To this day, Kallan is hypo sensitive, and Kian is hyper, displaying much of the same characteristics I did as a child. From what I have pieced together, SPD can be traced back to the Aarskog syndrome, but Kian does not have this syndrome so, the trauma of his illnesses would have been the cause to have triggered this.

I learned my body, mind, and spirit idled on hyperarousal. I always had to be on the move, and sitting for even short periods, would make me feel sick and lethargic. I could never sit down and always thought it was a good character trait, but I never realized it was a significant burnout source. My insomnia was the leading cause of my irritability and inability to control my impulses. So, she had me map out a behavior pattern that reflected a breaking point after long periods of little to no sleep. I was told I suffered from IBS (irritable bowel syndrome). This resulted from my ongoing stress, although I later found out that I suffered from ulcerous colitis.

My mind always stopped functioning correctly. I would experience a breakdown that had me isolated for days, so she put me on a medication that suppressed my central nervous system, and I was on it for several months. I hated the idea of being on the pill again, but I had tried everything else so, I went against my nature and chose to keep the faith. I detested everything about this medication. I was always so tired and gained close to sixty pounds, but I actually slept for the first time ever. Jack took care of the kid's morning routines for the following six months, so I'd catch up on thirty-five years of sleep.

One of the most significant stressors was that every time Jack got angry, upset, stressed out, or yelled, I would subconsciously go into full crisis mode. My flight or fight mode would trigger; I'd then lash out and verbally attack him every time.

Eventually, he was the one to back down and was always the first to apologize. But even then, I wouldn't accept his regret right away. It was almost as if I had to punish him for making me feel unsafe and further reinforcing my inability to trust him. On a conscious level, I knew deep down he would never hurt me, but his anger and stress had a way of bringing me back to my trauma state, triggering my PTSD. This matter subconsciously got me angry with Jack. I kept him at a reasonable distance so I could protect myself and stay safe.

As far as his brother Léo and I was concerned, he was a considerable threat. At first, I thought he was the sweetest man I ever met, and oh how much he reminded me of my brother. I used to admire him, but I now understood that this was just one facet of his personality; there were many, many more. He was my go-to anytime I needed support for years, but then he would disappear into his little world, and we wouldn't hear from him for a time.

I don't know if it was his explosive anger, which, for some reason, was always directed at his dad, or I could not fit in. His father had earned my utmost respect. It hurt to see him sound off on his dad. By looking at it from a different perspective, I realized that we took our anger out on the ones we felt the safest with. I with Jack and Léo with his dad!

It is much easier to point the finger at others' wrongdoings than to identify one's own. I don't know what has had the most impact on Léo growing up. Thus it is not my job to judge him. The most substantial fear factor was getting rejected. I tried a few times to let him in, and he brushed me off every time I was hurt, wounded! The result was that we could not get along; we were both too unhealthy for one another.

I learned that my bucket was always full of everything I had going on, which didn't take much to put me over the edge. Even though I thought I had it all together, I found myself picking fights with strangers I felt were ignorant or rude. It was a smart way to make sure I didn't take it out on my kids, but it also manifested into other things, like controlling my environment.

Ever since I can remember, I have always had a compulsion to clean. Everything had to be organized and in its proper place. When I had anxiety attacks or escalating out of control, I automatically targeted my environment and everyone in it. I always had one outlet and often left my clothes in a pile on my floor, whether clean or dirty. Matt, (my work husband from the group home) calls me the messiest neat freak he ever met. When I forced him to fold towels a certain way but leave my stuff in a pile, he would just laugh. Even Jack loved to poke fun at my OCD. I always arranged my cups by size and color. He got a kick out of mixing them up. This drove me nuts, so I got rid of them and replaced them with cups of all the same size and color.

Me being a runner and Jack being a fixer had its issues. Whenever we fought, I would retreat, and Jack would pursue to repair our disconnection. We would get lost in our push-pull (power struggle) until I came out on top. Unfortunately for Jack, this method suited my needs at the time just fine but did nothing to help him resolve his.

Jack and I found out a great deal about his health issues from day one. When Dr. Sharon asked him about headaches, back issues, and chronic neck pain, both of us were intrigued about where she was going. We knew he had suffered from all of the above for years.

Sharon explained that most of his health issues were directly related to his inability to identify or meet his own emotional and biological needs. A few years back, he woke up one-morning peeing blood. Shortly after, he doubled over in pain and couldn't get up, so we rushed him to the hospital. It turned out he had massive kidney stones that were dislodged and told he would require surgery to remove them. Knowing the procedure would put him out of commission for several weeks, he opted to wait until hockey season was over.

Before a game, I was up in the stands when one of his players shouted that Jack had collapsed. He asked me to come right away. I ran downstairs and found him doubled up in the fetal position on the bench in front of his players. He was still trying to direct them in hopes the pain would pass. One of my parents offered to take him home, and I stayed behind to coach his game. Anyone who knew

Jack understood he had to have been in unbelievable pain to let someone else coach his beloved team. He had to miss several other games due to his condition. When he finally had the surgery, the doctor rushed out to the waiting room to show me the stones and proudly claimed they were real beauties. It made me laugh and put my mind at ease. Typically, they only do one side at a time, so he had the other side operated on later. To this date, he has undergone five surgeries to remove kidney stones and is on medication to prevent new ones.

In 2012, he was rushed to the hospital in an ambulance after he woke me up at four a.m., drenched in his own sweat, and told me the room wouldn't stop spinning. I had never seen him so disoriented and frightened before and jumped into action. I woke up with my sons and called an ambulance. Our neighbor had seen Kian pacing outside and asked if everything is all right. Kian responded that his dad was really sick, and he was waiting for the ambulance. The neighbor asked if it would be ok to see if I needed help, and Kian replied, "Go ahead, he's not dead yet."

We laugh when we recall this story. Kian says he does not remember saying this. We understood our son and knew what he really meant. I was trying to keep Jack calm when my neighbor walked in and relayed what happened. Jack was still dripping, disoriented, and was becoming agitated. He yelled at us to shut up, which was way out of character for him.

The ambulance showed up and immediately ruled out a heart attack but told us it might be a stroke. I looked at my neighbor for a moment in disbelief and ran to call Papa. When he didn't pick up his phone, I drove over to get him to help out with my two younger boys. On the way to the hospital, I begged karma not to take him from me and prayed he was still alive but realized I had shut down and felt no emotions. I felt nothing, and I figured it was from the shock. I got to the hospital and was glad a bereavement counselor did not meet me. I was taken in to see him right away. He was lying down on a hospital gurney and was already being examined by the doctor.

We were informed that it was something called Vertigo. She then confirmed it after some extensive testing. She explained what the symptoms were like for him and assured me his agitation level was reasonable under the circumstances. In all the commotion, he was justifiably scared and was trying to gain his balance to center himself in an attempt to make sense of what was happening to him.

The next few days were tough, and I was extremely irritable towards him. I didn't know how to handle him or his situation. I felt utterly helpless and suggested calling his mother and have her come down to help out. I honestly couldn't make sense of my rationale and didn't know how to support him. I could barely contain myself and saved all my energy for our four boys. When we got to therapy, everyone could feel the tension between us and that Jack was walking on eggshells. I was ultimately on edge. Both Sharon and Amy tried to identify how scared he was, but I was reeling and couldn't connect with how he felt. I just kept telling them he needed to ask his mother for support.

I felt they were looking at me like I was a monster and just kept getting angrier, more defensive, and wanted to run and hide. I remember walking out, feeling defeated, picked on, and angry with Jack for not defending me.

The next week they apologized to me for not recognizing that I was also in crisis and realized I could not process what had happened. I finally broke down in therapy and identified that I had not allowed myself to feel. I had covered my emotions up with anger and directed it all out on the person who needed me the most. I was hiding from the fear of potentially losing the person who meant everything to me in this world and entirely disconnected from him. The reality of caring this much about one person was more than my mind could process, so I had shut down completely.

The guilt I had afterward was so overwhelming. I was so ashamed of myself that I completely retreated. I did what I always did and told him he deserved better than me. I still had so much guilt over how I treat him. I spent all those years tending to my addiction and spent less time with him or my children and not being there for them. Both physically and emotionally, I lived in contempt.

The more I looked at myself, the more I beat myself up for it. My negative mindset tempered my feelings of inadequacy as a wife and mother. It always circled back to thinking they deserved better. This came up frequently in therapy, and I was told I had no right to make that decision for them. Then it was disclosed that when things got terrible, I used to threaten the one thing I knew he valued most, and that was our marriage. It was never about me wanting to leave. It was my language telling him how desperate, scared, and disconnected I was.

Nobody Special

Our therapists taught me that it was all or nothing. If we were to continue therapy, the discussion of divorce had to be taken entirely off the table. I was not allowed to use it as a weapon in an argument again. One of the most pivotal moments in our therapy was where we identified the traditional dance. We called it our bench brawl. When one of us retreated, the other perused with the expectation that one of us would always back down to the other's needs and wants. The fact that we were so cleverly in sync with one another was, in a way, brilliant. All we needed now was to learn to channel that energy into building each other up, not tear the other down, and learn how to communicate with one another productively.

It wasn't always bad. We had this fantastic way of using humor and surprising one another to stay connected. One such surprise reminded me of when Kian was sick, and we had to cancel our movie plans. I knew Jack was disappointed and was really looking forward to our outing, but our baby needed us.

Having a chronically sick child usually meant we stayed in since he had particular needs that required both of our focus and energy. I had to go out and get him meds, so I stopped by the theatre on my way home and grabbed Jack a bag of his favorite popcorn. It was a little thing, but it was one of his favorite treats and made his entire night to him.

I discovered in my recovery how important the little things are and the significant impact they have on building people up. My fondest memory to date was when I was out running errands at the grocery store, and he called me for one of his idol chitchats. It was not unusual for him to ask me where I was in the store. It often reminded him of the things he needed from that area. I had just gotten to the frozen section and was chatting him up when out of nowhere, he popped out from around the corner and grabbed me. He then planted the mother of all kisses on me, saluted the gentleman behind us, and left. Everyone around me started clapping.

He completely blew me away from a shy guy in crowds and gave me the most cherished gift he had ever given me in the form of a memory; I would revisit often. I'm not sure Jack ever realized it, but he taught me the most valuable lesson. I learned what it means to build someone up, and the best part was, it didn't take words. It didn't cost a thing. He simply thought of me first. Our therapists would preach that touch was one of the greatest healers of disconnect and taught us how to hug properly. She encouraged us to play through contact. She challenged us to do this every time we came together.

Before this exercise, my favorite place, believe it or not, was my husband's arms. Mostly when things got challenging, it wasn't often, but it was there whenever I needed him. He was there, but now this place no longer felt sacred, and I found myself trying to avoid it. We were told that this would get better, but the more we did it, the further I needed to step out of my comfort zone, and it became debilitating.

To this day, I am open to doing it for him but still struggle with the concept of doing it for myself. It's a work in progress. I questioned why I could hug my children freely and give them affection but not to him and was told it was because they were not a threat. I have noticed that ever since Jack and I started hugging, my children have joined in and started wanting to connect in the same way.

That is a huge deal for Kallan since he was never affectionate, especially as a wee lad. He is such an awkward hugger, but we take whatever we can get. On the other hand, Kian was always an emotionally needy child and required a great deal of affection. This was easy to give to him when he was younger, but I found out that the older he got, the more conscientious I became about touching him. The reason for this, I'm told, is because his developmental age is not yet caught up with his chronological age, and his emotional needs are like a twelve-year-old. Biologically, he is 19, and subconsciously that is a potential threat. The thought in my mind, looking at my child as a potential threat, is incomprehensible. I'm grateful that my motherly instincts continued to override my fears of intimacy. One thing is sure; I love him and will continue to give him whatever he needs. No matter what, I will always be there for him. The funny thing was when they were little; my favorite thing in the world was one of their hugs. I could never get enough of it and think it's where I first learned to appreciate the warmth of an embrace.

I had always prided myself on my ability to read people. I felt stripped of my identity the day they said that my perception was based on an illusion. This was because everyone's experiences were different, and no two people thought or acted the same. As if intimacy wasn't tricky enough, I often got caught up in second-guessing myself. Especially when I would try to gauge people's cues or when it came to physical forms of affection. I still can't help but feel unsure and insecure when I do it now.

Nobody Special

The most ground-breaking piece was a chart we did base on the people I identified as those who hurt me the most. Mapping it out was the natural part. Then I was asked to rank them in order based on who had the most significant impact on me. The list went from Dean, Kristine, Sean, Nan, Beth, Child Services, Léo, Jack, Eline, and then myself.

Then I was asked to rank each one according to how much anger I had towards them. The list changed significantly to Léo, Eline, Sean, Jack, Child Services, Kristine, Beth, Nan, and Dean. The part that struck everyone was that Jason didn't make it on my list. I was a judge, jury, and executioner. Dean had the most negative impact, yet, I had the least amount of anger towards him. The two individuals with who I was most angry were tied between Léo and myself.

As it turned out, I was displacing all of my anger externally. I was projecting it all on the wrong individuals. I got sober based on the preconceived notion that each of my parents did the best they could with what they had. Any treatment I received at the hands of both Dean and Kristine had nothing to do with me. It was all about them, which made perfect sense and served its purpose at the time.

This matter holds merit when looking at the rationale. Still, I never came to terms with my anger, eventually projecting it onto myself and the people closest to me. I never held my mother accountable for her actions all these years and made up excuses for her behavior. I always felt pity for her and didn't think any of her attitudes or behaviors were her fault. I felt like I owed her.

The hardest part of my therapy was wrapping my head around the fact that she was in charge of making her own decisions. I couldn't comprehend any parent choosing the path she did. I had to believe there is an underlined reason to explain her behavior. Despite all my knowledge and experience, I couldn't accept any part of this to be true. I kept the hold on the illusion that none of it was her fault. All my life led me to believe that she was a helpless victim and blamed me for the way her life turned out.

All those years of torment and abuse happened because she allowed it and simply chose not to protect us. My mother had options and never once put any of us first. Jack and I took her in for several months when Bruce cheated on her, but she and I were very unhealthy and clashed. I chose to put my family first and stopped enabling her.

My therapists at the time told me that I exhibit symptoms of something called Stockholm syndrome. This meant I was conditioned to empathize and feel sorry for my abusers putting their thoughts, feelings, and needs ahead of my own. The DSM5 does not recognize this syndrome, but there is a lot of research to back it up. I knew it all too often in my field of work.

A lot of the anger I have for my mother, I have admittingly directed Eline. The passion I have for Dean has been projected onto myself and Léo. As far as my sister, Beth, was concerned, I never realized that our mother raised her during the most influential years of her life. She had not completely separated from her until she was almost five or six. It made sense that I would recognize many of our mother's characteristics in her, which was one of the contributing reasons we could never get along.

I have taken each of their character flaws and turned their actions into a personal vendetta against me. Their rejection continues to reinforce my false belief system. Sure, they have done things to justify a reasonable amount of anger, especially Léo but, they have been tried for treason. In return, they are serving a life sentence for someone else's crimes. Unfortunately, Kian doesn't understand why I choose to deny my half of the family. The truth is, it's easier to pretend they don't exist than accept the fact that my family didn't want me. I've tried to explain things to him and told him a bit about my history but warned my therapist not to. They explained he would figure things out for himself in due time.

Before therapy, I thought I was in good shape, but I didn't realize it was just how much I was still hurting. I wasn't aware that every time I lashed out or retreated from people, it was because of my fears. It was primarily due to fear of rejection. It is harsh for some individuals like me as rejection brings me back to solitude and the rationale that I was imprisoned all those years. I needed to take a step back from my behaviors and develop safety guided by tough love and compassion. The rest of the pieces would take time to fall into place. The majority of my guilt, remorse, and healing were based on forgiving myself. I beat myself up for who I was, how I raised my boys, and how I treated my family. In reality, I overcame unbelievable odds just to be with them. I know I still have lots of healing to do, but I am better equipped to recognize when I need support and ask for it.

Nobody Special

After a therapy session, I remember driving home and telling Jack how badly I wished I could see myself through his eyes instead of everyone else's. I started to cry, and he reached out to try and comfort me like he always did. I would pull away and retreat into my head; this was our dance.

CHAPTER TWENTY-THREE
Reflection

Many people have asked me what it is like to live with attachment disorder and bipolar disorder? I feel this is an important piece and a difficult one to connect with since it requires me to dig deep and to be open and honest about who I am. For me, living with this disorder feels like you're an outsider, always looking in. No matter what you do, whom you know, or how hard you try, you'll never fit in or belong anywhere. Intimacy is taboo and can turn the most innocent questions or conversations into a breeding ground of conflict. I'm forced to back off or shut down completely, primarily if the topic centers on family, lifestyles, or my past.

A simple question like how many siblings do I have can easily trigger my emotions. I am at a loss for words playing out every conversation I've had in the past and how each of them leads to being more invasive and interrogational. Everything had to be based on who, what, where, when, and it was was hard for me. I try to live in the moment by telling people a variation of the truth by leaving out bits and pieces. I found it easier sometimes just to change the subject and avoid the topic altogether. The conflict for me has always been the disclosure piece. I find it easier to keep people at arm's length and like how this allows for distance. I don't like how it isolates me.

I've tried letting people in, but what they discover after scratching at the surface spooks them, and their response is usually guarded and chalked with skepticism. It's ingrained into my subconscious to lash out at people or find fault with them first. This way, I don't have to feel responsible for the breakdown. I would rather have someone think negatively about me, knowing they're just going to end up abandoning me anyway. When I was younger, I always found it easier to lie, especially to strangers. I used to tell them that I was an only child, adopted by parents who passed away when I was in my teens. I eliminated the need to discuss two otherwise raw subjects that no one liked to discuss: adoption and death. Now, I tell them that I am in recovery. I am always intrigued by how fast people's attention is diverted elsewhere.

The moment I learned to talk, I was conditioned to lie and was forced by my caregivers to invent stories about who I was and where I came from. I just had to mask the horrible reality that was my life. Eventually, as I got older, I continued to make things up as I went along. This was without even realizing it. I only became aware and was able to address it after I got sober. I always made up little things like what I did that day to add spice to an otherwise dull conversation or makeup something funny that happened just to make people laugh.

In retrospect, by entering recovery, lying was the most straightforward issue to fix. The difficult one was learning to cope with the idea that I no longer had alcohol to numb the grief I had been running from. I had to come to terms with my pain head-on. The impossible part was knowing that even though I was the direct outcome of those who had a hand in raising me, I had to assume responsibility for my own life. I was forced to accept that I was a product of their choices and that some of the damage they did to me could never be fixed.

For years, I lived in fear within the confines of my bedroom walls. I was restricted physically. Over time, due to my undiagnosed anxiety disorders and SPD, I started to develop a heightened sense of awareness.

My understanding of this is that my mind was in constant arousal and became rewired to this state as a new norm. This continued as a child well into my teens. The only thing I had that would help soothe my anxiety was to suck my thumb and retreat into my head. This eventually caused acute damage to my psychological development and significantly hindered my ability to read my surroundings accurately. It made me a massive target for bullies, but I lived as a prisoner in my head and spent years in one depressive state after another. To this day, I struggle with stimulating and containing my mind. I live on constant autopilot.

I have this relentless need to have something on the go and must be stimulated at all times. If I'm not physically active and sit for long periods, I become lethargic. If my mind is not preoccupied,

Nobody Special

I have to be very conscious of my negative thought process. This tends to bring me back to my childhood state of sitting in that room all alone. A few years ago, I discovered the use of weighted blankets (I used two down-filled comforters in addition to a quilt) on my bed. This was even in the summer as I couldn't sleep, especially in hotels, unless I had several layers of soft blankets. The weight and texture were so essential and needed to be just right. This has, to this day, helped tremendously with my anxiety of sleeping in strange places and allows me to relax enough to fall asleep.

I know I'm supposed to feel things, but I simply don't, and if I do, its responsiveness is so strong that it consumes me. In the quest to define what it means to be healthy, I have spent most of my life pretending to be something I'm not. As far back as I can remember, I have always been incapable of establishing a healthy connection with another human being. Any of the dysfunctional relationships I endured were short-lived due to my inability to withstand any connection, bond, or even the most superficial level. Depending on how you look at it, I guess, in a way, I was lucky. My inability to connect with others kept me from staying in unhealthy relationships as well. I just wish it kept me from attracting those who destroyed my spirit for their own personal gratification.

I lived in a constant state of paranoia; everyone was out to get me and inevitably would hurt me so, I built an impenetrable wall to protect myself. For individuals like me who idol on the edge of fear and uncertainty, I am in constant awe of people who break up years of loyal friendship out of displaced anger. Don't they realize how fortunate they are to have that kind of connection to another human being? When it comes to conflict, I often tell my kids, if it's not going to matter in a year, then let it go. The difficulty is being able to follow through on my advice. I have an aptitude to hold on to my fears.

Every time Jack and the boys tell me they love me, I know I love them back, but it is not a feeling as much as it is a state of mind. I know I am capable of love but, to feel it, I have to reach deep down and connect with the devastation of what it would feel like to lose them and who needs that! That is why I don't go there. When Jack and I are apart, he tells me how much he loves and misses me, and I wish I could relate, but I don't. All I feel is being inadequate and empty. I even have questioned whether or not I am human. In a desperate attempt to make sense of the emptiness I felt, I once asked one of my therapists if I had psychopathic characteristics illustrating a narrow appreciation for mental illness complexities. She told me that it was unlikely that, based on our therapy, the feelings were there but were buried under layers upon layers of pain. It would take time to resurface, although it was still unclear how much of my brain was rewired during my years of torture and abuse.

When I am hurting or scared, I continue to retreat, isolate, and lash out. On a conscious level, I am capable of giving affection, especially to my kids. However, I still can't be on the receiving end of it and have backed off from them when they have reached out to me without realizing I'm doing it. I have experienced so much grief in my life that I have become irreversibly numb. I have convinced myself that it makes little difference to me what people think of me anymore. The fact is, I do feel. I just think on a much deeper, more painful level, and it is easier to shut down and pretend that I don't.

I learned that people with traumatic backgrounds tend to be drawn to shows and careers that are centered around people who have had or are experiencing trauma as a way to cope with their own. In the past, I learned to dismiss it and do whatever I could to avoid drawing attention to myself. I discovered that I had very little to no sympathy for their discomfort when it came to people's somatic pain and became irritated when they complained about it.

On the flip side, I have been the first on the scene of 5 major car accidents and have thrown myself into action, with no regard for the blood and broken, twisted limbs. When my boys (preteen) have cut themselves or broke a bone, I have gotten into a nuclear meltdown and have had an all-out panic attack. I feel like it's the end of the world. It kills me to think of them in any amount of pain or discomfort, and I struggle to contain my anxiety.

I have very little in the way of sympathy and patience for people in general. Still, especially those who hide behind their ignorance and I often come across as cold, angry, and abrasive when, in reality, I am just insecure, lonely, scared, and debilitating guarded. During the rare occasions when someone does pay forward their kindness, I become overwhelmed with gratitude. I have been known to overestimate their generosity.

I rarely feel the excitement, so I don't usually feel anything until the day when gearing up for trips or events. What often surfaces is again anxiety. When I'm busy, and away from my kids, I have to post reminders to connect with them, or I don't think to call them at all. I love them, and I prefer to be around them, but I lack the aptitude to dwell on being away from them.

We could be apart for days at a time, and I don't miss them until the day arrives. Only then do I feel an overwhelming urge to be near them. I can't shake until they're in my arms. Jack wrote letters every day while I was in the first rehab; I always knew they were getting the special care they needed. I can only assume this urge is what it's like to miss them all the time. On the other hand, I am one of the few parents who genuinely look forward to the summer when I can have my kids all to myself and like having them home with me. Sometimes, if we haven't connected in a while, I will give them the day off of school even if they just hang around the house doing their own thing. I just like having them close.

Before we moved, it was not unusual to have a house full of kids on the weekends. As much as I hate the mess, it was worth seeing them happy. I preferred them to sleep in their beds at night. I may not fully understand sympathy or what it is like to feel certain things, but I understand respect and tried to put myself in their place. I treated them how I would have liked to be treated at their age.

I never really learned how to play. Even as a kid, I could never grasp the concept of make-belief and get so annoyed with Stephanie when all she ever wanted to do was play with Barbies. When and if we ever did play a board game, I always had to control and use violence and intimidation just to get my way. To this day, I'm told she still holds a grudge and refuses to play certain games because of it. When my boys were little, I tried hard to play make-belief games with them but couldn't connect and became impatient. We eventually would crank up the music and dance instead.

One of my biggest challenges to date after all those years of living in survival mode is trying to figure out who I am. At 44, self-discovery is not as easy as identifying that I have a passion for dance. It often leads to thoughts of what I could have done with my life based on my interests now if I had a supportive upbringing.

Those are the times when I need my perspective the most. They help me identify that it's okay to feel cheated but that I still have so much to be grateful for despite all the negatives in my life. I pray for the faith to accept that karma had other plans for me. This mindset is not something that could have been lectured or taught. I had to come to terms with it on my own. No matter how much Jack wanted to make the hurt go away, it was not going to happen. In therapy, we learned that he needed to let me go through the stages of grief. He understood I needed to feel the emotions that came with each stage.

One of the things that made me successful as a parent is compassion to accept my children for who they are and the ability to identify and work within their limitations. Yet, I still struggle to do this for myself. I expect change to be instantaneous and vent my anxiety out on my partner like a child does her parent. For trauma survivors, the process of change is debilitatingly slow, making it hard for those who are rooting for us from the sidelines. The difference is a process that is meant to be hard, so we know how far we've come.

Putting it into perspective, you cannot learn to skate until you first learn to balance. I can tell you how to balance and hold you until you're ready to venture out on your own, but you won't learn for yourself until you take that first initial step. Some kids are quick learners with the right supports, some not so much, especially without supports.

The problem is, in helping our loved ones reach what we consider obtainable goals, we tend to hold them back in the quest to protect them. We overlook some essential steps. As caregivers, we want to protect them until we're ready to let them go. Based on our own experiences, fears, and insecurities (at the risk of them developing further dependence), we enable them and force them to hold on to the boards. We have fear they will fall and hurt themselves. We also push them out before they are ready (forced independence).

Some kids are content learning how to skate for fun, but they want to play with the big kids and experience the world of hockey for others. You cannot learn to play hockey until you learn the fundamentals of skating, stick handling, and team play. The same holds in everyday life; there is a process to child development. Each child learns at their own pace. If a child is delayed in one area, any good coach will tell you that fundamentally they will need to start from the beginning with a mentor they can trust. Sometimes one of the biggest challenges we face with today's youth who are forced to grow up independently as I did, is trying to reel them back in. Especially after they're convinced they've taught themselves everything there is to know about the real world.

Nobody Special

I don't allow myself to feel emotions on a relative level. I have learned to compensate by processing emotions regarding thought. This would be comparable to someone who has lost the use of one of their senses. Because of that, the other ones heightens to compensate for the loss. The term living in your own head is especially true for someone like me who tends to overthink things and have to depend on my brand of deductive reasoning to problem-solve emotionally complex issues. For this reason, I have a higher tolerance towards behaviors of aggression over drama. Before therapy, my mind was in permanent overdrive and never shut down unless I could suppress it with alcohol. It would keep me up for weeks at a time. This has slowed down tremendously with medication and coping mechanisms such as meditation to curb insomnia.

I am not a multi-tasker, although I'd like to think I am. In the middle of a crisis, I am almost always the calmest one in the room. I can defuse a situation faster than most. My mind is a constant battlefield of conflict between good and evil; its contenders are my healthier vs. my unhealthy mindset. In my healthier mindset, I understand that there are multiple facets to an individual's personality. In studying human behavior and working in the field, I have learned how important it is to hone in on the more positive characteristics.

I have found that educating myself on human development and evolving spiritually has given me better insight. Still, the truth is that I remain at a deficit socially and will always be a prisoner of my unhealthy mindset. As a child, I could never handle decisions and become extremely irritated and stressed out if faced with too many choices and overthought things. As a result, I failed miserably at multiple-choice when it came to academics but always excelled in short answers. The same holds true today.

For this reason, When it comes to decision-making, I tend to stick close to home. I don't stray too far outside of my comfort zone. Or I am incredibly impulsive and do not hesitate to do things on the spur of the moment.

When eating out, I played it safe and ordered the same thing off the menu. No matter where we went, I would do the same. I could never appreciate why people enjoyed dining out unless there was a buffet event, where I could pick and choose what I wanted. I'd be happier at home with a can of baked beans and a bottle of ketchup. In the same regard, I detest shopping and seldom ever did it for myself. If I did need clothes and happened to find something I liked, I always bought several of the same outfits in different shades and colors. My therapist called it my uniform.

The more I educate myself on SPD (sensory processing disorder), the more I discover that my disorder can explain a great deal of my psychosis. The problem is educating everyone else, especially since SPD is neurological, and there is no cure. For as long as I can remember, I have always had an aversion to certain textures and stimuli such as popsicle sticks, wooden spoons, wool, and especially cotton balls (to name a few). As an adult, I absolutely cannot touch a cotton ball or know a ball is near me without losing my mind. Often, medicine bottles have cotton in them, so my partner has to take it out and wet it before throwing it out. I even have to soak cotton swabs before I can use them on my kids. Beth and I discovered that we both shared the same affliction with cotton.

As a child/adult, I am overly sensitive to touch, bright lights, and certain smells like vanilla and have physiological reactions if I am exposed to it. One of the worst days of my life was when they invented vanilla-scented fabric softener and air fresheners. I cannot function outside on a bright day without sunglasses. I was first clinically diagnosed, as a teenager, with something called hypersensitivity. This translates to having a heightened sensitivity to touch, light, sound textures, and smell.

As an adult, The sound of snoring makes my head spin and gives me anxiety. This is likely from all the years I spent listening to Dean snore in the room next to mine. If I hear it, I tense up and cannot relax enough to fall asleep, and I cannot wear plugs in my ears due to my sensitivity to texture.

When I was younger, corduroy was popular, and my parents made me wear them to school. I used to sneak clothes and change before class because the feeling I got when my legs rubbed together would drive me insane. My parents found out I was changing at school when my teacher took a picture of the class on a school trip. She gave a copy of the picture to all the parents. No one understood what my hang-up was. The best way I can describe this is when you have the flu, your skin is sensitive to touch, and you have an aversion to anything it comes in contact with. Well, this is what it feels like for me, but all the time.

Nobody Special

My latest therapist supported this diagnosis and told me it could affect those who have suffered severe trauma, including PTSD. It is prevalent in individuals who have or are born with ADD/ADHD or Autism spectrum disorder like my son.

My SPD characteristics are heightened aversions to touch, taste, smell, the need for space, and my inability to process my environment properly, including color. I have always had difficulty telling the difference between yellow and orange, green and blue. I'm not colorblind, but when the two colors are side by side. My brain can't tell them apart and requires more time differentiating between the two.

My favorite colors are earth tones, and when combining shapes and textures, they simply have to make sense, or my mind won't accept it. One of my favorite places in my house is my living room. I have worked hard to make it visually appealing. I have found that Christmas time takes a significant toll on my anxiety. I start moving furniture around to put up the tree and discover the decorations clutter up my space. I reluctantly chose to do it for my kids. As a compromise, I put up the tree on Dec 1st and am allowed to take it down on Boxing Day.

All was well in my world until a few years ago when the kids decided that they wanted to decorate the tree with colored lights. I keep Christmas lights up all year round. I find the soft glow of light far less stimulating than regular lights, which are harsh on the eyes and give me headaches. I tried protesting, arguing that the change was stressful enough without changing the decor but lost that battle by a landslide.

Ever since I was little, I hated colored lights. I was okay with solid color, but the dizzying array of bright colors would send my head spinning, unlike beautiful autumn. I became increasingly agitated every time I set foot in my living room, even if the tree wasn't lit up. This wouldn't make a huge difference to a typical person and could take it or leave it, but for a person like me, my mind either accepts it or rejects it; there is no in-between. Some could argue this is a power and control thing, and I have no doubt that could factor somewhere, but this is entirely different for those who suffer from SPD.

Pick a strong smell or texture you don't like. Now imagine yourself in your favorite place, but everywhere you turn, there is that distinct odor. You're always on edge because everything you touch your mind rejects, causing you to react negatively to it. Your anxiety levels increase, and your favorite place is no longer warm and inviting. You try to leave, but the same things happen everywhere you go, and your sense of likes and dislikes is magnified and heightened. This is what it means to live with SPD.

The smell of asphalt is particularly harsh and so strong that I can't breathe altogether. I have an all-out panic attack and go into crisis mode. Even my poor dog isn't safe and is subjected to several baths a month because he has issues with his glands, and I can't be near him. On top of being allergic to him, I continue to suffer because, unlike humans, he loves and accepts me unconditionally for who I am, and I repay him in kindness.

There is no telling what my turning point or what combination of events allowed me to choose the paths I did, especially given what I had gone through. The fact is, the odds of being able to overcome my circumstances were stacked heavily against me. The bottom line is that I was a kid who spent my entire childhood living in fear with absolutely no empathetic skillset. It was an unlimited supply of shame, and it forced me to grow up in a world without compassion or trust. Somehow, I was able to find calmness in helping others who needed my support, even when I had next to nothing to offer them. This alone defined my humanity.

I quickly learned that everyone has something to offer you in recovery, but only if you're open to it. Sometimes it's a simple reminder of how far you've come, where you've been, and what you no longer want. Again, with everything I experienced, the one thing that got me through the worst of it was knowing that no matter how bad I had it, someone out there had it a lot worse than I ever did. This is what gave me the strength to move forward. It allowed me to get sober and was the driving force behind my decision to help youth, so they don't have to suffer as I had.

This matter came up in therapy quite often. I got called on undermining what I went through but learned that I needed to give the same compassion I was giving to others to myself. Only then could I start healing.

On a good day, I embraced the world and all its challenges. I am patient, warm, and don't generally let things bother me. I feel tranquil, open, and feel like I can do anything. I am typically well-liked. I am polite, curious and find people respond accordingly. I am confident and can usually find one thing I like about myself and tend to take better care of my appearance. I'm funny, easy-going. I love to sing, laugh, dance, pull pranks on my husband, and go out of my way to do something special for people, especially my kids, who love to be around their momma when I am in this space. I love this mindset, but I am terrified of it because it doesn't last very long. I feel like I'm on a roller-coaster ride clinging to the edge of my seat, trying to chase that next high and waiting for my car to derail. I never know when it's going to happen, and when it does, I become consumed by grief and despair in its absence. When I am in a negative mindset, I feel like I am drowning in quicksand, the mood is dark, and there is no reprieve. I become reserved and guarded and tend to take everything personally, even if people's comments and glances aren't directed towards me.

I internalize and blame myself for everything that is wrong with my life. I start to feel tired, defeated, and look for things to distract me from the constant furry of negativity that continues to consume me. In the past, I would drink, smoke, or gamble as a coping mechanism but have long since given most of my vices and recently turned to food.

The funny thing about food is when I am upset, I have absolutely no appetite. When I get really depressed, I get sucked into my suicidal adulations instead, often thinking the world would be much better off without me. I fantasize about what that would look like. I am strong enough in my recovery that I know when to go for support and when I need it. The issue is and always has been reaching out and communicating to others what my problem is. I struggle pinpointing it for myself and who do I trust. I've learned to stick up for myself. I've become the type of person who isn't afraid to speak my mind. I am told that I am too direct, challenging to read, intimidating, and standoffish. These attributes have become my default personality type and have gotten me into my fair share of trouble.

I hate what I see when I look into the mirror. Jack likes to point out how often I glance at myself, but it's not because I like what I see. I'm trying to come to terms with its distorted image. I have been going gray ever since I was 15 years old. I hardly ever wear makeup. I spent most of my adulthood battling my weight, so when people, especially Jack, pay me a compliment, I automatically assume they are lying.

Siobhan O'Regan

Trusting people goes beyond debilitating. I sometimes put myself out there hoping that someone will notice, but what often happens is people don't respond to my subtleties. I feel rejected and shut down entirely to protect myself. For this reason, I try only to keep positive people around me who value me, especially when I am feeling down. It is challenging to do when I'm hiding behind my walls and shut them out instead. My preferred method of communication is text and email. I hate talking on the phone or face to face and prefer to be alone with my thoughts before putting them out for the world to see. I find that it keeps me out of mischief since I'm not afraid to speak my mind.

No one knows better than I do that without Jack and his dad, there is absolutely no way I would be where I am today. Without their support, I have no doubt I would be dead. The fact is, humans are social creatures, and we depend on each other for our survival. The chances are that if I didn't meet my partner, I would have eventually gotten pregnant on purpose to create my own ready-made family. I would have lost the baby to the same system I supported due to my addictive coping mechanisms. Someone else would be justifiably raising my child, and I would have seen their intervention as more of a hostile takeover. My drinking would have excelled faster, and I would have found other ways to numb the pain.

Between the B-strep and the Aarskog, I would have likely given birth to a special needs child. Knowing what I know now, raising a child with Aarskog would have been tricky. Meeting his needs financially in a two-parent home without having to do it by myself would have been almost impossible. The cost to repair his teeth was in the thousands (and that didn't even include braces); without treatment, he would have suffered chronic pain and severe deformities. Countless research hours, dedication, patience, trial, and error were needed to understand his unique needs and behaviors. I would have never been able to raise both him and his brother, in addition to Kian's specific needs, on my own without the support of family, let alone hold a job. It was unlikely, having had no experience with boys and possessing limited access to resources, that I would have never detected a tumor. The outcome could have been devastating. Without the support, trust, or the proper assessment tools to identify my specific needs, my demeanor alone would have made me appear unwilling to cooperate. There was no way I could have survived the further loss.

Nobody Special

Every story needs a hero, and in my eyes, that is Jack. He stuck it out to support me. He put up with unspeakable abuse and stayed all in the name of love. He refused to give up on us, especially after finding out how damaged I was. He was the only person to find something in me I could not identify in myself.

After all these years, I am still reserved for letting him in because my negative mindset won't fully trust him. This continues to protect me from the fear of potentially losing him. It took me a long time to learn and appreciate how it was possible for him to love someone like me. By relating it to how I felt about my kids, I only found out that you cannot give what you don't have in therapy. Deep down inside, I hated myself, and I needed to come to terms with what that meant to me so I could start the healing process. I learned that I could never really honestly give myself over to him. As long as I hated myself and had an attachment disorder, It didn't just keep me from attaching to others; it also kept me from connecting to myself.

There is no pill or quick fix to repair this much damage. The only way I know I'll be able to heal fully is to identify and address my issues head-on. That recovery is a process and takes time. There are still times that knowing how much work I have ahead of me makes me feel tired, depleted, exhausted, and defeated. I still depend heavily on Jack for support.

Something I try to identify is who I am based on my core values. It is impossible when I struggle to determine what my core values are. Coming to terms with who I am without learning this basic fundamental is extremely difficult. This is especially true when you look at it from the perspective of someone who lives in constant conflict in the context of mental health. My healthier mindset wants to see trust as a core value, but my unhealthy counterpart says that trust is unsafe and won't allow me to go there.

Living life after abuse, mental illness, and addiction are not just about turning your life around and making better choices for yourself. Sometimes you have to go back and unlearn what has been instilled in you before you can rewrite a new chapter and run the risk of making several mistakes over again.

In my circles, we call this the definition of insanity, doing the same thing repeatedly and expecting a different result. Some don't realize that mistakes are sometimes necessary to establish a pattern and often crucial to the recovery process. When looking at the relationship from the eyes of the primary attachment, there is a level of expectation or myth that dictates, if you love someone enough or are pushed hard enough in the right direction, you can somehow alter his or her path of destruction.

In my experience, this statement is false, especially in working with kids and adults with severe trauma issues. No amount of love alone can force a person to change, only impact them. You can manipulate their environment to keep them safe or attempt to rehabilitate them. Still, the only way for someone to change their way of thinking is to identify and acknowledge that for themselves. A good therapist can introduce tools and show you how to use them to build a solid foundation in your recovery. Still, it's up to you to do the work and decide for yourself what the rest of the structure will look like. This is why I genuinely believe a crisis is a good thing. It tells us when things are not okay and gives us the autonomy to take personal inventory. This inventory is what challenges us to realize that change needs to happen. Still, it requires the capacity to make mistakes and learn in the process. Mistakes are proof you are trying and a necessary part of growing up to navigate the world.

CHAPTER TWENTY FOUR

Then And Now

In 2011, the first year as a foster parent was the same year I quit running the hockey program and attended my Foster Family Association annual AGM (annual general meeting) meet and greet. I had never been to an AGM meeting before and had never served on board. I found myself intrigued by the entire process. I had gotten to know a few of the general members through our mutual kids and looked to find a volunteer position. I had some idle time on my hands. We were sitting there chatting amongst ourselves when suddenly a member of my table nominated me for the president's position. I know I had a look of sheer disbelief on my face and laughed it off, figuring she was pulling a prank until it was first and seconded. Then the gentleman turned to me and asked if I accepted the nomination. I must have nodded yes because the next thing I heard was all in favor. I watched as every hand went up, and I listened to the words motion carried. From that moment on, I was the president of an organization.

I had no idea what I signed up for but, I was thrown in headfirst and learned quickly to sink or swim. I learned to do my fair share of both. From the very beginning, keeping the board afloat seemed like an impossible task since everyone had abandoned the ship. The only people still on board were the captain and its first mate, who wanted off the boat as fast as possible. He had been sailing without a crew for quite some time.

When I came on board, the current president jumped off at the first port, and the vice president stayed back to offer support. He wanted to move forward, too but agreed to stay on long enough to train me. I tried to learn as much from him as possible, but I couldn't connect with his teaching style. We agreed I would ask as many questions as I needed and would disregard the rest. I didn't have enough knowledge of procedures to navigate the system, so I read every manual and tried to enlist as much feedback as possible. Despite my lack of diplomacy, I was left to figure everything out old-school, so I sat back in many meetings and watched how things worked before I started offering my input.

One of the first things I teach my kids is the change they wish to see in the world. When they come to me with their issues, I try to make them understand they can't change those around them and be accountable for their own thoughts, actions, and feelings. I applied the same logic to the new position. When I first came on, I did my best to feel around, but I still stepped on plenty of toes. Only with the best of intentions, unfortunately, I couldn't please everyone, no matter what I did. I admit I made my fair share of mistakes, but there was no growth without challenges.

As it turns out, I was good at my position. I single-handedly accomplished what the previous board members had tried to do in four years. I broke attendance records and caught the attention of other presidents from all over who enlist our advice to reproduce what we did in such a short time frame. Within a year, I became the only board member left after one resigned for health reasons and another left due to overwhelming family demands. I was left on my own to carry the weight of the organization on my shoulders. I dedicated countless hours to maintaining, repairing, and rebuilding it from the ground up. From restructuring to rewriting our policy procedures and bylaws, I did it all. I enlisted the support of our provincial body and a group of foster parents who gave up an entire weekend, working around the clock to offer up their input and support.

As the president, I have had my fair share of challenges but trudged past them, and I am blessed to have the support of some incredible individuals on my team. They have qualities I have grown to admire. Together, we have changed the face of our organization and continue to rebuild. I tell them how valuable their contributions are and how much I appreciate them because I know how difficult it is to do on my own.

The biggest challenge I have to date is the imbalance of power and the overwhelming consensus that foster parents are under constant scrutiny and replaceable. I have had the experience of both perspectives as a child in care and as a foster parent. I would agree that their concerns are both valid and accurate. It is also my experience that we must implement what I call solution-focused ideas to implement this change. We have worked very hard to eliminate the us vs. them mentality that plagues a great deal of the overall thinking in my field. I often tell my foster parents and workers to offer a solution for conflict resolution. When bringing forth their concerns or issues, we can usually problem-solve independently without further input. Others I've discovered just need to be validated and heard.

Foster parents take in children who exhibit severe emotional and behavioral issues, mental health issues, attachment disorders and are medically fragile. They do it happily with little to no regard for themselves. I've personally had kids redecorate my home with urine and feces, hide weapons under their pillow, and attempt to throw me down a flight of stairs. I've had them hug a stranger and ask them to take them home, claiming we don't feed them.

It takes a particular breed of human to take on a challenging child who is not their own. These same individuals are skilled at unmasking the behaviors to see a frightened child underneath all that anger. They just want to be accepted and loved for who they are. If there is one thing a foster parent identifies, no two children are ever alike regardless of their similarities. Therefore, no matter how much experience you have with other children, each child brings forth their brand of challenges. There is strength in numbers, and there is no better reserve of support and resources than from your foster parents. I have those days when I know we both need repair, but I am exhausted, and all I want is to put them to bed. I want to distance myself from them to get a break.

My favorite part of the week was and always will be watching my kids play their sports. I do my best to attend every activity. I've taken full advantage of every training opportunity and hone in on my foster parent skills, knowing there is always room for growth. I base everything I do around structure, discipline, and emphasis on laughter and play. One of the most challenging parts of my role as a foster parent is developing the ability to see what is beneath the behaviors and identify the underlying issues. I focus on how to address them and not the actual actions. There isn't a single day that we are not laughing and carrying on. If there is one thing each of my kids got to take with them, it was knowing that someone outside of themselves cares about them no matter what. I never had this growing up, but they will always have a place in our hearts and home. I am still in contact with the kids I worked with in the group homes. I keep in touch with them and check in every time I get a chance. They let me know they're still alive and thinking about me. That's one of the reasons why I do what I do and will continue to do so as long as I can.

Fostering, for me, was the turning point, and it was pivotal to my healing process. The kids have enriched my life in countless ways, and I can pull unlimited positives out of every one of them. I can relate to these kids on a much deeper level. We have had some very challenging moments, and my kids have threatened to move in with their Papa a few times, but they always adjusted and came to their dad and me. They came to recharge their internal batteries. I genuinely believe they will become more reliable, more accepting, and compassionate individuals for it. Understanding my sons' individualistic needs, I find creative ways to build them up and spend time with each of them. That way, they never question their place in my heart and are more open to understanding that I have lots of room to care for other kids.

I also believe it has brought us closer together as a family, and I tell every one of them every day. I remind them how special they are and how unconditionally they are cared for. However, my kids hold a much different perspective and believe that fostering took a great deal of my time and energy from them. We did have some very high-needs placements that required supervision 24/7. I always believed my kids were stable, and their needs were well taken care of. I didn't consider what kind of a toll the youth's behaviors had on my kids and its impact on them.

Several caregivers come to me desperate for answers and at a loss for what to do for their RAD (Reactive Attachment Disorder) kids. I find them, more often than not, being traumatized too. A majority of these parents have already experienced multiple traumas in the form of infertility, miscarriages, or couldn't conceive a child of their own for genetic reasons. Some have entered a relationship and found themselves thrust into the role of caregiver of this unique creature only to find themselves in way over their head and subject to unspeakable abuse. Others (like me) had a chronically sick child, suffered mental health issues, substance abuse problems, and had mended their ways but not before the damage was already done. Going through the process of trying to adopt is highly intrusive and vulnerable. It does not guarantee that there will be a healthy baby in the end, and it often takes years before a child's status can be established. It takes even more time before an adoption is finalized. Generally speaking, the overall goal is to establish permanency for these traumatized children in a healthy and nurturing environment. While preserving ethnicity, culture and turning to outside adoption as a last resort, all other means of family reunification have been exhausted.

There are court decisions based on the burden of proof, the child's best interest, accumulated data, lack of information, disclosures, and community supports in the grand scheme of things. There are many different workers, lawyers, family members, kin placements, temporary care agreements, society wards, and crown wards provided: training, contingencies, appeals, considerations, treatment, drug screening, visitations, and personality clashes.

There is little to no security in looking to adopt through society. When all is said and done to a prospective parent and the child that comes their way, it is a welcomed gift. They genuinely believe their love for this child can overcome any trauma they may have suffered along the way.

The unfortunate reality is these kids simply don't trust. For them, trust is unreliable, dangerous, and any act of kindness triggers their primal fight or flight response. Then you have a child idling in survival mode. These exceptional children with unique needs come across as abrasive, angry, and require an abundance of power and control. Their survival depends on it. These are not your typical kids and need a particular approach to parenting that involves a lot of patents, skill, compassion, and above all else, tough love.

The kind of parenting that comes with experience and requires the proper tools, assessments, and support is needed. Without appropriate diagnosis and supports for both the child and the caregiver, it's no wonder there is such a high turnover in adoption breakdowns. Kids stop growing developmentally the moment they're impacted by trauma. The more extended intervention is delayed, the harder it is to repair the damage in the long term.

For a traumatized child, they say it can take up to two years of intense therapy, countless I love you's, structure, and relentless routines to buy in and establish safety. Only then can they securely attach and continue to grow where they left off before the initial trauma began. Add more trauma roots and recovery, and it takes substantially longer. In terms of placing a child in group care, think about how much damage is done each time a child is placed in an environment with multiple caregivers? Those who come and go are forced to adapt and move several times; thereby, more trauma roots are added. They are forced to start the process numerous times over.

How are kids in group-based care supposed to grow roots? Where is the stability? How does someone establish safety in an environment where there is an unlimited supply of chaos? The turnover rate is inevitable and substantially high. That is the biggest flaw I see with our system today. It is why I put so much emphasis on retention based on the number of kids who are being turned over to fend for themselves in the real world. They have to fight at the age of 16 when developmentally, they are significantly younger.

Could you ever consider sending a child who is 9 or 10 to live out on their own based on their skillset and narrow worldview? Can you leave them attracting the type of companion I did who will prey on their vulnerability to fulfill their basic need to belong and to fit in? Yet, we continue to do it every day from the moment we send a child out into the real world based on their chronological age rather than their developmental age. We justify it by saying sorry, kiddo, no room in the budget. To make things worse, we diagnose and medicate a child incorrectly based on their behaviors because officials are not adequately trained or are ill-equipped to identify and meet a child's needs with significant trauma history.

I spent my whole life mistrustful of authority figures. I was unable to maintain even one relationship that was remotely functional. I find out that I had a severe attachment disorder alongside other mental health issues. I was left to fend for myself because no one understood how to identify or deal with my unique needs or behaviors. I did not conform to society's ideal of how I should change according to laden standards. Ask any caregiver who has a child with RADs if traditional parenting techniques work. Chances are they have an even longer list of what doesn't work. Very few have access to the type of treatments that can help their child develop and grow to their full potential. There are fantastic support groups for any parent looking to explore creative ideas on connecting with their kids' behaviors. Through the eyes of someone who has been there or just having someone validate how you feel, I think support groups are an invaluable tool for any caregiver.

Jack and I agree we have so much love to offer the right child. We toyed with the thought of adoption and thought we came close a couple of times. Two of them were under the age of 2, but karma had other plans for both of them. The first one indescribably broke our hearts and took us completely by surprise. The courts gave a verdict one way when we were sure they were going in another direction. We raised that baby from birth until after their first birthday and were groomed to adopt them. We spent Christmas and New year's in sick kid's hospital, nursing them back to health, and just like that, they were gone. We never got to see them again. Just thinking about them now is a painful reminder of how much I loved and missed them. I am so grateful to have had them in my life, even if it was for a short while. I miss their tiny arms around my neck and how it felt when they called out to me. When you decide to adopt and accept a child unconditionally as your own, you are permanently attached to that child. When taken away, there is no real closure, and the healing process is debilitating hard.

Absolutely nothing will ever define you for the moment when you look into the eyes of someone else's child. You realize you love them unconditionally as your own, knowing that they belong to someone who loves them too. We had the second child in our care from birth until he was four and a half months. It was time for this tiny human to transition home. We asked his Grandma if we could still have visitation on the weekends. To our surprise, she said yes so, we started taking him on overnights. When daycare fell through, we offered to take him during the week too. He is now five years old, and we have such a secure connection to him. It's like he is one of our own, so we didn't just adopt this young lad in retrospect. We took his entire family and started including them as part of our own.

We have a unique situation and wouldn't trade it for anything in the world. I wouldn't change anything, and I'd do it again in a heartbeat. They both made me a better person just by being near them. We adopted the third child that came to us. He was 12 years old and officially became ours after he turned 16. The court process was long and slow, but in the end, he officially became our son, and we couldn't imagine our lives without him. I decided not to include him in this book to one day tell his own story.

Our foster care system has changed significantly since I was placed as a child. I had an attachment piece that allowed the child to have a sense of belonging and establish roots. You take these children in and make them part of your family even if you are tearing your world upside down, knowing there will always be uncertainty. There may come a day where you'll have to say goodbye. It takes a particular breed of human beings to knowingly subject themselves to that kind of heartache in the quest to make a difference.

After eight years of dedicated service, our doors were closed. It was disclosed that my boys were smoking pot just a few months shy of legalization, and I went against the agency directive to take back one of their own kids. When we accepted a young person's profile, my boys weren't exposed to pot. We understood they smoked pot shortly after this youth moved in. A young lad in our neighborhood introduced hardcore drugs to all my boys. Two of them rejected the invitation to try. Unfortunately, Kian did not pass on the opportunity and became addicted to cocaine and prescription drugs. He attended a great program but had to withdraw when we got hit with COVID-19. When he left treatment, his life was met with one challenge after another. He had no support and no way to meet supports. Despite many hurdles, he is still going strong and is doing exceptionally well in his recovery under the circumstances. We are exploring different treatment options, but our choices are limited due to our new temporary normal.

I look at my son, who has had his fair share of trauma, and how much it has impacted his life. He is a carbon cutout of his mother; he has PTSD and severe anxiety (separation, generalized and social). Unfortunately, he was severely bullied, feels minimal self-worth, and always thinks no one likes him. I like him; I like him a lot. He is so talented so funny, and I love it when he just acts like himself. School officials used to call us multiple times to say he was found crying in the stairwells at school and refused to go to class. He only attended a French school in Lonsdale, so Jack or I would trek the 45-minute drive to get him and bring him home. Anytime I tried to intervene, he would cry that it would only make things worse, so we had him transferred to an English school. That's when I'm told smoking pot and experimenting with drugs really began.

When I became aware of my kids using pot, I called the agency to ask about protocol and was told to use risk control. I took their advice, locked everything up in a lockbox, and bought a cabinet to lock up their lockboxes. Everything was double-locked, and I allowed the kids to smoke on the property in our shed to keep them from smoking in public. I wanted to prevent them from running into smaller youth.

Nobody Special

I kept in touch with the agency worker and let her know what steps had been taken to ensure everyone's safety. There were absolutely no concerns until the agency showed up at my home unannounced. I was being investigated to provide the youth in my house were not supervising our 3-year-old while under the influence.

I was so confused. My worker had just retired, and I reached out to the worker I had the strongest rapport with who profiled my youth. It stood to reason I would reach out to the individual I worked with most when interacting with the agency. I was taken back when I was told that I received the wrong information. I should have contacted my new worker about my concerns. I was forced to remove the cabinet and all its contents. I stand behind the fact that I did get the agency when I discovered that my kids were smoking, and I did my due diligence. In the end, the agency reprimanded me for not reaching out to the correct worker.

Another complicated matter was that I went against an agency directive to save a child from slipping through the cracks. This was a child who lived with us off and on for five years. I am sorry that we are no longer fostering. The reality is that I put a child's life first. I was told this youth is a survivor and that "They'll get by." That was not good enough for me. We were all they had.

In 2012, I asked my psychiatrist if she could refer me to one of the hospital's mental health social workers for further counseling. There was still so much for me to work on. Bridget and I connected from day one. She was unlike any therapist I had ever encountered. Until now, she has been teaching me how to cope with my disorder using the same method of cognitive-behavioral therapy we use daily with my kids who suffer from ADD/ADHD. I have been seeing her for the better part of 5 years, which has become an integral part of my ongoing recovery. Sometimes, I feel I would be completely and utterly lost without her constant support.

A good therapist can introduce tools and show you how to build a solid foundation in your recovery. It's up to you to do the work and decide for yourself what the rest of the structure will look like. This is why I genuinely believe the crisis is a good thing. It tells us when things are not okay and gives us the autonomy to take personal inventory. This inventory challenges us to realize that change needs to happen. This requires making mistakes and learning in the process, especially since mistakes are proof you are trying and a necessary part of growing up to navigate the world. She has taught me that recovery is a process. Even though it has taken me years and multiple therapists to get there, each one had something to offer me in the form of a perspective. I have learned to appreciate every time she challenges my outlook. It's never about getting me to see things her way, but it's about taking a step back and looking at things from a different angle. For the first time, with her insight and support, I actually learned how to care about myself and learned quite a bit about who I am as a person.

For my whole life, I disliked who I was. I couldn't grasp the concept of loving myself. With her support, I reached deep down and went through one layer at a time. For five years, I shed more tears than I ever thought I had. When I was angry, she was there. When I was confused, she was there. Every emotion you can think of, she was there. Now I have the skill and ability to identify when I go into crisis. I know just what to do and have learned how to act to my anger. I know how to take responsibility for my thoughts, actions, feelings, and environment. Sometimes, I still don't know when to hold back because of my all-or-nothing personality. I am still working on it. She has taken such fantastic care of me, but now it's time for me to venture out on my own. I have more than enough tools to be okay, and I can still connect with her for support or give her updates.

In 2013, Jack's stepfather Vincent was diagnosed with lung cancer and had an operation to remove the cancer tissue. It ultimately spread, and he became terminal. Kian took it the hardest and wanted to visit him near the end, but I wanted to spare my son the pain and heartache of seeing him waste away. I felt his loyalty was displaced, given Vincent did not care for him the way Kian thought he did. Kian had a method of overestimating how much people cared for him so he could feel special. Unfortunately, Vincent never really invested in him and didn't go out of his way to pay him any special attention, even on our yearly visits. Vincent passed away a couple of months later on Kian's twelfth birthday. We tried to hide the date from him and told him that he passed away a day after his birth date, but he found out after reading his obituary. He was devastated. I learned a valuable lesson that day. No matter how much you want to protect your children, to a child, a lie can be far more damaging than the truth. Sometimes you need to let them feel things even if you know it's going to hurt them.

In 2015, Jack's mother eventually sold the house and moved down to Ontario to be closer to her boys. After attempting a few conversations with her through Jack, it became evident that she and I will never be on the same page. In her eyes, I was never good enough for her son. She never had much of a connection with the boys and never really called them between visits. This was except for birthdays and holidays. Otherwise, I had to remind them to call her. Her attitude and demeanor often reminded me of my own mother. She had made it very clear, through her actions, that she had no use for me. I choose to keep my distance.

I like to remind myself that a communication breakdown is never the sole responsibility of just one person, and neither is the repair. The moment one person holds back, it becomes closed off. Suppose they refuse to be accountable for their part. In that case, the relationship suffers, and the people directly linked to it will also endure it.

We chose to keep our distance for several years. This was rather difficult for Jack as he saw her every time he went to work. Since the business was in his father's home, he held to his word and didn't speak to his mother for almost five years. I understood that Jack's connection with his mother pre-dated me and was separate from us. So, I learned to appreciate that my role was to support and respect their relationship by trusting his judgment. As long as he understood, I no longer choose to be subject to her abuse. The same went for the rest of his family. I did my best not to get involved, even though I often felt responsible that Jack had chosen to distance himself from his family. I was grateful that he always had his dad. I wished I could be more accepting, but a part of me was still guarded and unwilling to let some of my walls down. I was mostly this way to those who were determined to misunderstand me. I was optimistic and hopeful. The more I grew, the more I wanted to inspire change.

In 2017, on July 2nd, I upheld a childhood dream. I had made myself a childhood promise and bought a 13-year-old Appendix Quarter horse who just happened to be named Kallan. He had the same name as my oldest son, but we just called him Kal. Kal was a rare beauty, gentle inside and out, and I fell head over heels in love with him. As a child, for all those years I spent riding horses like Rudy. I was given basic instructions and was sent on my way. I became a self-taught rider and picked up some very unusual habits on the way. Kal was such a trained horse, and I learned that I was way out of my league. I sure had my work cut out for me trying to work on my technique.

One afternoon, I was out riding with a group of fellow riders, I directed Kal to go one-way, but he went the opposite. I was not prepared, and I ended up falling off of him, landing square on my back bouncing off the ground. It knocked the wind out of me, but I was able to get up and walk away. I was ever so grateful that I was wearing my riding helmet. The following day, I woke up, and I couldn't walk at all. A trip to the hospital discovered I had a dislocated tail bone and several dislocated ribs. As a person with diabetes, it takes forever to heal and being an active person, I always push my limits. It took me the better part of 8 months to fully recover, and at that point, I was so scared of my horse that I didn't see him for a little over a year. Kal had this little quirk about him. He loved to test limits. Being inexperienced, I didn't quite know how to work through this challenge. I gained some knowledge with the help of two trainers. My memory was so slow; it was hard to retain and learn, especially when my mind switched to survival mode. For nearly ten years, Kal was a barrel racer, probably not the best for an intermediate beginner, as I called myself. Still, in the end, the decision was mine. Unfortunately, I depended heavily on my trainer's expertise, and I wasn't equipped to ask the right questions. He was beautiful and perfect on the ground in every way, but I would learn the hard way that he was considered a term called "hot under the saddle." We experienced more bad times than good, and I spent a total of almost two years recovering from one accident or another. In total, I fell off of him five times, one of those times; my stirrup broke when we attempted to lope for the first time together; I flew off my saddle into the bars of the sand ring where we were riding.

My second trainer convinced me to sell him and told me I wouldn't get half of what I paid for him; she would be wrong about many things, this being one of them. They offered to help me to buy another horse and had one trailered in just for me to consider, but I didn't walk away from this horse feeling excited. In the end, I ended up selling Kal to an amazing young lady who was an up-and-coming barrel racer, and when she mounted him, it was like they were meant for each other. I knew letting him go was the right thing to do and that I was holding him back.

She had a beautiful 7-year-old quarter horse named Duke she was selling, they tried to make a barrel horse out of him, but he wouldn't have it; unlike Kal, he had more whoa than go. He checked off all of my boxes as far as what I wanted in a horse, so I made arrangements to see him. At the time, my trainer was against me meeting him; she said we weren't trading one barrel horse in for another. I went with my gut on this one and fell instantly in love with him. He was much smaller than Kal, who was 16.3 hands, topping at 14.3 hands. At my age, I don't bounce as I used to, so a more miniature horse was very appealing. He rode like a dream and stopped on a dime when it was time to go; I didn't want to dismount and could have ridden him all afternoon. We agreed to an even trade and created adoption certificates that each one of us signed. My trainer was not happy with my decision and fired me on the spot. My trainer, now Susan, is irreplaceable; we are starting Duke from the ground up, meaning I am learning how to become in tune with him like we are with our kids. Not 10 minutes into our first lesson, we were lunging Duke and Susan voiced a concern that he might be something called unsound. Unsoundness means he would not be able to perform because of a condition. We discovered that he had an undisclosed injury that was getting worse with time. It was not that he was incapable but that he was in a world of pain. Regardless of his diagnosis or the recovery process, he is mine, and I will do everything in my power to help and support him. I have been spending so much time getting to know my boy horse. I am happy and content just to be near him, touch him, and hug him. He is such an incredible horse on the ground. My dream is to be able to ride him like I did Rudy; at the end of the day, there is nothing more utopic than galloping across an open field. I just want to ride and be one with my beautiful companion.

In 2018, I relapsed for six months. This was after 13 years of sobriety. When life got to me, we put ourselves on hold for new placements. I wanted to focus more on the kids I already had. I lost my beloved Jessie and my Nan on the same weekend. I was struggling with my former foster child because I had to turn them over to the authorities. It was more grief than I could handle.

Jessie was a god-fearing woman who loved her church and was like a grandmother to me. She and I were close up until her passing, and I took it hard. She never judged me. She gave me space when I needed it and was there to listen to my stories. I was careful about what I told her because I didn't want her to worry about me. I took good care of Jessie by taking her on outings and bringing her to get groceries. I did this, especially when she gave up her driver's license to live independently as long as she could. Her family lived further up north, and she wanted to stay in the home that she and her late husband occupied. Jessie used to come over for the holidays and made my favorite cabbage rolls. Typically, I despise rice, but when she cooked, it was delicious.

She was starting to have accidents around the house and unexplained bruises. When I asked about them, she was never dishonest with me but always brushed them off. If I hadn't seen her for a short while, I would go find out things from her biological granddaughter. She and Jessie were very,

very close and would tell her everything. She didn't want me to worry either. I got to know Jessie's granddaughter very well, and we often texted.

Jessie called me up one morning and asked if I could come over. She needed some help, but she wouldn't say what for. I got there, and she greeted me with her head full of dried blood. She had fallen down the stairs the night before and called EMS by herself. She had earned herself quite a few staples. I grabbed a cloth and some warm water and started washing the blood out of her hair. I had to be as gentle as I could, sometimes strand by strand. I was so triggered. The smell of the iron in the blood reminds me so much of my many busted lips. It took everything in my power not to be sick. I held my breath, and away I went. You never know what you're capable of when a member of your tribe needs you. You know it took me six hours to get most of the blood out of her hair. Later that night, I called her son and told him I thought it was time. I wanted to keep her down here with me, but he wanted her up north where he lived. I took a step back. I knew she would be happy with her family too. I took care of her property and kept it clean and neat for potential home buyers to see the home. That Christmas was a Christmas indeed. She mailed me a money order for five thousand dollars when the house sold for taking care of the property and paid for all of my trips to go and see her. There are no words to express my gratitude to the only person who ever cared about me outside of my immediate family. She passed away just before her 96th birthday.

With Nan, as luck would have it, I just happen to be in Main visiting my brother, and just like that, I decided to check in on her. I hadn't seen her in over 10+ years. I was so nervous, but for the first time, she was polite and welcoming. She looked very apprehensive at first but relaxed as the conversation flowed. Most of it was small talk, but I did manage to slip in a little bit about the past. Her demeanor changed, and she looked despondent. Nan went stern and said, "forget about the past; it's not your fault; it's not my fault, so let's move on." I had many unresolved feelings about the past. I was hoping to discuss it so that I could have some closure, but this was the closest I would get to an apology. I don't know how to explain what happened in the next moment. It was incomprehensible when she hugged me for the first time. It was as if years of dead weight suddenly lifted, and I could breathe a little bit deeper. I promised to bring the boys by to see her but didn't get the chance. She died three weeks later. My only regret was that she never met her youngest grandchild Caleb, the child we adopted.

Nobody Special

After the 6th-month mark, I told Bridget that I noticed some old behavior patterns when I drank. Although this time was different, I was content to sing, dance, and clean whenever I drank. However, I drank almost every night and started drinking consistently. I sincerely thought I could manage my alcohol consumption by just drinking wine, only drinking in the evening and on special occasions. It turns out every night was a special occasion. This was a crucial point in my recovery. I found myself looking at a fork in the road—a road to lead me back to regeneration and the second road that was grim and uncertain. I always knew I had another drunk in me, but I was never sure I had another sober.

This was a slogan I picked up in NA (Narcotics Anonymous), and I was scared. I was afraid to lose my autonomy. I had convinced myself that for the first time in 13 years, I felt like them. I fit in like them, and I was normal, like them. Only I was deceiving myself. I couldn't be like them because I am foremost an alcoholic/addict first. I could do almost anything except I couldn't drink or do drugs. I always felt like an outsider when I went to parties and disillusioned myself into thinking drinking made me fit in. The fact of the matter is, I still struggle navigating humans. All alcohol ever did is lower my inhabitations. At gatherings, when I'm drinking, I'm told I am more outgoing and hilarious. When I'm sober, I am quieter, more reserved, and withdrawn. I feel like an outcast.

I stopped taking my meds. They made me feel tired all the time. After I found out I was suffering from burnout, my focus was not there, and I fell into an intense depression. I can be around alcohol. I lost all desire for it. It's as if karma (the god of my understanding) took it away. I had no desire for it for the first 13 years either, but the first drink was almost like a compulsion. My spirit couldn't handle everything that was happening all at once. My father-in-law and I now have a standing deal; I will go to him first if the compulsion ever happens again.

Bridget and I did a few questionnaires together. She did some fantastic research and found a great facility. It was a 3-month program and 2.5 hours away. I needed it to get off the alcohol and to get my meds adjusted correctly. Finally, this facility specialized in concurrent disorders (addiction and mental health). After much thought and many discussions with Jack and the boys, we decided I would go. It turns out there was a great deal of change to my medication, and for the first time, I went months symptom-free. There was some tweaking to do but no major depressive or manic states. I completed the program in Feb 2019 and have been sober ever since. I don't regret my mistake; it was a lesson learned. I took in some valuable tools I would not have learned had I not attended the program. It has made me stronger in my recovery. However, I've been told I will never be able to go off my medications ever again. We have enough documentation of my symptoms when I don't take them. I know now they serve a useful purpose, and were still investigating why I'm so tired all the time. I don't ever remember a time when I woke up feeling refreshed. It's a working progress.

In 2019, we lost our house, where I developed roots for 15 years. We took in a young lass and her two children for almost a year. She was one of my girls from the group home I used to work at years ago. This young lady got into her third domestic, and I had no placements, so I told her to come to live with us to get on her feet. She made incredible gains with our support, but the cost of living with nine people in one house just mounted the bills. It was nothing we couldn't manage. However, while volunteering for Child Services, when they did their investigation, one of our community members complained about safety concerns. I had a lot of teenagers. They were there to make sure the boys weren't supervising our (then) 3-year-old while under the influence of pot. They preach about being upfront and honest, which I was, which I get in return. This was not our first investigation, so I knew what to expect. It's inevitable when you are a foster parent to be investigated. It's just a matter of when. While being investigated, I was not permitted to work for Child Services, so I was suspended. The investigation took almost six months.

I lost out on 5+ months of income because it was summer, and workers stated they needed their time off. Jack's income paid for all the bills, mortgage, utilities, etc. My income paid for all the extras, food, sports, credit, etc. Like many, we live paycheck to paycheck. I had five teenagers, and they are so expensive. As far as the multitude of teenagers, I had five teenagers living with me at the time, and each teen had friends/girlfriends. It stands to reason that my house was a little bit busy at the time. My house was a haven for some and somewhere to hang out for others.

I sat down and got to know all of the kids; they often came to me for support or constructive venting. When Child Services decided to stop by, I had seven kids and another parent. Three of the kids were going to Wonderworld, and the other four were just hanging out. I often preferred that the kids and their friends hang out at my place, so I knew exactly what they are up to. We needed to pull money from somewhere and were living off of credit and went into debt very fast. There was no way to recover. We remortgaged our house for two years before paying for a new roof. Our only option was to sell the house so we could breathe. Of course, the investigation came back unverified, which meant they couldn't find any safety concerns in their terms. The kids were always respectful of the toddler and often hung out in the basement where the wee one couldn't go. Jack or I were still the primary caretakers when he was with us. They often say things happen for a reason. We were able to find a beautiful house to rent that happily pleased my kids because, for the first time, they all had their own rooms. The downside was, we were living in a new construction area. There was not much in the way of transportation unless you could drive. Kallan had his license, so he drives his brothers around. For the most part, my kids are homebodies. When we moved to this house, we had five children. Two left to further his aspirations, which left me with just the 5 of us.

In 2016, my mother reached out to me. She had finally left Bruce and asked us to help her move in with her best friend. She was now living in a home that should have been condemned but was given to her friend when her beloved parents passed away. She made the best of her accommodations. I helped her apply to subsidized housing and visited her periodically to ensure she was taken care of. She was becoming a shut-in, so I started taking her to Al-Anon or out to do some shopping. The more I hung out with her, the more I noticed a massive difference in her attitude and demeanor. If I didn't know any different, I would say she was almost human. During one of my visits with her, I couldn't help but notice how old and frail she was sitting across the table from me. She looks up as if to say something, pauses, and then says, thank you! For what I asked? She looks me right in the eyes and says for being able to love me after everything I ever did to you.

I was no longer under her spell. I had no reason to forgive her, but I had a few things to say, and I wasn't feeling shy. I told her that she destroyed my spirit. She did unspeakable things, stripped me of my childhood, and damaged me well into adulthood. There was a moment of silence. She nodded her head and then explained to me that she spent eight years in Al-Anon. While in her program, she did a great deal of self-reflecting, healing, and growing with her sponsor. She validated everything I had said to her and told me repeatedly how sorry she was and really wanted to know how to move forward.

Siobhan O'Regan

I had no feelings, no aches, and pains, no anger or resentment. I can thank Bridget for that, and I could see that she was genuine. I took in some air, blew it out slowly, and closed my eyes to center myself. I just sat there deep in thought. My mother was a very sick individual for many years and worked hard to overcome most of it. After all the years I spent in therapy, I could respect that.

It turns out she is a sweet, warm, and generous human being and a great conversationalist. I enjoy her company very much. She has long since apologized to Jack for any of her negative participation in his life. Jack is still guarded but has let most of it all go. I don't look at her as a Nazi anymore. She has long paid penitence with everything she has been through. She is a great grandmother to her grandsons. To them, that is how it should be. Sometimes the past comes back to haunt us in conversation, but we could sort through the emotions together and talk about it as adults. I would say I am 70% healed; the other 30% is the scarring left behind.

As miracles would have it while I was in rehab, I decided to write Léo a letter. It wasn't a letter to explain myself necessarily, but a message to let him know I wanted to reach out. I spent so many years hating the man. I tried to make amends somehow. All that anger I had for Dean was projected at him. Justifiably every time he did something that somehow impacted me negatively. Like my brother, there was a time I wanted to be just like him. From my perspective, he was funny, social, and carefree. I couldn't be any of those things, so I started resenting him for it. Every time he left the girls with me and then took them away from me, it severely impacted me. I was many things in my unhealthy state, but the bottom line is I was incredibly sick, and in a way, so was he. We never know how things impact people, too, had visible trauma roots. I could never see it outside of my own misery at the time, nor did I have the tools to navigate as such.

I heard he disagreed with some of what was written in my letter, but we decided to put our swords down and declared an armistice. In 2008 Léo met and fell in love with a beautiful woman named Megan. She became public enemy number one. Anyone associated with Léo was no friend of mine, and I didn't give her a fair chance. Partly because of my attachment issues and second, because she was attached to him. We attempted to be friends at one point, but it didn't work out because of the Leo conflict, and we parted ways.

Nobody Special

She broke the silence first and invited our then 3-year-old nephew and me on a playdate with her and her 3-year-old. Our kids were two months apart to the day. I am so grateful to know her. She is such a hard-working human being and a remarkable mother to her three kids. I had to stop by the house for something, and he came out. For the first time in more years than I can count, we were face to face. I had no words, but then words weren't unnecessary. He took me into his arms, and we just held each other for a while. When it was over, he said, "I love you," and I said, "I love you," back. There was a time when the very mention of his name would cause a great deal of upheaval in my spirit, and I would be angry and resentful and explode in anger. Now all of that anger just blew away in one genuinely sincere hug embrace. Jack got his brother back, and I know how much he missed him.

His mother followed suit when everyone broke their silence. She and I have been trying hard to communicate amicably with one another. She spent a great deal of time with her youngest grandkids, and I was surprised by how good her English had become. She was very friendly towards me, and when I stopped by the house, she came up, and we chat away. It was mainly about the kids, but I truly appreciate her effort. We all spent Christmas together in 2019; it was beautiful to have the entire family under one roof. Kian was beside himself. He was so delighted, and truth be told, so was I.

I no longer have any connection to my sister Beth or our father anymore. I invited Beth to my wedding renewal last October, celebrating the day we met rather than the day we actually married. It was also the year that marked the halfway point when I had been with Jack. I was 22 when I met him, and we celebrated being together for 21 years. She texted back to have a wonderful life making it clear it was to be without her involvement.

I see my brother from time to time but not since Covid. Sean always told me to go after my rightful inheritance if Nan died. Just like when I was young, when everything was said and done, my father was all talk and no action. All her children and grandchildren stood to inherit a modest amount, and when push came to shove, he chose the money over me.

There is a directional sign in the road that points forward instead of looking both forward and backward. As for my relationship with Jack, it has weathered its fair share of a storm. Through years of therapy and perseverance, we have developed a solid and impenetrable foundation that neither one of us takes for granted.

The serenity prayer states: Grant me the serenity to accept the things we cannot change, the courage to change the things we can, and the wisdom to know the difference. I spent the better part of my life mourning the loss of my childhood, family, freedom, friendships, ability to trust, and the ability to connect with others. I cried for my kid's lack of normalcy, the normality of a connection with my husband, and the readiness to move on with my life. I decided a long time ago to channel all the years of anger and torment into something I could be proud of, and for the most part, I did. If my journey ends tomorrow, I get to own that.

PERSPECTIVE

Healthier vs. Unhealthier Mindset

Sometimes it takes a great deal of energy to be me, to combat my ailments, my medication, my mood disorder, to stay active, and to keep focused. No one can truly understand what I have gone through, only relate. Even if you experience the exact same incident in time, you're seeing and sensing everything based on your life, past history, and perspective, which is fueled by your own temperament. The impact will be different for everyone, and so will the degree of resiliency. Through openness, experience, and education, one can absolutely comprehend what it means to live with trauma and how it significantly impacts life if there is awareness, lived experience, well-trained, well-seasoned, and compassionate individuals to fill these roles.

    I feel we are just scratching the surface regarding identifying trauma, its impact, and its toll on mental health. We need more educated peer support roles with individuals who have lived experience. We live in a society where normalcy dictates you are raised in a relatively healthy environment with good core values and ample supports. Unfortunately, this is not a reality for far too many people. Remember what I wrote about human developmental delay? I am still healing from my trauma; even with extensive therapy, I was lucky and knew the right questions to ask to get the resources I needed. The demand for supports is so immeasurably high. Still, there are not enough resources to go around. (Many of these resources are funded—the more people who utilize these resources, the more funding they can receive to continue services).

Siobhan O'Regan

I struggle with simple things like boundaries. For most of my life, I was at a huge deficit. I was never really taught or modeled boundaries. Instead, I was taught barriers. This is an area I struggle with the most, especially in my field.

My whole purpose in life has always been to help others. I don't want anyone to suffer needlessly like I did, especially little humans. I have learned to appreciate, however, that some individuals need to learn at their own pace. We've had remarkable outcomes as foster parents; not all interventions were a bad thing; in fact, I truly believe something good comes out of every negative if you have the right perspective.

Perspective is everything; I always try and look for the positive in every situation and take accountability for my own thoughts, actions, and feelings.

As foster parents, we were molded to understand the trauma and attachment piece. We learned how to incorporate each youth as part of our family and work closely with the youth's caregivers to integrate them home whenever it was possible. I understood this as the gospel. Nobody ever really framed the toll it would take on you emotionally.

My partner is my voice of reason, and in my healthier mindset, I do well to understand when he warns me of the potential outcomes of my choices. My unhealthy mindset wants to help and believes the goodwill outweighs all. Sometimes I am told I should know better. You're only as good as the last and the next individuals who invest their time into you. Some take the time to mentor you; others can't wait to complete the task and move you to the next person.

I remember back in the day when my sponsor used to drill into to me, "I am Responsible. When anyone, anywhere, reaches out for help, I want the hand of A.A. always to be there. And for that, I am responsible." This was honestly the first time I remember someone taking me under their wing to really mentor me. Since then, it's been the amazing foster parents at their annual foster parent conference…and, of course, Bridget.

I was never more excepted, understood, and felt more belonged than when I was amongst our provincial body of foster parents. I went to quite a few of their conferences. I felt I was amongst like-minded people who understood trauma and openly related to my trauma history. I never felt judged;

I only ever felt validated and heard. I understood my youth's trauma. I could see how much it impacted their lives, how much hurt was underneath all that anger, and the unquenchable thirst for that sense of belonging. I've seen it with my adopted son. We spent many months talking through the night until he didn't need me to sit up with him anymore. I was intuned to the fact that my son was more than just struggling; he was trying to work through his trauma. Nighttime was especially difficult for him. I was able to be that person for him.

This saga isn't about how I overcame everything or how I got everything I wanted in life. It's a testament of strength, courage, survival, trauma, and its impact. For my entire life, I hid behind walls of shame that I built to protect myself. It wasn't until I found the right person to open up and begin the healing process. I learned that I could not do this alone on my journey and that as much as I was afraid to let Jack in, it became imperative to have him as support for my recovery.

You are not alone; there will always be someone with wisdom guiding you and who needs your insight as well. There are many resources out there and people with compassion and experience who genuinely want to help support you. You can reach out, tell somebody, or contact me at "Nobody Special, from a trauma perspective" via Facebook Or siobhanoregan@nobodyspecial.ca

Together, we will find the right resources to meet your needs.

Please always be kind with your words.

www.ingramcontent.com/pod-product-compliance
Lightning Source LLC
Chambersburg PA
CBHW071411070526
44578CB00003B/548